# Contents

# How to use this book

Welcome to your BTEC National Business course!

A BTEC National in Business course is one of the most popular BTEC courses. There are many reasons why this course is in such demand, and you will experience some of these at first hand during the next year or so.

Your qualification will help you succeed in your future career, no matter what you choose to go on to do. The principles of business that you will learn on your course underpin every shop, office and organisation in the UK economy – from being able to make effective decisions in business and understanding management and leadership styles, to creating effective training programmes and building your own business. The skills you will develop on your course will be valued by employers in every sector.

Your BTEC National in Business is a vocational or work-related qualification. This does not mean that you will be given all the skills you need to do a job, but that you will have the opportunity to gain specific knowledge, understanding and skills that are relevant to your chosen subject or area of work.

## How your BTEC is structured

Your BTEC National is divided into **mandatory units** (M, the ones you must do) and **optional units** (O, the ones you can choose to do). The number of units you need to do, and the units you cover, will depend on the type of BTEC National qualification you are doing.

▶ BTEC Level 3 National Certificate in Business (180 GLH): two units, both mandatory, of which one is external

▶ BTEC Level National Extended Certificate in Business (360 GLH): four units of which three are mandatory and two are external

▶ BTEC Level 3 National Foundation Diploma in Business (510 GLH): six units of which four are mandatory and two are external

▶ BTEC Level 3 National Diploma in Business (720 GLH): eight units of which six are mandatory and three are external

▶ BTEC Level 3 National Extended Diploma in Business (1080 GLH): thirteen units of which seven are mandatory and four are external

The table below shows how the units covered by the books in this series cover the different types of BTEC qualifications.

| Unit number | GLH | Unit name | Cert | Ext Cert | Foundation Dip | Dip | Ext Dip |
|---|---|---|---|---|---|---|---|
| 1 | 90 | Exploring Business | M | M | M | M | M |
| 2 | 90 | Developing a Marketing Campaign | M | M | M | M | M |
| 3 | 120 | Personal and Business Finance | | M | M | M | M |
| 4 | 90 | Managing an Event | | | M | M | M |
| 5 | 90 | International Business | | | | M | M |
| 6 | 120 | Principles of Management | | | | M | M |
| 7 | 120 | Business Decision Making | | | | | M |
| 8 | 60 | Recruitment and Selection Process | | O | O | O | O |
| 14 | 60 | Investigating Customer Service | | O | O | O | O |
| 16 | 60 | Visual Merchandising | | | O | O | O |

| 19 | 60 | Pitching for a New Business | | O | O | O |
| 21 | 60 | Training and Development | | | O | O |
| 22 | 60 | Market Research | O | O | O | O |
| 23 | 60 | The English Legal System | O | O | O | O |

Units in grey are covered in this book. Units in white are covered in BTEC Nationals Business Student Book 1 (ISBN: 978 1 292 12624 1).

# Your learning experience

You may not realise it but you are always learning. Your educational and life experiences are constantly shaping you, your ideas, your thinking, and how you view and engage with the world around you.

You are the person most responsible for your own learning experience so it is really important you understand what you are learning, why you are learning it and why it is important both to your course and your personal development.

Your learning can be seen as a journey which moves through four phases.

| Phase 1 | Phase 2 | Phase 3 | Phase 4 |
|---|---|---|---|
| You are introduced to a topic or concept; you start to develop an awareness of what learning is required. | You explore the topic or concept through different methods (e.g. research, questioning, analysis, deep thinking, critical evaluation) and form your own understanding. | You apply your knowledge and skills to a task designed to test your understanding. | You reflect on your learning, evaluate your efforts, identify gaps in your knowledge and look for ways to improve. |

During each phase, you will use different learning strategies. As you go through your course, these strategies will combine to help you secure the core knowledge and skills you need.

This student book has been written using similar learning principles, strategies and tools. It has been designed to support your learning journey, to give you control over your own learning and to equip you with the knowledge, understanding and tools to be successful in your future studies or career.

# Features of this book

In this student book there are lots of different features. They are there to help you learn about the topics in your course in different ways and understand it from multiple perspectives. Together these features:
▶ explain what your learning is about
▶ help you to build your knowledge
▶ help you understand how to succeed in your assessment
▶ help you to reflect on and evaluate your learning
▶ help you to link your learning to the workplace

In addition, each individual feature has a specific purpose, designed to support important learning strategies. For example, some features will:
▶ get you to question assumptions around what you are learning
▶ make you think beyond what you are reading about
▶ help you make connections across your learning and across units
▶ draw comparisons between your own learning and real-world workplace environments
▶ help you to develop some of the important skills you will need for the workplace, including team work, effective communication and problem solving.

## Features that explain what your learning is about

### Getting to know your unit

This section introduces the unit and explains how you will be assessed. It gives an overview of what will be covered and will help you to understand *why* you are doing the things you are asked to do in this unit.

### Getting started

This appears at the start of every unit and is designed to get you thinking about the unit and what it involves. This feature will also help you to identify what you may already know about some of the topics in the unit and acts as a starting point for understanding the skills and knowledge you will need to develop to complete the unit.

## Features that help you to build your knowledge

### Research

This asks you to research a topic in greater depth. Using these features will help to expand your understanding of a topic as well as developing your research and investigation skills. All of these will be invaluable for your future progression, both professionally and academically.

### Worked example

Our worked examples show the process you need to follow to solve a problem, such as a maths equation or the process for writing a letter or memo. This will also help you to develop your understanding and your numeracy and literacy skills.

### Theory into practice

In this feature you are asked to consider the workplace or industry implications of a topic or concept from the unit. This will help you to understand the close links between what you are learning in the classroom and the affects it will have on a future career in your chosen sector.

### Discussion

Discussion features encourage you to talk to other students about a topic in greater detail, working together to increase your understanding of the topic and to understand other people's perspectives on an issue. This will also help to build your teamworking skills, which will be invaluable in your future professional and academic career.

**Key terms**

Concise and simple definitions are provided for key words, phrases and concepts, allowing you to have, at a glance, a clear understanding of the key ideas in each unit.

**Link**

This shows any links between units or within the same unit, helping you to identify where the knowledge you have learned elsewhere will help you to achieve the requirements of the unit. Remember, although your BTEC National is made up of several units, there are common themes that are explored from different perspectives across the whole of your course.

**Step by step:**

This practical feature gives step-by-step descriptions of particular processes or tasks in the unit, including a photo or artwork for each step. This will help you to understand the key stages in the process and help you to carry out the process yourself.

**Further reading and resources**

This contains a list of other resources – such as books, journals, articles or websites – you can use to expand your knowledge of the unit content. This is a good opportunity for you to take responsibility for your own learning, as well as preparing you for research tasks you may need to do academically or professionally.

# Features connected to your assessment

Your course is made up of a series of mandatory and optional units. There are two different types of mandatory unit:

▶ externally assessed
▶ internally assessed.

The features that support you in preparing for assessment are below. But first, what is the difference between these two different types of units?

## Externally assessed units

These units give you the opportunity to present what you have learned in the unit in a different way. They can be challenging, but will really give you the opportunity to demonstrate your knowledge and understanding, or your skills in a direct way. For these units you will complete an assessment, set directly by Pearson, in controlled conditions. This could take the form of an exam or it could be a type of task. You may have the opportunity in advance to research and prepare notes around a topic, which can be used when completing the assessment.

### Internally assessed units

Most of your units will be internally assessed. This involves you completing a series of assignments, set and marked by your teacher. The assignments you complete could allow you to demonstrate your learning in a number of different ways, from a written report to a presentation to a video recording and observation statements of you completing a practical task. Whatever the method, you will need to make sure you have clear evidence of what you have achieved and how you did it.

## Assessment practice

These features give you the opportunity to practise some of the skills you will need when you are assessed on your unit. They do not fully reflect the actual assessment tasks, but will help you get ready for doing them.

### Plan – Do – Review

You'll also find handy advice on how to plan, complete and evaluate your work after you have completed it. This is designed to get you thinking about the best way to complete your work and to build your skills and experience before doing the actual assessment. These prompt questions are designed to get you started with thinking about how the way you work, as well as understand why you do things.

## Getting ready for assessment

For internally assessed units, this is a case study from a BTEC National student, talking about how they planned and carried out their assignment work and what they would do differently if they were to do it again. It will give you advice on preparing for the kind of work you will need to for your internal assessments, including Think about it points for you to consider for your own development.

## Getting ready for assessment

This section will help you to prepare for external assessment. It gives practical advice on preparing for and sitting exams or a set task. It provides a series of sample answers for the types of questions you will need to answer in your external assessments, including guidance on the good points of these answers and how these answers could be improved.

# Features to help you reflect on and evaluate your learning

**⏸ PAUSE POINT**

Pause Points appear after a section of each unit and give you the opportunity to review and reflect upon your own learning. The ability to reflect on your own performance is a key skill you'll need to develop and use throughout your life, and will be essential whatever your future plans are.

Hint
Extend

These also give you suggestions to help cement your knowledge and indicate other areas you can look at to expand it.

**Reflect**

This allows you to reflect on how the knowledge you have gained in this unit may impact your behaviour in a workplace situation. This will help not only to place the topic in a professional context, but also help you to review your own conduct and develop your employability skills.

# Features which link your learning with the workplace

**Case study**

Case studies are used throughout the book to allow you to apply the learning and knowledge from the unit to a scenario from the workplace or the industry. Case studies include questions to help you consider the wider context of a topic. This is an opportunity to see how the unit's content is reflected in the real world, and for you to build familiarity with issues you may find in a real-world workplace.

# THINK ▶FUTURE

This is a special case study where someone working in the industry talks about the job role they do and the skills they need. This comes with a *Focusing your skills* section, which gives suggestions for how you can begin to develop the employability skills and experiences that are needed to be successful in a career in your chosen sector. This is an excellent opportunity to help you identify what you could do, inside and outside of your BTEC National studies, to build up your employability skills.

# International Business 5

# Getting to know your unit

International business has a huge impact on the national as well as world-wide economy for small and large businesses. This unit gives you the chance to investigate the benefits and issues concerned with international business, including the economic and cultural factors that influence the way in which business is conducted. You will also have the chance to gain a greater understanding of the strategic and operational approaches to developing businesses. Finally, being aware of options in the global business environment will help you to choose whether to specialise in international business in higher education or seek employment in this area after your BTEC.

## How you will be assessed

This unit will be assessed through a series of internally assessed tasks set by your tutor. Throughout this unit, you will find assessment practices that will help you to practise and to develop your knowledge and skills ready for assessment. Completing these practices will help you to be fully prepared for assessment as you will have practised the activities before you complete your final assessment.

In order to successfully pass this unit, you must make sure that you have met the requirements of all the Pass grading criteria. You can do this yourself by checking against the criteria.

To gain a Merit or a Distinction, you must extend your work further. For Merit criteria you must analyse different elements of the unit. For Distinction you must evaluate. This means that you must make judgements about different criteria in the unit.

The assignment(s) set by your tutor will consist of a number of tasks designed to meet the criteria in the table. This is likely to consist of activities such as:

- writing an individual report that researches the context of businesses operating internationally, including how international business is financed and the support given to it
- writing a journal article giving situational analysis of contrasting markets supported by a report on the results of the analysis and how cultural factors influence businesses operating internationally
- giving a presentation comparing the strategies and resources used by two contrasting businesses operating internationally.

## Assessment criteria

This table shows you what you must do in order to achieve a **Pass**, **Merit** or **Distinction** grade, and where you can find activities to help you.

| **Pass** | **Merit** | **Distinction** |
|---|---|---|
| **Learning aim** **A** Explore the international context for business operations | | |
| **A.P1** Explain why two businesses operate in contrasting international markets. **Assessment practice 5.1** | **A.M1** Analyse the support that is available to contrasting businesses that operate internationally. **Assessment practice 5.1** | |
| **A.P2** Explain the types of finance available for international business. **Assessment practice 5.1** | | **AB.D1** Evaluate the impact of globalisation on a business. **Assessment practice 5.1** |
| **Learning aim** **B** Investigate international economic environment in which business operates | | |
| **B.P3** Explain the main features of globalisation that affect two contrasting businesses. **Assessment practice 5.1** | **B.M2** Analyse the barriers of operating internationally for two contrasting businesses. **Assessment practice 5.1** | |
| **B.P4** Explore the role of trading blocs on international trade. **Assessment practice 5.1** | | |
| **Learning aim** **C** Investigate the external factors that influence international businesses | | |
| **C.P5** Explain the external factors that influence a selected business considering trading internationally. **Assessment practice 5.2** | **C.M3** Carry out a situational analysis on two countries that a selected business may consider trading in. **Assessment practice 5.2** | **C.D2** Recommend one country that a selected business could target for international trade, justifying your decision. **Assessment practice 5.2** |
| **C.P6** Explain how business support systems enable a selected business to trade internationally. **Assessment practice 5.2** | | |
| **Learning aim** **D** Investigate the cultural factors that influence international businesses | | |
| **D.P7** Explore the cultural differences affecting international businesses. **Assessment practice 5.2** | **D.M4** Analyse how cultural differences affect international businesses. **Assessment practice 5.2** | **D.D3** Evaluate the impact of cultural differences on international business. **Assessment practice 5.2** |
| **Learning aim** **E** Examine the strategic and operational approaches to developing international businesses | | |
| **E.P8** Explain how products and processes have to be adapted for international markets by a selected business. **Assessment practice 5.3** | **E.M5** Analyse the effectiveness of the strategies and resources used by a selected international business. **Assessment practice 5.3** | **E.D4** Evaluate the success of the strategies and resources used by a selected international business in one of its markets. **Assessment practice 5.3** |

## Getting started

International business takes place every day and includes movement of physical goods from one country to another and provision of services that often take place online using email or communication such as Skype. Write down as many different ways of trading as you can think of. At the end of the unit, review your list and see how many new types you have learned about, to measure your learning progress.

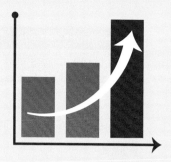

# A Explore the international context for business operations

In this section, you will explore the different ways that international business takes place, and the reasons why businesses choose to operate in this way. Choosing the right markets and the factors that influence those markets are also considered, as well as the finance and support needed for international business to take place.

## International business

International business can take many different forms and these include sending things overseas (exporting), bringing them in (importing), operating in different countries (multinational) and being involved with the support for businesses operating in multiple countries, through activities such as marketing or logistics.

### Types of business activity

Businesses will be involved in one or more different activities when they operate internationally. This may mean that they need offices in different locations or that they will use **subcontractors** to carry out work on their behalf, for example Fugro operate the cable laying for the Rampion offshore wind farm operated by E.On UK plc.

### Exporting businesses

When a business decides to export, it can do this within the European Union (EU) or outside the EU. Operating within the EU means that there are no customs checks on the goods that are moving into Europe and also that goods can be freely moved. This type of export is called dispatches. You will learn more about the EU and how this affects international business later in this unit.

If a business decides to export outside the EU, different rules apply and the countries where goods are sent to are called 'third countries'. Businesses deciding to export to these countries may need:

▶ an export declaration

▶ an export licence

▶ to pay customs duties

▶ to pay taxes in the country where the goods are being sent.

Many different businesses export throughout the EU and worldwide, including Pipe Source UK Ltd, which works with other partners to deliver piping and other related equipment to businesses all over the world.

## Importing businesses

Importing goods from an EU country into the UK usually means that the business does not need a licence or to pay import duties, but value added tax (VAT) must be paid and the business needs to have a **commodity** code attached to the import so that the right VAT level can be paid. Plater Chemicals, for example, is a leading importer of chemicals from the EU and throughout the rest of the world.

Commodities are given codes that are used to give additional guidelines or show how much VAT is to be paid. For example:

> the code for importing playing cards is 9504400000:
>  • 95 relates to toys and games
>  • 04 table or parlour games
>  • 40 00 00 relates to playing cards.

The amount of VAT is determined by the code that is given to that commodity.

Importing goods from outside the EU requires:

> an import declaration

> an import licence

> commodity codes to be allocated to the goods

> customs duties to be declared and paid to Her Majesty's Revenue and Customs (HMRC)

> VAT to be paid.

| Key term |
| --- |
| **Commodity** – a raw material or product that can be bought or sold. |

## Multinational enterprises

Multinational businesses are those that operate in more than one country, and they can often operate in a number of different markets globally. Multinational enterprises have to be very careful to adapt the way that they trade to the different countries in which they are operating. Each country will have different rules for importation, tax and other duties that need to be paid. They also have different customs, laws and cultures which will affect their operations.

## Associated businesses

Sometimes businesses will offer their support to other organisations through offering services or working in partnership. Businesses that associate with others to help with international trade may offer specialist services such as those relating to marketing or **logistics**.

For example, GBS Freight operates throughout Europe and the rest of the world, moving goods on behalf of others.

| Key term |
| --- |
| **Logistics** – the movement of people, goods or facilities. |

**⏸ PAUSE POINT**  Think of four key reasons why a business might choose to export within the EU rather than exporting to the rest of the world.

> Hint  Compare the movement of goods and people that is possible throughout Europe compared with outside Europe.

> Extend  'Trading outside the EU is a very high risk business.' To what extent do you agree with this view?

## Reasons for conducting business internationally

Conducting business internationally offers lots of different opportunities for growth and development that may not be possible from working in the UK alone. For example, AstraZeneca plc is a British–Swedish company that is one of the largest pharmaceutical companies in the world and which benefits significantly from international business operations.

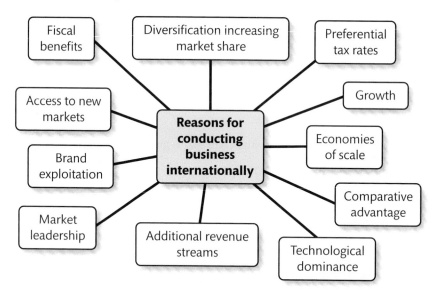

▶ **Figure 5.1:** There are many good reasons to conduct business internationally

### Growth

Offering goods and services in other areas outside the UK offers potential for organisations to grow, and growing sales should lead, in the longer term, to growing profits. Most businesses operate to make a profit, so taking something that is being sold successfully in one country and offering it in another should lead to more sales and eventually more profits, if the business operates carefully. Businesses operating outside the UK can also offer new goods and services from outside the country. This can offer growth in particular markets for them as well as growth for the associated companies that are required to help them, for example in distribution or marketing.

### Additional revenue streams

Choosing to sell goods or services in other countries also gives companies more opportunities to generate **revenue**. New revenue streams are methods to generate new income. The more ways that an organisation has to generate income, the more stable the business is likely to be. If one revenue stream is not working well, then there are others that can be used to generate income instead: for example, companies such as Virgin choose to offer different products and services that complement one another, such as trains, flights and gyms.

### Brand exploitation

Exploiting **brands** means making the most of the name of the brand across different countries. This means that a brand name may be used for sponsorship in different countries, which is commonly used in sports, so different brands will sponsor different teams. Brands may also be exploited by using a brand name that is associated with one country and then having it licensed to be made or offered in another country by other companies on behalf of the business.

### Key terms

**Revenue** – the amount of money that a company receives during a specific period of time.

**Brand** – a distinctive name or trademark that is given to a particular product or service.

General Mills is an American company that owns many well-known food brands manufactured under licence across the world. In the UK, for example, one of their brand items, Old El Paso Refried Beans, is manufactured in Spain for General Mills International, Switzerland and is then distributed to the UK.

Research other brands owned by General Mills and list the different places where they are manufactured and then distributed. Discuss what you find out with other members of your class.

### Access to new markets

Trading on an international basis gives businesses the chance to expand their sales and offer goods and services that may be common in one country and sell them in another. Accessing new markets offers new opportunities, as people in those countries may not have come across those products before.

▶ List as many internationally recognisable brand names as possible.

**Discussion**

#### The tale of two salespeople

There is a business story that tells of two shoe salespeople who went to another country. When they got there they found that no one was wearing shoes.

One salesperson was very disappointed and returned back to the UK, saying sadly 'we will never make sales in this country because no one wears shoes'.

The other salesperson was very happy and she telephoned back to the UK telling them to send the whole sales team to this country – because no one was wearing shoes and there were many sales to be made!

- Discuss the story above in small groups.
- What are the advantages and disadvantages of trying to sell a product or service in a country where it is not already sold?

### Diversification

Diversification means taking a new product or service into a new market. Diversifying can help a business to reduce risks as they will then offer different types of product or service so they are not reliant on one or two, but it can also increase risks if that product or service does not take off in a particular country.

### Increasing market share and market leadership

International businesses, as you have already learned in this unit, often work across many different countries and even regions. Having a greater share of the market means that they have more sales in that particular market and they are more dominant over the other businesses that are operating in that market. By becoming the leader in a market, the business has the most control over a particular market and can make sure that they are first to make changes to a particular product or service.

### Technological dominance

To have the position of the market leader, as you have learned, means that you are the most powerful business in a particular market sector. Having dominance may make it hard for other businesses to come into the market in which you are operating and one of the other effects that often follows is technological dominance. When a business trades across countries and becomes large, it is able to invest in technology to make processes work more efficiently. This often leads to higher profits as sales go up and costs go down. Technological dominance can also be gained by businesses operating internationally as they source supplies or carry out research in one country and then sell goods or services in another.

▶ How are processes made more efficient by technological dominance?

🅤 **PAUSE POINT**

Why is the ability to increase market share important for a business thinking of trading overseas?

**Hint**    Think about the potential for revenue and increasing costs of trading at higher levels.

**Extend**    Market leadership is the single most important aim for any business entering a new market. Discuss this view.

**Comparative advantage**

Being able to produce goods or services across more than one country and then sell them in another reduces costs for a business and supports the potential for higher profits to be made. This is called comparative advantage.

---

**Theory into practice**

**Comparative advantage**

Compare these two businesses in the UK.

**Business 1** has a toy bear manufactured in the UK for £3 per bear. They sell these for £4 per bear to retail stores. The retailer then sells them for £6 per bear.

**Business 2** has a toy bear manufactured in Europe for £1 per bear. They have to import the toy bears at an additional cost of £1 per bear. They sell them for £3.50 to retail stores that sell them for £6 per bear.

- How much cheaper is it to manufacture a toy bear in Europe than in the UK?
- How much additional money is made by Business 2 when the manufacturing costs are taken away from the sales price?
- How much additional money is made by the retailer?
- What are factors to consider when selling a toy bear in the UK that has been made in another country?

'Keeping the selling price of a product high while keeping the costs low is the aim of any business trading internationally.' Discuss this view in small groups.

---

## Economies of scale

Economies of scale mean that the more of a product or service that you sell, the lower the cost per unit to make it. This is because, whether you produce one product or 1000 products, your overheads will remain the same. Being able to produce large volumes of goods means costs go down, as shown in the Worked Example.

## Worked Example

If you produce one tin of beans in a factory per day and the factory costs £1000 per day to run, that tin of beans would need to be sold for at least £1000 to cover its costs. If you produced 1000 tins of beans in that factory per day the cost per tin would be £1 per tin plus the costs of the tin, the beans and the label (variable costs, for example £0.25). The cost would then be £1.25. If the factory produced 50,000 tins of beans per day, then the cost per tin would be £0.02 per tin plus the variable cost of £0.20 (this would also usually go down due to being able to buy materials more cheaply), and the cost to produce the beans would be £0.22.

1 tin = £1000.25 per tin    1000 tins = £1.25 per tin    50,000 tins = £0.22 per tin

**Research**

In small groups carry out research into what is meant by diseconomies of scale and how this might affect a business wishing to trade on an international basis.

## Fiscal benefits and preferential tax rates

Fiscal benefits and enhancements relate to the amount of spending and tax that a government of a country is seeking to make. If a business is choosing to export outside the UK, they may be given support by the UK government to do so, as this has a positive impact on the performance of the UK as a whole. If an international business chooses to come to the UK and is a large employer, so will create a lot of jobs, the UK government may offer an incentive for them to come. One of the ways in which this can be done is for them to have a preferential tax rate on profits that they have made in the UK. The same is true for businesses operating outside the UK that will seek to pay lower charges and taxes overseas if they are able to do so.

**Research**

The island of Jersey has different rates of tax for businesses, compared with mainland UK. Carry out research, in pairs, into the rates of tax for businesses in Jersey. What implications does this have for businesses operating there? What are the advantages or disadvantages for businesses choosing to work in Jersey or sell goods from Jersey?

▶ How many companies can you find that export flowers from the Channel Islands?

## Choice of markets in which to operate

Throughout this unit so far, you have learned the different reasons why businesses choose to trade overseas. Choosing which market to operate in is the next decision for any business thinking about moving into, or expanding to trade in more international markets. There are three main types of market in which businesses can operate, as shown in Table 5.1.

▶ **Table 5.1:** Different markets for international business

| Type of market | Examples | Potential advantages | Possible disadvantages |
|---|---|---|---|
| Developed economies | • Europe<br>• UK | • Already established and support available from agencies to help trade here.<br>• Higher employment rates.<br>• Established trading rules. | • Market already very competitive (unless a unique or new service).<br>• Higher tax levels than other countries. |
| Less developed economies or developing economies | • Brazil<br>• Russia<br>• India<br>• China | • Potential for high sales, e.g. there are 1.5 billion people living in China.<br>• Structures in place to continue expansion and existing knowledge. | • Different tax or legal systems that present risks.<br>• Protection of the country for its own products and services or reluctance to adopt products and services from other countries. |
| Emerging markets | • Turkey<br>• Mexico<br>• Iran | • Opportunities to be the first entrant into that market.<br>• Government incentives offered there to create jobs or reduced taxes. | • Ethical considerations, for example the use of child labour if in existence.<br>• Lower employment rates or lower wages that may restrict sales growth.<br>• International relationships or restrictions on trading with that country. |

## Factors influencing the choice of market

Choosing which markets to operate in needs very careful thought. For example, a business that is considering extending into China will need to have all the necessary support and local knowledge to ensure that it operates within the Chinese legal system. It must also ensure that any cultural differences between the UK and China are understood in order to avoid any problems. You will learn more about cultural differences later in this unit. The type of market choice will be affected by:

▶ the type of product of service: some products and services may not be appropriate for particular markets (for example, it would not be appropriate for a sausage manufacturer to choose a market where pork is not eaten)

▶ costs: the cost of exporting goods may be prohibitive to particular markets

▶ the size of the market: all businesses need to consider how many potential customers they will have in a particular market before deciding whether to enter that market.

> **Discussion**
>
> How could a UK supplier of sun hats grow their business by operating in different overseas markets?
>
> Divide your group into two, with half of the group thinking of ways in which a UK business could grow their business by selling overseas and the other half of the group thinking of the barriers to sales.
>
> Hold a class debate 'A UK sun hat supplier is unlikely to be successful when trading outside the UK.'

**❶ PAUSE POINT**    Describe the three most important reasons why businesses choose to engage in international business.

> (Hint)    Think back to all the different reasons why they may choose to get involved and the benefits to them of doing so.

> (Extend)    To what extent do you think choosing the right market is more important than the product or service itself?

# Financing of international business

Once a business has decided that it wishes to trade internationally, and has researched all the possible options, the next stage of the process is to ensure that the finances are in place so that the international trade can be financed. There are four key ways to finance international business and the appropriateness of the different methods very much depends on the products or services that are being offered and the market in which the business is operating.

## Methods used to finance international trade

### Prepayment by the importer

If a business decides it wishes to import goods into the UK to sell, or if an overseas business wants to import British goods, it is sometimes required to pay in advance in total or in part-payment. Paying cash in advance for goods does involve a lot of trust between the two organisations. Total or part-payment in advance may be necessary when importing goods if:

▸ there is little trust by the company sending the goods to the importer

▸ the political situation in either country is challenging

▸ there is a high demand for the goods and, by paying in advance, the price can be fixed at a particular level

▸ the importer is a new business or new to the market and cannot negotiate better terms.

Part-payments may be more acceptable to both parties, depending on the size of the payment required in advance.

> **Discussion**
>
> When businesses trade overseas, they have to choose between trading in their own currency or the local currency of the country to which they are exporting. Discuss the benefits of trading in the different types of currency.

### Letters of credit

Letters of credit are very commonly used for international trade. Under an import letter of credit, the bank of the importer agrees that they will pay the supplier as soon as the order has been completed and the terms and conditions of the letter of credit are met. The bank working with the importer will not check the goods that have been received but will make sure that the importer is paid. The bank monitors the agreement between the two different businesses and acts as a form of intermediary to make things easier for both parties.

Letters of credit are also used as evidence for customs and other legal practices in the countries where the businesses are operating.

### Export credits

Export credits are when a business agrees with a supplier or customer that credit is offered or given for a specific amount of time and related to pre-set terms and conditions. Export credits may be offered to a business overseas when a UK company allows them to have the goods up front and allows them to pay for them after an agreed period of time. Export credits may also be used if the businesses are supplying to each other to save monies being moved between the two organisations.

Export credits may also be provided by an export credit agency. These agencies offer finance to help exports take place and their role includes helping to negotiate terms and also to provide insurance to make sure that payment is received. This is very important if the country with which the business is working is politically unstable and the transaction is high risk. Export credits negotiated through Export Credit Agencies may have short-, medium- or long-term payment periods, depending on the risk involved.

> **Research**
>
> Carry out research into UK Export Finance to find out their role and how they help UK businesses to export, and businesses overseas to buy, products from the UK. In small groups, outline how UK Export Finance helps each type of business and why.

### Bank loans

Bank loans are another source of finance to expand internationally. The type of loan and the type of terms that are offered depends on a number of different factors: size of the loan required, type of products or service on offer, knowledge of the market/country where the goods are being sent or experience and track record of the business trading overseas. Some loans may be taken directly by the businesses through their existing banking arrangements. Others need more specialist loans and insurance, which is available from agencies such as UK Export Finance. Bank loans offer funding to support expansion of businesses overseas, but it is important for businesses to ensure that they sign up to the best terms and conditions that they can to support their business.

▶ Why are bank loans a common source of finance for businesses to use to expand?

## PAUSE POINT

Why might a business use a letter of credit in preference to a part-payment for an international order?

**Hint**   Think about the risks involved when using each method of payment.

**Extend**   'Bank loans are the most efficient way of accessing finance for international business.' Discuss this view.

**Case study**

### British Chambers of Commerce

The British Chambers of Commerce have been offering support for businesses to trade internationally for more than 150 years and promote partnerships between organisations in different countries. The support offered aims to give practical and on-the-ground advice about how to work in different markets in the world. Businesses wishing to operate overseas can get access to specific support to operate in a particular country including:

- market information
- practical tips about how to trade in a country
- building the share of a market in a particular country
- building the share of a market in a region.

Go to their website and check your knowledge.

### Check your knowledge

1 Why do you think the British Chambers of Commerce offer support for businesses?

2 What are the advantages of providing information and support for businesses to trade in other countries?

3 Are there any potential disadvantages?

4 Carry out research online to find information on the nearest Chamber of Commerce to where you live. In small groups, discuss the different types of support available for organisations wanting to trade internationally in your area.

## Support for international business

You have already learned, during this unit, about two of the agencies that support UK businesses to export goods and services: Chambers of Commerce and UK Export Finance. There are also other agencies that can offer help: UK Trade and Investment and Regional Advisory Organisations.

### Agencies that support international business

#### Department for International Trade

Department for International Trade offers support to UK businesses that trade internationally and also to overseas entrepreneurs wishing to set up their businesses in the UK. Department for International Trade has advisors in each of the regional areas of the UK and offers a service of workshops, videos and information packs to help any business thinking of trading internationally to have support to do so. Accessing support from Department for International Trade saves businesses time, and also therefore money, as they are able to trade more quickly and gain support to do so.

#### Regional advisory councils

You have already learned about some of the regional advisory councils that help businesses in your area to export. As well as having a national Chamber of Commerce that represents the UK as a whole, there are also local Chambers of Commerce that serve the needs of the different regions. Local Chambers of Commerce offer specific training and opportunities for the areas which they serve.

Local enterprise partnerships are also available in each of the regional areas. Networking and support is on offer to help businesses from the regions to gain access to support and funding through partnership working to help increase the number of exports from the UK from those particular areas.

## Greater Cambridge/Greater Peterborough Local Enterprise Partnership

Local enterprise partnerships operate across the UK and bring together representatives from business, local government and social enterprise, the voluntary sector and education. The purpose of all Local Enterprise Partnerships is to tackle barriers to growth in their areas by supporting growth, developing skills and setting up local support, including support for exporting overseas.

Greater Cambridge/Greater Peterborough Local Enterprise Partnership (GCGP LEP) offers support to businesses to help them export from the local area all over the world.

Go to their website and check your knowledge.

**Check your knowledge**

1  Why do you think the GCGP LEP offers support for businesses to export?

2  What are the advantages of providing information and support for businesses to trade in other countries?

3  Are there any potential disadvantages?

4  Now compare the support in your area with that offered in Great Cambridge/Greater Peterborough – how does your area compare?

### Open to Export

Open to Export is a community interest company (CIC) that is run as a not-for-profit organisation. It is supported by many different agencies including the Federation of Small Businesses, the Institute of Export and the HSBC bank. The organisation supports businesses going into export by providing training, practical information, webinars and different forums so that ideas can be shared.

**Research**

Open to Export offers a wide range of advice, information, webinars and support, such as 'Ask the Expert'. In pairs, go to the website and find out information about how a small business such as a dog bakery would export its products from the UK to France. Produce a poster of what you have found to present to your class.

### Types of support provided

There is a huge range of support on offer for businesses wanting to get involved in international trade, and advisors are available too. You have already learned about UK Export Finance earlier in this unit. They have advisers who are allocated to help businesses. Help is also available for businesses from other sources.

▶ **Table 5.2:** Support for international business

| Trade fairs | Export Britain (part of the British Chamber of Commerce) organises local export trade fairs all over the UK. |
|---|---|
| | The trade fairs vary from single focused fairs, such as Discover Columbia: Business Opportunities for British Companies, to the International Festival of Business 2016 held in Liverpool. |
| | Export Britain also offers trade missions to countries such as China and Vietnam where UK businesses are given the opportunity to meet representatives from businesses overseas. |
| | Trade Fairs are also organised by trade associations and there are many different trade associations that can support the development of international trade: for example, Associated Independent Stores is an association that works to help smaller retailers by combining expertise, knowledge and purchasing power. |

▶ **Table 5.2:** – *continued*

| | |
|---|---|
| Identifying international partners | Visits to different international countries, and becoming aware of the different opportunities there, are ways to help to identify international partners for businesses.<br><br>British embassies are based in most international countries and they are also there to help to support international trade with Britain. They are able to offer support and information to businesses about countries that they are working with.<br><br>Other companies or agents are also available to help establish businesses overseas and look for partners for them to work with: for example, Intro International offers support to businesses wishing to establish themselves in Singapore. |
| Grants for international promotions | Grants are available for UK businesses to start operating overseas. For example, grants may be available for small businesses wishing to grow by exporting overseas through the Growth Programme which aims to support new or existing small businesses in rural areas. |

 **PAUSE POINT**    Describe as many different types of support as you can that are available for businesses wishing to trade internationally.

> **Hint**    Think about all the different types of support available under different categories and the impact of support for businesses.

> **Extend**    Research the support available for businesses offering different types of goods or services in your local area.

# B Investigate the international economic environment in which business operates

You have already learned about the benefits for businesses of trading internationally, and the many different reasons that they choose to do so, from their individual or group perspectives. Across the world, globalisation affects all businesses and this section outlines what is meant by globalisation, how countries work together to help each other in different parts of the world and, finally, what restricts or stops international trade from taking place. Restrictions and support are important for UK businesses to consider when they are operating internationally as their influence may help a business to decide if it is going to choose to go into a particular market or not!

## Globalisation

You have probably heard people say that the world is getting smaller all the time. Globalisation means that, through better communication, financing and links between countries, world trade and partnerships are becoming easier. Improvements in technology that are happening on a daily basis mean that trading with businesses in other countries is much easier now, in many instances, than at other times in history.

Globalisation has a number of features and these include countries working together, people moving for work, organisations working across borders and payment systems being worldwide. Examples of companies that trade globally include Apple (technology), Actavis (health care) and Nike (consumer goods).

### Trading blocs

A trading bloc is a group of countries in a geographical area that get together to protect themselves from countries outside their group, working together to make goods or services move more easily and placing restrictions on the number of goods or services being brought into the area. You will learn more about trading blocs in this unit.

### International mobility of labour and capital

Globalisation also means that it is possible to have people working in different countries around the world for different organisations. The mobility of labour makes it easier for people to work in other countries around the world. Citizens of the UK may require permits to work outside the EU. Citizens of member states of the EU are able to move and work where they wish within the EU. As the UK has decided to leave the EU, it is unclear what requirements there may be in the future for UK citizens to work in EU countries. The same is true of capital. It means uncertainty as to whether investment is possible in countries outside the UK to set up businesses by UK citizens, or for business people outside the UK to come in to the UK and invest in a new business.

### International currencies

There are more than 150 different currencies in the world. Globalisation means that businesses are aware of the different ways to trade and the currencies that can be used. Sometimes common currencies are chosen for trading, such as dollars, the euro or sterling (pound).

### Multinational corporations

Another feature of globalisation is that companies now regularly trade across the UK, the EU and even the world. Very large multinational corporations will have offices throughout the United States, the EU, Australia, Asia and Africa. Some of these multinational corporations are so large that the turnover they make per year is greater than the wealth of some of the countries of the world.

---

### Case study

### Walmart

Walmart is the largest retailer in the world. It trades in 28 countries under 65 different brand names. In 2015, it had net sales of nearly $500 billion. Walmart employs 2.2 million staff worldwide and has 260 million customers. In the UK, Walmart trades as Asda. In Africa, it trades in South Africa and 12 other sub-Saharan countries as Massmart.

Carry out research into Walmart and how it operates as a multinational corporation.

#### Check your knowledge

1   What are the benefits for Walmart of operating across the world?

2   Are there any potential disadvantages?

3   'Companies trading across the world is the natural progression for all large companies in the UK.' Discuss this view.

## International business communications

International business communications happen on a daily basis online through websites, social media and other communication systems such as Skype. Skype allows companies and people to communicate all over the world using WiFi; this is a cost-effective and efficient way to work. Communication can take place using systems such as Skype through audio, text chat or video. Many organisations choose to operate in common languages, such as English, or it is possible to communicate using translator software online that can almost instantaneously translate what you are saying into another language.

**PAUSE POINT**    Many companies are now trading in Mandarin. What are the benefits to businesses of trading in a language like Mandarin?

Hint    Think about all the different potential customers that speak Mandarin.

Extend    'Businesses can communicate worldwide now with only the use of instant translation services online; they do not need to rely on local knowledge or people.' Discuss this view and decide whether or not you agree.

## International payment systems

Paying for goods and having them shipped from overseas was much more challenging in the past and involved having different bank accounts and arrangements for exchanging money. Many businesses today, even very large ones, such as Argos or British Airways, use organisations such as PayPal to help them manage these payments.

### Case study

#### PayPal

PayPal had 173 million users worldwide in 2015. It offers a free service for customers to be able to pay for their goods or services online securely by using the network that PayPal has linked across the world. PayPal offers businesses the ability to trade in 203 countries in 26 different currencies and 24/7, so orders can be made and payments taken 24 hours a day.

Carry out research into PayPal and find out more about some of the companies that they support, from very small organisations through to multinational organisations.

**Check your knowledge**

1   What are the benefits for businesses of using a service like PayPal when they are trading globally?

2   Are there any potential concerns they may have?

3   'Purchasing goods online is just as safe as using cash offline.' Make a judgement about this view.

## International trading blocs

You have already learned that a trading bloc is a group of countries in a geographical area that get together to protect themselves from countries outside their group; working together to make goods or services move more easily and placing restrictions on the number of goods or services being brought into the area. Some organisations help these countries to work together to move goods and services more easily. These organisations include the World Trade Organization and other common markets that you will have heard of, such as the EU.

## World Trade Organization (WTO)

The WTO makes sure that countries can trade with each other as smoothly, predictably and freely as possible so that businesses can sell their goods all over the world. The WTO has negotiated agreements between countries so that businesses trading have legal rights and agreements that can protect them, and the laws of different countries can be recognised and adhered too. Many countries have the trade agreements voted on and confirmed by their parliaments.

If there is a problem or dispute between two countries, the WTO will step in and try to help. The WTO has 160 member countries and these countries are responsible for approximately 95 per cent of all world trade that takes place. More countries want to join the organisation as it helps businesses to trade more easily.

The WTO aims to help people throughout the world to trade effectively with each other by keeping costs low and ensuring that countries trade fairly with others, as well as maintaining the health of their populations and the world environment.

### Research

Carry out research into the WTO. Find the latest news and information that has been published to help countries trade with each other. Find out the settlement arrangements for the latest disputes between different countries and watch some of the WTO videos to find out more. Can you identify the key things that the WTO offers? Put together a brief presentation to display your findings.

## Customs unions and common markets

In some areas of the world, customs unions and common markets have been established to allow free trade to take place between those different countries. You have already learned a little about the EU earlier in this unit and you will also learn about Mercosur (South American Nations).

### The EU

The EU was first established through the European Economic Community after the Second World War. The more formal move towards the EU of today started in 1957 when six countries joined together: France, Germany, Italy, Belgium, the Netherlands and Luxembourg. Over the next 60 years or so, that number increased to 28 different countries including the UK (which joined in 1973). The EU is important as it created its own internal market which allows goods and services to move even more freely between the 28 different countries. It does this through the following ways.

▶ It has its own currency: the euro.

▶ There are some areas of the EU where border controls are not required at all: the Schengen Area is an area of the EU where people do not need to have their passports checked and they can move freely.

▶ It gives citizens EU rights and responsibilities as well as those of their own individual countries.

▶ There are common policies and agreements on many different aspects of EU life from agriculture through to food safety.

▶ Common paperwork and arrangements make recognition between the different countries easier, for example, common driving licences.

**Mercosur**

Rather like the EU, Mercosur is a group of countries that has joined together to help each other trade. These countries are grouped in South America and the countries are:

▶ Argentina

▶ Brazil

▶ Paraguay

▶ Uruguay

▶ Venezuela.

The Mercosur area allows the countries to trade with each other more easily and, like the EU, Mercosur has countries that are associate countries that work with the group, again to help support trade. These include other South American countries, such as Peru, Chile and Columbia. The size of the land involved in Mercosur is a lot larger than the EU (in fact, four times as big) and although the group has been established for more than 20 years, it has not yet made as much progress as the EU. However, the vision is to have a similar way of working to allow people to move freely between the different countries and to support growth and trading effectively across all the different countries.

## Free trade areas

The idea of moving goods, services and, indeed, people, in areas with limited or no restrictions, can also be applied to other free trade areas that have been established in the world. These include the Northern American Free Trade Agreement (NAFTA) area and the Asia Pacific Economic Cooperation (APEC) area.

### North American Free Trade Area (NAFTA)

This agreement is between Canada, the United States of America (USA) and Mexico. The purpose is to make trading between the countries easier and to remove tariffs, particularly those that relate to Mexico, to allow goods to be traded more easily between Mexico and the other two countries. NAFTA supports movement of people between the countries but requires citizens moving to work in the USA to have temporary employment status which lasts for only three years.

NAFTA has ensured that Canada, the USA and Mexico have benefited from free trade by:

▶ reducing the cost of goods and therefore inflation in the member countries

▶ increasing competition for government contracts between the three countries which lowers costs between them

▶ promoting investment by companies outside the area by encouraging multinationals to invest in the NAFTA area

▶ increasing the trade between the three countries so that they benefit from supporting each other even more

▶ creating more jobs in the three countries as the trade between them develops

▶ creating specialist skills in the area, for example mining, agriculture and car manufacturing.

### Asia Pacific Economic Cooperation (APEC)

The Asia Pacific Economic Cooperation area consists of 21 very varied countries. The purpose of this regional economic forum is to give greater prosperity to the people of those countries by building inclusive communities, so that everyone in those communities can be supported to live with better living standards, reducing poverty and improving health standards.

APEC seeks to enhance economic integration which means that it tries to ensure that all 21 countries in the region work with each other to trade as much as possible and, by doing this, it helps small- and medium-sized businesses to grow. This means that across those countries more people are in work and are able to contribute to the wealth of the area. APEC also develops the skills and expertise of people, particularly relating to technology, to make sure that the region has the skills it requires to ensure that it can work effectively in the future. Finally, it also seeks to build sustainable and resilient communities. This means communities that can flex and change according to the needs of the area. The aim is also to support communities after disasters and other environmental problems so that they can survive and not require significant amounts of external assistance, as they will be able to cope with such impacts.

▶ **Table 5.3:** Asia Pacific Economic Cooperation: APEC countries

| Australia | Japan | Phillipines |
|---|---|---|
| Brunei Darussalam | Korea | Russia |
| Canada | Malaysia | Singapore |
| Chile | Mexico | Chinese Taipei |
| China | New Zealand | Thailand |
| Hong Kong | Papua New Guinea | USA |
| Indonesia | Peru | Vietnam |

**Research**

Carry out research into one of the APEC countries listed in Table 5.3 above. Find out when it joined APEC and the background to its economy. Present this information as a poster and share it with your group.

**Key term**

**Supply chain** – the chain of organisations that link together to produce a product or service and which includes raw materials, information, processes and people. For example, a yoghurt producer will have a farm for milk, and the chain will be between the farm and the manufacturer. The chain continues to the retailer to sell the goods to the consumer and may also involve a distributor.

There are many benefits for the 21 countries that are part of APEC, these include:

▶ reducing trading barriers between countries
▶ developing more common regulations between countries and reducing time in customs
▶ promoting economic integration and trade
▶ making it simpler for people to travel between the countries with a special APEC visa
▶ making it easier to make links in the **supply chain** between businesses that have raw materials through to those that need them for manufacturing
▶ training people in communities where skills are low to increase social equality
▶ developing energy-efficient towns and ways of working to protect the environment and reduce costs.

**⏸ PAUSE POINT**

The USA is a member of NAFTA and APEC. What are the advantages of being a member of more than one free trade area agreement?

**Hint**

Think about the benefits of being members of each individual agreement and of being members of both.

**Extend**

'Membership of more than one free trade agreement area by the USA inevitably leads to a conflict for USA multinational organisations.' Discuss this view and the extent to which you agree.

# Barriers to international business

You have already learned about many of the benefits of trade agreements that operate in the EU, North America and Asia and the way in which they benefit the countries and organisations that operate within those areas, but there are still barriers to trade that restrict where and how international business takes place. These restrictions, or barriers, sometimes operate within the trade bloc areas where negotiations are underway, or operate to stop businesses trading in a particular area. This type of restriction in international markets is known as protectionism.

## Reasons for protectionism in international markets

There are many different reasons why countries may wish to block others from trading in their country. These include protecting infant industries, protecting jobs in the country, protecting local businesses in that country, differences in consumer laws and cultural reasons.

### Protecting infant industries

Infant industries are new industries that are developing in a particular country. Countries may decide to not allow rival businesses from other countries to trade with those countries to allow the infant industries to become established. You have already learned about economies of scale; and economies of scale can only happen when businesses are large enough to compete. By protecting their infant industries, countries allow them to grow so that they can compete with businesses from other parts of the world. Sometimes infant industries will also be given special trade subsidies in their countries to help them trade more easily and these are not available to other international businesses. Infant industries that have been operating in areas of the world recently include those involved with renewable energy, such as solar power and electric cars.

▶ Infant industries that have been protected include solar power.

### Protecting employment

Countries may also restrict imports from international businesses because that country needs to protect employment. Sometimes cheaper imported goods can mean that people do not buy local products. This can result in businesses reducing the number of people they employ or even closing completely. When businesses close, employees may not be able to get other jobs and may become dependent on the state for help. To avoid this, sometimes countries will place restrictions on imports to help organisations that are struggling to survive.

### Protecting local businesses

Sometimes countries put into place particular restrictions on industries that they believe are very important for them and stop imports from other countries coming in, if they can. For example, in 2015, Canada was still placing many restrictions on imports that related to the food industry to protect its own local businesses. The dairy industry is particularly important to Canada and this is the area of industry where imports from the EU were restricted to help Canadian farmers. Argentina also has many restrictions on imports from sparkling wine through to textiles; these are all in place to protect the country from cheaper imports.

### Differences in laws

Another reason why a country may choose to protect itself from imports is because the products that may be imported do not comply with its own laws. For example, potassium bromate is a substance used in flour for baking in the USA that is permitted by the US Food and Drug Administration but is banned in the EU and many other countries around the world due to fears about its possible link to cancers. Olestra is a product used in the USA as one of the ingredients in crisps and chips. This ingredient is banned in the UK by the Food Standards Agency and in Canada. Marmite was banned in Denmark for more than three years owing to it containing extra vitamins and minerals. It was only returned to general sale in 2014 when the ban was overturned.

### Cultural reasons

Sometimes products and industries are prevented from being imported due to cultural differences: for example in the EU, Africa and Asia, raw milk (milk which has not been pasteurised) can be sold directly to consumers. In the USA and Canada, it is banned as it is perceived to be unhealthy due to the high levels of bacteria. Restrictions are also made in some countries on products containing alcohol, as these are not permitted for religious reasons.

## Methods for protecting markets

You have already learned some of the reasons why countries use protectionism to support their businesses and people, but the methods that can be used vary widely. Key methods used by different countries are shown in Table 5.4.

▶ **Table 5.4:** Methods used to protect markets

| Method of protection | How it works |
|---|---|
| Tariffs | Tariffs are additional payments or taxes that are added to goods that are imported. This means that local goods are at an advantage and often cheaper so that local people will buy them instead of more expensive imports. |
| Customs duties | Customs duties are added to goods, like tariffs and, therefore, can make goods more expensive. In 2015, a pair of leather boots being imported from Bangladesh that cost £200 plus insurance and delivery charges of £75 would require the importer to pay £46.75 duty and £64.35 of VAT. This means that the original boots costing £200 would now actually have cost £386.10 to bring to the UK. That is £186.10 more than they originally cost. The difference may mean that the boots are then cheaper to produce in the UK. |
| Currency restrictions | This is when countries will try to lower their currency value so that their goods become cheaper when they are imported by another country. For example, if a product sells at £1 and the exchange rate is £1=$1 and then the value of the currency becomes £1=$2, the product would now need to be sold for $2 instead of $1 making it more expensive and less attractive to buy for local people, in this case, in the USA. Sometimes countries will try to manipulate their currencies by allowing more or less of their money to be available to change the exchange rates to their benefit. |

▶ **Table 5.4:** – *continued*

| | |
|---|---|
| Quotas | Sometimes countries or trading blocs will introduce quotas for how much of a product or service is allowed to be brought into the country or area such as the EU. There are restrictions in place that limit the amount of seafood that may be brought in from Brazil or the number of vegetables that can be imported to the EU from Thailand. These restrictions mean that the quantity of these goods is reduced and that consumers can only purchase items from their own country so the price of these goods will be higher. |
| Subsidies | Subsidies can be used in the opposite way to quotas. Subsidies are there to support particular groups or types of industry to ensure that they can survive. It is common in the USA and EU to have subsidies for the food industry to help it continue and provide for populations in the future. |
| Legal restrictions | Having different laws in different countries affects the ability of businesses to import goods. You have already learned about different restrictions for food additives and other products that can be used to limit supply. |

## Barriers to trade

You have already learned about the different methods that can be used to protect markets but there are also other barriers to trade that can affect the ability of a business to operate in a particular country, and these are divided into six main categories.

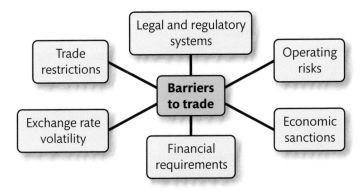

▶ **Figure 5.2:** Barriers to trade can be very varied and have a significant impact on international businesses.

### Trade restrictions

In some countries, governments may choose to have trade restrictions in place to stop businesses either importing or exporting to those countries. For example, there are long standing trade restrictions on military equipment being sent from the UK to countries such as Myanmar. Some trade restrictions have also been in place for a number of years for political or other reasons: for example, the USA has had trade restrictions in place against Cuba for many years and although these were relaxed in September 2015, they remain in place.

### Exchange rate volatility

You have already learned that governments can make changes to the value of currency to make exports cheaper and imports more expensive, but a business may be prevented from trading in a particular country because of general changes in the value of currency that has not been manipulated by governments at all. The supply and demand for money across the world affects the value of currency. If a country has a very volatile currency then, this means that its value changes often. A predictable currency means that a business can work out and effectively plan the costs of imports or exports so that they can estimate the likely profits that they will make. If a country has a currency that changes value a lot, then this is a bigger risk to the businesses trading there: for example, the Turkish Lira and Brazilian Real both devalued by 20 per cent during 2015. Such huge changes in exchange rate can have a big impact on businesses exporting or importing goods as this could result in unplanned losses that would have a negative impact on the business.

### Legal and regulatory systems

Laws and changes to legal regulations also have an impact on the way in which businesses trade, and this can be a barrier to trade. Sometimes goods may be restricted in a particular country.

## Case study

### Chewing gum in Singapore

Due to the maintenance problems that discarded chewing gum was causing on their public transport system, in 2004, Singapore began enforcing a ban on chewing gum. The import of chewing gum was immediately halted, although shops were given the opportunity to clear their existing stock. Initially, some consumers would travel to neighbouring Malaysia to purchase chewing gum, although no 'black market' or underground economy for the product ever really emerged.

In 1999, Wm Wrigley Jr Company, the chewing gum supplier, had enlisted the help of Washington DC lobbyists to include chewing gum on the United States–Singapore Free Trade Agreement. Singapore chose to recognise the health benefits of medicinal and sugar-free gum. Chewing gum is now only permitted for therapeutic reasons and must be prescribed by a doctor or dentist, for example for the purposes of giving up smoking. There are large fines in place for any citizens found to be spitting gum into the street.

#### Check your knowledge

1 How might the legal ban on chewing gum except for dental purposes affect businesses trading in Singapore?

2 What are the possible opportunities for a business trading in Singapore with this type of ban?

3 Why do you think Wrigley lobbied for the inclusion of chewing gum to the FTA, despite Singapore's small chewing gum market?

4 Carry out research into products or services that are banned in countries and consider the potential opportunities for businesses in those countries. Present your ideas to your class for discussion.

▶ Natural disasters can be one of the operating risks for businesses to take into account when operating internationally.

### Financial requirements

Another barrier to trade that can have a negative influence on a business is that of being able to access investment within a particular country, or being required to have participation in a particular project by citizens of that country. Some countries may also place financial restrictions on how much profit may be taken out of a country and require all profits to be reinvested in that country. This makes investment in that country less attractive to businesses thinking of trading there.

### Operating risks

Another barrier that impacts on international businesses is that of the threat of local operating conditions themselves. In some countries the risks of operating are higher than others and this depends on the nature of the product or service being offered and the stability of that country. In some countries, the risks of generating a loss rather than a profit may be higher due to the way in which processes operate in that business, or external events that may affect them, for example the higher likelihood of terrorism, or damage to goods through natural disaster or sudden increases or decreases in demand. If the level of operating risk is high, a business may be prevented from entering the market there and this is a form of trade barrier. Local knowledge and trading information can help to reduce these risks but they may not be eradicated totally.

### Economic sanctions

Sometimes economic sanctions are introduced to stop trade taking place between countries – this is another form of trade barrier. Sanctions are restrictive measures that are placed on countries to reduce trade happening in particular countries. Economic sanctions can influence international business as they can have a negative impact on the success of a business in a particular country. For example, until July 2015, the UK had financial restrictions placed on Iran but these have since been relaxed in exchange for limitations on Iran's developments in nuclear weapons. The relaxing of restrictions on Iran gives opportunities for businesses wishing to invest money in Iran and the transfer of monies from Iran to the UK. However, these sanctions may change at any time if the political climate changes and, therefore, economic sanctions still remain as a trade barrier and a potential high risk for businesses trading in Iran.

---

**❚❚ PAUSE POINT**　　Think of a country where there are trade restrictions in place. What are they and why have they been put into place?

　　Hint　　Think of the political and economic situations in that country and find out more about their exchange rate.

　　Extend　　'Imposing trade restrictions on countries is a necessary and inevitable part of business trading.' Evaluate how much you think this is true.

---

## Assessment practice 5.1　　　A.P1 | A.P2 | B.P3 | B.P4 | A.M1 | B.M2 | AB.D1

Operating businesses internationally is heavily influenced by the markets in which a business operates. Having access to finance and being able to trade in areas where trade is supported can all lead to business success.

You have been asked to write a report using your own research evidence to explain the impact of international business on two different businesses and provide a detailed evaluation about the impact of globalisation on one of those two businesses over a period of 5 to 10 years.

You should select two businesses that operate in contrasting international markets. Your report should explain all the main features of globalisation and consider how it has affected both businesses. In your report, you will need to ensure that you cover all aspects of international trade and globalisation for two businesses including:

- an explanation of why each business has chosen to operate in their market, with an identification of their target market and a discussion of how the characteristics of this market has impacted on business operations and management practices
- an explanation of the types of finance available for international businesses
- an explanation of the role of trading blocs in the practices and operations of the business internationally
- an analysis of the support that is available and the barriers to each business operating internationally.

You should explore the similarities and differences in approaches between your two selected businesses and consider how their structure is affected by how they engage with global businesses. You will need to ensure that you have selected relevant research sources and keep an accurate bibliography. When writing your report, you must ensure that you consider all relevant factors.

### Plan

- Where can I gain the most information about organisations that trade internationally?
- How do I reference my sources appropriately?
- How can I structure my report appropriately and include a wide range of research material that covers trading in the last 5 to 10 years?
- When are my deadlines?

### Do

- How can I check that my sources are appropriate, accurate and up to date?
- How often shall I check on my word count, page numbers and progress?
- How do I know that I am keeping to my deadlines?

### Review

- Did I include all the necessary research sources?
- Did I include enough analysis and evaluation to help me to develop my argument fully?
- What would I do differently next time to make sure that I improve in future assignments?

# C Investigate the external factors that influence international businesses

**Link**

You learnt about PESTLE in *Unit 1: Exploring Business* and *Unit 2: Developing a Marketing Campaign*.

In this section, you will continue to explore the impact of factors outside the control of a business when it operates internationally – factors that can have a major impact on the success or failure of any business. You have already learned about some of the economic influences, earlier in this chapter, but there are others that also need to be taken into account and these are represented using the PESTLE analysis tool. The acronym PESTLE stands for:

▶ Political
▶ Economic
▶ Social
▶ Technological
▶ Legal and regulatory
▶ Environmental and ethical.

Other factors that also affect businesses include the business support systems that are used to help businesses trade and, particularly, methods of payment and the use of the internet.

## External influences

PESTLE is a good tool that can be used to analyse the impact of external factors on a business. You will need to learn how to apply this type of analysis tool to a business. Each of the elements of PESTLE is very important and is outlined for you in turn.

### Political

The political influence of the government of a country or the president of a group of countries, such as the EU or APEC, has a significant influence on the way in which the country does business and the type of businesses that are able to trade there on an international basis. Understanding the political system in a country or group of countries is very important: for example, China and Cuba are both communist states so this means that trading with them is more challenging than with other countries and potentially has more restrictions.

**Research**

Carry out research into a communist country such as China, Cuba, Vietnam or Laos. Find out about the way that the political system works there. How does this system affect trade in your chosen country? Discuss your answers with another member of your class.

▶ Communist countries have different political viewpoints.

Most countries around the world are democracies rather than communist. However, even these countries are influenced by different political viewpoints with regard to international trade. Some governments may seek to protect jobs in their economies and, therefore, may be less positive about international businesses coming into their countries. Depending on their viewpoint, governments may decide to increase spending on the **public sector** (more left-wing policies) or reduce spending on the public sector (more right-wing policies) and encourage higher levels of private investment and competition.

### Economic

International businesses are also affected by the economic conditions of the country in which they operate. Economic conditions can have a huge impact on the ability of customers to buy products in that country and also on the business as a whole. The economic conditions that can have a significant influence include:

▶ level of taxation

▶ interest rates

▶ inflation

▶ the stage of the economic cycle that the business is in, such as growth or decline

▶ levels of employment/unemployment that affect the demand for products or services.

Each of the economic influences above are likely to have an impact on the demand for a product or service, particularly if it is a luxury item. If levels of tax, interest rates and inflation are all high, the cost of those products or services will be higher and this may affect demand. Businesses need adequate levels of demand to make sure that all their costs are covered. The point at which the costs and the income are the same is called **break-even**. To be a profitable international business, more income must be made than costs.

International businesses are also affected by the different levels of taxation, including corporation tax, that they must pay in different countries. Even within the EU, the level of VAT that is paid in different member states is very different and varies according to the type of goods for sale. The Standard VAT Rate 1 at September 2015 is as follows in these countries:

▶ Luxembourg: 17 per cent

▶ UK: 20 per cent

▶ Hungary: 27 per cent.

> **Research**
>
> In the past, large multinational businesses have been accused of not paying enough corporation tax in the UK as they have been able to claim higher levels of expenses or have declared their profits in countries where corporation tax is lower than in the UK. Research one multinational company that has been accused of this type of tax avoidance practice. How and why did they allegedly avoid paying tax in the UK?

▶ Interest rates also affect international businesses, as interest rates affect the amount it costs a company to borrow money and also the amount of money that potential customers have left over after they have paid their bills. High interest rates mean that the cost of loans and mortgages is high and this affects the spending power of people with those costs. However, for luxury goods, high interest rates may also

> **Key terms**
>
> **Public sector** – the services provided on behalf of the government of a country that are mostly paid for through taxation, such as hospitals (in the UK – NHS), police, education and government itself.
>
> **Break-even** – the point at which costs and income are the same.

mean that some people have more money to spend as they make higher amounts of interest on their savings: for example, retired people with high levels of savings in the bank may be more likely to buy goods or services.

▶ Inflation is the cost of living and is worked out in the UK using the CPI (consumer price index) or RPI (retail price index). If inflation is high, then the cost of everyday items goes up and, if wages do not go up at the same rate, the amount of money that people have left over goes down. Most of the time, inflation is positive as costs go up. However, in 2015, for the first time since the 1960s, inflation became negative and the cost of products and services actually went down. The reduction of prices is not necessarily good for businesses as sometimes consumers may decide to not buy a product or service now in the hope that the price will go down in the future.

<table>
<tr><td>⏸ PAUSE POINT</td><td>Tax avoidance is not a crime but tax evasion is. What are the differences between the two?</td></tr>
<tr><td>Hint</td><td>Compare businesses avoiding paying tax with businesses deliberately choosing not to pay taxes.</td></tr>
<tr><td>Extend</td><td>'Tax avoidance is as bad as stealing from a country.' To what extent do you agree with this view?</td></tr>
</table>

### Theory into practice

In 2015, some international businesses were trading in countries with negative inflation and others with very positive inflation, for example:
- in April 2015, UK inflation was –0.1 per cent
- in Egypt, inflation was +11 per cent.

- What impact could negative inflation have on a business trading in the UK in April 2015?
- What impact could positive inflation have on a business trading in Egypt during 2015?

The stage of the economic cycle will have an external influence on a business. If a business is trading during growth, predictions for future sales are likely to be optimistic and the outlook positive for jobs and for profit making. However, if a business enters an economy that is declining or even going into a **recession**, then sales, profits and investment are likely to be declining and this will probably have a negative impact on that business.

### Key term

**Recession** – when the economic cycle of a country is declining, sales are falling, unemployment is increasing, output is reducing and interest rates are falling. At this time, inflation is also falling.

The final key economic factor that can affect a business trading internationally is that of the level of employment/unemployment in a particular country and the age and type of people that are unemployed. Higher levels of unemployment mean that fewer taxes are being paid, spending is lower (especially on luxury goods) and the amount of public sector spending on benefits and other welfare support goes up. When unemployment is high, some businesses may not be able to grow as their sales are too low.

## Social

Social external influences on international businesses vary depending on the country in which an international business is operating. Social external influences can be very far reaching and include everything from health factors in a particular country, for example levels of obesity or smoking rates, through to other social factors, such as attitudes to work and leisure, or the make-up of the population, such as the extent to which the population is ageing or growing. External social influences on business are affected by the general population of a country and are influenced by:

▶ the level of education and attitude towards education

▶ spending power

▶ lifestyle habits

▶ religion or beliefs

▶ environmental attitudes

▶ population decline or growth

▶ approach to immigration/emigration

▶ family sizes

▶ income available to spend (disposable income).

> **Research**
>
> Carry out research into internet technology, specifically, the impact of faster speed broadband connections on the UK population and its effect on the way people spend their money.

## Technological

Technology has a big impact on businesses and technological change is often very rapid. The pace of change and the ability to communicate change is rapidly increasing through the use of the internet and, in particular, through online communications and social media. Access to rapidly changing technology, particularly in relation to communications, means that international business may be positively or negatively affected.

▶ Technology can have positive and negative impacts on international business depending on the type of technology and the acceptance of users in that country.

▶ **Table 5.5:** The positive and negative impacts of technology

| Positive | Negative |
|---|---|
| • Information can be exchanged and updates can be made very quickly. | • Too many unnecessary email messages which can be distracting in the workplace. |
| • Software can be used to communicate quickly, for example automatic translation software. | • More competition from global companies. |
| • Sales can take place 24/7 – there is no concept of a business being closed. | • Customers ordering online and not visiting businesses, especially retailers. |
| • A worldwide marketing audience is available and customers can be found in areas of the world that were not possible to access before. | • Communication problems as people do not get to meet and only communicate online. |
| • It is cheaper and faster to send an email than send out a publication in the post. | • Pressure to respond more quickly than the business can cope with. |
| • Virtual meetings can keep international businesses in touch with each other through online meetings and conferencing, so reducing transport and meeting costs. | • Staff may need more training and/or skills than they have. |
| • Less paper and filing is required as documents are stored online. | • Crime can take place online and businesses need to protect themselves from the copying of an idea or from having their systems hacked and important details stolen. |
| • Social media has offered a new way to conduct business through different forums. | |
| • Tracking of different points is possible through GPS or other methods, for example the delivery of parcels. | |

The acceptance or dislike of technology can have a huge impact on the way that businesses operate on an international scale. In some countries, the use of technology is very well received and in others it is less well developed. Therefore, the acceptance of technology at a local and national level has a big impact on the way that businesses can trade internationally, and the extent to which they can operate within countries using local people, or whether they need to bring in external people to train others.

**Link**

See also *Unit 23: The English Legal System* and *Unit 1: Exploring Business.*

### Legal and regulatory

Legal systems and legislation vary widely around the world and the countries where international businesses are trading will have very different influences on the way that international businesses operate. Laws and regulatory frameworks cover many different areas of international business including:

▶ employment law

▶ regulations about how businesses operate and the licences required

▶ legal structures of businesses in countries

▶ the way that contracts operate and contract law relating to the country in which a business is operating

▶ tax that needs to be paid

▶ reporting regulations, including how accounts are produced and returns made to governments

▶ criminal law and what is permissible in one country compared with another.

**Research**

Countries around the world operate using very different legal systems.

The UK, the USA and India use common law, which means that the law is interpreted according to cases that have been ruled upon in the past in a court, in addition to statute law or laws made by Parliament.

Other countries, such as France and Germany, operate using a civil system. This means that they have a list of written rules about what is allowed or not and how these are applied.

Some countries have a legal system based on religious teachings, for example in Pakistan and Saudi Arabi. This is called Islamic Sharia Law and is based on the principles of the Koran.

In pairs or small groups, choose one of the different types of legal system. Find as many ways as you can in which an international business will be affected when it is working within the legal system of that country.

Compare your answers with members of different groups and produce a chart or table showing the potential impact of different legal systems on international businesses.

Now challenge yourself to find out more about how businesses working internationally can ensure that they are compliant with the different laws around the world when they trade globally.

## Environmental and ethical

International businesses are affected by and have an impact on the environment and ethical pressures within the countries in which they are operating: for example, generating high levels of waste through offering services or production, or through emissions from machinery operating or transportation of goods. Laws and policies in particular countries or groups of countries can have a significant impact on the way in which a business operates.

The influence of the environment on an international business can be in terms of its ability to look after its environment, and the extent to which it is required to operate in a way that does not damage the local environment or has to recycle or use recycled products in its delivery or production.

The environment may also affect international businesses in terms of the climate of that country and the type of products and services that can be offered at different times of year, including the impact of the geography – such as the likelihood of snow, rain or extreme temperatures.

Other environmental factors that affect international businesses operating in different areas may also include:

▶ transport links
▶ infrastructure such as communication links, including provision for electricity, water and other energies
▶ access to housing and medical services
▶ location of the country and its ability to serve other countries or communities, for example, if an international business sets up in mainland EU, then it has access to many countries around it, but, if it sets up in an island country, it may have to use water or air transport to move goods around.

▶ Why do you think it costs more to transport goods by air than by road?

Ethical factors also affect the way international businesses operate. This can range from the way in which employees are treated and their rights and working conditions through to the type of products that are offered to consumers in those countries. You will have probably seen ethical issues highlighted that relate to the way that goods are:

- sourced
- sustained
- manufactured
- distributed
- used
- recycled.

> **Discussion**
>
> In small groups or pairs, discuss the ethics of:
> - selling tobacco or nicotine products to people in developing countries
> - employing children to manufacture shoes and clothing
> - cutting down rainforests to give more space for cattle to graze for beef production
> - cutting down forests to grow palm oil for food production.
>
> Present the case for and against each.
>
> Extend your thinking by making a judgement about the statement:
> 'Creating a desire for luxury goods that are not essential for life is always unethical.'

▶ Ethical practices vary internationally and businesses need to make judgements about their own ethical practice in different countries.

## Situational analysis

You have already learned about PESTLE as a business tool and how it can be applied to international business. PESTLE is one tool that can be used as part of a business situational analysis, but there are other tools that may also be applied to different external environments to help leaders and managers make decisions about operating in different countries.

Various business tools help international businesses to understand more about their:
- markets
- marketing strategies
- industry analysis
- business capabilities.

Additional tools that can be used by businesses include a SWOT Analysis, 5C Analysis and Porter's Five Forces Model.

## SWOT Analysis

SWOT stands for: Strengths, Weaknesses, Opportunities and Threats. When international businesses are thinking about trading in new countries, they will carry out a SWOT analysis to review their likely success in that particular country. When applying SWOT to an international business reviewing whether to enter a new country, the strengths and weaknesses apply to the international business itself, and the opportunities and threats relate to aspects outside the business.

**Link**

See also *Unit 1: Exploring Business*, on SWOT analysis.

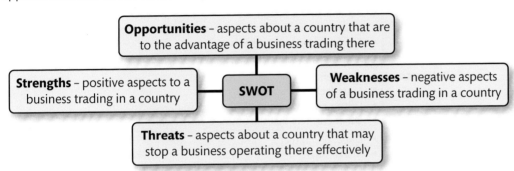

**Opportunities** – aspects about a country that are to the advantage of a business trading there

**Strengths** – positive aspects to a business trading in a country

**SWOT**

**Weaknesses** – negative aspects of a business trading in a country

**Threats** – aspects about a country that may stop a business operating there effectively

▶ **Figure 5.3:** SWOT analysis is essential when a business is considering new markets.

**Theory into practice**

### Fluffy Toys Ltd

Fluffy Toys Ltd currently trade in England, Scotland and Wales. They produce soft toys in Manchester that are distributed by road.

They are currently reviewing the decision to increase sales and expand their business further by selling their toys in the Republic of Ireland. To review their likely success in Ireland, they have used a SWOT analysis to review their likely chances of success.

| Strengths | Weaknesses |
|---|---|
| • Existing brand reputation in current markets.<br>• High market share in current markets.<br>• High quality manufacturing processes.<br>• Good transport networks.<br>• Strong cash position with investment.<br>• Loyal existing staff. | • Lack of knowledge of business processes outside England, Scotland and Wales.<br>• No knowledge of customs or import regulations for Ireland. |
| Opportunities | Threats |
| • Develop market share in Ireland through higher sales.<br>• Work in partnership with one or more toy manufacturers to produce toys under licence.<br>• Work in partnership with a retailer to distribute the toys.<br>• Access to grants to establish a manufacturing base in Ireland. | • Exchange rate fluctuations owing to trading in the euro.<br>• Competition from other manufacturers.<br>• Need to establish a new brand. |

### 5C Analysis

The 5C situational analysis considers five elements that are applied in the international business context. These are: Customers, Collaborators, Competition, Company and Climate.

▶ **Table 5.6:** The different elements of 5C analysis

| | |
|---|---|
| **Customer** | • Market size<br>• Market profile and segments<br>• Benefits to the customers<br>• Where and how customers buy the products or services (channels)<br>• The frequency of purchases<br>• The number of purchases |
| **Collaborators** | • Suppliers<br>• Manufacturers<br>• Distributors<br>• Other partners that the business works with |
| **Competition** | • Direct or indirect<br>• Market share<br>• Products or services offered, including benefits<br>• Weaknesses of products or services offered<br>• Type of product or service, e.g. luxury or basic (positioning)<br>• Unique selling points |
| **Company** | • Mission, culture and ethos of the company<br>• Products or services offered<br>• Image of the company in the market<br>• Technical expertise |
| **Climate** | • Political<br>• Economic<br>• Social<br>• Technological<br>• Legal<br>• Environmental |

**PAUSE POINT**

What are the strengths and weaknesses of using SWOT and 5C analysis when making decisions about a business's position in an international country?

 Hint

What information in these analyses helps a business in their thinking? What are the limits of the information provided and what is missing?

 Extend

Judge the extent to which situational analysis can help businesses to make decisions over longer periods, such as 5 to 10 years.

### Porter's Five Forces Model

The final model that can be used is that of Porter's Five Forces.

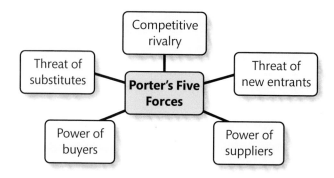

▶ **Figure 5.4:** Porter's Five Forces Model can help businesses to analyse their position in a market.

Porter's Five Forces Model helps businesses to be aware of the influences of competition from five different aspects.

▶ Threat of new entrants means how easy it is to get the structures and finance in place to start offering a similar product or service in a country: for example, is it easy to copy and easy to offer or make.

▶ Power of suppliers means how easy it is to control suppliers, the number of suppliers and the costs that they can charge. Fewer suppliers often means that businesses have to pay more.

▶ Power of buyers means how easily buyers can drive down prices by having too much choice or by being able to switch to an alternative product or service.

▶ Threat of substitutes means how easily a customer can change to buying another product or something similar and therefore not need the product or service at all.

▶ Competitive rivalry means the number of competitors to a business both nationally and globally, and also the products and services offered by the competitors.

These forces all influence international businesses in their home countries and can also help to reveal the likely competition if going into a new market in a different country.

> **Link**
>
> For more information on Porter's Five Forces model, see *Unit 19: Pitching for a New Business.*

> **Research**
>
> Carry out research into the mobile phone market by applying Porter's Five Forces Model. Find out how many mobile phone suppliers operate in the UK and the impact of the influences outlined by Porter on how they operate.
>
> Make your own judgement about the extent to which you agree or disagree that the mobile phone market is very difficult to enter in the UK.

# International business support systems

International business support systems refer to those systems that help international trade to take place. You saw the phrase 'the world is getting smaller' before earlier in this unit. This phrase highlights that it is becoming easier to communicate with customers in different countries and to trade with them for two main reasons: the internet and international methods of payment.

### Influence of the internet

Businesses are now able to trade all over the world in a number of countries that have never been accessible to them before. The internet, through social media and websites, is constantly evolving and means that businesses are very quickly and easily able to attract new customers in other parts of the world.

The internet has also supported the idea of customers being able to buy products or receive services 24/7, as they do not need to have a physical store containing the products or services on offer. Even if those products are required physically, it is possible to have them delivered by a third party, such as the Royal Mail in the UK, or customers can actually download or access the products themselves online. It is very important that international businesses keep up to date with the way that customers can operate and can adapt to new circumstances or they risk losing business and, ultimately, ceasing to trade.

▶ How many different businesses do you deal with online?

## Blockbuster UK

The company Blockbuster UK ceased trading in the UK in 2013 when it went bankrupt. The reason it gave for its bankruptcy was the change in the way people bought and viewed videos. However, it did have a significant number of competitors at the time, including Netflix which started to offer a DVD rental service through the post that became very popular.

Blockbuster UK's main business was to loan out DVDs and games to customers through a chain of retail stores. These stores also sold sweets and drinks to customers. As a result of the internet, instead of borrowing DVDs, customers were able to download and stream their films directly to their televisions or laptops to watch for lower fees. Other competitors made good use of download times and facilities and Blockbuster were slow to change the way that they operated the business. Other competitors, such as BT and Virgin, also saw a gap in the rental market and started to offer rental services through cable and satellite services.

Blockbuster also operated in the USA, where it had gone bankrupt three years before, in 2010, but it was bought by a company called DISH and was relaunched as a postal DVD service. But again, in 2014, this service was closed. DISH retained the Blockbuster name and then launched Blockbuster On Demand which uses 'Sling TV' in the USA to allow customers to download films to their television. This service is only available in the USA.

### Check your knowledge

1 How could Porter's Five Forces Model have been used to explain to Blockbuster what was happening in the market?

2 What was the influence of the internet on business, in this instance, and how did it change the way the services were offered/business processes?

3 What could Blockbuster have done, if anything, to have avoided bankruptcy in the UK?

4 Carry out research on the internet to find information on the future of the rental film industry, the current competitors in the UK and what they can and should be doing to protect themselves internationally going into the future. Share three of your findings with your class.

5 Extend your thinking further by considering how this same situation could be applied to photograph printing and companies such as Bonus Print. Make a judgement about the extent to which you think companies must innovate and be creative to survive in the future.

## International payment methods

You learned, earlier in this unit, about some of the ways in which international payment methods influence the way that businesses operate internationally. You will remember that businesses need to consider different payment methods for different countries, and some of these methods are outlined in Table 5.7 below.

▶ **Table 5.7:** The different methods of international payments

| Method of payment | Influence on international business |
|---|---|
| Cash in advance | • Businesses can do bank transfers in advance.<br>• This method may be necessary in countries where cash is needed to produce the goods.<br>• It relies on high levels of trust.<br>• Cash may be preferred by the supplier.<br>• Cash may be used as part of the negotiations to get the best deal for the international business. |

▶ **Table 5.7:** *continued*

| Letters of credit | • Letters of credit give a guarantee that a seller will receive payment from a buyer within a certain amount of time. |
| | • Banks will guarantee the payment in return for making sure that strict terms are met for shipping from the seller in the other country. |
| | • Letters of credit are less risky for buyers and also for sellers. |
| Open account | • An open account is when the goods are shipped and delivered by a supplier without receiving any payment. |
| | • Payment is usually made within 30, 60 or 90 days. |
| | • Cash flow problems can happen if payment is not paid quickly enough. |
| | • Exporters who do not give credit may lose sales. |
| | • Exporters using open accounts may get more sales. |
| | • High risk of the customer not paying. |
| | • The political climate in the country where the goods are being sent will have a big influence. |
| Consignment | • Consignment is a type of open account. |
| | • Payment is only sent after the goods have been sold to the customer. |
| | • A contract is in place ensuring that the seller is the legal owner until the goods have been sold. |
| | • High level of risk as a distributor looks after the goods until they are sold. |
| | • Using consignment means that sellers can be available more quickly. |
| | • Goods are sold more quickly. |
| | • The distributor stores and then sells the goods to customers and this reduces storage costs. |
| International credit card | • Businesses can use international credit cards that have different rates and benefits. |
| | • Some cards are pre-paid which lowers the risk. |
| | • Other cards have low fees when different currencies are used. |
| | • Credit cards can provide additional payment protection for businesses trading overseas as they often include additional insurances, but may also have extra charges. |
| International bank transfer | • International bank transfers are secure ways to move money from one country to another. |
| | • Businesses may choose to operate with international bank accounts so that they can get access to lower fees for transfers. |
| | • International bank accounts can avoid changes in exchange rates affecting the business, which makes planning easier. |
| | • Sometimes only major currencies are accepted, such as the euro and dollar. |
| | • Banks may charge to receive the money into another account, even if it was free to send, so this needs to be taken into account. |
| Commercial payment systems | • These are systems that help to move payments from one country to another. |
| | • Other systems that can be used overseas include Google Wallet, Apple Pay, Android Pay and Bitcoin. |

---

**Ⅱ PAUSE POINT**   What are the advantages of using letters of credit compared with open accounts for an international business trading in Europe?

      **Hint**   Why are letters of credit are used by businesses when trading internationally? Are there any disadvantages?

      **Extend**   'Cash in advance is the best payment method as it secures the best terms.' Discuss this view with a member of your class.

**Discussion**

Carry out research into the different types of commercial payment systems that can be used by international businesses, including Google Wallet and Bitcoin. What are the advantages and disadvantages of each?

'Commercial payment systems are not necessary, as banks can transfer money.' Discuss this view with a member of your class.

## D  Investigate the cultural factors that influence international businesses

In this section, you will explore the way in which culture affects businesses when they are trading and also how they interact in other countries. Culture means the way that things work in a particular business or, indeed, in a country or a group of countries, such as Europe. All over the world, there are subtle differences in the way people interact with each other based on the individual histories of those countries, how people work and, sometimes, other factors, such as the religious beliefs or attitudes in those countries.

### Cultural factors

Cultural factors come from the different ways in which countries operate, and these are divided into eight key factors that you will explore in this unit.

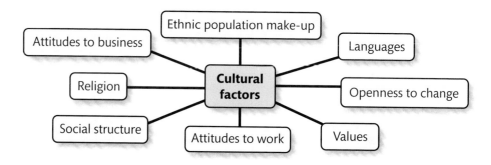

▶ **Figure 5.5:** There are eight key cultural factors that affect international businesses.

### Languages

There are 7000 different languages in the world, so operating internationally means that being able to communicate in the right language is important. There are about 150 to 200 languages that are spoken by at least one million people.

Language can be distinguished in two ways: those that are spoken by native speakers (their first language) and those that are second languages. The most popular native speaking language in the world in 2016 was Mandarin, followed by English and Spanish.

Being able to communicate in the relevant languages is very important in order to:

▶ avoid misunderstandings

▶ make business communications happen faster and more clearly

▶ build trust and the appreciation of different perspectives

▶ build teams made up of individuals from wide geographical locations.

It is interesting that, even when countries share the same language, it does not necessarily mean that there will be full understanding between them. In France and Canada, French is spoken, but the type of French is very different between the two, and the impact of language and culture is also very different. The UK and the USA both use English, but words in American English can be very different from UK English. For example, if someone in a business meeting in the USA were to use the phrase 'let's table this idea' they would intend for it be discussed later. In a business meeting in the UK, this phrase would mean the exact opposite, and the idea should be discussed immediately.

| **Ⅱ  PAUSE POINT** | English is often referred to as the language of business. A new version of English called 'international English' has been developed where both parties are not native speakers but communicate and negotiate in English. Why do you think that English has become the language of business? |
|---|---|
| Hint | What has been the impact of the history of the UK and America on why English is spoken in business frequently? |
| Extend | Mandarin is the most widely spoken language in the world. Do you think that the language of business will become Mandarin? |

## Ethnic population makeup

Different countries have different numbers of ethnic groups and this affects the way that international businesses operate in these countries.

▶ **Table 5.8:** Ethnic make-up of some different countries

| Country | Native group: % | Other ethnic groups: % |
|---|---|---|
| UK | 87.2% White British | 12.8% |
| Poland | 96.9% Polish | 3.1% |
| United Arab Emirates | 19% Emirati | 81% |
| USA | 79.96% White USA | 20.04% |

The ethnic make-up of a country will affect whether or not a product or service may be popular there or how that product or service is sold or promoted. There are large variations between countries, so it is important that businesses operating internationally understand these differences and their impact on how they work.

▶ The ethnic makeup of different countries will influence the way that international businesses operate in those countries.

## Social structure

Social structures in countries mean the class systems that are operating in those countries. In the UK, for example, there is a class structure that operates and goes from the elite social class, which is the top six per cent of British society, where people have access to high amounts of wealth, to the lower levels of working class society, where qualification levels are low and economic wealth is poor. In Japan, the class structure has been very traditional and, like the UK, includes different hierarchical levels such as the middle and upper classes. Knowing the class structure of different countries helps businesses to work out where partnerships need to be made, which business people to approach and work with in terms of partnership, and how to develop more specific, targeted marketing for their product or service based on the class structure of that country.

> **Research**
>
> Find out more about the class structures operating in Austria, the USA and Morocco.
>
> Compare your results and what do you notice? How would these differences have affected international businesses trading in these countries?

## Religion

There are many different worldwide religions and each has its own influence over the people that follow it. In some religions, such as Islam and Buddhism, alcohol consumption is not permitted. For other religions, such as Christianity, it is allowed. Knowing the religious preferences of business people meeting for a corporate dinner can have a big impact on the way that such dinners are held. Corporate dinners often take place to help participants network, so it is important that these events comply with the religious expectations of all parties, to avoid offence. Religion can influence the way that businesses operate. Some countries operate their laws based on religion more than others. For example, in some countries that are Muslim, Sharia Law operates and this affects the ability of businesses to borrow money or to have mortgages.

## Values

The values of people living in particular countries also affect the way that they trade. These values come from historical traditions and the way that people have been brought up in these countries. In some countries, it is perfectly acceptable to give bribes as part of business trading; in fact, if an international country does not do this, they will not be able to trade there. In other countries, such as the UK, this is illegal and any monies paid to employees to ensure that business goes ahead, particularly in public sector businesses, need to be declared and made public to ensure that those businesses are not treated differently as a result.

 **PAUSE POINT**

Bribery is commonly used in some countries. What is the disadvantage to UK businesses of operating internationally in these countries?

**Hint**

Think of the difficulties that businesses may have when operating in this type of environment. What is the impact of UK law on how these businesses operate in the UK?

**Extend**

'All forms of discount or promotion are types of bribery.' To what extent do you agree with this view?

## Attitudes to business

Attitudes to business are also extremely varied internationally and these attitudes shape the way that business is carried out.

In Japan, business is conducted using high levels of respect and through relationship building. Lengthy discussions are required to take place, and patience is needed when operating with Japanese companies to ensure that the correct decisions are made and that all avenues are covered. Women tend to be paid less than men in Japan and often, therefore, perform lower paid duties. This means that when women are working in Japan on business, they may be viewed differently from men.

In Norway, business must be carried out on time, each member of a meeting must be allowed to put their point forward and any interruptions are viewed as rude. Men and women are treated as equals during negotiations and in business.

In Mexico, it is perfectly acceptable to attend meetings late and for the agenda not to be followed. Sub-meetings may take place within a meeting. Interrupting and speaking loudly are seen as actively engaging in the meeting. Being emotional in a meeting is not viewed negatively but is seen as a Mexican characteristic, showing that they are committed and interested. Women and men are treated relatively equally and, therefore, there are not usually any issues in this area for women working internationally.

### Research

Produce a poster showing the attitudes that are present in business for a country of your choice, including information related to:

- behaviour in meetings
- attitudes towards women
- management style
- team working
- any other useful information.

Share your findings with other members of your class and produce a wall display of your posters.

## Attitudes to work

In some countries around the world, attitudes to work are very different and this includes the average working week, the amount of holiday that is given to business people (e.g. see Table 5.9) and the way in which business negotiations are carried out. For example, in Spain, it has been common to have a siesta (which is a form of rest) during the middle of the day and work later into the evening, and, in France, to have a long meal at lunchtime. However, in many cities this is now starting to become less common.

▶ **Table 5.9:** Working hours and holidays in some different countries

| Country | Average collectively agreed working hours (updated July 2015) | Actual working hours (2014) | Minimum number of days paid leave (2014) | Public holidays |
|---------|---------------------------------------------------------------|------------------------------|-------------------------------------------|-----------------|
| UK | 37.4 | 40.9 | 20 | 8 |
| France | 35.6 | 37.3 | 25 | 13 |
| Slovakia | 38.9 | 39.3 | 20 but many employees have 25 days | 15 |
| Romania | 40 | 41 | 20 | 13 |

**PAUSE POINT**

Working hours and leave arrangements vary from country to country. What impact do you think this has on international businesses?

**Hint**

Think of the availability of staff, resources and meetings.

**Extend**

'All EU countries should have the same working hours and public holidays to help support international business.' Discuss.

## Openness to change

Due to the pace of change that is happening around the world, some countries are more open to change and, indeed, some businesses are more open than others. With rapid continued expansion, it is important that, as the 'world is getting smaller', businesses can keep up to date with what is happening in their own countries and others. Trends that happen in some countries can be quickly replicated in others and so, by operating internationally, businesses must be more and more open to change in order to be successful.

According to INSEAD Knowledge 2015, the four most talent-ready countries in the world in 2015 were:

▶ Switzerland

▶ Singapore

▶ Luxembourg

▶ USA.

These countries, through the use of technology, were seeking to change the most quickly and to be entrepreneurial in their approaches, for example, through the use of fast broadband and the ability to communicate using online methods. The UK was placed in the top ten of the countries in the world. Technology has had a significant impact on change and the pace and rate of change that is possible within businesses, countries and internationally.

## Impact of cultural factors

You have already learned, in this unit, that there are key cultural factors that influence businesses and some of the ways in which they have an impact, but for, international businesses, making clear assessments about how to change the way that they work based on these factors is extremely important.

**PAUSE POINT**

Which of the eight different cultural factors has the biggest impact on businesses when they trade internationally?

**Hint**

Think of the impact on populations of these factors – which have the most influence and which have the least influence?

**Extend**

Do you agree that it is not the influence of the cultural factors themselves that affects international business but the approach by businesses towards those factors that makes a difference?

Cultural factors have an influence on key ways that businesses operate, including:

▶ contract negotiations
▶ composition of the workforce
▶ management style
▶ workforce practices
▶ organisational culture
▶ marketing strategies and brand names
▶ advertising.

## Contract negotiations

You have already learned that, in some countries, bribery is acceptable and in others it is not. Negotiating contracts is a very important part of business and, therefore, being aware of what is acceptable business practice in different countries is very important. In the UK, in 2010, the Bribery Act was passed in order to avoid this practice being used.

## Composition of the workforce

The composition of the workforce will have a big impact on the way that it operates. The culture, expectations and ways of working will affect the way that the business operates. An international business may have a view about sending workers to a particular country to start trading, according to the values that it holds, or may take the view that they will employ a local workforce to make sure that they have greater knowledge and understanding of the local area and also of the business expectations.

Sometimes international businesses may choose, through the existing use of technology, to have some of their workforce based in one country and some in another. A common example of where this has happened in the past has been call centres that have been able to operate in countries such as India, in collaboration with call centres run in the UK.

### Research

Find out more about the Bribery Act 2010 and how it affects businesses operating in the UK and worldwide.

Make a judgement about how it would affect a business operating in a country where bribery is common.

What would the business need to do and what would the impact be on how it trades with that country?

### Case study

#### EE

In 2014, EE took the decision to move 1000 jobs back to the UK following many complaints about the way that call centre operators supported customers, as their level of English did not meet the expectations of customers. These call centre operators were based in India and the Philippines. Although the staff were highly trained in these countries, UK customers were frustrated with levels of service that they did not think were good enough. The many complaints that were received from customers, because they were being cut off or not able to communicate effectively, led to EE's customer service rating going down.

Carry out research into EE and other phone companies that have chosen to move their call centre operations back from overseas to the UK.

#### Check your knowledge

1 What were the reasons why EE decided to bring back their call centre operations to the UK?

2 How did cultural factors affect this decision?

3 Many companies underestimate the impact of culture when considering communications between staff in different countries and languages. Discuss this view.

## Link

This section links to *Unit 1: Exploring Business* and *Unit 6: Principles of Management*.

## Management style

Management styles in companies in the UK vary widely. Some companies operate a very directed and controlled structure. This is called an autocratic management style. Others opt for much more consultation and collaboration, known as democratic style. Differences in management style are very common between businesses in the UK, but add in the cultural factors that are present when working overseas and the impact of these differences can be felt even more strongly.

▶ **Table 5.10:** Typical management style in three different countries

| Country | Typical management style |
|---------|--------------------------|
| India | • Clear need for a boss<br>• Very hierarchical approach<br>• Instructions should be given<br>• Micromanagement is common |
| Russia | • Clear need for a boss<br>• Instructions given with little consultation as this would be seen as a weakness<br>• Specific tasks are given<br>• Employees are told what to do and must follow instructions |
| Sweden | • Managers seek consensus<br>• Bosses do not necessarily know all the answers<br>• Discussions are open<br>• Social distance between managers and employees is close |

 **PAUSE POINT**

Think about the type of manager that you have worked for. What were the advantages and disadvantages of their management style? How would this management style work in India, Russia or Sweden?

 Hint

Think of the extent to which you were told what to do, or were given the ability to choose by yourself.

Extend

'Management style depends on the product or service being offered rather than the culture of the country in which it operates.' Discuss this view.

## Workforce practices

Workforce practices include the way that businesses operate on a day-to-day basis and the extent to which they follow different procedures, rules or even the legislation that operates in the country in which they are based.

Daily operating practices in different countries can have a huge impact on the reputation and ways of working in that business; for example, health and safety practices are much stricter in some countries, and therefore there are fewer accidents than there are in others. A business operating internationally may decide that it wishes to adopt health and safety practices that are more stringent than those in the country in which it is operating. Management style is affected by operating practices, so it may be necessary to have a more direct or autocratic style when working in some countries as this is the expectation, for example in China, and a more democratic or cooperative style in others, such as Sweden.

Other areas of business working practice that also may be very different are those that relate to the way that pay and working conditions are negotiated. In some countries, such as France and Germany, there are very strong unions in operation that negotiate pay and terms of employment on behalf of groups of employees. The laws of these countries relating to the way that people are treated are also very strong and this has an impact on businesses operating there.

▶ Health and safety practices may be very different in other countries compared with those in the UK.

## Organisational culture

Organisational culture, as you have already learned, is the way that 'people do things around here'. This means the day-to-day way that workers behave in the workplace and the influences that they bring in from outside.

The impact of organisational culture is felt in two ways. First, the impact of the culture of the country where the international business is operating comes into the organisation and, secondly, the culture of the international business and how it influences the business in the country in which it is operating.

American businesses, for example, may celebrate Independence Day on 4 July or have associations with American companies rather than those locally. They may also not trade on those days. The culture of a business is often set by the parent company, so a British company trading in another country may decide to operate in the way that British companies would rather than following local expectations.

**⏸ PAUSE POINT**    Think of companies that are not from the UK. How does their culture affect the service and products that you receive?

    Hint    Think of the link back to the original country and how it affects the business and staff working there.

    Extend    'Culture is always set locally and not from the parent company.' To what extent do you agree with this view?

Local culture will also affect the way that any international business operates in a country. This is because different cultures and people have different ideas and tastes. The influence of local tastes will mean that the products and services on offer are adapted to meet local needs.

### Theory into practice

**Local culture meets fast food**

Think of fast food restaurants that you or members of your class have visited in the UK and abroad.

What did you find was the same in the fast food restaurant in the two different countries?

What was different (what was on offer/not on offer) compared with the UK?

How much influence did local culture have on the menu at the restaurant?

Local culture also affects the days of the week that are worked by businesses, and the working hours and lunches taken. In Islamic countries, most people have their weekends on Friday and Saturday. Friday is a day of prayer and Saturday is the second day of the weekend. In Christian countries, it is common to have Saturday and Sunday as the weekend.

### Research

Find out the official weekends for three countries: one from Europe, one from the Middle East and another of your choice.

- When do the weekends start and finish?
- What impact does this have on the working week of international business employees?
- Are there any advantages or disadvantages of having different weekends and working hours operating in different parts of the world?

Businesses may also be affected in their sales numbers by local customs or practices in terms of the tastes or attitudes towards different products or services. For example, in France, restaurants offer frogs' legs and snails, in China, snakes and bees are delicacies eaten at street markets. In the USA, it is acceptable to turn right even when a traffic light is red.

## Marketing strategies and brand names

Marketing strategies and brand names are another element that is heavily influenced by cultural factors. Sometimes it is possible for businesses trading internationally to use the same advertising and brand names. For example, McDonald's uses the same name to trade in many countries and it does not need to be translated for different countries.

In other instances, it may not be possible to translate the name from the original language. For example Schwarzkopf Hair Care products translates as 'Black Head' Hair Care and blackheads are spots or pimples in English. Other expressions or idioms that may be used are also not always possible to translate exactly from one language to another, for example, in English, you know that when a person says it is raining cats and dogs, they do not mean that it is actually raining animals; it means the rain is heavy.

Historically, many brand names were changed as companies were concerned that people in the UK would not buy their products or services if they could not ask for them. Now it is much more common to have European names and products traded internationally. People are happier to ask for them. For example, Prezzo means price in Italian – Prezzo sounds much more appealing for a restaurant chain than Price!

## Advertising

Trading internationally is also affected by cultural factors that relate to how advertising takes place. In advertising in Islamic countries, women are often shown with their hair and shoulders covered. This is not commonly the case in the UK. Cultural differences, such as views relating to the role of women, homosexuality and ageing, for example, all influence how advertising takes place and its likely success.

It is also very important that the appropriate hand gestures are used in advertising, so as not to offend. The 'thumbs up' sign in the UK and USA is a positive gesture showing that someone is happy. In the Middle East, it is an insult and, therefore, would upset local people.

There are many examples of where this sort of advertising has gone wrong, so it is important to try to get local people to look at advertising and to check it before it is published.

▶ **Table 5.11:** How to get it wrong in advertising

| | |
|---|---|
| Baby food in Africa was sold with pictures of babies on the label. | In Africa, it is common to put the picture of what is in the jar to help people who cannot read understand what they are buying. |
| Pepsi changed their vending machines from dark blue to light blue. | Light blue is a symbol of death and mourning in South-east Asia, so sales went down. |
| Braniff International Airways had the phrase 'Fly in leather'. | When it was translated to Spanish, it read, 'Fly naked'. |

▶ Putting your thumb up in a Middle Eastern country is an insult rather than a positive gesture in advertising.

The external and cultural factors that affect international businesses are very important. They can make the difference between a business working well in the international context and not working well. They can lead to better communication or total misunderstanding.

Using one of the businesses that you investigated earlier, produce a case study as a journal article, using your own research evidence, to explain the impact of international business, and make a detailed evaluation about the impact of external influences and cultural differences on that business.

In your article, you will need to ensure that you cover external influences and cultural factors that influence the way your business trades. You should ensure that you incorporate a wide range of research evidence and select appropriate research sources.

In your article you need to make sure you cover:
- external influences that affect whether a business trades internationally
- business support systems that help international trade to take place
- an exploration of the cultural differences, and an analysis of how these affect international businesses.

Using your research, you should carry out a situational analysis, using relevant models, on two different countries that your chosen business may trade in, including your recommendations for which country would best fit the needs of that business. Ensure that you fully justify your recommendations.

### Plan
- Have I chosen the most appropriate business from assessment practice 5.1 for this task?
- Have I made sure that I can source enough research about the countries that I have chosen?
- Do I know where/how I am going to find the information I need about cultural differences?
- When are my deadlines?

### Do
- How do I know I am on task?
- Where can I get my research?
- Who do I know that can help me with first hand research into cultural differences?
- Where can I get images and other information to enhance my work?
- How do I know I am keeping to my deadlines?

### Review
- Did I include as much research evidence as possible?
- How did I approach it?
- What would I do differently next time to make sure that I improve in future assignments?

# Examine the strategic and operational approaches to developing international trade

In this section, you will learn about the different strategies that need to be used when operating internationally, and how businesses decide which ones best meet their needs. You will also learn some of the additional adaptations that are made to meet local demand and the costs and structures that are put into place to support businesses operating in this way.

## Strategies for operating internationally

There are many different ways that businesses can operate strategically and these do not necessarily mean that the business has to trade in a particular country or countries.

### Strategies

There are eight main ways that businesses can operate internationally and these are outlined below.

▶ **Figure 5.6:** Businesses can use different strategies for operating internationally.

### Subsidiary businesses

A subsidiary business is one where the parent company has got a holding in its shares of 50 per cent or more. A subsidiary business is controlled by the parent company but can operate in another country. The subsidiary has to follow the laws of the country in which they are based and pay relevant taxes and other business expenses accordingly.

There are two ways to establish a subsidiary business of a parent company – a business can be set up in the new country as a subsidiary of an existing business or an existing business can be taken over.

In terms of legal liabilities, the subsidiary business operates in its own right so this means that it has its own legal liabilities. There are benefits to buying and, therefore, owning a subsidiary for international operations:

▶ limits risks
▶ good controls in place to expand the business internationally
▶ investment can be made in an existing subsidiary, so the international business takes over existing experience and knowledge of the country in which they want to trade
▶ supply chain relationships and supplier networks are purchased as they are existing.

There are also concerns with operating a subsidiary for international operations:

▶ business knowledge locally may not satisfy the needs of the parent company
▶ the subsidiary company may be hostile to being taken over.

### Joint ventures

A joint venture is when two or more businesses come together by contractual arrangement to focus on a particular business transaction or deal. Businesses enter into joint ventures to reduce risk and share expertise. A company that produces an item may enter into a joint venture with a trading company as their businesses complement each other.

Another type of joint venture might be an arrangement between a producer and a supplier of goods.

▶ **Table 5.12:** Benefits and concerns in joint ventures

| Benefits to an international business | Concerns for an international business |
|---|---|
| • Growth of the business without borrowing money from banks or other third parties.<br>• Increased capacity.<br>• Shared risk of the new venture.<br>• Access to new resources such as people and technology in the new country.<br>• Can be a win–win performance solution. | • Communication problems may occur.<br>• Balance of power between the two powers; one may have more knowledge and expertise than the other.<br>• Different cultures and management styles of the businesses. |

**Research**

Jaguar Land Rover and Cherry entered into a joint venture in 2012 to build Range Rovers near Shanghai for the Chinese market only. Carry out research into the joint venture and find out the benefits for Jaguar Land Rover and also for Cherry Automobile Ltd.

## Partnerships

Partnerships, like joint ventures, are used to bring different parties together. However, partnerships are usually for the longer term and join the different businesses together more closely through legal processes. Partnerships can be brought together for commercial reasons or to share expertise, for example Norfolk police have worked with Lithuanian and Polish police to share training and expertise. Partnerships can be brought together with unlimited liability for the actions of each partner, or more commonly, with **limited liability.**

Partnerships are different from joint ventures as they usually:

▶ are indefinite in length

▶ are multiple project focused

▶ have joint profits and liabilities

▶ share resources, such as staff

▶ have voting rights and ownership with the partnership.

## Agencies

Agencies are another way of expanding internationally, for example Export to Japan. Export agencies or agents help businesses to trade internationally by:

▶ giving information and contacts for the markets in particular countries

▶ identifying opportunities in countries for business to take place

▶ using their own offices and staff to promote sales

▶ keeping control of the goods that the business is trying to sell in the new country.

Agencies do charge international businesses for this service and this charge can be quite expensive. It can range from 2.5 per cent to 15 per cent, depending on the countries where trade is happening and the type of product or service.

There are other areas of concern that may also stop an international business from using an agent, these include:

▶ loss of control over the marketing

▶ additional costs, such as distribution costs

▶ services for customers after purchase may be difficult to offer.

**Key term**

**Limited liability** – having a restricted amount of money that the business is liable for that can be paid out if the partnership goes wrong. This means that directors do not put their own personal wealth at risk if the partnership were to go wrong and each individual business going into the partnership only has a set level of financial responsibility in the event that the partnership does not work well.

⏸ **PAUSE POINT**   Businesses can choose whether they go into a joint venture or a partnership. What are the differences between each? Why might a business choose a joint venture in preference to a partnership?

Hint   Think of the legal differences between the two different ways of working and compare them.

Extend   'Partnerships indicate that working together is going to be more sustained and this leads to higher levels of motivation and collaboration than joint ventures.' To what extent do you agree with this view

## Licensing

Sometimes businesses will decide that licensing is a better way to expand internationally. Licensing means that a business enters into an agreement to let another business manufacture their product or market their services in another country as a **licensee**. Burton's Biscuits produce American brands in the UK under licence.

Licensing can give permission to another business to sell services, expertise or even ideas on behalf of the licensor. Licensing agreements can be used to cover copyright, patents and other forms of agreement. They can also be offered exclusively or non-exclusively in different countries. Exclusively means that only the licensee can produce the goods or offer those services. Licensing payments can vary but it may cost a set amount to buy the licence or it may represent a percentage of sales made. Fees may also be charged to the licensee for technical expertise and initial agreement payments that are made as a one-off. Agreements can also vary: they can be open-ended and therefore long term, or be set for a fixed period of time.

▶ **Table 5.13:** Advantages and disadvantages of licensing arrangements

| Advantages | Disadvantages |
|---|---|
| <ul><li>Support on offer for the licensee.</li><li>Easy access for the licensor to new markets through the licensee.</li><li>Cheap for the licensor to expand using other companies to help them.</li><li>Low investment required in the new country.</li></ul> | <ul><li>Loss of control for the licensor.</li><li>Potential lower income (only %) not all of the sales.</li><li>Licensee may damage the reputation of the licensor if not carried out correctly.</li><li>Potential for additional competition from the licensee if they decide to stop operating under licence.</li></ul> |

**Research**

Mizkan Euro Ltd produce goods under licence in the UK and Europe. Find out the type of goods that they produce under licence and more about the history of the business.

## Franchising

Franchising is similar to licensing in that businesses agree to pay to run a franchise in another country on behalf of another. The franchise itself is an agreement to sell or distribute goods through a legal agreement between a franchisor (the person offering the goods or services) and the franchisee (the person offering those goods or services in the other country).

Franchising is very popular throughout the world and many companies use franchising arrangements to expand their services and make their brand names more well known across the world. These include:

▶ McDonald's

▶ Subway

▶ Dunkin' Doughnuts

▶ Papa John's Pizza

▶ Harry Ramsden's.

Franchising means that the franchisee agrees to buy all of their products and services from the franchisor, by arrangement, and that the business should be operated in the same way as the franchisor expects.

The only difference is that the profit that the business makes under the franchising agreement, and the legal status of the business running the franchise operation, are separate from that of the franchisor.

### Papa John's Pizza

In 2016, the minimum expected investment to enter into a franchising agreement with Papa John's Pizza was £70,000.

Papa John's Pizza have over 300 restaurants in the UK and have used franchising to expand their presence in the UK. Papa John's Pizza have operated in the UK since 2000 and have won awards for their pizzas. Signing up to a franchising agreement has various incentives for the franchisee, which have included free ovens and marketing support.

Training is offered centrally by Papa John's Pizza and this includes online and offline training to help franchisees to run their businesses effectively. Franchisees need to be good communicators and must be very organised.

**Check your knowledge**

1 What are the benefits for Papa John's Pizza of operating this model to expand their business internationally?

2 What are the benefits for the franchisees of entering into an agreement with Papa John's Pizza?

3 Can you think of any potential disadvantages?

4 'Franchising is a low risk way to expand a business internationally.' To what extent do you agree with this view?

### Subcontracting

Subcontracting is another potential way for a business to expand internationally. It means that one business undertakes work on behalf of another, and is commonly used in the construction industry, where a large business may negotiate a contract and then ask smaller companies to carry out parts of the work on the ground.

Subcontracting can be carried out for services as well as for manufacturing, for example for financial services or technology consulting. A subcontractor may be asked to give advice or oversee a project for a specific period of time.

Subcontracting has many advantages including:

▶ being useful for specific projects/periods of time

▶ low investment required in advance

▶ subcontractors are usually **self-employed** so costs are lower

▶ costs are fixed as the business only needs to pay the contract costs and not additional costs such as holiday or sickness pay for employees

▶ faster and easier to buy in expertise.

There are also some disadvantages including:

▶ it may be more expensive in the longer term

▶ subcontractors may not be as loyal as employed staff

▶ less control potentially over the quality of the service offered or product manufactured

▶ subcontractors may be less motivated than permanent staff.

**Key term**

**Self-employed** – a person who earns their living from charging fees or commissions rather than being employed and earning a salary.

**PAUSE POINT**

Franchising, subcontracting and licensing are all ways for international businesses to expand. What would the best method be for a cupcake manufacturer to use when expanding from the UK to Slovakia?

**Hint**    Think of the level of control, costs and customer service.

**Extend**    'Franchising is the best way to expand a business internationally with minimal cost and maximum satisfaction.' Discuss.

## Outsourcing

Outsourcing is another way of choosing another business or agency to run services on behalf of another business. Outsourcing can be used to perform certain functions such as producing accounts, running a payroll system, call centres or telesales. Outsourcing can also be used to perform other functions, such as research and development, or marketing on behalf of the business.

Outsourcing allows the core business to continue to focus on what it needs to do. By using outsourcing, for example in marketing, a business could expand the sales volumes for their product or service whilst being able to focus on their core business purpose.

▶ **Table 5.14:** Advantages and disadvantages of outsourcing

| Advantages | Disadvantages |
|---|---|
| • Keeps the business focused.<br>• Flexible.<br>• Less risk.<br>• Keeps costs under control through arrangement.<br>• Access to specialist skills or expertise. | • Lack of control.<br>• Reliance on third party and potential to be tied to that third party contractually.<br>• Hidden costs.<br>• Problems with quality. |

## Reasons for using a selected strategy

You have already learned some of the different methods that can be used to expand a business internationally. It is very important that a business chooses the right type of strategy to expand effectively. Choosing the right strategy needs to be thought about carefully and it needs to take into account the factors shown in the table below.

▶ **Table 5.15:** Choosing the right strategy for business expansion

| Factor | Areas to consider |
|---|---|
| Speed of establishing operations | • Time allowed in the business strategy – short or long term?<br>• Competitor strategy and ability to copy the product or idea – first or follower?<br>• Threats from markets in existing countries – expanding or declining?<br>• Money available for the project to ensure that the operation can go forward quickly. |
| Access to local business knowledge and expertise | • Ability to communicate in the country, including language barriers.<br>• Local culture or traditions around the service or product offered.<br>• Local business conditions and working arrangements. |
| Cost control | • Capacity for a business to expand and invest in itself versus the ability to go out and get additional investment through third parties.<br>• Cash flow of the business.<br>• Requirements of the business for **capital investment** or expertise.<br>• Need for economies of scale across geographical areas. |
| Risk control | • Reputation of the product or service.<br>• Ability to control or influence the relationship between the customer and the business.<br>• Level of investment available.<br>• Capacity to take a risk in a new market.<br>• Levels of risk traditionally adopted by the business. |

## Re-engineering products and services to meet demands and preferences

**Key term**

**Capital investment** – the amount of money that needs to be spent on investment in assets such as land, buildings, machinery or technology.

Although it is important to consider the different models of expansion when deciding to go into a new market, new country or even new geographical area of the world, it is also essential to consider the demands and preferences of customers in those areas.

Across the world, there are differences and adaptations that must be made in order to satisfy local tastes and needs. Businesses trading internationally should consider the impact of these adaptations and the extent to which they need to make changes. Changes can incur an additional cost that might be essential to trade in a new market.

Car manufacturing is a good example of re-engineering a product as some countries have left-hand drive cars and others, like the UK, have right-hand drive cars. A car manufacturer operating in the UK would need to re-engineer their products in order to produce an appropriate car.

Another example is that, in some countries, certain food additives, dyes or ingredients are not permitted and it is important that changes are made for local customers.

**Discussion**

Fast-food restaurants, such as McDonald's, have different menus for different countries. For example, in Abu Dhabi (United Arab Emirates) the food is produced and certificated as Halal and there is a selection of additional choices. These include haloumi for breakfast.

What are the advantages and disadvantages of re-engineering menus for McDonald's worldwide?

To what extent do you agree that it is impossible for a business to behave in the same way in each of the countries it operates within?

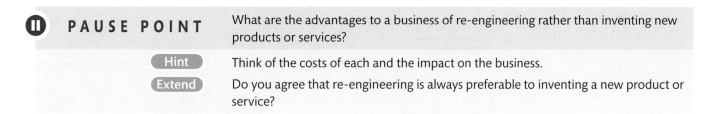

**❚❚ PAUSE POINT**     What are the advantages to a business of re-engineering rather than inventing new products or services?

      **Hint**     Think of the costs of each and the impact on the business.

      **Extend**     Do you agree that re-engineering is always preferable to inventing a new product or service?

# Resource considerations

As well as thinking about strategy and the way in which any international business wishes to expand, including the timescales involved, another critical area that the business needs to review before choosing its final strategy for expansion is resources. Resourcing has a huge impact on the potential choices of a business as, without appropriate resources, it is difficult for any business to expand within its own country and certainly very difficult internationally.

## Capital costs

Capital costs are those costs that represent high levels of investment in assets that are needed to run the business.

If a business requires high investment in capital costs and equipment, it will need to choose the most appropriate way to expand. Using methods such as franchising or licensing may be most appropriate.

Capital costs that businesses commonly incur include:

- computers and printers
- buildings
- plant and machinery
- cars
- furniture and fixtures.

Capital costs may be paid for with a business loan that can be paid back over a number of years. **Depreciation** also needs to be taken into account when valuing the assets.

## Revenue costs

Businesses also have to consider revenue costs when they are thinking about expanding. These are all the costs that need to be paid for from sales by the business. The type of revenue costs that a business may expect to incur include:

- staff wages
- utilities including gas, heat or light
- raw materials
- rent
- advertising.

These are all costs that usually need to be paid immediately and, therefore, the business needs to have money available. Making sure that a business has a healthy **cash flow** is very important, or it may risk not being able to pay these costs.

**Key term**

**Cash flow** – the amount of available money flowing in and out of the business. Having a positive cash flow means that a business can always pay its costs. If a business has a negative cash flow for a long time, it means that it is spending out more cash than it receives in income and this can lead to the business not being able to cover its shorter term costs.

**Discussion**

'Cash is king' is a common phrase used in business. Discuss, in small groups, what you think is meant by this phrase. To what extent do you agree that 'cash is king' for any business trying to expand into international markets?

## Expertise and intellectual capital

You have already learned about the capital and revenue costs that a business must take into account when expanding overseas, but there are also the costs of the expertise and knowledge of staff working in any business. Expertise and intellectual capital refers to the cost of expert knowledge and the skills that have been developed in the business that cannot be immediately transferred, or the need to bring in specialist knowledge, for example when working in particular countries.

Intellectual capital is also the term used to try to put a price on the relationships and knowledge that employees themselves have. It is sometimes difficult to actually calculate the costs of this type of expertise but it is important that any business planning to expand into international markets not only considers the cost of the intellectual capital and expertise in the current markets within which it works, but also the cost of this expertise, if they decide to move into a new market.

▶ Intellectual capital is an important cost within a business that must not be underestimated when expanding internationally.

In some countries, intellectual capital might be higher than in others, as specific expertise for how to work effectively in those countries may be more important than in others. International businesses may also put a cost on intellectual capital when pricing the expertise that they are offering in a country. In a country where skills levels are low, intellectual capital is likely to be higher and worth more than in countries where there are a lot of skilled workers. Being aware of the skills levels of local people, including levels of literacy and numeracy, can have a huge influence on intellectual capital costs.

## Training costs for local labour

Deciding to move into new international markets can take place by asking existing employees to move from one country to another and also by investing in training new employees in the local area. When a business decides to invest in a new country, they may need to invest in specific training, such as sales training, how to operate machinery or to offer particular services.

Some businesses have also made a commitment to ensuring that they invest in local people and the local population, to enhance the skills of workers there.

> **Research**
>
> Nestlé have a commitment to support employees in various countries around the world. In Mexico, for example, they have provided basic education in their factories to try to help improve the educational levels of their employees. In Turkey, employees have been given basic administration and health and safety training.
>
> Find out more about the types of programme that Nestlé and other companies offer.
>
> - What are the benefits to Nestlé of investing in education in these countries?
> - Are there any disadvantages?
>
> To what extent to you agree that investing in local people to improve their skills and support training is a good idea for companies?

## Organisational structure of international business

When businesses decide to operate internationally, they can do so in many different ways. They can decide that they are going to run the operations themselves or they can use a third party to help them, such as using subcontractors or franchise arrangements.

The type of structure that a business decides to use is heavily influenced by the way that the business chooses to expand and the countries in which it chooses to operate. The structure of the business is also significantly influenced by the type of decision making that the business wants to use and the control that they feel will be necessary in the future. There are two types of decision making that a business structure can use going forward.

### Centralised decision making

This means that all decisions are made from the central or core business. A business offering a franchise in another country makes many decisions centrally and the level of control in terms of the packing, products and service delivery method are relatively well controlled. Central decision making can also be operated when a business opens its own branch or office in another country.

The benefits of centralised decision making for international business are:
▶ consistent decisions are made from the 'head office' or by the franchisor
▶ stakeholders are dealt with consistently regardless of where the business is operating
▶ deals or agreements can be negotiated across a number of countries and areas
▶ clear recognition of the brand or way of working world-wide.

The disadvantage of centralised decision making for businesses is that the decisions made may not be appropriate for the country in which the business is operating, due to a lack of local knowledge.

### Decentralised decision making

This means the opposite to centralised, and decisions are made more locally by the managers, leaders and employees in the relevant countries. The benefits of decentralised decision making are:
▶ greater leadership and management potential at a local level
▶ enhanced ability by the business to match to local needs
▶ more flexibility to adapt to change
▶ higher levels of motivation for employees.

The disadvantages of decentralised decision making are:
▶ potential for confusion about the use of the brand or the service
▶ lack of control for the international business in the new country or countries
▶ international damage due to lack of care in one country may negatively affect the reputation or sales in another.

The type of structure with which an international business will choose to operate heavily depends on the type of decision making that they wish to use. By being clear about the types of decision and how they can be taken, the business can ensure that the structure that they choose meets their needs. The structures themselves will depend on the following factors.

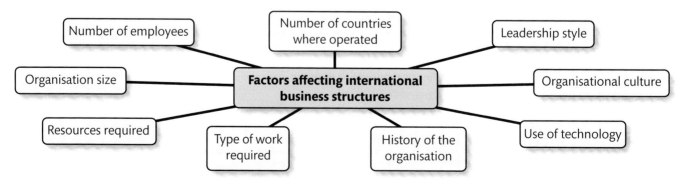

▶ **Figure 5.7:** Factors affecting business structure

The types of structure that are used by international businesses will also depend on whether or not a business chooses to operate a hierarchical, matrix or flat structure.

▶ **Table 5.16:** Features of international business structures

| Hierarchical | Matrix | Flat |
|---|---|---|
| • Many layers of management.<br>• Clear definition of roles/specialisation.<br>• Clear authority.<br>• Long chain of command.<br>• Limited span of control.<br>• Challenges for communicating from the top to the bottom.<br>• Potentially slow decision making. | • Team structure drawn of specialists, especially good for project working.<br>• Different specialists brought together in a team.<br>• Shared expertise and knowledge.<br>• Team working using specialists being brought together. | • Fewer layers of management.<br>• Wide span of control which can be challenging.<br>• Fast decision making.<br>• Fast communication.<br>• Cheaper to run.<br>• More team spirited ethos. |

Traditionally, many businesses – including those operating internationally – would have opted for a hierarchical (also known as tall) structure, as these types of organisation would have had lots of command and control when operating at the head office and also within the countries in which they were operating.

▶ Technology has changed the way that international businesses operate.

However, today, with many changes in technology and the ability to work online using webinars and web communication between countries, the need to have more controlled tall structures when operating in multiple countries has changed. It is now possible to have flatter structures or matrix structures operating across more than one country with the ability to monitor and check progress.

**Ⅱ PAUSE POINT**    The impact of online communications has changed the face and shape of international businesses. Teams can now meet virtually. What are the advantages and disadvantages of meeting in this way?

> **Hint**    Think of the costs of travel, time and accommodation.

> **Extend**    Do you think that having meetings in person is no longer necessary for multinational businesses operating in the virtual world?

Now carry out a research study into an international business of your choice, looking in depth at the way that it is resourced, and the strategies it adopts. Explain and make judgements about the impact of strategy and resourcing on that business. You will need to produce a presentation of your findings.

In your presentation, ensure that you include detailed information showing how decisions are made and the impact of resourcing decisions on strategy. You may wish to use a business that you have researched previously. Before you begin, ensure that you are able to research your chosen business to the depth required for this assignment.

In your presentation, you need to make sure that you cover:

- an explanation of how businesses make adaptations to products and processes when they operate internationally
- the strategies used with regard to the way that the business operates using different types of international agreements, such licensing or subcontracting
- the resources that have been considered, including those that relate to people, physical assets such as building, and investment required.

Your presentation should conclude with an analysis and evaluation of the extent to which you believe these strategies and resources have worked successfully and effectively in your chosen business.

## Plan

- Can I find plenty of research and information about the resourcing, structures and ways of working within my chosen businesses?
- Do I have enough information about levels of resourcing, on and offline, to enable me to answer all of the elements of the activity?
- Have I reviewed and got access to enough information on the different types of agreement and structure that the business is using?

## Do

- Am I looking at the positives/negatives, advantages/ disadvantages of the ways in which resources are used, so making sure that it is possible to show both viewpoints to give detailed analysis in my work?
- Is my information responding to all the elements of the question, including structures, resources and ways of working, such as those legal agreements that could be put into place?
- Are my judgements or conclusions backed up by research evidence including book references and websites and are these included at the end of the work as a bibliography or references list?
- Have I used judgement words within my work to show the clear thinking needed for work at the higher levels?

## Review

- Did I include as much research evidence as possible?
- How did I approach it?
- What would I do differently next time to make sure that I improve in future assignments?

### Websites

The official website of the European Union.
europa.eu/index_en.htm

A website giving details about culture in different countries.
www.worldbusinessculture.com

# THINK ▶FUTURE

## Evie May

International Sales Manager of Fruit Juice Company

Evie has been working at the Fruit Juice Company for 10 years. During this time, she has been lucky enough to travel around the world and to spend time working in different countries. The Fruit Juice Company operates in Europe and further afield, so this has given her a good idea about the different cultures and ways of working.

Working for an international business gives her opportunities to progress her career in the UK but she has also had the chance to work and line-manage people in other countries. This has meant that she has had the chance to help motivate teams all over the world.

Working for an international business means that she is also very good when using technology. There are weekly meetings of the sales teams and these are all done using Skype. This means that no one has to travel and they can spend their time concentrating on sales targets and ensuring that their customers are happy. Evie can speak three languages and being able to speak at least one additional language is a very useful skill. She recommends being involved in an international business because you never know where it might take you and she still enjoys seeing her organisation's fruit juices on the tables of customers all around the world!

# Focusing your skills

### The impact of culture on international business

Working in international business means it is important to focus on the way that cultural differences can be used positively. When working with people from other countries it is important to think about:

- communication methods that show you are respectful and polite towards others
- the influence of religion, for example on working practices, holidays in that country or even appropriate dress
- the way people view work and their working methods at work
- the way that managers need to lead their employees, giving lots or little direction.

### When working with colleagues or customers from other countries

When you are working with people from other countries as colleagues or customers what should you do?

- Find out as much as possible about their culture so that you are aware of differences and common ground.
- Try to be as respectful as possible and, if you get something wrong, apologise as soon as you can.
- Try to think of as many questions about the organisation or person you are working with in advance, by doing lots of research and asking questions of others, where appropriate.

# Getting ready for assessment

Sidney is working towards a BTEC National in Business. He was given an assignment on strategic and operational approaches for developing international trade, and needed to include reasons for selecting different approaches, including changes to products and services and resource considerations. He had to give a presentation with an accompanying report on his findings. He had to make sure that he covered:

▶ how his chosen food manufacturing business has adapted its products and services for different markets, including the way that resources have been used to support this

▶ an analysis of the impact of the strategies that have been used, including an overall judgement about the extent to which these strategies have been effective for his food manufacturing business.

Sidney shares his experience below.

## How I got started

First, I looked back at everything I had learned from my textbook. There were lots of strategies I had learned about, including joint ventures, partnerships and agencies. I reviewed each of these types of strategy. I narrowed it down to three different types that were relevant and then gave the strengths and weaknesses of how these strategies were applied to my business. This helped me to review why my business had made its choices regarding strategy and also to look at associated resourcing areas, such as access to finance and staff. Reviewing the different types of strategy first before narrowing it down meant that I was also able to make judgements about why my food manufacturing business discounted some of the methods and gave an opportunity for me to really be clear in my thinking.

I did lots of research online into the different resource implications, including the capital, revenue, and staff and training costs including that had a big impact on my business, particularly when it moved into new markets. I realised that the impact of international business accounts and exchange rates was important so I ensured that I added this to my work. The research also confirmed my thinking about the importance of ensuring that the right skills were available in countries in which international businesses operate or that there is the capacity to transfer people and skills on or offline.

## How I brought it all together

I needed to give a presentation and write an accompanying report. I chose to start with the presentation and use PowerPoint so that I was able to be clear in my thinking about the strategies and resources that had been used. Putting the presentation together also made me realise where there were gaps in my knowledge so that I could carry out more research online and using my BTEC National textbook.

When I had completed the draft PowerPoint presentation, I started to write the accompanying report. This included a clear introduction, a summary and conclusions at the end. Writing the report to go with my presentation enabled me to review my thinking and helped me to analyse the different strategies and add conclusions to enhance my higher level thinking towards distinction.

At the end of my report, I made sure that all the sources of information, including my BTEC National textbook, were referenced.

## What I learned from the experience

I found researching and investigating different ways to develop strategy and use resources in international businesses really interesting. It has made me think that I might want to get involved in international business in the future. Researching international business has made me realise how important it is to have a second language and that practising speaking in other languages or communicating in writing would really help me in my career. I have family members who can speak Mandarin so I have decided that, as well as working on my grades, I am going to try to improve my speaking of Mandarin so that I can use it in my future career.

## Think about it

▶ Have you included a bibliography in your work to make sure that you reference your sources at the end of your work?

▶ Do you know how to reference quotes and other material clearly?

▶ Is your report written in your own words to make sure that you have not included any information that has not been written by you (unless it has been referenced correctly as a direct quote)?

▶ Have you looked back over other units to see if there are elements that connect to this work?

# Principles of
# Management 6

# Getting to know your unit

Managers are vital to the running of any business; they shape and influence it through their managerial performance and leadership.

In this unit, you will examine how businesses adapt their approaches to management in response to challenges in their environment. Depending on their roles and responsibilities, managers need to develop skill sets that enable them to work effectively in areas such as people, financial, resource and quality management, and managing change. You will investigate some of the issues that managers and leaders have to deal with in the workplace to make businesses more efficient and ensure their survival and growth. The effective planning and organising of a business' activity can significantly influence the success of a business.

This unit will help you to progress either to employment, by considering a career working in supervision and management and/or to vocational training. Additionally you might move on to related higher education having developed a knowledge and understanding of management.

This unit will enable you to understand how the role of management and leadership in the workplace contributes towards business success.

## How you will be assessed

This unit is assessed under supervised conditions. You will be given a case study before the supervised assessment period so that you can carry out research. During the supervised assessment period, you will carry out a task which is set and marked by Pearson.

As the guidelines for assessment can change, you should refer to the official assessment guidance on the Pearson Qualifications website for the latest definitive guidance.

This table lists the essential content areas that you must be familiar with prior to assessment.

| **Essential content** | |
|---|---|
| A | The definitions and functions of management |
| B | Management and leadership styles and skills |
| C | Managing human resources |
| D | Factors influencing management, motivation and performance of the workforce |
| E | Impact of change |
| F | Quality management |

Identify what you already know about the principles of management. For example, what do you mean by management, does it differ from leadership? Reflect on the business experience you already have and consider the types of managers you have encountered.

As you work through this unit, develop your ideas and initial impressions and extend your explorations across a wider business culture.

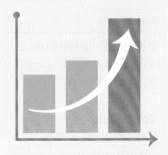

# A The definitions and functions of management

## Definitions of management and leadership

Managers are often required to also be leaders as the two functions go hand in hand, but in the business world there is a distinction between being a manager and being a leader. Leaders are often considered the innovators of the business, while the manager's job is to plan, organise and coordinate.

Conflicts exist between the definitions and functions of management and leadership. In essence, managers are usually responsible for making things happen, but those things are mostly determined by leaders. Managers will identify resources needed for an action to occur, including:

▶ physical – equipment required for the task
▶ human – the people best suited to the task
▶ financial – working within a budget.

Leaders focus on the bigger picture, such as where the business fits within the global marketplace. Leaders plan ahead longer term, while managers have a shorter-term view and focus on getting the job done now and its fairly immediate consequences.

In effect, everyone is a manager of something as they have responsibility, not only for themselves and their actions, but also a responsibility to others and the aims of the business. A manager usually has authority over somebody or something which means they can make decisions about business practice, for example a retailer offering a discount.

Employees have responsibilities but may not have the authority to make decisions without consulting others. The same is true of managers, according to their level of responsibility and hierarchy within an organisation. Having responsibility without authority can be difficult to manage but, likewise, when you have the authority you are also responsible for the impact and outcome of the decisions you make.

### Management by objectives

Management by objectives (MBO) is a business term for a system of agreeing objectives so that everyone moves forward in a consistent manner. Managers set and pass on objectives that have been put in place to help achieve business goals. These objectives must be linked to strategic plans set out by those managers or leaders at the top of the hierarchical structure. It is then the responsibility of managers to work out how the strategies will be implemented by identifying the objectives, for example to promote a new product or service.

Managers do not spend their entire time giving orders and **delegating** responsibility for achieving tasks. Managers are responsible for defining the purpose of tasks so that the workforce understand why they are completing something, and so are likely to act more enthusiastically.

## Situational and contingency

Situational and contingency leadership is a theory introduced by Blanchard and Hersey in 1969 about how the situation is related to a leader's (or manager's) personality and behaviours. For example, just as you are likely to vary your personality or behaviour according to any given situation, so will a manager or leader. Consider if you were a customer in a bank and just about to pay some money into your account, when the bank was suddenly under threat of robbery. You would be highly likely to change your behaviour to match the situation, or find a contingency for what you thought best matched the situation. Managers and leaders have to react to situations in a similar way.

We shall explore several different management and leadership styles later in the unit in the section Management and leadership styles.

## Functional and action-centred

John Adair developed a model for team leadership and management in 1979 demonstrating in a simple, Venn diagram-type model the roles of a leader or manager.

Adair defines action-centred management by three core responsibilities, which are represented in Figure 6.1:

▶ achieving the task
▶ managing the team or group, and
▶ managing individuals.

As you work through this unit, you will learn more about how managers and leaders do this and the skills they need to achieve the planned outcome.

▶ **Figure 6.1:** John Adair's action-centred model
(Source: *Action-Centred Leadership*, McGraw-Hill (Adair, J.E. 1973), with permission from John Adair)

## Transformational and transactional

These are two types of leadership or management approach which are distinctly different, as shown in Table 6.1. It could be argued that one style complements the other.

▶ **Table 6.1:** Transformational and transactional styles of leadership

| Transformational style | Transactional style |
|---|---|
| Considers the much bigger picture and takes a more strategic view to achieving greater goals. This style adopts an approach of investing time and effort now to reap rewards in the longer term. Targets are important to push employees to aspire to greater things and receive rewards which are commensurate. This style is likely to produce tomorrow's managers and leaders. | Concerned about getting the job done with little disruption to normal operations. Likely to follow process and systems and will use various techniques or incentives to encourage employees to give their best by being motivated. Generally short-term goal focused and responds quickly. |

**Discussion**

In a small group discuss the advantages and disadvantages of each style of leadership: transformational and transactional.

## The concept of leadership continuum for management behaviour

Leadership **continuum** is a concept originally defined by Tannenbaum and Schmidt in 1958 and updated in 1973. Like many theories on management and leadership, it has been studied and critiqued by theorists and concepts vary according to situational factors and developments in business practice.

This theory suggests an imaginary line along which various styles of management or leadership can be placed to help explain how behaviours influence the decisions made.

▸ **Figure 6.2:** The leadership continuum

For example, a manager or leader who lets their subordinates suggest or try out new ways of working sits at the far right-hand side of the continuum. However, a manager who likes to keep control and tell their subordinates how it will be done sits on the far left-hand side and adopts an **autocratic** style. There are several stages in the process along the continuum which will vary according to behaviours. It is suggested that the more successful and effective managers are those who know which behaviour is appropriate to the situation. Douglas McGregor developed 'Theory X' and 'Theory Y' in the 1960s. They are management theories that describe two models of how managers motivate their workforce. Theory X stresses the importance of strict supervision, external rewards and penalities. Theory Y, on the other hand, stresses the importance of job satisfaction and working without direct supervision.

> **Key term**
>
> **Autocratic** – controlling, not taking views of others into account.

> **Reflect**
>
> What style of management do you think you would prefer to work under? Why?

## Functions of management and leadership

You have considered some differences and similarities between managers and leaders and will now explore the functions relating to those roles.

### Functions of management

#### Planning

Planning is a management function. Managers need to plan to implement strategic objectives. As suggested earlier, part of a management role is to ensure a task can be carried out within pre-determined boundaries. For example, when BT decided they should move some of their off-shore overseas call centres back to the UK, following perceived customer service issues, it would be the managers' responsibility to make this happen. To initiate a plan to execute this large-scale operation, managers would have needed to consider many different factors, although this would be the case regardless of the size of the operation.

#### Organising

The plan provides a framework for managers, which in this example of BT would involve several managers, to organise teams, schedules, resources, budgets, and every other aspect of the operation. Managers would need to organise a series of events before moving their call centres to UK sites. The plan would need to ensure sufficient stages were in place so that customers could still continue to make contact with BT without disruption to services.

#### Coordinating

The team of managers in this example would need to work together to coordinate such a large task. On a much smaller scale, for example a department manager in a store such as House of Fraser, the manager would be responsible for coordinating the entire operation and would delegate duties to team members.

### Controlling

An important function of management is taking control of different parts of the business. This could be a manager controlling their team, ensuring they are all working effectively and behaving appropriately. Managers also often have control of projects or particular business functions and within this the budgets and processes of those projects and functions. It is important that managers understand what they need to control and take appropriate steps in order to do so.

### Monitoring

Every plan requires monitoring to review its effectiveness and progress towards meeting objectives within the timeframe, just as you and your tutor monitor your progress to ensure you meet your deadlines. Managers will need to monitor the effectiveness of teams, evaluate what is working well and where gaps or weaknesses appear. Plans may need to be changed and milestones shifted.

> **Reflect**
>
> What skills do you think are crucial for managers? How effective are your skills in these areas?

### Delegating

A key part of a manager's role is to delegate. All managers will have tasks and elements of the job they must do themselves, for which they are given responsibility, but it is also their job to delegate some tasks to their subordinates. Managers will often be delegated tasks by their own senior managers, but part of a manager's role is to act as an interface and identify the best-suited subordinate for certain tasks. This might include identifying who has capacity, the skills or even who already has that sort of task as part of their job description.

**PAUSE POINT**  Cover this page and draw a mind map of the different functions of management.

**Hint**  Think about a manager's day-to-day job. What functions do you think they use the most?

**Extend**  Consider how the plans for the Olympic Stadium were monitored to ensure work was completed on time and within budget. Which function do you think is most important to a manager on a project of that scale?

## Functions of leadership

### Inspiring

Leaders are expected to inspire and innovate. They are the driving force of the business, looking at the long-term vision and devising strategies to achieve the business goals. They make the top level decisions which directly affect the business and have the power to change the business' direction by challenging suitability of decisions. Leaders look at the bigger picture. They have much more **autonomy** than managers.

### Energising

Leaders must energise their teams. What this means is by bringing inspiration and innovation to business ideas, they indirectly inspire. Leaders have direct responsibility and management of those immediately below them who are managers. Depending on the structure of the organisation, there can be few or many managers and in a very large organisation they may have managers beneath them. Consider the BT scenario where there are thousands of managers employed. Leaders will energise their direct subordinates and expect managers to cascade that energy downwards.

> **Key term**
>
> **Autonomy** – the freedom to make decisions and take action, independent of others.

### Influencing stakeholders

Another leadership function is to influence stakeholders. Stakeholders take an interest in the business and want to know whether the products or service they purchased are secure. It is up to leaders to influence stakeholders in their view that the business is going in the right direction. If the business is like BT and has shareholders, they will pay particularly close interest to the business as they want to see a greater return on their investments.

### Envisioning

This is the term for looking to the future to envision what the consequences of actions and proposals are likely to be. Leaders will rely on having credible information to base their judgements on, such as a financial forecast or analysis of competitors' operations.

### Determining best path/route to achieve success

It is the leader's responsibility to determine the best path or route to achieve business success. They will need to convey their intentions to managers in order for the vision to become reality. Leaders need to have a complete overview of business operations – what has worked, what has not worked and why. Based on this knowledge, which is established by frequent monitoring and evaluation of sales figures, productivity, profits, costs, market share etc, leaders can make informed decisions which affect the success of the business.

## Business culture

### Definition

Business culture can be defined as the way in which things are done in a company or organisation – its style or ethos. As a model of business operations, business culture will influence how employees deal with customers, other staff and management. Take, for example, the business culture of McDonald's or various different travel agents and the major cruise lines, where employees are valued and recognised for a job well done through recognition schemes ('employee of the week/month'), just as the retail sector often offers staff discounts. This recognition fosters a culture and a sense of belonging, like a large family, which bonds employees and has a positive effect on customer relations.

▶ The Tupperware 'family' spread across the world in the 1960s

American-founded business Tupperware became a household name in the UK during the 1960s. Despite being sold directly to the public through home parties by individuals known as Tupperware dealers, the ethos of belonging to the Tupperware family was a well-engrained culture.

**Model** – copy, behave in a similar way, replicate the intentions of the vision.

**Intonation** – what can be inferred from, or is implied by, an indication of intention of a communication.

**Paternalistic** – a management approach that involves a dominant figure who treats employees like members of an extended family and expects loyalty, trust and obedience in return.

## Business vision, mission and values/ethos

A business culture is determined by its vision, mission, and associated values or ethos. A positive business culture can easily be destroyed, so it is crucial to communicate the vision so it is understood by all stakeholders. Consider how well staff in McDonald's **model** the values and ethos of the business; while in a similar vein, it is claimed that the workforce for a major soft drinks brand are not allowed to be seen drinking their major competitor's brand.

## Influence of business culture on management practices

The business culture influences management practices, for example, the way managers communicate, behave and value their employees and customers. Consider the business culture of Volkswagen with the 2015 revelation that vehicle emissions were fraudulently portrayed. It takes a strong management team to instil confidence back into its teams and stakeholders in such adverse circumstances.

### Link

When you consider the positive practice by management and employees in the Little Italy Case Study in *Unit 1: Exploring Business*, the influence of business culture is evident.

## Policies and procedures

Business culture influences policies and procedures. Although these are built around a framework of legislation and regulations, how they are interpreted represents the culture of the business. For example, consider the notices you might have observed when visiting a hospital or perhaps a doctor's surgery around the zero tolerance of any aggressive behaviour towards staff members. Messages conveyed represent the culture of the organisation and influence how its employees are likely to behave.

### Discussion

Discuss the message or **intonation** of some policies from part-time jobs or places of study and the business culture they reflect. Do you see any similarities or differences between the types of companies?

## Management styles

Business culture affects and influences management styles. First, the country and demographic has an effect, which is seen when considering the examples of McDonald's and Tupperware. American-born leaders and companies often encourage use of first names and a friendly manner whereas in Germany, this might be considered to be impolite. In some British businesses, the use of titles and last names is still common, such as senior airline staff and some doctors' surgeries, dental practices and solicitors.

The structure of a business is often influenced by national characteristics and this is likely to be reflected in both the way the business operates and the titles used. In parts of Asia and Europe, the management style is likely to be autocratic, whereas in the United Arab Emirates (UAE) the style is directive and **paternalistic**, where instructions are given and it is expected that they will be followed.

## Structure of the workforce

The structure of the workforce also reflects the business culture. Where individuals are placed on the organisational structure reflects and impacts on the business culture. Hierarchical structures tend to have very few people, sometimes only one person, in charge of the entire workforce or with a single layer of managers in between. As this type of structure is associated with one person in overall charge, and speedy decision-making, it is likely to generate a culture that is autocratic. On the other hand, a holocratic structure encourages a business culture which is open and democratic.

> **Link**
>
> You will have covered holocratic structures in *Unit 1: Exploring Business*. Take a look at Figure 1.5 to remind yourself.

> **Research**
>
> Carry out research into at least one business for each type of management and leadership style. Suggest reasons why these businesses use the style they do.

### How people work

Organisational structure impacts on the way people work. Consider an example of an open and democratic structure with a culture that encourages new ideas, proposing changes and creating new opportunities. Employees are likely to be motivated and willing to try new things. This can be seen at Google, where staff are encouraged to be innovative and to propose ideas through the use of creative workspaces in multiple environments (for example, outside spaces). Staff members there might be more likely to demonstrate creativity and propose new ways of working, whereas this may be less likely in a more autocratic business culture. Many companies operate somewhere in the middle, where people are often willing to offer ideas but not at the expense of business success.

The way a business treats its employees also impacts on how employees feel. For example, Virgin, despite their huge workforce, often report employees feeling as though they are part of a family.

> **Discussion**
>
> In a small group or pairs, discuss the type of culture in your place of study or work and its relationship with the way people work.

▶ How does it help a business if employees feel part of a family?

> **Case study**
>
> ## About turn!
>
> Within the armed forces the functions and culture of its people are clearly defined.
>
> The British Army consists of the General Staff and the deployable Field Army and the Regional Forces that support them, as well as Joint Elements that work with the Royal Navy and Royal Air Force. The Army carries out tasks given to it by the UK government. Its primary task is to help defend the interests of the UK, which consists of England, Wales, Scotland and Northern Ireland.
>
> The command structure is hierarchical with divisions and brigades responsible for administering groupings of smaller units. Major Units are regiment or battalion-sized with minor units being smaller, either company sized sub-units or platoons. All units within the service are either Regular (full-time) or Army Reserve (part-time), or a combination with sub-units of each type.

Unit names differ for historical reasons. An infantry regiment is an administrative and ceremonial organisation only and may include several battalions. An infantry battalion is equivalent to a cavalry regiment. For operational tasks a battle group will be formed around a combat unit, supported by units or sub-units from other areas. Such an example would be a squadron of tanks attached to an armoured infantry battle group, together with a reconnaissance troop, artillery battery and engineering support.

The Army Reserve has two clearly defined roles. Firstly, it provides highly trained soldiers who can work alongside the Regulars on missions in the UK and overseas. Secondly, it gives people who have specialist skills, like medics and engineers, a range of exciting opportunities to use them in new ways.

Each unit is reliant on clear goals and directive leadership, drawing on multiple skills. New recruits are transformed into fully trained and highly skilled personnel. Management and leadership roles are functional and action-centred, with the ability to perform multiple functions, from careful planning through to execution of every manoeuvre. Leaders closely monitor the effectiveness of individuals and how they interact as teams. They are expected to inspire and energise and use an enormous amount of personal energy on motivating their teams. Most of all they need to ensure success and will involve teams in deciding upon the most appropriate route and suitable contingencies. In essence they are risk managers.

Being able to form teams who can work efficiently and effectively together requires refined observation skills and the ability to interpret behaviours and anticipate reactions. Managers and leaders expect full compliance with the policies and procedures and employ strategies to ensure they are implemented for maximum impact. For example, they will need to undertake risk assessments to make allowances for different situational factors according to the terrain or the territory, whether at home or overseas. They need to plan for, and coordinate, resources and delegate tasks to teams and individuals.

Source: British Army Structure, www.army.mod.uk/structure/structure.aspx, © Crown copyright. Contains public sector information licensed under the Open Government Licence (OGL) v3.0. www.nationalarchives.gov.uk/doc/open-government-licence/version/3/

### Check your knowledge

1 How would you define the management and leadership in this example of the Army Reserve?

2 What are the main functions of the officers as managers?

3 Why do officers and troops need to plan thoroughly for their manoeuvres?

4 What contributes to the culture of the Army Reserve?

5 What are the main functions of the officers as leaders?

**PAUSE POINT**

Think about your centre's management or leadership team. List the functions of management they use within their jobs.

**Hint**

Does your centre have a mission or vision statement? How does this impact on how managers or leaders work within your centre?

**Extend**

What sort of impact do you think a new leader would have on a business' culture?

'Pleated' is a small fashion business devoted to replicating vintage clothes. It is a partnership run by Matthew and Thula who ensure the staff know exactly what they are aiming for and that quality is paramount.

They value their staff and are willing to listen to their ideas especially when it comes to production, although they need to get the job done on time. The partners are flexible but do find they spend considerable time having to adapt to the workforce, rather than the other way round.

The partners are seeking some guidance about their roles and the functions of management and leadership, as they would like the workforce to be driven by them without being too bossy. Currently they believe they run a 'happy ship' and are concerned this could all change if they get it wrong.

Matthew and Thula want a presentation with some speaker notes and a handout for future reference. They want to understand the different definitions and functions of management and have asked for examples of different approaches in practice.

*Plan*
- What are you being asked to do?
- Have you read through the assessment outcome and highlighted or underlined key words in the activity?
- Can you prepare a timed action plan and build in a contingency to make sure you meet the deadline?
- Can you identify the resources and where to get the sources of information you will need?
- Have you sketched out a rough plan for your presentation?

*Do*
- Have you carried out enough research?
- Have you documented and kept all your sources for your bibliography?
- Can you provide lots of examples to explain concepts, benefits and disadvantages?
- Have you spent enough time on the content compared to the presentation?

*Review*
- How did it go?
- Did you manage to complete the objectives within the deadline comfortably?
- What would you change?
- What do you need to learn to understand better?

 **B    Management and leadership styles and skills**

## Management and leadership styles

You have started to learn about different types of management and leadership styles. You will now explore seven different types of style and some of their pros and cons, plus some examples of where these styles might exist. Kurt Lewin and David McLelland are often associated with theories of leadership styles although thousands of books and articles have been published. Their research explored the relationships between different styles of leadership and the impact on performance and behaviour.

### Autocratic

An autocratic style of leadership adopts an **authoritarian** approach, examples include former leaders of China, Russia and North Korea. This style is often associated with power and control over others although, as you saw earlier in the unit, there is a continuum of autocratic styles just as there is with each type of leadership and management style.

> **Key term**
>
> **Authoritarian** – enforcing strict obedience to authority.

▷ What political systems are associated with an authoritarian style of leadership?

This style is likely to be in evidence where a small business team are working on a project which needs to be completed quickly and where instructions need to be given clearly and executed efficiently. For example, if a major water leak occurs on the M25, a team of workers will be drafted in rapidly. The team leader will need to manage the team, and ensure the least disruption possible to traffic, limited water loss, and that everyone is safe, all within a very tight deadline. The armed forces operate this style of leadership.

The negative side to this style is that workers can resent being told what to do, especially when they might have their own ideas about improving the process. It is felt that this style lacks creativity as it focuses on systems and processes and, while deadlines might be met, it is often at the expense of job satisfaction.

## Democratic/participative

This type of leadership and management style sits at the other end of the continuum. A **democratic** approach invites participation from others, seeking ideas and involvement in decision making and problem-solving. As you started to learn earlier, this approach, while considered favourable by many, can take up so much time and energy that tasks do not get done within deadlines.

A democratic or participative leadership style is viewed as being inclusive by sharing responsibility and involving everyone. The Prime Minister is expected to portray a democratic leadership style. Members of parliament are encouraged to contribute with their views, opinions and solutions, as are members of the public, for example when discussing the EU Referendum.

Businesses which benefit from a controlled method of democracy are creative industries such as advertising, consultancy and service industries. John Lewis Partnership (JLP) is also an example of a retail business displaying this type of management style in the way in which they involve their employees and other stakeholders.

## Paternalistic

This type of leadership and management style often appears as a large 'family' with the leader or manager acting as a dominant paternal or maternal figure. Employees are treated as part of this family and are expected to demonstrate trust and loyalty in return.

For example, an employee in a business may get disciplined for not delivering complete customer satisfaction. However, a paternalistic leader will endeavour to protect staff and while the customer would be treated appropriately with an apology or remediation, the employee is likely to be forgiven and trained to act appropriately in future, rather than merely censured.

▷ Have you seen extracts from debates in Parliament on the news?

A paternalistic style is one which historically has brought a feeling of family, protection and lifetime commitment to its employees, such as the ethos instilled by Earl Tupper when he founded Tupperware. Due to the economic climate, few businesses are able to offer such a commitment nowadays.

## Laissez-faire

As the term suggests, this type of management and leadership style is hands-off, where employees are delegated free-reign to decide how to go about their business and make decisions, such as Facebook and to some extent Microsoft. The music business and other creative industries are likely to adopt this type of management style.

The advantages might appear to be a feeling of freedom and entrepreneurship but in reality the outcome is very often slow productivity and higher costs due to an inefficient workforce. One reason for this might be lack of clear job roles and boundaries; imagine the disruption which would occur in an army of ants without clear roles and leadership.

## Transactional

You were introduced earlier to the definition of a transactional leader (see Table 6.1). Theorists Bass and colleagues (1976) and Burns (1978) are well known in academic circles for their studies.

This style of leadership comes from the path-goal theory of Robert House who in 1971 suggested that, for leaders to be effective, they must adapt their own behaviour to suit both the situation and their employees' abilities and skills. He based his theory on previous works by Victor Vroom. By changing their behaviour to cover any gaps in the business environment or employees' performance these leaders are able to introduce contingencies that help to make the business run smoothly.

▶ Would ants survive if they all did different things rather than working together?

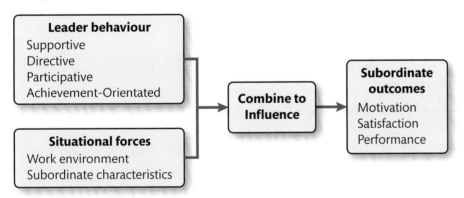

▶ **Figure 6.3:** The path-goal leadership model
From *Management and Organizational Behavior: An Integrated Perspective*, South-Western (Pierce, J.L., Gardner, D. and Dunham, R.B. 2001) figure 11-7, reproduced with permission of South-Western College Pub in the format Republish in a book via Copyright Clearance Center.

This theory suggests that four different leadership behaviours are called upon:
▶ participative
▶ goal or achievement-oriented
▶ directive
▶ supportive.

Examples of areas where this style is demonstrated in business are likely to be where the people are the biggest assets, for example, a football manager whose players are critical to the success of the team, a music or film industry agent or a manager at a modelling agency.

## Transformational

A transformational style (Bass, 1978; Burns, et al, 1976) is one where the leader or manager demonstrates concern for employees and is focused on developing individuals to fulfil the vision of the business. The overall aim is to transform the business by investing in its employees. Businesses evidently displaying this style are often family-run businesses, but larger examples include M&S and Legoland.

This style of leadership ensures employees know where the business is going and how it will get there. Leaders value their employees and reward them accordingly. The possible disadvantages of this type of leadership is that the business may be so focused on their long-term goals that they have overlooked the core **competencies** they need today, whether that is training employees appropriately, or diversification in products or services. Examples of this, where a business has moved away from its core activity, include Polaroid and Kodak, which delayed their joining the digital market.

## Charismatic

A charismatic leader is one who pushes boundaries and engages and motivates people through their personal attitude and approach to business.

Leaders described as charismatic often include Martin Luther King, Richard Branson and Barack Obama. This style of leadership can be unpredictable, leaving employees feeling insecure and not knowing what will happen next. Rules and regulations can appear to get ignored or interpretations stretched beyond all recognition. Employee motivation can be affected, especially if a project is shelved after extensive involvement. Some people find charismatic behaviour exhausting, stressful and even intimidating. However, this style of leadership can inject motivation in employees by changing business culture. Just as negative behaviours are infectious, so are positive ones.

▶ What are the benefits to employees of having a charismatic leader?

**❙❙ PAUSE POINT**

Close your book and list each of the management and leadership styles, plus key features of each.

Hint    You could do this as a list or as a mind map. Save your notes and use them when revising for your assessment.

Extend    Can you think of a real example (modern or historical) for each type of style?

**Reflect**

What type of style does your tutor or employer display? What style do you prefer?

## Management and leadership skills

Each management and leadership style requires a set of skills. This section looks at examples of the skills needed to be an effective manager or leader.

### Setting objectives

The ability to set objectives which are SMART (specific, measurable, achievable, realistic and time-bound) is one of the skills leaders and managers need to demonstrate. The skills required to set SMART objectives include:

▶ problem-solving (you need to know how to analyse a problem and solve it)
▶ creativity (you need to be able to think 'outside the box' when required)

▶ innovation (you need to be able to think about, and implement, new ways of working if necessary)

▶ team working (you need to be able to work as part of a team)

▶ clear communication (you need to be able to communicate clearly so that others know what you are doing at any given time)

▶ diligence (you need to give your full attention to the job in hand)

▶ attention to detail (you need to make sure that details are correct and nothing is missed)

▶ time management (you need to be able to manage your time effectively in order to make sure you cover what you need to do in a given time)

▶ organisation (you need to be organised in the way you approach your work)

▶ forecasting (you need to be able to look ahead and answer 'what if?' questions)

▶ integrity (you need to be honest and have strong moral principles).

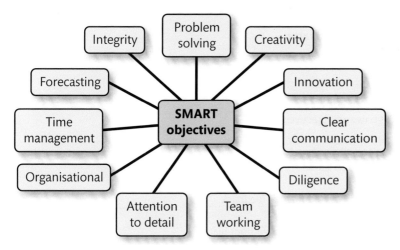

▶ **Figure 6.4:** Setting SMART objectives is an essential leadership skill

Objectives are generally to set to:

▶ achieve a solution to a problem

▶ improve processes and systems

▶ develop individuals.

The difference between an aim and an objective is often confused. One simple way to differentiate between the two is to think about an example. If the aim is to learn to drive, the objectives identify how you will do that in small stages:

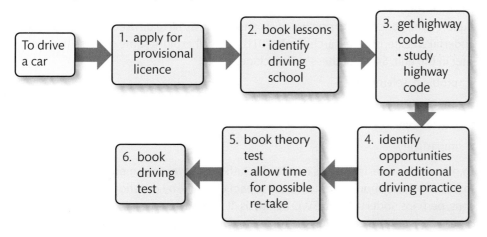

▶ **Figure 6.5:** Learning to drive: aims and objectives

Objectives should always be SMART. For example, if you consider the steps listed above, you will see how some of those stages are broken down further. Other steps will also need to be identified until the objectives are 'specific' and each one is SMART. Managers apply similar principles to setting business objectives to make actions more manageable and to aid business planning.

## Motivating

Managers and leaders who are positive, enthusiastic, have integrity and credibility are likely to be natural motivators. However, these are skills which may need developing for others. It could be argued that there are skills which a person is born with, such as charisma, and that these are not easily developed.

To be an effective motivator requires a special skill-set which can be developed (Fuller, 2008), as shown in Table 6.2.

▶ **Table 6.2:** Skills required for an effective motivator

| Skillset for an effective motivator |
| --- |
| • giving encouragement |
| • belief |
| • value |
| • clear communication |
| • setting SMART goals and objectives |
| • autonomy |
| • giving stretching and challenging tasks |
| • creating opportunities to learn |
| • giving praise |
| • giving constructive and developmental feedback |
| • showing equality and no favouritism |
| • allowing the opportunity to takes risks without blame |
| • finding interesting and varied work |

Managers need to be able to motivate teams and individuals otherwise the work may not get done. To be a self-motivator requires willpower and self-belief.

## Decision making

A manager's role is to make decisions, and though these are at a different level and complexity from those a leader must make, a manager without the skills to make decisions will demotivate teams and have an impact on productivity. A poor decision maker lacks integrity and credibility and is unlikely to progress within the business.

The skills required for decision making are very complex. Many academics have explored the concept and psychologists and scientists have devised theories and undertaken extensive research (Bush, 2011). You will explore some of these theories later in the unit. Some of these skills include:

▶ problem-solving

▶ intuition and reasoning

▶ critical thinking

▶ impartiality.

To make a decision, managers need to be sufficiently well informed about the problem to be solved and should consider each aspect critically, by questioning the pros and cons, perhaps undertaking a SWOT analysis. It is important to remain impartial, otherwise emotions can get in the way of making the right decision.

▶ How can you be sure you'll make the right decision?

For example, imagine you have devised a system or product which is proving problematic or someone suggests it should be done differently. You might feel somewhat put out and find it difficult to focus on the needs of the business and individuals if you are not impartial.

Figure 6.6 suggests a decision-making model that includes a series of processes involved in making a decision. The arrows indicate the importance of reflecting at each stage in arriving at a well-considered decision.

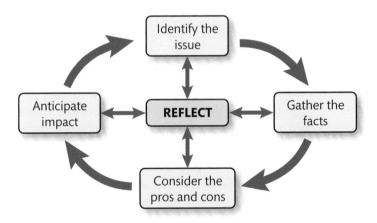

▶ **Figure 6.6:** A suggested model for a decision-making process

---

**Theory into practice**

You are considering your next steps after you have completed your BTEC Nationals Level 3. There are many options you could choose after your course, but for this activity you are choosing between:

- work
- apprenticeship
- university.

Whichever route you are planning will require an application. To help make your decision use the decision-making outline in Figure 6.6. Once you have come to a choice, evaluate the skills you need to make your decisions and any changes you made to the model which made it more useful to you.

## Team building

Businesses rely on effective team working just as you need to do to function in life. Leaders and managers with the skills to build effective teams contribute to successful businesses. Rather like pieces of a jigsaw, individuals in a team come together to make something that is not possible on their own and, as with a jigsaw, every part is different.

This idea could represent any level of employee and later in this unit (see Factors influencing management, motivation and performance of the workforce) you will learn about some of the tools developed by psychologists for selecting the right people to do a job by the skills and **traits** they display.

To be an effective team builder requires effective skills such as:

▶ interpersonal skills – to convey the goals of the team, individual roles and responsibilities and monitoring mechanisms
▶ the ability to manage conflict and power struggles
▶ analytical skills – to make accurate judgements about the dynamics of team players which will affect productivity
▶ trust in the team's abilities to get the task done
▶ understanding of your own behaviours and traits.

A manager also requires knowledge about each individual and their performance, skills and traits to make an informed decision about who will form the best team to suit the task, situation and goals. This may require managers to involve employees in various team-building exercises to observe interaction and productivity. You may have been involved in some team-building exercises during your induction period.

One particular well known team builder is Jack Welch, who was the Chairman and CEO of General Electric in the USA. Through his expertise in building and motivating teams, it is claimed he increased the turnover of the organisation in the 20 years up to 2001, by several thousand per cent.

## Leading by example

Some leaders or managers are conspicuous by their absence, in other words they appear to hide away in their offices 'doing things' and 'giving orders'. Not being visible to the workforce does little to build integrity and credibility and successful managers and leaders are likely to be those who lead by example.

They tend to positively represent the corporate image and demonstrate the values of the company. They often go beyond what is expected and act as advocates for the organisation. By acting as a role model for their employees they encourage those employees to also lead by example. This level of visibility requires leaders to have some humility as if they are more visible, then so are any problems that arise. However, this can also endear leaders to their employees and foster a team or family business community.

> ### Research
>
> Search for the TV show 'Back to the Floor' on YouTube and watch examples of leaders working among their employees. What positive outcomes do you see at the end of some episodes?

## Consulting

Managers and leaders need to consult with others. Those others include internal and external customers but also specialists who might be involved to help with resolving specific problems, such as financial matters, subject or product specialists, engineers etc.

> ### Key term
>
> **Trait** – a distinguishing quality or characteristic.

Admitting you do not know all the answers might be a useful tactic to seek out others' opinions and expertise. The skills required to make the right decision based on the information gathered from consulting may result in confirming your original thoughts. To consult with others requires a variety of effective skills, as shown in Table 6.3.

▶ **Table 6.3:** Skills required for consulting

| **Skills for consulting with others** |
| --- |
| • understanding your own limitations |
| • speaking |
| • questioning |
| • listening |
| • interpreting |
| • comparing |
| • **synthesising** |
| • analysing |
| • summarising |
| • critical thinking |
| • evaluating |
| • decision making |

<table>
<tr><td>

**Key term**

**Synthesise** – to pull together, to combine, for example information from different sources.
</td></tr>
</table>

## Problem solving

Problems require solutions and leaders are mostly interested in managers finding those solutions. Everyone needs to solve problems on a daily basis, at work and in life. For example, someone stacking supermarket shelves will need to avoid customers, move boxes, sort display-by dates, move product lines according to promotions and replenish faster moving stocks.

Problem-solving requires solutions to the barriers which get in the way of something running smoothly. Possibly the biggest barrier is identifying the problem in the first place. Leaders operate at a strategic level, while managers mostly work at an operational level. In practice, this means that leaders identify problems and will require managers to present solutions. However, managers will also have to solve problems on a daily basis, for example, covering someone's sick leave, issues with customers or orders etc.

The skills required to be an effective problem solver are numerous, including those shown in Table 6.4.

▶ **Table 6.4:** Skills required for problem solving

| **Essential problem-solving skills** |
| --- |
| • thinking |
| • creativity |
| • planning |
| • forecasting |
| • organising |
| • analysing |
| • assessing risks |
| • communicating |
| • observing |
| • listening |
| • reflecting |

## Valuing and supporting others

Everyone likes to know that they are valued and so effective managers and leaders value and support others. However, there is a fine line between supporting someone and being patronising. The skill lies in providing support in a way which empowers the individual and does not take away their autonomy. Part of the role of a manager and leader is to ensure that all their staff feel valued and supported. They might do this by regular catch-ups, recognition schemes and through performance appraisals.

## Managing conflict

Managers and leaders will often have to manage conflict at various levels within a business.

Part of the skill of managing conflict is being able to understand the behaviour of others and ourselves. The root of resolving conflict lies with the cause and so ensuring that you engage in **active listening** is key to discovering the cause of conflict. Another skill that is required is the ability to anticipate potential conflicts. In business, the cause of the conflict might be that a team has been put together with incompatible team members. As a manager you may need to help resolve conflicts within this team after they have started working together. Even if you had anticipated that the conflict would arise, sometimes people get impatient with each other for other reasons, perhaps because they are over-stretched, too busy or stressed owing to personal issues; but it may still be necessary to form that team based on the needs of the business. It would be reasonable to argue that as adults, the individuals should learn to get along and find ways to resolve their differences without interfering with or compromising business operations.

As a manager, there are four key steps to managing conflict.

1 Identify the issue or problem.
2 Identify those in conflict.
3 Express concerns to those involved – usually together.
4 Listen actively.

Resolving conflict may require compromise and needs both parties to agree to the resolution. If the conflict continues, businesses usually have procedures for dealing with such matters and you will learn more about these in the section Managing human resources.

## Building positive interpersonal relationships

Possibly the most important role of any employee, regardless of management status, is to build positive interpersonal relationships, ie to get along with people. The benefits include job satisfaction, productivity and progress. The skills needed could include tolerance, honesty, **empathy**, respect and humility. Though managers and effective employees may not be able to show these skills at all times, they should work hard at maintaining and developing their own skills through personal development and reflecting on their own actions to assess effectiveness.

> **Reflect**
>
> Consider what makes some managers more effective than others and why it is that some managers do not bring out the best in their workforce. What do you think are the top three most important skills for managers and leaders?

## Using emotional intelligence

Among multiple theorists, Daniel Goleman (1995, 2001) is one particularly well-known authority on emotional intelligence. Emotional intelligence is the ability to accurately read someone else's emotions, wants and needs. However, in order to be able to assess how someone else is feeling, you have to be able to accurately assess your own behaviours. In other words, you must be self-aware.

> **Key terms**
>
> **Active listening** – paying full attention to what someone is saying so you can paraphrase and respond to the important points.
>
> **Empathy** – the ability to understand and share the feelings of another.

> **Link**
>
> See *Unit 8: Recruitment and Selection Process.*

Goleman's (2001) definition of emotional intelligence is: 'The capacity for recognising our own feelings and those of others, for motivating ourselves, for managing emotions well in ourselves and in our relationships'.

Being emotionally intelligent enables change to take place, by convincing others of the benefits, being optimistic and collaborating effectively. Goleman's simple model places four key skills at the heart of emotional intelligence which lead to a positive impact on others.

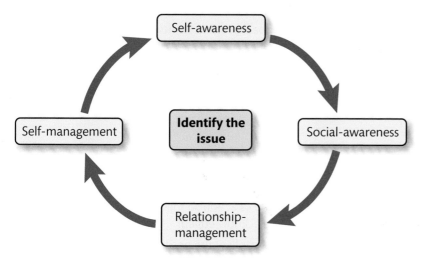

▶ **Figure 6.7:** Adapted from Goleman's (2001) model of emotional intelligence

**Reflect**

How emotionally intelligent are you? Using Goleman's simple model, assess your skills under each category and identify a plan for your own personal skills development. Remind yourself of where your strengths lie.

## Communicating

How well you communicate is dependent upon many factors. For example, an emotionally intelligent person is far more likely to be tactful and diplomatic than one who is less skilled. Communication is not all about what you say or how you say it, but combines many other skills such as:

▶ non-verbal signals
▶ active listening
▶ speaking
▶ observing
▶ interpreting what is being communicated to you
▶ articulation
▶ thinking
▶ synthesising.

The skills you use to communicate will also vary depending on the situation. Managers must ensure that they adopt the correct method and tone of communication for the situation they are in. For example, managers are likely to use different communication methods when presenting an idea to their immediate subordinates or to colleagues at the same level, compared to a group of senior managers. They also have to consider the method. It would be inappropriate to offer a job in a text message, but this may be an effective way to communicate an issue at the office that day.

**Discussion**

Discuss in a small group how you adapt your ways of communication according to the audience and situation. Consider the strategies you use to communicate effectively and which ones are less successful.

## Providing feedback

Feedback is one of the methods used to motivate teams and individuals. The skill in giving the right sort of feedback is complex. Just as feedback can motivate, it can easily demotivate and alienate. It is not unusual to feel uncomfortable when giving feedback, possibly due to the potential for conflict. Managers often have to provide feedback as part of a formal appraisal process, in which they can structure the feedback given by the goals and standards that were expected of the employee. They may also have to provide more informal feedback to employees.

Some of the key rules in providing feedback are that it must be:

▶ well considered
▶ justifiable
▶ easy to understand
▶ impartial
▶ honest
▶ tactful
▶ SMART.

For feedback to be meaningful and lead to improvement it must be both constructive and developmental. To make a difference and recognise progress, feedback should include timeframes and require evidence of action so that recognition of improvement and continuing positive practice can be acknowledged.

Several theorists work on the simple principle of the positive, negative, positive feedback sandwich to ensure the feedback is focused and well balanced.

> ### Link
> The importance of honest, justifiable feedback is covered in *Unit 8: Recruitment and Selection Process.*

> ### Reflect
> How willing are you to receive feedback? Does your reaction to the feedback depend on who is giving it? Why is that? What do you think you could do to use the feedback positively?

**PAUSE POINT**

Consider a manager or leader you know in a part-time job or at your centre. What skills can you identify that they use?

**Hint**

Think about what this person does on a day-to-day basis. What skills do they need?

**Extend**

Think of two famous business leaders and identify their leadership style. What differences and similarities between the two can you see? Suggest alternative management and leadership styles and why they could also be effective.

### Case study

#### The other way round

Patrick Tame, who founded headhunting organisation Beringer Tame in 2004, describes his leadership style as 'alternative'. 'My company is here to serve the employee, not the other way around' he says – in a statement some might find counter-intuitive. 'It's my role to identify three things staff are doing each week and then publicise the hell out of it,' he explains.

Beringer Tame is a niche company with an ambition to be the most respected brand in their market, using specialists to get to know applicants and give long-term advice that's right for them. They focus on integrity, service and delivery and have worked hard to build their reputation over the years because in this highly competitive market, reputation is everything.

As someone who recruits other leaders for a living, it's perhaps to be expected that Tame has a good idea about what modern leadership looks like. He was the first in the UK to recruit a CEO by asking candidates to create Vine videos, to get a better feel for 'who they really were'.

'The success of Beringer Tame is based on our strong focus on people. We treat people as we'd expect to be treated and whether you are a client looking to hire, a candidate looking for career advice or even a supplier to us, we strive to make that experience as good as it can be', says Patrick Tame.

According to Tame, leaders must accept talent is transitory and recognise that attracting and retaining skilled individuals requires commitment. He says leaders need to recognise they are lucky to have their talent for the time they do. It's this view that needs to be mainstream and not be the exception to the rule. Understanding this, he says, is the secret to creating winning teams.

According to academics, by 2020, 50 per cent of the global workforce will be 'millennials' – those born between 1980 and 2000. For these people, job-hopping to find employers whose values align with their own will be the norm [91 per cent of millennials expect to stay in a job for less than three years according to futureworkplace. com]. Leadership styles must respond to this in terms of authenticity and being the 'real you'.

Being authentic increasingly means letting staff take responsibility. Richard Branson cites his success as surrounding himself with people that have skills he doesn't have and then trusting them to run with it.

It has adopted holocracy, where job titles and traditional leadership hierarchy are replaced with staff being invited to join projects according to the skills they can bring. The idea is that responsibility comes from staff being accountable to all their co-workers rather than to a specific boss (who simply has a direction-setting role). In other words, work doesn't originate from top-down orders, it comes from individuals themselves.
Source: www.investorsinpeople.com/resources/ideas-and-inspiration/may-best-team-win, Investors in People

### Check your knowledge

1  What theories would you use to describe Beringer Tame's management and leadership styles?

2  What are the skills Patrick Tame relies on as a leader and manager?

3  What are the functions of management and leadership at Beringer Tame?

4  Name some of the factors which lead to a positive business culture.

---

## Assessment practice 6.2   AO1  AO2

Parker-Jones is a medium-sized manufacturer of high-end jewellery. A 95-year-old family business, it has operated in the same way since inception, with the owner controlling all business matters.

MD Miles Parker-Jones, the current owner, is very fixed in his ways and is resistant to change within the company. The highly skilled workforce know there are quicker ways of carrying out some of the processes but find that their ideas are ignored. There are rumblings of dissatisfaction among employees, including the admin staff and their single sales executive.

Miles' son George has decided to seek advice about better ways of managing the workforce. George has asked you to put together a report which clearly describes the different management and leadership styles with examples of how they work in other business situations.

George is also interested in highlighting some of the skills that might indicate management training needs but overall wants a happy workforce and a continuing business.

### Plan
- Have you read through the brief and identified what you need to do and produce?
- Can you identify your sources and order any books you will need?
- Do you know the order you will undertake the task, and dates for review and completion?
- Can you find out about writing an executive summary – the tone you should use, its content and length?

### Do
- Can you provide examples of several different types of management and leadership styles and their relationship to business culture?
- Have you identified some suitable recommendations with your reasons for them?
- Have you read through your report very carefully to ensure there are no mistakes and the tone is right?
- Have you checked the report for any changes needed to layout, format and balance of paragraphs and headings to ensure it is professional and fit for purpose?
- Have you written your executive summary?

### Review
- How would you feel receiving your report if you were George or Miles?
- What would you do differently next time?
- What areas should you consider for your personal development, knowledge and skills?
- What did you find most rewarding?

# C Managing human resources

## Human resources (HR)

Larger businesses usually have whole departments dedicated to managing HR (such as Top Shop; KwikFit; Apple; BT) and some businesses choose to outsource the management of their HR, either entirely or just for specific functions, such as payroll or recruitment, to specialist businesses. They may do this to save money or to draw on specialist expertise which they do not have within their business.

The functions of HR are numerous and have evolved over the years from taking over personnel matters to more of a consultative and possibly strategic role since businesses began to recognise the conflict between informal methods of managing employees and a more ethical formal process.

HR personnel require specialist training, and dedicated qualifications accredit different functions of the role. Businesses recognised that their biggest and possibly most expensive resource is their workforce and the investment of specialist HR services could impact greatly on the success of the business.

HR functions include monitoring, coordinating, advising and possible intervening in a variety of situations as shown in Table 6.5. (See also the section on appraisals.)

▸ **Table 6.5:** Situations requiring HR

| HR functions are needed for: |
|---|
| • appraisals |
| • promotions |
| • holidays, sick leave |
| • reward, pay, pensions etc |
| • employee relations |
| • recruitment and selection |
| • organisation structure |
| • compliance with legislation |
| • budgets |
| • professional development. |

### Human resources as a factor of production

Resource is a term used in economics, and human resources as a factor of production relates to the resources required to produce goods or deliver services. Resources can be both human and physical and include equipment, technology etc.

The HR department is involved in managing physical resources by monitoring the effectiveness of teams and individuals, involving human managers primarily. For example, managers are directly responsible for their teams and therefore any requests for increased resources usually require approval from HR. HR will either have a budget for resources or monitor managers' spending against the budget for resourcing.

Take an example where a member of staff is on extended sick leave, resulting in a department being under-resourced to meet deadlines and demands. In some businesses, managers will have the authority to take on a temporary member of staff to cover the period needed although the HR department is likely to have a preferred list of agencies to use. In other businesses, possibly due to the size of the organisation, the request will have to go to HR for them to deal with, although the manager may still be involved in selecting the right individual, or following initial screening by HR.

HR departments will use various forms of information to make decisions about the suitability of the resources and advise leaders and managers on whether or not departments should be re-structured.

**Links**

*Unit 8: Recruitment and Selection Process* covers the different functions of HR departments.

See also *Unit 21: Training and Development.*

## Labour market analyses

HR departments rely on analyses of labour market information to evaluate the supply and demand for skills and the effect of regulatory changes on businesses. Gathering and analysing this type of data is not solely the responsibility of HR departments as it is required for all departments and especially managers, to plan for **sustainability**. The gathering of this information is often referred to as **market intelligence**.

HR departments use data analyses to evaluate and plan strategically for:

▶ workforce requirements
▶ policy changes in light of government legislation
▶ anticipating contingencies for future government intentions, such as elections and party mandates
▶ measuring the availability of skills in the global market and possible impact on the organisation (for example, the gaps in literacy and numeracy skills in the UK)
▶ forecasting skills which will be needed in the future (such as international trade and export and areas that have skills gaps)
▶ education and training impact for future employees (for example, the shortage of skilled employees since the early 2000s due to limited opportunities for developing new engineers; future shortages in computing and manufacturing).

As well gathering external data, HR departments will compare it with internal data, often produced by departmental managers such as:

▶ performance against targets
▶ budgets
▶ health and safety reports
▶ customer and employee feedback
▶ employee movements, such as holidays, sick or maternity leave, punctuality, performance, resignations etc.

As data flows upwards it becomes more simplified, as shown in Figure 6.8, so that managers or leaders at the top of the organisation can make decisions based on the most important information.

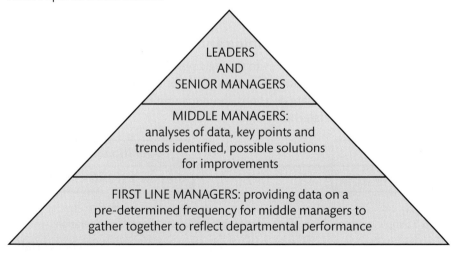

▶ **Figure 6.8:** Simple flow chart of data in an organisation

Depending on the size of the organisation, first line managers (or team leaders) might be the same people as the managers in the middle of this example. In a small manufacturing or engineering business, the manager will rely on employees' job sheets to provide information about productivity and performance. All the reports gathered from each manager will create a bigger picture for those in strategic roles to better evaluate.

> **Key terms**
>
> **Sustainability** – ability to function with sufficient resources including finance to maintain a certain level or rate.
>
> **Market intelligence** – factual information based on analyses and evaluations of multiple data, providing a big picture view of the economic climate which is used for planning, forecasting and to enable decision making.

## Forecasting labour demand

You should be starting to develop an image of how HR departments (and other managers) forecast and plan for the future of the business. Forecasting labour demand is another key factor as a business cannot survive if the labour is neither available nor sufficiently well skilled.

The construction industry is generally effective in anticipating labour needs, such as for the building of the Olympic Stadium. In this case as well, businesses within the park, such as restaurants, will have needed to forecast the amount of labour they would need to cover the Games. Managers will also need to forecast demand for unforeseen events, such as Volkswagen having to reassess labour needs in light of additional work from the emissions issue in 2015.

## Sources of information available to conduct labour market analyses

Some of the likely places where HR departments access their data to conduct their analyses include (websites can be found at the end of this unit):

▶ Department of Trade and Industry
▶ Department for Business, Innovation and Skills
▶ Office for National Statistics
▶ Information about competitors
▶ Institute for Fiscal Studies
▶ International Labour Organization (ILO)
▶ Organisation for Economic Co-operation and Development (OECD)

HR departments may also rely on local business intelligence from sources such as:

▶ Chambers of Commerce
▶ BusinessLinks
▶ sector-specific organisations such as the Construction Industry and Training Board (CITB), which is highly respected by the constructed industry.

## The link between business planning and human resources

The functions performed by HR are key to strategic planning. Strategic planning is based on using the judgements formed from the analyses and evaluation of various forms of data to make appropriate decisions about the route the business will take in the future. It can be simply stated as in Figure 6.9.

| **Strategy is** | **Operational is** |
|---|---|
| the what and by when | the how and with what |

▶ **Figure 6.9** Simple representation of the relationship between strategy and operations

Take, for example, an HR department in a chain of cycle shops dealing with an unexpected fall in sales of bicycles in the summer of 2015. Suppose that after analysing external data, plus data from the marketing and sales departments, the potential for bike sales in five years' time suggested the trend would continue. HR would advise leaders on appropriate strategies for suitable **deployment** of the workforce solely responsible for bicycles. They might suggest a strategy for redundancies or retraining to meet other business demands over a period of time.

HR are concerned with **succession planning**. They use the data to help plan for how the business will remain successful by advising on the strategies for succession. It is their role to spot talent, in collaboration with managers, and to guide or advise on ways that individuals can progress within the organisation in the short, medium and long term. Promoting from within means businesses can benefit from knowledgeable and talented employees who are familiar with the business' ethos and practices rather than having to invest heavily in recruiting externally.

### The impact of globalisation on human resource planning

Globalisation in business means the integration of operations, processes and strategies into diverse cultures, products, services and ideas. Human resource planning that considers diversity results in a workforce which generates fresh ideas and cultural insights, languages and skills which complement each other. Globalisation allows for the easier hiring of the most skilled and appropriate candidate from a much larger pool. Tools such as global job websites and video conferencing (for interviews) mean that it is much easier to establish whether a candidate from another country is suitable.

The increasing importance of video conferencing and other tools also means that it is much easier for businesses to operate globally, and candidates may not even need to move countries to be able to work for a business. The impact of having a global workforce is that HR departments will need to not only take into account cultural differences when establishing procedures but also national laws and regulations, such as those around working hours and benefits.

Easier links to other parts of the world also allow businesses the opportunity to outsource work, and to maintain control and communication more easily.

## Human resource planning

### The nature of the work and the characteristics required to perform work roles

You have been exploring the role of HR and its functions. You will now look at several of the factors associated with the planning for human resourcing.

### Skill levels

For HR to plan effectively, it is important to identify the skill levels commensurate to the position. For example, the expectation is that the higher up the structure the employee is, the greater the demands on their skills. In addition, according to the role to be undertaken, the skills would also need to be commensurate. One example is where a job role as a column editor or copywriter for a magazine publisher or copywriting agency relies on a higher level of literacy than the managerial role.

### Experience

According to the role to be filled, experience can be:
▶ essential
▶ desirable
▶ not required.

If the position available is for a skilled carpet fitter, for example, then experience would be essential; but if the job role was for a sales assistant, or trainee carpet fitter, experience might be desirable but not essential. There are occasions where HR planning includes openings for applicants without experience, not just to pay a lower salary than an experienced employee but to train the individual in their own business practices. This might be the case particularly in a specialist or niche business, such as an antiques shop or a taxidermist.

▶ Have you ever used video conferencing?

However, the decision whether experience meets one of the three criteria is a little more complicated than this. Consider how to define experience, using the example of a teacher, from these options:

1 Number of years in the role.
2 Number of hours teaching.
3 Variety of subjects or topics taught.
4 Range of students, eg age, ability, level, specialist needs.
5 Types of places where applicant has taught, eg college, school, training provider, workplace.
6 Qualifications held.
7 Length of continuous service.
8 Outcomes of students taught.

Consider these options and what they might reveal or hide. Qualifications are not the same as experience but can mask the ability to be effective. Item one is too often the first criterion to influence a positive decision but might disguise a limited amount of experience. For example, if the teacher only worked four hours a week for half of each year, then the experience is less than a full-time teacher, teaching 26 hours for 36 weeks a year. However, if the teacher has only a few years in the role but teaches in many different places for 40 hours a week, their experience might be considerably greater.

### Educational level

As briefly considered already, HR planning involves making judgements about the educational level necessary for the job to be undertaken.

Educational level relates to the academic level attained and accredited. These levels range from entry-level qualifications such as Skills for Life to a 'Level 8' Doctorate. As you are probably aware, there are qualifications which are designed to prepare you for different types of job roles. Some qualifications are purely academic, which means becoming very knowledgeable about a topic; while others are designed to prepare you for work by developing transferable skills and specialist knowledge.

### Aptitude

An educational level does not automatically assume an employee or job applicant can operate at that level. Partly this is due to experience but also competency and **aptitude**.

Consider celebrities, such as Oscar-winning actors or successful entrepreneurs, who could all be described as having an aptitude which contributes to their success. HR planning will take into account which employees demonstrate a talent that makes them suitable candidates for promotion or successful applicants for a job offer.

> **Key term**
>
> **Aptitude** – the natural ability to do something.

> **Reflect**
>
> Review the Beringer Tame case study again and how the business relies on skills and talent when selecting applicants for jobs.

Managers might be selected for the role due to a particular aptitude, such as emotional intelligence, despite not having experience in management. The latter can be learnt on the job and with additional training. HR will often structure assessment activities for job applicants to undertake to demonstrate their aptitude. These tasks might be totally unrelated to the job depending on what is deemed more important.

## Need for flexibility in the workforce

HR planning involves structuring a workforce who can be flexible, as no individual works in isolation of others and is always part of a larger team when you consider both internal and external customers. A sole trader is still part of a team otherwise they wouldn't have a business.

In the service industry, such as the catering sector, everyone will need to pull together to ensure customers get the right meals and on time. This might require flexibility when short staffed or overwhelmed with business. Kitchen equipment has to be cleaned thoroughly, supplies ordered, food prepared for cooking, washing up to be done etc.

HR want individuals who are flexible to meet business demands, work in different teams and respond to requests from management. This may include being flexible in working beyond your normal hours when required.

▶ What would happen in a restaurant kitchen if staff did not work together as a team?

## Core versus peripheral workers

Core workers are those who are employed on full-time, permanent contracts and **peripheral workers** are those who are contracted differently on a part-time or flexible working basis. Blue chip company Microsoft rates very highly in employee satisfaction partly due to its flexibility in working arrangements.

You might consider the core workers to be the hub of the business and peripheral workers as cogs who keep the wheels turning but that can be increased or decreased as necessary according to business needs.

HR's planning strategy for employing peripheral workers has changed over recent years by shifting the balance between full- and part-time employees or those with flexible working arrangements. With the trend towards dedicated HR departments that are specialists in resource management, businesses have found ways of becoming more cost effective by employing people to meet the demands on the workforce only when they are required.

However, it was not until 2000 that part-time employees were protected from less favourable treatment than their full-time counterparts with the introduction of new legislation to protect their rights.

> **Key term**
>
> **Peripheral workers** – flexible working, contracted, not permanent.

## Full-time versus part-time workers

There is no specified number of hours worked per week to define someone as full-time or part-time. A full-time worker will usually work 35 hours a week or more (with an average of 39 hours according to 2015 figures published by the Office for National Statistics (ONS)). A part-time worker is someone who works fewer hours than a full-time worker.

The reasons for employing part-time workers are similar to those for employing peripheral workers. This may not solely be to reduce costs but also means that two employees could share the same job but at different times. This provides opportunities to tap into a wider range of skills and abilities. Part-time working can also be useful for employees who do not wish to work full-time, such as parents returning to work, or those who wish to fit employment around other interests.

## Subcontracting

Subcontracting involves  paying another individual (or company) outside the business to help complete particular projects. A subcontractor is paid for the period of time or for the job they undertake as part of a project. The construction industry relies heavily on subcontracting.

Over recent years, HR strategies have shifted from employing permanent workers and mostly only employing temporary staff on a contract to cover holidays and sickness. Businesses have adopted the strategy of reducing their **headcount** to reduce ongoing costs, such as wages, national insurance, and other additional costs associated with employing people.

Subcontracting is one way HR departments have been able to plan for responding to demand in productivity and also tapping into a wider range of specialist skills, such as accountancy, building maintenance and the construction industry.

Other reasons include the costs associated with material resources, such as engineering equipment. Garages commonly subcontract body work to specialists who have the right equipment and expertise to undertake body repairs to damaged vehicles rather than purchasing, maintaining and housing the equipment on site themselves.

## Zero hours contracts

Zero hours contracts are issued by HR departments on the basis that they could call on specialists for a specific project if they were required. These types of contract offer no promise of work or payment and the workers are not obliged to accept the work offered. Also known as casual contracts, around 37 per cent are likely to be issued to students (ONS, 2014).

This was a fairly common practice with consultants who would **tender** for work in response to the contractor promoting a forthcoming project. The contractor would then be able to confidently bid for the work by demonstrating a team of specialists who they would use to deliver the contract. When the contractor won the bid for the project, they would then issue zero hours contracts to the consultants to ensure they could fulfil the project requirements. All this was part of the planning process, before the details of how the work would be undertaken was finalised.

The strategy in this type of scenario is that HR would have a contingency by seeking a commitment from those being given contracts, in this case the consultants, without any guarantee of payment or work. Other examples include bar and restaurant work, and work for actors and musicians.

**Discussion**

In a small group, discuss the risks associated with zero hours contracts – both to the contractor and to the person being offered the contract.

## Temporary staff

Temporary staff are those who are contracted to cover gaps in the workforce usually for short periods of time. Contracting with temporary staff has its advantages and some businesses, such as local authorities, use temporary staff to provide cover when a permanent position comes available partly to cover a need but also to test out an employee's suitability as an applicant. While equality laws require jobs to be advertised so that interested parties all receive an equal chance of being selected, this does offer useful insights into selecting the right person for the job.

Temporary staff require some training for the work they are to undertake; they will be unfamiliar with the business culture, policies and procedures and many temporary workers lack commitment to the organisation. All these factors and others, impact on managers, co-workers and HR departments.

## Agency staff

Businesses using temporary staff often rely on agencies to provide a list of potentially suitable applicants for the job to be undertaken. The benefits for HR departments include:

▸ specialist screening of individuals prior to being recommended
▸ access to an often instant list of potentially suitable applicants
▸ saving costs on advertising
▸ saving time
▸ reducing HR workload
▸ information about applicants' work ethics can be discussed based on the relationship existing between agency and applicant.

However, businesses usually have to pay more per hour for temporary staff than they would for a permanent member of staff, especially when agency fees are on top of the wage. While the business saves on other overheads, such as pension contributions and holiday or sick pay, which the agency will be responsible for, in the same way as for temporary workers, there are other risks involved.

## Management actions to address human resource issues at an operational level

As discussed earlier, HR departments advise on strategy and the direct responsibility for employees lies with their manager at operational level.

Managers are responsible for the smooth operation of their department which includes all its resources. In the case of human resources, while HR make the decisions about the ability for the business to sustain recruiting additional staff or the need to reduce numbers or restructure, it will be the responsibility of the manager to action the changes. The process might be:

1  Manager learns about employee resignation and informs HR.
2  HR advises replacement can be recruited and the salary to be offered.
3  Manager informs HR of any changes to job role or person specification.
4  HR drafts advert and amends job description for manager to approve.
5  Applicants apply to HR which involves manager in pre-selection for interview.
6  Manager and possibly HR representative carry out interview.
7  Suitable applicant is decided upon, possibly in negotiation with HR.
8  HR make formal offer to applicant.
9  HR receive acceptance and prepare contract of employment, agree start date etc.
10 Manager inducts new employee and liaises with HR regarding any external training required.

Consider a different example, where a member of staff has complained about unfair treatment by another individual. While the matter might have come to the attention of the HR department as a formal complaint and therefore been passed back to the manager to resolve, it may also have been reported directly to the manager informally. Either way the manager is required to sort out the issue to the satisfaction of all parties.

> **Link**
>
> You learnt about recruitment processes in *Unit 8: Recruitment and selection process*.

**❚❚  PAUSE POINT**

Research different job roles online and look at the employment terms. Organise your research by industry. Are there any similarities or differences between industries, eg around salary or the type of contract?

**Hint**  Some industries will tell you more about the employment terms of a role than others. Why do you think this is?

**Extend**  Are there any advantages to the employee of zero hours contracts? You might want to research this further online.

## Labour turnover (expressed in words and numbers)

Earlier you were learning about the functions of HR and how they gather and analyse data to plan accordingly. One of the areas they are especially interested in is labour turnover. That means the rate at which the workforce remains stable and is retained, just as your place of study is interested in the number of learners who stay on their courses until the end.

To calculate labour turnover requires a set of calculations based upon the number of employees who leave the company due to:

▶ resignation

▶ dismissal

▶ **attrition**.

A calculation based on these figures in relation to the number of employees on the payroll can produce a ratio of turnover which HR departments compare over periods of time. This data invites managers to ask questions about why the turnover is as it is and what they can do about reducing it. HR and managers will set targets based on the improvements they plan for and in relation to the objectives.

| | A | B | C | D | E | F | G | H | I | J | K | L |
|---|---|---|---|---|---|---|---|---|---|---|---|---|
| | Jun-16 | | Jan-16 | | Jun-15 | | Jan-15 | | Jun-14 | | Jan-14 | |
| # on payroll | 120 | | 135 | | 86 | | 106 | | 89 | | 76 | |
| # resignations | 8 | 7% | 5 | 4% | 11 | 13% | 1 | 1% | 3 | 3% | 9 | 12% |
| # dismissals | 4 | 3% | 0 | 0% | 9 | 10% | 0 | 0% | 0 | 0% | 2 | 3% |
| # left due to attrition | 3 | 3% | 1 | 1% | 0 | 0% | 3 | 3% | 0 | 0% | 4 | 5% |
| **Totals** | **15** | **13%** | **6** | **5%** | **20** | **23%** | **4** | **4%** | **3** | **3%** | **15** | **20%** |

▶ **Figure 6.9:** An example of labour turnover figures over three years

Note how Figure 6.9 shows three years' data so managers can compare labour movements year-on-year at the same time of year in each case, and the most recent date appears first in this example.

Using the basic data presented in Figure 6.9, certain information should already be apparent to HR and managers, for example the fluctuation in payroll numbers, possibly due to growth in the company. Both numbers and percentages are crucial to provide an overview of labour turnover. For example, the percentage rates of turnover in columns B, F and L would otherwise be considered even more significant without numbers to provide some degree of context.

Examples of some of the questions HR (and managers) are likely to ask include:

▶ What are the reasons for an increase in mid-year resignations and dismissals over the last two years?

▶ What reasons do employees offer for resigning from their positions?

▶ Which departments reflect the greatest fluctuation in labour and why?

▶ What types of job roles are at greatest risk of turnover?

▶ What is the relationship between those leaving the organisation and the time of year?

▶ How does the labour turnover for the business compare with regional and national figures?

▶ With the numbers currently on payroll, do we have sufficient capacity to meet demand?

In pairs or in small groups, discuss what you would need to know to plan for sufficient resources to manage a business. What questions should you ask to get this information?

To present the figures to inform managers and leaders, a graph might be included. However, without a summary of the conclusions drawn from analysis, graphs can often confuse or mislead.

Therefore both quantitative and qualitative data are relied upon to inform strategic planning and decision making. Note also that numbers can also be rounded up or down and therefore do not always balance. The accountancy term is 'roundings'.

HR and managers would consider the ratio between the number on payroll and those who have left employment during a given period. To calculate the ratio between column A and B:

## Worked Example

Find the ratio between the total number of employees and those leaving the organisation in June 2016.

Note that the top, smaller number in a fraction is known as the numerator and the whole number is known as the denominator.

**Step 1:** Write the total number leaving (15) as a fraction by drawing a line underneath and placing the total number on payroll (120) below. $\frac{15}{120}$

**Step 2:** Reduce the fraction, if possible, by finding a common number which can be divided into both top and bottom number, in this case 5.

**Step 3:** Having reduced the original figure to 3 over 24, try a different number which can be divided into both top and bottom figures or try dividing the top figure into the bottom figure. In this case you get 1 over 8. $\frac{1}{8}$

**Step 4:** A fraction can be presented as a ratio just by writing the top (smaller) number first followed by a colon which represents the ratio and then the bottom figure. You now have a ratio of 1:8 left the business in June 2016.

**Step 5:** Reflect on the power of the different messages by presenting figures in different ways.

Therefore asking questions such as those suggested will encourage **drilling down** into the data to get a satisfactory answer and provide HR and managers with the ability to anticipate recruitment drives, when based on trends over time.

**Key term**

**Drilling down** – in statistical terms this refers to analysing the more detailed data which has been summarised to produce the headline data.

## Productivity

HR planning is essential for the business to meet its objectives. For HR to do this effectively, they not only rely on analyses of internal and external data to identify patterns and trends historically and the reasons why, but also look to forecast future needs.

HR will need to have a clear picture of how each function of the business relates to the others and the impact on productivity when one department is under-resourced. For example, the business will struggle with their **cash flow** if a business delays sending out invoices for payment if they are short staffed in the finance department.

HR do not solely rely on the data of labour turnover but also other factors such as the impact on productivity when, for instance, government legislation changes. For example, from 30 June 2014, employees gained the legal right to request flexible working hours if they have worked continuously for the same employer for more than 26 weeks. For HR planning, this provides an opportunity to extend the period of productivity and maximise office space by introducing **hot desking**. It also presents challenges, as HR have to consider whether flexible working hours are appropriate for employees who need to interact with other teams or customers.

### Skill shortages

You have been exploring ways to question data and also to think about the information that data does not supply. Figure 6.9 is an example of where headline data does not give you sufficient information or context. In this case, while it might provide you with the numbers of employees leaving in order to inform planning for recruitment, it does not provide information on the skills leaving the organisation. Therefore, while the period June 2014 to January 2015 might appear to be positive in terms of few people leaving, those seven employees might have the largest proportion of necessary skills and expertise when compared with the needs of the business.

HR departments rely on employees to provide and frequently update their CVs with an honest and clear account of their abilities and employment record. However, these are not sufficient to provide HR departments with sufficient detailed information about employees' abilities and aptitudes. To obtain this information, HR rely on appraisal information, skills audits and possibly other means to build a more comprehensive overview of the workforce. From this information, they can plan for restructure, promotion, progression, training and the skills required for recruiting new members of staff as business needs change.

### Workplace stress

Human resources are concerned with the welfare and wellbeing of the workforce. Workplace stress contributes to a loss of productivity, as reported by the Health and Safety Executive:

▶ stress affects one in five of the working population from the newest recruit in the post room to the board of directors
▶ it is now the single biggest cause of sickness in the UK
▶ over 105 million days are lost to stress each year – costing UK employers £1.24 billion.

HR can offer information on ways to prevent workplace stress and also how employees can manage their stress levels. They will help advise managers in specific cases where workplace stress is an issue for an employee.

### Absenteeism (expressed in words and numbers)

When you explored labour market analyses, one of the factors referred to as being of interest to HR was absenteeism. When resource planning, the number of days lost through sickness and other reasons also impacts on productivity. For example, you might assume the winter is the time when more people are absent from work due to illness, but it does not reflect the number who may be away due to other reasons, such as maternity and **compassionate leave**.

Consider the example for a sales department during the first six months of 2015.

**SALES DEPARTMENT**

| | A | B | C | D | E | F | G | H | I | J | K | L |
|---|---|---|---|---|---|---|---|---|---|---|---|---|
| | **Jun-15** | | **May-15** | | **Apr-15** | | **Mar-15** | | **Feb-15** | | **Jan-15** | |
| # on payroll | 18 | | 18 | | 18 | | 18 | | 18 | | 18 | |
| # sick | 1 | 6% | 0 | 0% | 3 | 18% | 8 | 47% | 6 | 33% | 0 | 0% |
| # maternity | 2 | 11% | 2 | 0% | 2 | 11% | 2 | 11% | 2 | 11% | 2 | 11% |
| # holidays | 1 | 6% | 0 | 0% | 2 | 12% | 1 | 6% | 1 | 6% | 2 | 11% |
| # compassionate leave | 1 | 6% | 1 | 6% | 0 | 0% | 1 | 6% | 2 | 11% | 0 | 0% |
| **Totals** | **5** | **29%** | **3** | **6%** | **14** | **41%** | **12** | **70%** | **11** | **61%** | **4** | **22%** |

▶ **Figure 6.10:** An example of absenteeism data for a sales department

Figure 6.10 provides the numbers and percentages of those personnel absent and the reason why. What is obvious almost immediately is the high percentage of sales personnel who are absent, although the table does not show whether it was for one day or longer or whether it was the same individual. What it does tell you though is that the sales department is never up to full capacity. HR and managers would want to investigate why that is and take action accordingly.

There are certain assumptions that HR might make, especially about holidays, depending on the demographic of the employees. For example, those with young families are more likely to take their holidays during allotted school holidays while those without are less likely to do so. Depending on when Easter falls each year, that might also be an indicator of when leave will be taken or possibly non-authorised leave.

HR will have a policy stating when leave can be taken and how much notice must be given for a request to take leave. Many organisations will state in the policy the maximum number of employees who can be away at any one time. This will also depend on the type of role and department they are in.

Some of the questions HR will want answered include the following.

▶ Is there a pattern between absenteeism and individual employees?

▶ How do these figures compare with the same period last year and the previous year?

▶ Which personnel are on extended periods of leave and what is the likelihood of them returning next week, month and so on?

▶ Is there anything in common between the absenteeism and the job roles in that department?

▶ What is the forecast for planned (holiday) leave and how will that impact on productivity?

HR will also involve the departmental sales manager and comparisons will be made between sales performance and absenteeism in order to anticipate labour needed to maintain productivity over the next six to twelve months. The outcomes of analyses will be used to consider changes to policy, procedure and also used for planning for sustainability of the workforce to meet strategic objectives.

## Motivation

HR planning involves development and training of the workforce. Businesses where employees receive little or no personal development, or where there are few opportunities to progress within the organisation, will lack a motivated and stimulated workforce, and these employees are also less likely to be retained. Although it may be assumed that many small businesses or sole traders may lack capacity to train their employees, the government highlighted that two-fifths of UK businesses do not train their staff, including more than half those at managerial level and even in the public sector staff can be missing out on **continuing professional development** (CPD).

Developing individuals provides value to a business that is prepared to invest in their future and help employees to realise their aspirations. It is also more cost effective than taking on new employees and enables HR to plan for both sustainability and succession. Businesses in the private sector that provide extensive CPD for all members of staff at all levels and job roles include: McDonald's, M&S, John Lewis Partnership (JLP), Nike and PricewaterhouseCoopers (PwC). Several of these businesses and others offer formal management training programmes.

## Engagement with business culture

HR play a major role in the business culture through successful planning and ensuring employees are maximising opportunities for job satisfaction and striving for continuous improvement. It is not an HR function to engage with business culture but rather to generate an ethos which employees recognise and portray. Reflecting on the characteristics explored throughout this unit, you might consider HR to be the hub of a business.

## Employee satisfaction

You should by now have an image of how HR planning relates to employee satisfaction through its functions in informing management decisions and business objectives. It might be considered that HR are the key to improving employee satisfaction, right from the time employees join the business, with an induction process which settles them in quickly, to the interest and investment in their future. HR also have some responsibility for ensuring that the best potential applicants apply in the first instance by giving the best impression of the business as a place to work; for example, attracting graduates or learners considering their options for management training programmes before they leave university, school or college. Examples of businesses that demonstrate consistently high levels of employee satisfaction include Google and John Lewis Partnership (JLP).

**PAUSE POINT**

Pick an industry. Which factors do you think influence the motivation of a workforce working in that industry?

**Hint**

Refer to the theories and motivational factors you have just studied and think about how they will differ between industries.

**Extend**

How would you describe the management and leadership styles that are most prevalent in your chosen industry?

# Making its Mark

London's five-star Landmark Hotel wanted to increase employee engagement and to define a clear vision for the future direction of the business. They also wanted to increase guest satisfaction rates to make a sustainable business that was able to grow in a challenging and competitive market place.

Through assessment methods the Landmark London was able to obtain clear information about the true feelings and understanding of the business direction from team members at all levels. Working groups and taskforces were created throughout the hotel to focus on areas of the business that needed significant improvement.

By changing the management style and including all team members in business decisions, as well as empowering team members to take decisions for the good of the guests, the Landmark London can see a clear proactive approach to the targets within the business. The Landmark London has created a culture where team members want to take ownership and responsibility for their actions. Employees teach others how to exceed expectations and create memorable moments for each other and the guests.

The Landmark London drives their business from the front line. They empower front-line teams to make decisions and have their own input on the operations with the guidance of Management and Executive teams.

Their team members are often involved in various Task Forces and ad hoc projects that foster personal and career development.

The Landmark believes it is important to foster an environment based on strong values that describe their culture: trust, awareness, respect, recognition, engagement, individualism, consistency, belonging and security. These values are underpinned by rules and principles to help them achieve their mission: people, service, product, profit, technical skills and environment.

Each of the values and principles are designed to ensure all employees strive for continuous ways to improve the guest experience. Standard Operating Procedures (SOPs for short) are used to ensure consistency and quality and ensure that team members are trained for the job. The SOPs are a detailed explanation of how a policy is to be implemented and communicates who will perform the task, what materials are necessary, where the task will take place, when the task shall be performed, and how the team member will execute the task. Each and every department within the hotel needs to follow a set of standards that are related to their functions.

As a result of the strategy, Landmark London's journey has highlighted its successes and areas for development. The process has allowed them to take positive actions to improve the business, through a cultural change and by engaging the workforce at all levels – listening and valuing everyone's contributions to the future of the business.

All staff have a personal development plan to ensure they receive the support and development required for career progression. The HR department is involved in what they describe as 'your journey' right from application. As staff are employed on different shifts and roles are variable, the website provides overviews of the responsibilities and duties attached to each role with the focus on both customer and employee satisfaction.

The Landmark London has seen significant improvements in various areas. Health and safety awareness has increased with the number of accidents throughout the hotel decreasing; guest satisfaction ratings have increased; mystery guest scores have improved, as have Trip Advisor ratings. They have achieved £35,000 savings, thanks to the rise in awareness and focused learning activity in teams, and increased their recycling of waste from 74 per cent to 86 per cent.

Source: https://www.investorsinpeople.com/resources/case-studies/landmark-london and https://www.investorsinpeople.com/file/2309/download?token=M_yNqioJ, Investors in People

## Check your understanding

1 What part do HR play in Landmark London's success as a business?

2 How do HR engage with employees and applicants so they belong to business culture?

3 What are the values of the business and how do managers ensure they are practised?

4 What methods does Landmark London use to meet skills requirements?

5 What have been the benefits and impact from the HR strategy?

'We have it covered' is a big logistics company which transports large concrete materials used in the infrastructure of motorways and major roads. The business has its own centralised HR department that manages the HR for all six branches based around the UK.

Senior management have asked HR to produce a plan to cope with their staffing issues. Primarily they need reliable lorry drivers who can work at a moment's notice and are willing to work over weekends. They also need drivers who will travel long distances across Europe. The business, which operates all year round, has had problems with unreliability and unskilled drivers. Some have been recruited in the past without HGV licences while other drivers have struggled to understand the instructions given or find the locations within the deadlines set.

One of the major problems managers have is not knowing who is working or not and they are concerned about the high labour turnover. Unfortunately they have no tangible data to compare with previous years and so management have asked for a plan or schedule which will help them monitor labour movements.

The HR department have asked you to produce a report identifying:

- a summary of labour market analyses
- the different ways of contracting staff which may resolve their staffing issues
- how management can monitor staff movements
- ways to engage employees in the business culture
- ideas for contingency planning in the case of skill shortages or cover for geographical and ethnic differences such as religious festivals.

### Plan
- Have you prepared a timed plan prioritising all your tasks to meet the required outcomes?
- Can you identify your information sources?

### Do
- Does your report justify the advantages and disadvantages of different ways of contracting staff, monitoring staff movements, methods for engaging employees in business culture, and your ideas for contingency planning?
- Are your analyses presented clearly so they can be read and understood by anyone without verbal explanation?
- Have you proofread for accuracy, omissions, punctuation, grammar, formatting etc?

### Review
- What have you gained from this activity?
- Did you have enough time?
- What did you find difficult?
- What will you do next?

# D Factors influencing management, motivation and performance of the workforce

## Motivation in the workplace

A workforce comprised of motivated employees is much more likely to result in a successful business. Motivated employees are more likely to respond to change and buy into the business ethos. Motivation is generated by a positive business culture with an effective and efficient workforce.

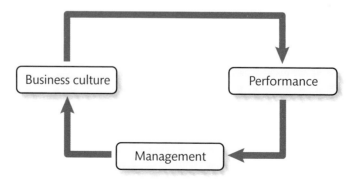

▶ **Figure 6.11:** Suggested model of the influence of management on productivity

The model in Figure 6.11 represents the impact management can have on the business culture and in motivating the entire workforce. There are many theories about factors for motivating the workforce and you will explore four of them in this section.

## Theories of motivation

There are more than two million articles and publications featuring aspects of motivation. Psychologists have been proposing motivational theories since the 1940s when struggling with understanding what motivates people to achieve goals. You will explore four of those theories here: Maslow, Herzberg, F.W. Taylor and E Mayo et al.

### Maslow

Maslow's 1943 theory is possibly one of the most well-known theories of motivation. Abraham Maslow argued that in order to strive to progressively higher achievements people must first have their basic needs met. Maslow presented his hierarchy of needs as a pyramid – see Figure 6.12.

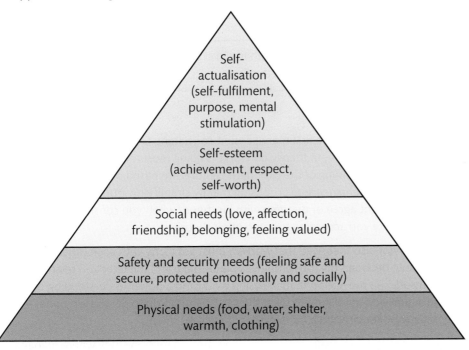

▶ **Figure 6.12:** Maslow's hierarchy of needs (1943)

Maslow claimed that people are driven by higher goals to remain motivated and unless they have their basic needs met they are unable to progress to the next levels. However, as with most theories which come under multiple challenges, there are those who criticise it as representing a linear model with only way to progress.

## Herzberg

American psychologist Frank Herzberg published his first book, with the support of two colleagues, *The Motivation to Work* in 1959. The two-factor theory on job satisfaction and job dissatisfaction was based on his research that the reasons people have for what motivates them are not automatically the opposite of the factors which demotivate them.

Herzberg presented the results of his research in graph format, displaying what he categorised as motivational and hygiene factors and the percentage which they motivate people most and least. To give you a selection of his results, before being updated in 2008, Table 6.6 provides a selection from most, middle and least motivational factors.

▶ **Table 6.6:** Summary of Herzberg's motivational factors

| Motivational factors | | |
|---|---|---|
| **Most** | **Middle range** | **Least** |
| Achievement of challenging work<br>Recognition<br>The work | Relationships at work<br>Job status | Working conditions<br>Personal life<br>Security of the job |

Herzberg's hygiene factors include supervision, interpersonal relations, security, company policies, pay, and working conditions. If you compare Maslow's theory with Herzberg's theory you might come to the conclusion that Maslow's theory is concerned with attitude while Herzberg's theory is concerned more about behaviour.

> **Reflect**
>
> Reflect on what factors affect your ability to study by applying both Maslow's and Herzberg's theories to your own situation.

## F. W. Taylor

American engineer, and the first management consultant, Frederick Winslow Taylor based his early management theory on workers being most motivated by their pay. His works, at the beginning of the twentieth century, are based on a management theory in industrial engineering, proposing that by simplifying jobs, productivity will increase. You might agree or disagree with his theory when you consider what is most likely to motivate you according to some other theorists.

However, Taylor also theorised that workers must get along with each other and saw a relationship between the jobs employees undertake and the effect on relationships. Taylor introduced the notion that analysing work, and a better understanding of what people actually do in relation to what they are meant to do to get the job done, leads to greater productivity and a happier working environment.

Taylor was the first to introduce the idea of a time and motion study where managers analyse employees' jobs by breaking down the tasks and timing how long each task takes. They look for overlaps and duplications or gaps in what is required to achieve greater efficiency. In other words, Taylor proposed **optimising the work** for a more efficient workforce.

> **Key term**
>
> **Optimising the work** – breaking down tasks into small chunks that can be timed so that workers know exactly what they are expected to achieve in a given timeframe.

▶ Industrial conditions like this can still be found in countries with poor workers' rights

Taylor upset many people when he stated his beliefs that management should control workers as they were more likely to understand what was required. He also believed workers should be rewarded according to their productivity. This type of business model is very typical of the industrial **piece work** such as was used in the motor vehicle, engineering and clothing industries. Similar working conditions still exist today.

You might argue that Taylor believed in dividing up the workforce and work to fit his scientific theory.

**Discussion**

Discuss in pairs, or in small groups, the pros and cons of Taylor's theory in different types of business sectors and explore examples.

### E. Mayo et al.

Australian-born psychologist, industrial researcher and organisational theorist, Elton Mayo and his colleagues were concerned about the effects of light on productivity when examining work conditions in a Chicago electric plant in the mid-1920s.

Mayo developed his experiments to find out what effect tiredness and monotony had on productivity which led him to question how they could be controlled through regular breaks, work hours, temperature and humidity under factory conditions.

Mayo's 1933 human relations theory is known as the Hawthorne Experiment and his subjects were controlled by introducing breaks and changing the conditions under which they worked – with some confusing results. As the conditions were varied, productivity mostly varied but not as you might expect. In fact, when they had more frequent breaks, workers became less efficient and they complained it interrupted their flow. (Workers also became more productive when researchers were interested in them.)

|  | Controlled breaks | Many breaks | Self-regulated breaks |
|---|---|---|---|
| Workforce response and productivity |  |  |  |

▶ **Figure 6.13:** Mayo's motivational theory – an interpretation

Research findings concluded that as workers became more motivated by increased productivity, due to how they regulated their own breaks, they also became more efficient when they took control of their own work patterns. Subsequently, the subjects for his experiments became an autonomous and responsible team.

## Impact of motivation on business performance

You have looked at four major theories about factors which influence management decisions and the effects those decisions can have on staff motivation and ultimately productivity.

Managers are required to consider a variety of justifiable and tested approaches for structuring the workforce based on factual evidence, so they can anticipate the benefits and risks to the business. Consider how different the outcome might be if managers radically changed the structure and ethos of the business based on a flimsy strategy. Some of the businesses that have been referred to in this unit, especially those with highly motivated staff such as Microsoft or Google, would possibly have decreased worker motivation if employees' autonomy was taken away by management control and their creativity suppressed.

### Research

Carry out research to discover what employees give as reasons for being especially satisfied with their working arrangements in each of these businesses: Microsoft, Google, Virgin and Expedia. Apply each of the four theories to anticipate any changes to performance. Share your findings with a peer and discuss.

## Financial motivators

As you learnt from the results of experiments undertaken by Herzberg, workers are not especially motivated by their pay if there are other more motivating factors, such as job satisfaction because of the work itself. However, this does not suggest that employees deliberately look for low-paid jobs or are satisfied with being paid less than their job is worth. Examples of well-publicised underpaid sectors include the care, security and hospitality sectors. Much of the criticism arises from poor working conditions, unsociable hours and risk to safety or workers' wellbeing.

If you consider the earlier example of piece work and the industries where overtime is still paid (for example those listed in this section, plus the construction and engineering industries), it might appear reasonable to pay more money to those with greater productivity. It is still the case that the types of jobs that attract these types of financial rewards, such as overtime, are generally the lower paid and physical jobs. In the UK this type of manual labour is categorised as blue-collar work. However those who come to rely on overtime pay may rapidly become demotivated if opportunities for overtime cease.

Employees in jobs which are classed as professional (traditionally referred to as white-collar workers) are less likely to receive overtime for any additional hours they contribute. However, in some professions, bonus payments are part of the financial package. These payments are based on achievement of targets whether personally or as a whole business. Therefore if the business does not meet its main objective, no-one receives a bonus, or just gets part of the bonus based on the profits, regardless of individual effort.

Some professions pay their employees a commission based on individual sales, such as estate agents, recruitment consultants and car salespeople. This commission is usually calculated by HR and management to assume an average salary for the job when combined with a lower wage. Therefore those who under-perform are penalised and those who are the higher performing sales personnel, achieve higher overall wages.

## Non-financial motivators

You have begun to consider how financial rewards are not necessarily the most important motivator for employees. According to the theorists explored, motivators include:

▶ working relationships
▶ job satisfaction
▶ sense of achievement
▶ challenging work
▶ autonomy
▶ sense of worth.

You might bundle these together under a label marked as **belongingness**.

Nevertheless, there are other types of rewards and recognition that are not money-related. These might be included in an employment package or offered as incentives or recognition of a job well done, such as subsidised meals (for example JLP, M&S), free or subsidised private healthcare or free membership to health and leisure clubs.

Some businesses reward those employees who put in additional hours beyond the call of duty with **time off in lieu** where overtime payments are not considered policy.

Time off in lieu can equate to a few hours, days or even longer depending on additional time spent in work or on special projects.

> **Key terms**
>
> **Belongingness** – an emotional feeling of belonging to a community or group.
>
> **Time off in lieu** – a predetermined length of time as compensation for unpaid overtime.

> **Research**
>
> Choose a job and identify what non-financial motivators there might be that would make you want to work in that organisation or particular business.

> **Reflect**
>
> What motivates you to work? Can you identify what, if anything, might demotivate you?

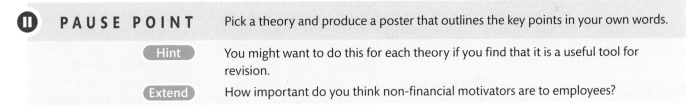

**⏸ PAUSE POINT**  Pick a theory and produce a poster that outlines the key points in your own words.

**Hint**  You might want to do this for each theory if you find that it is a useful tool for revision.

**Extend**  How important do you think non-financial motivators are to employees?

# Techniques to meet skills requirements

The different skills required to carry out a job role to the standard required by employers are numerous and variable. Managers use a number of techniques to meet skills requirements and shortages and you will explore some of those approaches next.

## Recruitment

Recruitment is one way of filling the skills gaps in the workplace, perhaps to:

▶ replace a leaver
▶ bring additional skills to a team for a new product line
▶ increase productivity
▶ respond to a change in business direction, or
▶ compete with other market forces.

Recruitment can put a strain on business finances, management time and especially the workforce as workers may need to make up for any shortages to maintain productivity. Making a decision to recruit someone with the skills the business needs may not result in suitably skilled candidates being available.

## Upskilling/reskilling/training

Businesses that invest in their existing workforce are more likely to retain them. Motivation theories suggest that achievement is possibly one of the main reasons for high levels of employee satisfaction, so it would seem that training of some form is especially appropriate. Table 6.7 looks at what these aspects mean.

▶ **Table 6.7** Different types of training

| Type of training | What this means |
|---|---|
| Upskilling | <ul><li>This means to teach additional skills or enhance the skills the employee already has.</li><li>Accounts personnel often upskill if they begin their working life as payroll or accounts clerks. As they progress up the ranks in the finance department they will receive training in-house from managers or colleagues on processes and terms while attending formal training to upskill them to the next level, each of which is externally regulated.</li><li>Job roles such as health and safety officers or tax advisors require regular upskilling in the latest legislation and regulations and require a formal certificate to operate as proof they have met the required standard.</li><li>Upskilling increases your capability to undertake functions at a higher level of competency and as a result could lead to progression opportunities.</li></ul> |
| Reskilling | <ul><li>This is a term given to teaching new skills. Suppose you are a computer programmer and the business is looking to increase the workforce with the skills to design their new website. The skills are different but there may also be an overlap, if you are required to produce the programming code that makes the website work. Therefore for website design you might need reskilling by undergoing some formal training which may possibly lead to additional qualifications.</li><li>Retailers are likely to reskill employees in-house, often relying on skilled members of staff to provide on-the-job training for duties such as operating the checkout, dealing with refunds and exchanges, stock control etc.</li></ul> |
| Training | <ul><li>Reskilling or upskilling employees where businesses do not have the spare capacity or the suitably skilled workforce in-house will require formal training bought in from specialist providers. According to the needs of the business and whether the employee needs to gain a formal qualification, this training might be **accredited** or **non-accredited**.</li><li>Accredited training often takes much longer and costs more than non-accredited but may be a requirement of the job function.</li><li>Non-accredited training is often much shorter and might just be a day or half day but could also extend over several weeks or longer. As these types of training are not externally regulated, they may vary in effectiveness, quality, value for money and impact on the employee and business.</li></ul> |

> **Key terms**
>
> **Accredited** – formally recognised by a regulated qualification.
>
> **Non-accredited** – does not lead to a qualification.

## Outsourcing

Another way for managers to meet skills requirements is to outsource. The examples used earlier related to mostly finance functions and often larger businesses will outsource legal advice. Outsourcing in the manufacturing industry is not uncommon. For example, several racing teams combine a chassis and engine from another manufacturer, such as McLaren-Honda and Scuderia Toro Rosso with Ferrari whereas Renault manufactures the entire car. The reason for this is to create a hybrid of a racing car constructor together with a precision-built engine, drawing on the specialist skills required for each.

Computer technology company Dell outsource their customer support, as do many other businesses. While it could be argued that outsourcing does not always meet customer needs, businesses are motivated to outsource for different reasons, often to reduce cost.

## Changing job roles

It may not suit all employees but changing job roles is not only an effective technique for maintaining motivation but also for getting the right people into a job with the skills to maximise productivity. For example, a family business will ensure that every member of the workforce is traceable back to the role they played. In order to maintain employee interest, upskill knowledge and reskill to ensure all job roles can be covered, they rotate job roles. As this occurs, employees become 'all-rounders' and are able to help each other out and take pride in the finished article. They have a much better understanding of their impact on their colleagues' roles and management are able to draw on a larger pool of resources to meet demand.

## Re-structuring

Re-structuring occurs when businesses need to re-position their workforce to where the skills are required. Unfortunately there are often negative connotations associated with re-structuring, implying that there will be a surplus workforce who do not have the right skills and therefore are no longer required. However, there can be other alternative approaches to meeting skills requirements with more positive options than **redundancy**.

Many areas of the public sector frequently undergo restructuring, especially local authorities, NHS and further education, owing to strategy decisions made by the government.

Any restructuring strategies put into place must be carefully thought through as, if long-term consequences are not considered, a reduced, or radically altered, workforce may prove unable to meet business demands.

Redundancies are expensive and not usually good for an individual's wellbeing because there are associated feelings of failure and lack of self-worth. Problems arise especially when the business finds they later need to recruit more personnel to meet demand but have lost a wealth of knowledge, experience and skill through redundancies.

> **Key term**
>
> **Redundancy** – when an employee is dismissed because the company no longer needs someone to do their job.

> **Link**
>
> See also *Unit 21: Training and Development.*

# Training and development

You have already considered skills audits and appraisals (see section on Skills shortages) and seen how training and developing individuals can contribute to employee motivation and loyalty to the business. You will now look at ways to upskill or reskill the workforce.

## The purpose of training needs analysis

A training needs analysis (TNA) is an analysis of what the business requires to meet its objectives and where the skills exist. When all the data are gathered, the existing skills, levels and gaps are then analysed to make decisions about training and development.

The tools for gathering the data vary considerably and are likely to reflect the nature of the business. The more creative industries might use spidergrams and similar, flexible tools whereas the more traditional businesses are likely to use templates.

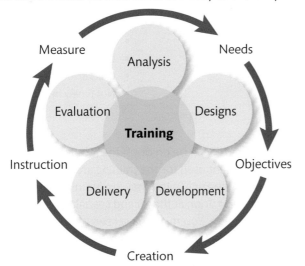

▸ **Figure 6.14:** Training needs analysis

**Link**

Another example of a TNA can be seen in *Unit 21: Training and Development*, Figure 21.3.

All these methods provide different information. For example, one tool may show how skills relate to business objectives to determine what training is required, and another may present an analysis of existing skills and gaps in relation to individuals. A simple staged process includes the following.

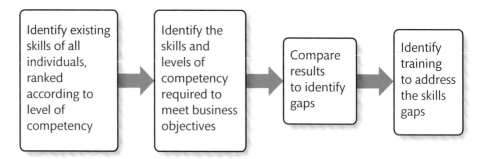

▶ **Figure 6.15:** Flowchart of skills analysis

## Types of training

There are different types of training which you will consider in a little more detail along with the potential pros and cons of each.

### Internal/external

Internal training might be delivered by another member of staff or sourced by paying for experts to come into the premises to deliver training. External training means where employees receive their training off-site, in other words outside of the business, perhaps at a commercial training centre, private training provider, college or even at another employer's premises.

▶ **Table 6.8** Some advantages and disadvantages of internal and external training

|  | **Advantages** | **Disadvantages** |
|---|---|---|
| **Internal training** | • Lower cost<br>• Saves time and cost travelling to external training<br>• Can respond more rapidly to urgent need | • Not valued by employees as much as external training<br>• Not always structured<br>• Training given by trainers who may not be qualified in the area |
| **External training** | • Structured<br>• Professional<br>• Trained trainers | • Higher cost<br>• Not easily applied back in the workplace<br>• Often too generic<br>• Quickly forgotten<br>• Not timely in responding to need |

### On the job/off the job

Even when training is internal, it can be on or off the job. Training on the job is where the situation and any equipment used for the training are in a real life situation so the employee can more rapidly apply what they are learning; for example, training a checkout assistant on the shop floor, at the till and scanning the products which results in an almost realistic transaction. You might have seen training such as this in some of the major supermarkets. Some of the pros and cons are shown in Table 6.9.

▶ **Table 6.9** Some advantages and disadvantages of on-the-job and off-the-job training

|  | Advantages | Disadvantages |
|---|---|---|
| **On the job** | • Rapid response<br>• Using familiar equipment<br>• More able to apply quickly<br>• Can resolve queries more rapidly | • Distractions<br>• Pressure of work building up<br>• Missed opportunities to network with employees from other businesses in similar roles<br>• Not taken seriously or valued the same as external training |
| **Off the job** | • Trying out new ways or using different equipment<br>• Less likelihood of distractions when removed from desk or work station<br>• Learning from others | • Unfamiliar equipment<br>• Simulated environment<br>• Takes longer to achieve competency<br>• Not so easy to identify questions which may arise when trying out new techniques<br>• Travelling time and costs |

Off-the-job training doesn't always mean external training. You can receive off-the-job training in your employer's business premises by being trained away from your normal work area. Examples of off-the-job training in the employee's business premises include simulated activities where training in a real situation might be inappropriate because of a safety or security risk. Examples might include:

▶ using a flight simulator

▶ anatomy students working on a cadaver

▶ surgeons practising on oranges to simulate keyhole surgery

▶ fire-fighting role play

▶ air tunnels to simulate weightlessness.

### Mentoring

You have already briefly looked at the use of a mentor to assist with training. The role of a mentor is shown in Figure 6.16.

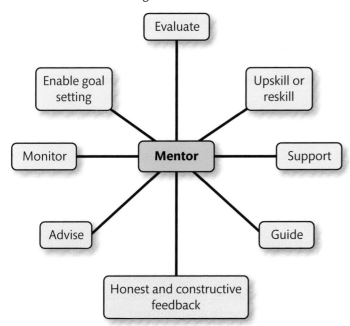

▶ **Figure 6.16:** The role of a mentor is many multi-faceted

A mentor is someone who can act as a role model, and is able to share their knowledge and aid your development. Businesses favouring mentors benefit from shared knowledge and colleagues developing their competences by receiving frequent monitoring and feedback. Mentors and the **mentee** can both find it a rewarding experience and the business may find this not only financially beneficial but also an effective form of succession planning.

The mentor does not have to be a manager or an employee from the same department but must be someone with the necessary skills required to develop the mentee. It is important that the mentor is given time to devote to their mentee and that the relationship is effective.

### Coaching

You will have heard the term coach, especially in the sports industry. In a business context, the coach does not have to be an expert in the subject. It is more important that the coach is a trained individual with the coaching skills required to:

▶ challenge the coachee

▶ listen actively

▶ paraphrase

▶ refrain from giving opinions and advice

▶ ask questions

▶ help provide focus

▶ encourage autonomy

▶ encourage problem solving

▶ enable goal setting.

A coach needs to be an exceptional listener and also be non-judgemental. Their role is specifically to encourage the person being coached – the coachee – to find their own solutions and resolve their own problems. The coach listens and poses questions to the coachee encouraging them to reflect on the issue and consider it from different perspectives, without imposing their own opinions or ideas on the coachee. The fundamental skill required by both coach and coachee is to reflect.

There are multiple different coaching models and many theories and publications about coaching (Goleman, Graham, Passmore). Possibly one of the most well-known is the GROW model, which the coachee uses to break down a problem into small stages by considering:

▶ G = goal

▶ R = reality

▶ O = obstacles and options

▶ W = way forward.

### Effectiveness of training

To evaluate whether or not the training has sufficient impact on the business, its effectiveness needs to be measured. You may have a part-time job where you have received training, on or off the job. Consider how the effectiveness is measured; it could involve your performance being observed and questioned for your evaluation and increased knowledge. Employees may undergo an updated skills audit to measure against an earlier audit to assess progress and distance travelled.

Businesses often do not perform this evaluation, which can limit the usefulness of training. Other ways businesses may not get the most from training is through:

▸ employees receiving training not passing their knowledge on to others

▸ employees not being monitored for implementing new ideas and skills

▸ ineffective training not being reported back to trainers.

---

**Ⅱ   PAUSE POINT**     Think about a part-time job you have had and produce a report detailing all the training you received.

> **Hint**     If you have not had a part-time job then try and pair up or join a small group with someone who has.

> **Extend**     How effective did you find the training? Outline some ideas as to how you would improve the training provided.

---

# Performance appraisal

A performance appraisal is a method by which an employee's performance in a particular role is documented and evaluated. You will now look more at what appraisals are for, different types of appraisal and the impact of their use.

## Purpose of performance appraisal

### Individual and group targets

Appraisals are a means of monitoring employees' performance against targets. You may have received an appraisal if you have a job. An appraisal is used to set targets which relate to the overall objectives of the business. Business objectives can only be met by deciding on the targets to meet the objectives and then sharing out the targets amongst the workforce.

These targets are shared among all employees according to their job roles and job descriptions, regardless of level in the organisation. Therefore a manager or director will share targets with those below them, who might be departmental managers, who will in turn share the targets with those beneath them. For example, a national sales manager, who may have an overall target of £6 million, will divide that between the four regions they manage and the regional manager in turn will divide that between the sales representatives. The targets will not automatically be split equally, but will depend on the potential sales in the region, based on previous performance, and individual sales representative experience.

The targets being shared are not the same as they will reflect the level of responsibility and authority of each employee. Some targets relate to groups of employees, which could be projects or whole tasks. Employees should also have personal development targets and these may lead to further training.

### Assessment of individual and group performance

Once targets are set, they are then used to assess performance of both the group or team and the individuals. When you experience an appraisal, or as you may have seen already, the targets set will be used to measure how you perform. Imagine you are one of the sales representatives in the previous example. You will be required to report your ongoing sales to your manager at regular intervals.

The manager will then be able to monitor how progress is being made towards the whole team's target and the impact on the overall sales department. This

> **Link**
>
> See *Unit 1: Exploring Business* and *Unit 22: Market Research* for more on setting business objectives.

measurement will be used by the manager to plan to meet or exceed the target. After all, targets can be wrong as the original targets could underestimate the potential for demand or simply be over-cautious or over-ambitious.

### Providing employee feedback

An appraisal is the opportunity for managers to give feedback to those they are responsible for, just as you receive feedback on your progress from your tutor or assessor.

An appraisal is a formal event and both parties involved in the process need to prepare otherwise the feedback is likely to have less relevance or value. It is likely that you, the **appraisee**, will be asked to evaluate your performance and your assessment will be compared with that of your manager, who is known as the **appraiser**.

As you considered earlier, providing effective feedback requires skill, so as not to offend with negative feedback. Feedback must be honest and factual but also developmental and constructive, reflecting strengths and weaknesses. Therefore feedback must be planned and prepared so it reflects the appraisee's performance against targets, just as your targets are reviewed and feedback given, perhaps during a tutorial or monitoring visit.

### Identifying training needs

The purpose of an appraisal, usually held once a year with a half-yearly review, is to appraise your performance and identify any training needs.

The appraiser will identify training to upskill or reskill the appraisee related to business objectives. The appraisee will be involved in deciding the training plan. In some organisations the appraisee can propose training and development to meet business objectives and for their own personal objectives.

## Types of appraisal

There are different types of appraisal. The following are four of the most commonly used appraisal systems and might be used independently or combined.

### Self-assessment

A self-assessment type of appraisal is one where the employee evaluates their own performance against their job description and targets. Although this method can be **subjective**, it provides a useful opportunity for the appraisee to reflect on their strengths and weaknesses.

This method might be used in the planning stage for an appraisal so the appraiser can compare their evaluation with that of the appraisee. This process provides the opportunity for the employee to identify actions which might be overlooked by the manager, such as helping others or using their initiative.

You may well be familiar with this type of process as you may have carried out a self-assessment before you began this course. Your tutor uses your self-assessment to help plan for your learning and help with setting targets.

### Management by objectives

This type of appraisal system was first promoted in the 1950s by management theorist Peter Drucker. It is often referred to as MBO and alternatively as MBR (management by results).

Drucker's view is that all parties of management, leadership and other employees should be involved in the setting of objectives, as you started to consider earlier.

---

### Key terms

**Appraisee** – the individual being appraised.

**Appraiser** – the individual carrying out the appraisal.

**Subjective** – based on or influenced by personal feelings, tastes or opinions.

---

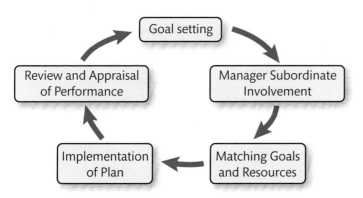

▶ **Figure 6.17:** Drucker's 5-step MBO process for appraisals

The benefit of management and employees collaborating is that all parties understand and know what is expected of them to achieve the goals. The difficulty with this type of approach is the amount of time it takes to involve all members of the workforce.

### Ratings scales

Ratings scales can be used in appraisals to provide a structure for measuring individual characteristics or traits. You are possibly familiar with this type of method if you have completed a skills audit or during your initial assessment before starting this or other courses.

The number of ratings options should be an even number so you have to think harder about which rating you will give to each question. Too many options can also be confusing as can the terms used for rating.

| Tick one option only. 1 is HIGH, 4 is LOW | 1 | 2 | 3 | 4 |
|---|---|---|---|---|
| Work unaided | | | | |
| Loyal | | | | |
| Problem solver | | | | |
| Punctual | | | | |
| Creative | | | | |
| Numerate | | | | |

▶ **Figure 6.18:** An example of a ratings scale form

The options do not have to be numbers – you may have seen some with smiley faces. The trouble with numbers is that there is no consistent use of which number represents high and which is low. If the appraisee has not read the instructions, or they are not clear, it can be an easy mistake to assume 1 is always low.

Although this method can be a useful starting point, the characteristics or traits can also be difficult to interpret and the results will be subjective.

### 360° appraisal

A 360 degree appraisal is where a bigger picture is built of the appraisee so their performance can be evaluated holistically, using other sources, rather than simply the judgement based mostly on two people's assessment: the appraiser and the appraisee. For example, the appraisal is likely to include the information shown in Figure 6.19.

**Research**

Carry out research to explore Drucker's MBO theory for other advantages and disadvantages of this process.

**Link**

See also *Unit 8: Recruitment and Selection Process.*

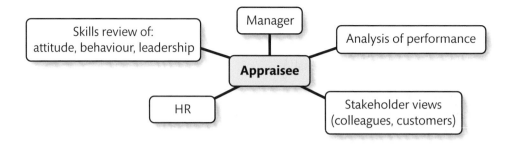

*Figure 6.19:* A 360° appraisal is likely to include these elements

Using this range of information for an appraisal provides a broader picture of the training and development needs the appraisee may have.

However, making judgements about someone's behaviour and attitude, and their skills, is not as reliable as measuring performance against, for example, a sales target. The difference between the two is that measuring sales against a target is **objective**, while the measurement of skills is subjective.

## Impact of performance appraisal

### Impact on the individual

As an appraisal is for the employee, it provides the opportunity for the individual to give feedback on their own performance and make suggestions for further development and targets. An appraisal is intended to be a positive experience and for some employees might be one of the few or only opportunities they get to spend quality time with their manager to discuss how things are going and what the future might hold. This should be a time of reassurance or the occasion to express concerns in an open and honest discussion.

However, some managers may not be an expert at conducting appraisals and some people can find it very difficult to accept criticism, which as you explored earlier, can be destructive if not carefully considered. Depending on the personality and characteristics of the appraisee, the feedback might be difficult to take even if it is mainly positive.

> **Reflect**
>
> Think back on the role play you will have completed for *Unit 8: Recruitment and Selection Process* or any other feedback opportunities you may have had. How did you deal with both presenting feedback and receiving it?

This is a time for reflection and for the employee to take responsibility for their own personal development. This development might include dealing with personality clashes between colleagues or with their manager.

### Impact on the business

Appraisals are considered essential business practice for both employees and the business. The outcomes from appraisals provide management with information about the current situation of the business in relation to objectives and what is needed in their planning.

Without formal appraisal systems in place, which involve every member of staff, the business cannot systematically monitor the effectiveness or efficiency of those they employ. Decisions can then be made about how the workforce will enable the

> It is not always easy to take feedback

business to meet its future objectives or whether those objectives are unrealistic or not sufficiently challenging.

However, the time taken to carry out appraisals is considerable and requires organisation. They are also costly as everything involving people and resources has a cost attached. Appraisals need to be planned to take place at the same time every year with a half-yearly review. Also, as appraisals are used to review performance and set new targets, they need to occur in the order of hierarchy. For example, the leaders and managers need to set their targets based on the overall business objectives before they can share these among the remaining employees.

**⏸ PAUSE POINT**    Consider what it might be like to be the appraiser. Evaluate which system or systems work best and who benefits most.

Hint    You could try a role play with a peer, taking turns to play different roles.

Extend    Try the same exercise in a group of three with the third person observing and taking notes. Give feedback on the role play to each party and ask them to evaluate the effectiveness of the feedback. Identify areas for further development.

**Key term**

**Artistic licence** – producing a piece of work based on your interpretation, which may not be based on actual facts.

## Assessment practice 6.4    AO3

'The Sky's the Limit' is an independent travel business struggling to make ends meet. It is faced with significant competition from major travel companies such as Thomas Cook, TUI and Virgin. Profits are down and so staff are demotivated and concerned about their job security. The business is now looking for an investor.

A major business has shown an interest, providing that the business can convince them they can boost staff morale and retain the expertise and face of the business. They have a long-standing customer base who travel frequently at high cost. The business needs to provide their potential investor with:

- a theory-based model for motivating the staff
- a strategy for training and development
- systematic and efficient performance appraisals.

The management have collected some data over the last three years in preparation for analysis but have not yet carried out any evaluation, see Table 6.10.

▶ **Table 6.10:** The Sky's the Limit performance indicators

|  | 2014–15 | 2013–14 | 2012–13 |
|---|---|---|---|
| Turnover (£) | 1,805,002 | 2,532,884 | 2,751,233 |
| Number of employees | 7 | 8 | 9 |
| Sickness days per year (#) | 198 | 82 | 40 |
| Repeat business (# of clients) | 78 | 94 | 115 |

*Plan*
- Can you identify what you need to provide?
- Can you create a plan of action with timeframes?
- Can you identify your sources and any revision you need to do?
- Can you sketch out what you want to produce?

*Do*
- Have you provided worked examples explaining theories, including the benefits and risks?
- Can you apply your own **artistic licence** to the demographic of the client base and workforce to justify your recommendations?
- Have you presented your final products in a combination of formats which best suit the task?

*Review*
- Where did your strengths lie in this diverse task?
- What have you learnt since the last activity?
- What do you still need to understand better?

# E Impact of change

## Managing change

**Discussion**

In a small group, discuss the occasions when you find it hard to change and explore why you think this is the case for each situation.

Possibly the most difficult challenge for any business and its employees is being able to manage change. You might be able to identify someone who always seems to resist any ideas or changes to plans, or perhaps you are like this yourself.

### The need to manage change for business survival and success

All businesses need to change in some shape or form in order to survive and be successful. Managers and leaders have to manage this process. It may be as simple as deciding to move to a different display shelving system, and signing off on this purchase, or it may be a wider restructuring of the business to take advantage of a new market opportunity. These changes will all need to be managed effectively, taking into account cost, feasibility and employees.

Some businesses manage to stay resistant to change and still survive, however this is unusual and might be because they operate in a niche market where demand does not change. However, even these businesses are likely to have had to manage change of business operations to some extent. For example, they will have had to deal with the onset of technological changes and may have had to move some of their sales operations online.

▶ What are the differences between this shop and a modern shop?

There are examples of some businesses that continue with traditional methods, such as solicitors sending handwritten letters to their clients, but these too are affected by modern day changes. Businesses can quickly find themselves left behind if they do not respond to change. For example, consider how estate agents work. The advent of digital photos and the internet means that a property can be photographed and the details are available within a few hours. In the past, photographs had to be developed, details of a property were handwritten and typed up later and then sent out with letters in the post. It all took more time and effort.

# Factors influencing change

## Internal factors

Some internal factors that may influence change include:

▶ growth or decline of business, e.g. specific products or the entire sector
▶ technology changes, e.g. a new technology replacing the business' product or the cost of implementing a new technology in the business
▶ demand for skills, e.g. the struggle to find appropriate staff
▶ poor leadership or management, e.g. staff leaving due to this or reduced profits due to bad decisions
▶ industrial action, e.g. staff walkout possibly leading to increased costs in wages
▶ cash flow management, e.g. as a consequence of poor leadership or management, or due to the impact of other factors.

## External factors

These factors are mostly outside human control. Consider how farmers might need to change when they harvest their crops in accordance with the weather and the way they have been forced to change their equipment and practices to respond to year-round demand.

Possibly some of the biggest external factors which force businesses to change include:

▶ changes to legislation (e.g. health and safety regulations which force businesses to make costly changes to equipment and premises)
▶ failure of a market (e.g. in obsolete products such as VHS recorders)
▶ economic instability such as a recession (risk to market share and profits)
▶ competition (risk to market share)
▶ media (e.g. health scares, pressure groups such as Greenpeace)
▶ availability of raw materials (e.g. animal, vegetable and mineral)
▶ economic changes and stock market changes (e.g. fluctuating price of fuel and its impact on transport costs, interest rate and currency rate changes)
▶ unforeseen events (e.g. Fukushima on the nuclear industry, the effects from Tungurahua volcanic activity in South America on the travel industry).

## Case study

### Lettuce grown by robots

When a sprawling new 'vegetable factory' opens near Kyoto, Japan in 2017, it will be the first farm with no farmers. Robots will plant lettuce seeds, transplant them, raise the vegetables and automatically carry the fully-grown lettuce heads to a packing line, where they can get ready to be sent to local grocery stores.

In a single day, the farm can harvest 30,000 heads of lettuce. On a traditional farm, a field of the same size can grow about 26,000 plants – but only harvest two or four crops a season. This robot-run indoor farm can grow 10 million heads of lettuce a year, saving water and energy, along with human labour.

Spread, the Japanese company planning the factory, opened its first indoor farm in 2006, and already supplies lettuce to 2000 stores around Tokyo. But it saw the opportunity to make its process even more efficient. It sees the new farm as a model for the future of farming.

'There are several reasons vegetable factories will be needed in the future in order to create a sustainable society', says Kiyoka Morita from Spread. Like other indoor farms, Spread's new factory uses far less water than traditional agriculture; the factory's new technology also allows them to recycle 98 per cent of that water. Because the factory is sealed, there's no need for pesticides or herbicides. The ultra-efficient lighting system can run on renewable energy. Japan imports about 60 per cent of its food each year, but the factory can supply it locally.

As climate change increases extreme weather like drought and floods, the fully sealed environment can grow a much more reliable supply of produce. The factory automatically controls temperature, humidity, the level of carbon dioxide, and light to optimise growth.

Those things are true of other vertical farms (farms producing food in vertically stacked layers), but the fact that the process is now fully automated also makes it cheap. Compared to Spread's current factory, the new one will cut labour costs by 50 per cent, so the company can sell lettuce at a lower price (now, it sells for the same cost as regular lettuce from the field).

The new system also protects the food from contamination from humans. 'Full automation also reduces the crops' exposure to human contact during cultivation, further reducing the risk of contamination, and increasing the hygienic levels in the area,' Morita says.

It is not easy to automate every step of the process, and Spread is still tweaking some of the steps, like planting

the seeds. The equipment had to be designed to carefully handle the plants, something that was a little hard for robotic arms to do. 'It's challenging to make sure that the machines all run quickly and efficiently without damaging the delicate vegetables,' she says.
Source: This robot-run indoor farm can grow 10 million heads of lettuce a year, http://www.fastcoexist.com/3050750/this-robot-run-indoor-farm-can-grow-10-million-heads-of-lettuce-a-year, Fast Company

### Check your understanding

1  What factors influenced the need for Spread to change the way they grow vegetables?

2  What techniques have managers at Spread used to meet skills requirements and increase productivity?

3  Who or what will benefit from the changes Spread is implementing by its revolutionary methods?

4  What are the features of management and leadership skills being employed by Spread's leaders?

---

 **PAUSE POINT**

What definitions and functions could you apply to the style of management at Spread?

**Hint**

Refer back to section A for the distinctions and justify your proposals.

**Extend**

What other factors would you consider essential for HR to consider in their planning?

**Link**

Look back at Unit 1: Exploring Business on different stakeholders and their influence.

## Stakeholders who influence change

### Owners

You might consider that those who own the business have the greatest influence on a business. While that could be the case with a sole trader or micro business, it is not always the case and certainly not with larger businesses. If the business has shareholders then they might have the majority share of the business (51 per cent or more) and therefore have the final say over what happens.

### Managers

Managers are involved in planning for the business strategy so they are a major stakeholder of the business. They report back to owners about plans and are in an influential position to shape the future of the business. They can use their knowledge of the position of the business using analyses of data, such as: sales figures, customer satisfaction, complaints and suggestions, to add strength to their arguments.

Consider how managers of a franchise are at the forefront of the business on behalf of the owners, for example fast food restaurants or retailers situated within large department stores. The owners rely on the franchise managers to inform them about what the customer does and does not want. There may be regional tastes or particular preferences from customers, such as those related to religious beliefs, special requests and owners can consider meeting local market demands.

## Customers

Customers have significant influence on the business. Think about when Coca Cola tried to change their long-standing recipe – this did not go down well with their customers. As a result Coca Cola were forced to return to their original recipe.

Other examples include the following:

▸ football fans influencing the removal of the club's manager

▸ software manufacturers relying on customers to test out software and recommend developments

▸ Walkers crisps inviting customer feedback by using social media such as Facebook and Twitter to test the popularity of their products and involve them in campaigns to suggest new flavours.

## Regulators

All businesses are influenced by some form of regulatory body. For example, your place of study is likely to be regulated by many bodies, such as those specific to educational provision: Ofsted, awarding organisations accrediting the qualifications, plus health and safety regulators, auditors and others.

Ofsted is responsible for regulating education services by inspecting them and publicly reporting their evaluations. The awarding organisations also regulate the quality of the training and education, and when they announce they will change their qualifications to ensure they are keeping up to date with industry needs, managers need to plan for changes to teaching and possibly resources.

The construction industry is governed by various regulators including the NHBC, which monitors the quality of building in the UK and provides a set of standards for businesses in the industry to follow. Builders register with NHBC, and they also run a recognition scheme, which recognises builders according to the quality of their build.

▸ What regulatory bodies govern the building industry?

## Financial institutions

Financial institutions are those organisations which provide financial services to businesses, for example in the form of mortgages, loans and other services. Businesses are reliant upon these services to maintain the flow of finances, for example, to pay employees' wages even when the business income is not sufficient to cover the salaries.

The Bank of England is responsible for determining the official bank rate. The percentage of interest paid on bank loans will then be decided by individual banks, varying their interest above this rate. Therefore businesses rely on skilled accountants to forecast their profits and income to ensure they can cover the commitments to these financial institutions, perhaps in the form of an overdraft.

Changes to the bank rate affect how businesses operate and plan for the future and now. Sudden and unforeseen changes can cripple businesses that need to pay mortgages on premises, interest on other loans and, when the bank rate is low, as it has been for several years because of the recession, this affects the interest businesses receive from any financial assets they may have.

**Link**

See *Unit 3: Personal and Business Finance.*

## Government

The government has a lot of influence over business activity through the rules and regulations imposed on industries. Consider the changes in law relating to the food industry, for example the Food Standards Act (1999). The government listens to major organisations, such as WWF UK on sustainable food sources, forcing businesses to find alternatives, such as Birds Eye's introduction of Hoki into their fish fingers.

Government has influenced the farming industry in many ways, such as the crops grown in return for increased levies to farmers, and affecting the returns dairy farmers now get, and this has led to half of Britain's dairy farms closing since the start of the 21st century.

### Employees

Employees do have power within their organisation. For example, some employees can use strikes to attempt to have their demands met, such as for improved working conditions, increased wages or holidays.

This is not to suggest that strikes are always successful and the ethics of workers striking in emergency services, such as firefighters, can be disputed.

## Case study

### How the DVLA managed change

The Driver and Vehicle Licensing Agency (DVLA) is a UK government organisation based in Swansea. It has four main responsibilities: maintaining records for more than 44 million drivers and 36 million registered vehicles, collecting nearly £6 billion per year in Vehicle Excise Duty, limiting vehicle tax evasion to no more than 1 percent, and supporting police and intelligence services in dealing with vehicle-related crime.

Historically, the DVLA has maintained its driver and vehicle registers by handling large numbers of emails, phone calls and paper forms, delivered by post and processed manually. It currently processes around 120 million transactions per year and issues more than 10 million driving licences and 17 million vehicle registration documents. To improve the services it provides to the public and to reduce operational costs, the agency has adopted a comprehensive modernisation agenda that aims to transform it into a more digital enterprise, where paper-based processing is the exception rather than the rule.

The planning stage began by identifying areas where cost reductions could be achieved, and employees from across the whole organisation contributed their ideas, which led to 69 initiatives, ranging from business process simplification to brand new digital services. The department adopted many of the new working practices, seeing increased efficiencies due to a more effective team structure and a simplified decision-making process. One of the biggest improvements was a shift towards the concept of business ownership – where specific people are given responsibility for their own domains and knowledge areas. This means that decisions are made by the people who have the most expertise in each area, and are less likely to be overturned later on.

Source: DVLA embarks on cost-reduction and transformation. IBM Global Business Services Case Study, http://www-935.ibm.com/services/multimedia/WR925831ED-DVLA_cost_reduction_GBC03094GBEN.pdf, IBM Corporation, reprint courtesy of International Business Machines Corporation, © (2012) International Business Machines Corporation

### Check your knowledge

1   What factors influenced the need for the DVLA to change the way they operated previously?
2   Who was involved in the changes that needed to be made?
3   What steps did the DVLA take to prepare for the changes?
4   How did the DVLA change the business culture?
5   What are the current and likely future impacts of these changes?

 **PAUSE POINT**     What are the skills the Programme Manager needed to implement this change?

Hint        Without referring to the case study, make a list of the steps the DVLA took to plan for change.

Extend      What management styles has the Programme Manager deployed to undertake this mammoth task?

# F  Quality management

Quality management is the process where businesses put systems in place to ensure the quality of their product or service is consistent. You are probably aware of some of the quality systems where you study, such as the moderation or verification procedures to confirm the standard of assessment of your work is reliable and accurate.

## Quality standards

There are regulated quality standards, in addition to those regulators you have already explored, and you will now look at these and why some businesses view them as important.

### British Standards Institution standard BS 7850-1:1992

As the UK National Standards Body, the British Standards Institution (BSI) provides a series of quality products tailored to different aspects of industry. The standard known as BS 7850-1 is a guide for management principles on how to organise the business structure. **TQM** is designed to involve the whole company in evaluating what works well and what they need to improve. TQM aims to make best use of the company's resources, including the workforce, to meet business objectives.

> **Key term**
>
> **TQM** – Total Quality Management.

▶ **Figure 6.20** TQM flowchart

If you consider the very simple representation in Figure 6.20, it tells you that all external operations relating to the business go through the process of quality checks on their pathway through the business. For example, a customer makes an enquiry about purchasing a further 1000 tons of steel within a set deadline and at a negotiated discounted price. The process provides the necessary checks, to ensure:

▸ finance check the reduced price is viable
▸ the materials are available
▸ production check the workforce have the capacity to meet the deadline
▸ operations check the discounted work does not interrupt more profitable work being carried out
▸ transport are able to deliver on time
▸ the raw materials are of the standard expected to produce a high quality product
▸ the finished product meets the standard previously produced

and so on throughout the business.

There is a cost to implement this system and the BSI will evaluate the systems in place against their standards to determine if the business meets their requirements. Rather like an annual medical, the business will undergo annual checks to ensure standards are being maintained and advise on any improvements.

### International Organization for Standardization standard ISO 9000:2015

ISO standards are internationally recognised for both quality management and quality assurance. An earlier ISO standard for quality management was 8402:1994. They also

**Discussion**

Discuss in a small group the risks associated with systems which require all employees to follow the same process, compared with the risks attached to those businesses having no standard systems in place.

provide a framework for quality processes and checks for consistency of standards across the business. As they are internationally recognisable, businesses awarded the standard are able to present an assurance to existing and potential customers of the quality of their products and services.

There are many parts to the ISO standards and these are mainly concerned about assuring statutory laws and regulations are being met. It is the most widely used quality standard internationally but like most quality systems is often blamed for being overly bureaucratic and costly.

## Kite marks – IiP

You can probably recall different places where you have seen the kite mark logo which is a British Standard quality mark which symbolises quality, safety and value for customers and businesses. The kite mark here is the one representing Investors in People (IiP) which is the quality standard for people management.

▶ Can you think of any businesses where you have seen this logo?

You may recognise the Investors in People (IiP) logo as one displayed at the place where you study or possibly work. It was established in 1991 to set the standard for the way in which businesses manage their biggest asset: people. Businesses subscribe to this standard as a way of being recognised for caring about their employees and their customers. It is known worldwide and involves businesses in demonstrating how they strive for continuous improvement by understanding the way they operate and how they plan for sustainability and growth.

To gain accreditation, businesses must provide evidence of how they meet the IiP framework, rather as you need to provide evidence of your achievements. One of the many ways they measure consistency in their standards is by using **mystery shoppers**. Examples of businesses awarded IiP include Geoplan, The Prince's Trust and Virgin Trains.

**Key term**

**Mystery shopper** – a person employed undercover as a customer to assess the quality of goods or services.

## Developing a quality culture

The term quality can generate many different interpretations and reactions depending on how well it is understood and the effectiveness of the system. The impact of a quality system should be one which evidently improves business practices for all stakeholders and not one which generates paper-work overload. The government and the public sector have been criticised considerably over the years for introducing too much bureaucracy, coined by the phrase 'complete in triplicate' from the days of paper form filling.

What quality systems do require from employees is that they are diligent and conscientious in following the procedures as prescribed. However, quality systems should allow for flexibility and initiative and not constrain users to the extent that they are completely controlled.

## Setting quality standards

Quality standards are based on two aspects of quality, defined by ISO as quality control (QC) and quality assurance (QA). Quality control concerns the operational means to fulfil quality requirements and QA aims at providing confidence in this fulfilment – both within the organisation and externally to customers and authorities.

▶  In the case of ISO expectations, QC processes not only occur between input and output but also before production is begun in how the business prepares for production. For example, the business anticipates risks and decides on contingencies to ensure customer needs and expectations are met.

▶  QA relates to all those planned and systematic actions necessary to provide adequate confidence that an entity will fulfil requirements for quality. All QA processes occur after production, as in the case of ISO standards, which is not consistent with all TQM systems.

The change in the way employees work will impact on the business culture and it might be the reason why the decision is made to seek quality management accreditation. For example:

▶  if the business is not cost effective

▶  there is too much waste

▶  customer complaints are high

▶  inefficient workforce practices.

Setting quality standards means writing policies and procedures for putting the standards into operation. Quality standards require a framework to enable all stakeholders to know how the business operates and what to expect. You have already explored some of the standards businesses must comply with, such as those set by government and other regulators.

Those businesses applying for accreditation from national or international standards will have a framework to guide them. Whether a business chooses or feels compelled to become accredited or not, they still should have a quality framework in place for themselves and their stakeholders. A quality framework should cover all aspects of business operations and some of the procedures include:

▶  instructions for every operation of the business

▶  complaints and grievances

▶  recruitment and selection

▶  how each operation is monitored and reviewed for its effectiveness

▶  finance operations.

Each business will tailor their quality framework and standards depending on several factors, including the type of business and where they operate. For example, a high street retailer will operate very differently from a residential care home.

**PAUSE POINT**    Choose a business, and consider the procedures they need to have in place to ensure quality is assured and improvements identified.

> Hint    Start by identifying how your chosen business would define 'quality'.

> Extend    Can you find any examples of other businesses in the same industry that have met certain quality standards, such as IiP? What will they have needed to do to achieve this?

**Link**

See also *Unit 21: Training and Development*.

## Managerial commitment and staff buy-in

To set quality standards requires **staff buy-in** for management to bring about change. It also requires commitment from managers as they are the ones who are responsible for deciding on the quality standards and how to implement them. Managers will be the ones who have to sell the changes to staff and offer reassurance of how the changes will occur with the least disruption to daily operations.

There are many different ways managers can gain staff buy-in and some structures are more likely to gain managerial commitment and subsequently employee buy-in. Some of the businesses which invite change include:

▶ Formula 1 racing teams
▶ software businesses
▶ fashion businesses
▶ businesses in the food industry
▶ businesses in the music and media sector.

Manufacturing organisation, Festo GB, has been awarded the Gold standard for IiP in recognition of their inclusivity, which has brought about strong business performance. The Landmark Hotel in London has also been awarded Gold status.

## Quality circles

Quality circles are a way of involving employees, usually those undertaking similar jobs or working in the same department, with problem-solving and resolutions. This can be a highly effective and efficient way of getting to the bottom of the problem by listening to those most closely related, as managers are often too far removed from the day-to-day operations.

Take, for example, the reference earlier to franchising (see Stakeholders who influence change) where the owner relies on the manager of the franchise to learn about what the customer wants and needs at a local level. When staff are encouraged to contribute to problem-solving through being listened to, they are more likely to feel valued. Staff can influence the way the business operates which impacts on their job satisfaction.

## Partnership working with suppliers and customers

The government is very keen to encourage partnership working and it continues to feature in their directives to businesses. The numerous benefits of partnership working with suppliers and customers include:

▶ stakeholders feeling listened to concerning what they want and expect
▶ learning from mistakes and constantly looking for ways to improve
▶ gaining trust from stakeholders
▶ gaining in competitiveness on a wider scale
▶ learning new ways to put things right
▶ being able to outsource specialist operations
▶ diversifying products and services
▶ contributing to the economy on a global scale
▶ ensuring sustainability.

## Transparent and open communication

You may have heard people talk about being transparent and open or you may have read it in a policy belonging to your place of study. It involves encouraging staff to own up to mistakes so that improvements can be made and to avoid any culture of blame and deceit. Businesses which are known for encouraging transparent and open communication include Google and Hewlett Packard (HP).

Some businesses rely on transparent and open communication to provide their services, such as air traffic control and the police force, especially with the introduction of The Police National Database and the sharing of information across regions. Information regarding police crime hotspots is now shared online, as is information on vehicle licensing tax evasion.

## The techniques and tools of quality management

The techniques and tools of quality management come under three categories:

▶ tools for data collection and interpretation
▶ tools for planning
▶ tools for continuous improvement.

### Quality control

Quality control is concerned with ensuring that not only products but also services are of an acceptable quality standard. Quality control was possibly the cornerstone of the motor vehicle industry emerging in the USA from around the 1940s. Whole quality departments were devoted to quality control of vehicle components, although this was mostly to do with finding problems and checking standards, rather than improving the quality.

The Japanese market showed its competitive and quality nature and was possibly instrumental in changing the way industry viewed quality.

### Lean manufacturing

The purpose of lean manufacturing is to ensure maximum value for minimum waste. It was used to describe Toyota's operations in the mid-1980s.

All types of businesses use lean manufacturing principles, not just the manufacturing industry, encouraging the whole workforce to focus on three different aspects.

▶ Purpose: what customer problems will the enterprise solve to achieve its own purpose of prospering?
▶ Process: how will the organisation assess each major value stream to make sure each step is valuable, capable, available, adequate, flexible, and that all the steps are linked by flow, pull, and levelling?
▶ People: how can the organisation ensure that every important process has someone responsible for continually evaluating that value stream in terms of business purpose and lean process? How can everyone touching the value stream be actively engaged in operating it correctly and continually improving it?

### Six Sigma

Six Sigma comprises quality techniques and tools for process improvement. It is a data-driven approach and methodology for eliminating defects. In essence, Six Sigma is a quality framework that a business will progress through, with the intention of reducing waste time and processes and so producing an end result that is fit for purpose. Its engineering founder, Bill Smith, introduced the quality process during his time at Motorola in the mid-1980s. Jack Welch recognised its scope and made it central to his business strategy at General Electric in 1995.

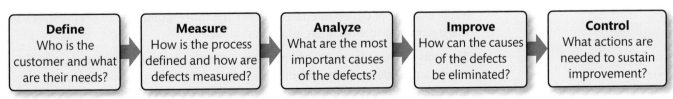

▶ **Figure 6.21:** Phases of Six Sigma

General Electric expect employees wishing to progress in the organisation to achieve the quality standard, which strives to meet near perfection, in order to be considered for higher positions.

# The importance and benefits of quality management

In business, it is important to have some quality control measures. These ensure that processes are clear and everyone understands what they are doing, that pre-planned checks are implemented at the right stages and that waste is kept to a minimum to enable everyone in the business to work towards producing an end result that is fit for purpose, whether this is a product or a service. Ensuring quality control measures are implemented is part of the manager's role.

## Zero defect production and output

The goal of this is to do precisely what it says – produce materials with zero defects, stemming from the work of a highly-skilled workforce.

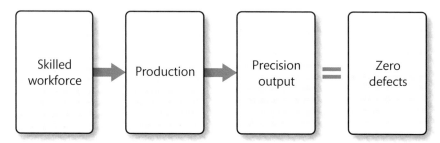

▶ **Figure 6.22:** Zero-defect output

The benefits to any business operating tight quality controls which result in zero-defects include:

▶ maximum profit

▶ customer satisfaction

▶ rapid production

▶ deadlines being met.

To achieve this high reaching aim, every member of the workforce needs to understand the part they play and that they are responsible for their contribution.

## Continuous improvement

Continuous improvement refers to the way that businesses will continuously monitor, review and evaluate their processes to look for ways to improve, to help reduce waste and increase efficiency and productivity. You are striving for continuous improvement with your studies and the place where you are studying is doing the same.

Regulators' oversight and monitoring pushes businesses to continuously improve, such as the example of Ofsted referred to earlier. It is the responsibility of all employees and management to identify areas for improvement.

The tools you have learnt about above are some of those used for systematic quality checks and analysis of data to anticipate problems and identify risks. A quality improvement cycle can look like this:

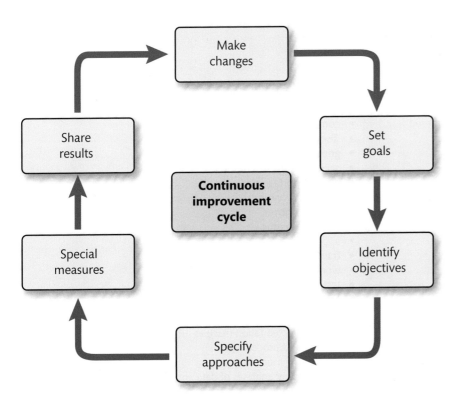

▶ **Figure 6.23:** Cycle for continuous improvement

## Improved output quality

One of the many benefits of aiming for continuous improvement is improved output quality, in other words the products and services are of improved quality.

Consider two examples of businesses where quality appears to be at the heart of their values:

▶ Budget Vets – staff have autonomy to support each other where their strengths lie, and the business offers them opportunities for CPD. They also have the opportunity to try and improve processes within the business, as managers welcome new ideas. There are seven branches that maintain close contact, working as an overall team.

▶ Unipart Aftermarket Logistics – promote efficiency and eliminating waste. One way they do this is by tracking performance over time, in one-hour intervals, which enables them to plan better and organise their workloads. This means they can rapidly respond to customer and employee needs.

## Reduced inspection requirements

Businesses which are able to demonstrate their ongoing commitment to continuous improvement are likely to experience fewer external inspection checks by regulators, such as IiP, BSI, ISO or Ofsted.

In order to do so, the regulators will need to be satisfied that the business has a consistent track record of improvement and that the analyses and evaluation of supporting evidence proves this is the case. Regulators, whether they are external or internal, will measure trends over time and thoroughly scrutinise the data using a variety of means such as those shown in Table 6.11.

**Table 6.11:** Methods used by regulators

| Interviews with | • customers<br>• suppliers<br>• employees<br>• management<br>• other stakeholders (eg parents in the case of Ofsted) |
|---|---|
| Data gathered | • complaints<br>• disciplinaries<br>• grievances<br>• accident and H&S reports<br>• waste reports<br>• financial records<br>• labour turnover<br>• sickness records<br>• appraisals<br>• training plans<br>• workforce skills and job descriptions<br>• testimonials from customers<br>• action plans and minutes of meetings |
| Systems | • quality frameworks<br>• external accreditation (such as IiP, BSI, ISO etc.)<br>• policies and procedures<br>• monitoring mechanisms<br>• robustness of analyses of data and evaluation<br>• business plans |

Whoever is carrying out the inspection wants to be satisfied that the business has robust and rigorous systems which are able to sustain business operations and future plans for maximum production and profit. Internal inspectors will comprise members of the workforce who carry out regular quality checks, as an additional responsibility to their main job role, which act to identify or validate checks. This way everyone is involved in the quality system.

## Supplier engagement and satisfaction

Engaging with suppliers requires a strategy which leads to supplier satisfaction. This is known as supply chain management. If a business does not have reliable suppliers to provide the raw materials at the required cost and quality, it either fails or has to find alternative sources. This of course takes time and costs money, not only in the loss of business by not being able to supply its customers, but also the cost of seeking out alternative sources and testing out the product for its quality.

One of the main benefits for a business of having quality kite marks is that like-minded businesses understand and appreciate the hard work and efficiency within that business that has led to them being accredited.

Businesses from approximately 75 countries around the globe are accredited with ISO standards; this enables outsourcing to be selective if the business strategy is to buy only from those with accreditation.

However, this does mean that businesses that do not have accreditation may not be considered, possibly for reasons such as:

▶ new business start-ups
▶ too costly for a small business
▶ business not yet accredited although undergoing the process
▶ not yet meeting the standards for accreditation.

As for all business operations, the key to satisfaction is communication.

▶ **Figure 6.24:** Model for supplier engagement

## Customer involvement and satisfaction

Customer involvement is beneficial for businesses and more likely to lead to customer satisfaction. The use of social media has been important here, especially Twitter or Facebook which, for example, invites customers to be involved and make recommendations. Customers are informed of how their contribution makes improvements to the operation of the business, such as the 2015 introduction of the 'Facebook reactions' button. Businesses often use customer feedback as part of a process of continuous improvement, taking on board comments and feedback from various sources, such as feedback cards, online reviews and focus groups.

## Improved efficiency and profitability

Quality systems often generate complaints from employees where they are not understood or where they are not well planned and so place a burden on the workforce. Quality systems are not all about paperwork although some degree of paperwork or electronic documentation is essential in order to track what is happening within an organisation.

The overall aim and benefits from quality management are improved efficiency and profitability. Businesses that operate without clear guidance from management about the processes workers should follow are likely to fail.

## Case study

### The Urbanists – achieving Investors in People accreditation

#### What was the IiP motivation?

The Urbanists are a town planning and design consultancy established in 2005. They take their name from "one who studies and seeks to influence the process of change in human settlements" and their mission is to design vibrant economic places with an active social context.

The Urbanists' objectives were to build on their emerging reputation and brand and to evaluate the ethos of the organisation to see how it added value to their client. Social responsibilty, continuous learning and work-life balance were all regarded as important attributes and they wanted to benchmark these against the Investors in People standard.

#### How did IiP help?

The Urbanists were surprised how straightforward their IiP journey was when compared with many other industry accreditations, having an emphasis on developing the culture of the organisation and developing the way people are managed and appreciated.

The IiP assessment process highlighted how people felt about such issues as communication, support and teamwork. From the results, an action plan for continuous improvement was put into place based on the company's objectives and priorities. Everyone appreciated what the company was trying to achieve and that their contribution was recognised and valued. IiP helped the organisation to learn that their overall ethos is one of strong team spirit, engagement of staff, listening and adding value to clients through collaboration and sustainability.

#### What was the impact?

Achieving Investors in People raised The Urbanists' profile. As a small company delivering major projects of high value, achieving IiP demonstrated to their clients a clear standard and level of ability.

The Urbanists are confidently promoting high business standards and demonstrating that Wales has a committed, skilled and flexible workforce that allows businesses to be competitive on a global scale.

Martin Sullivan, Managing Director of The Urbanists said that the whole team had worked hard to achieve the award, and it would add value to their objective of delivering projects that enhance the character of places and the lives of people who live there.

The Urbanists were able to demonstrate 'a leading edge in best people management practice in the UK, and that team spirit, engagement and continuous learning are built into the ethos of the company. This confidence would allow The Urbanists to expand beyond their borders' (IiP Assessor).

If you would like to know more about The Urbanists visit their website at http://www.theurbanists.net.

**Check your understanding:**

1 What is the emphasis on Investors in People accreditation?

2 What did the organisation learn from the process?

3 How has achieving the accreditation helped the business?

 **PAUSE POINT**    What evidence can you suggest contributed to The Urbanists being awarded IiP status?

         Hint    Produce a list or spidergram of evidence without referring to the case study.

         Extend    Produce a presentation persuading the management of a business of your choice to aim for formal accreditation of one of three quality standards.

## Assessment practice 6.5    AO4

'The Body Beautiful' has been operating as a franchise since 1982 and is based in rural Norfolk. While it has enjoyed a growing membership over the years, the fitness industry has also grown. The manager has heard a rumour that a major competitor is considering opening a new fitness and leisure centre in the town centre.

The manager and her team are always asking customers for feedback and they have heard about the difficulties getting to the centre, especially in bad weather when business profits drop considerably. The business struggles with its cash flow in the winter as the cost of heating is high and customers are few. They are also being told by customers that the potential new leisure centre will have the latest equipment and even a hydro-pool. However, their main USP is the customer service. The business prides itself in always giving value for money and the very best service.

The manager has decided to put forward a proposal to the owners to convince them of the best way forward. She knows it will require some investment but is positive it will work. She wants included in the proposal some external accreditation proving to the world they are as good as they say. She needs to present the owners with the solutions and recognises they will want to be able to measure impact if they are expected to invest.

She has asked you to prepare a summary report to accompany a very convincing argument in a presentation, which also includes speaker notes as she will be presenting it to the owners. She is expecting the notes, executive summary and any handouts to upskill her understanding of quality management tools and techniques and clearly demonstrate the impact.

### Plan

- What are you being asked to do?
- Can you identify all the areas you need to cover?
- Can you plot out a timeframe for each of the tasks to meet the overall timeframe?
- Can you identify your sources of information?

### Do

- Have you practised the different quality standards so you can explain to others?
- Have you prepared your outline presentation?
- Have you produced the speaker notes and handouts?
- Have you completed your executive report?
- Have you checked everything for accuracy and presentation/formatting?
- Have you considered the questions others are likely to ask? Can you explain the information clearly, perhaps by asking a family member to listen to you present your proposals?

### Review

- What did you enjoy most about this activity?
- In which areas are you most skilful?
- Which skills are you going to focus on improving further?

# THINK ▶FUTURE

## Shan
## Middle-level manager

When Shan gained his BTEC National at level 3 in Business, he was fortunate to find a job working in a bank – starting off as a cashier. He found the skills and understanding gained from his studies were invaluable, especially when learning how to work with business colleagues at different levels and most importantly customers.

His manager was really encouraging and Shan was rewarded by being promoted to team leader having demonstrated that he would be capable of managing people at different levels of the business. At that time he managed just two cashiers and although it was demanding, he also found it rewarding.

He has now worked for the bank for five years and has just been promoted again to middle manager. He is now in charge of a small department of five staff and one team leader. The bank has supported him in developing his people management skills and he has been offered a sponsored training programme to study towards a degree in Business Management.

# Focusing your skills

Shan is now managing a larger team, including a team leader, named Paul, who is directly responsible for managing the cashiers. How should Shan manage communication between all the different team members? Do you think he will need to vary how he communicates with Paul compared to the cashiers?

- What skills do you think Shan needs to manage any conflict that arises between the team leader and his direct reports, the cashiers, or between himself and Paul?
- Shan would like to make one of the cashiers Employee of Month. How should he do this?
- Paul asks Shan to complete a report for him that is actually his responsibility. What should Shan do in this situation?

### Preparing yourself

For his interview for the middle manager role, Shan had to be prepared for questions about:

- management and leadership principles and functions
- the types of data managers will use to monitor performance and methods of analysis
- how to apply theories of motivation
- the role of Human Resourcing in business planning.

Ahead of his interview, he also made sure he reflected on his experience managing the two cashiers so that he could provide examples of where he had been an effective manager.

# Getting ready for assessment

This section has been written to help you to do your best when you take the external examination. Read through it carefully and ask your tutor if there is anything you are not sure about.

## About the test

The assessment test will be split into two Parts: A and B. Part B is likely to be two activities worth 44 marks each. Part A contains material for completion of preparatory work for the set test which will be undertaken a set period of time before Part B. Part A will include a case study which you will use to prepare for the test and must be carried out independently and you will not be allowed to share your work with other learners.

Your tutor may give guidance on when you can complete the preparation but cannot give you feedback during the preparation period.

The case study will provide a scenario and you will be given activities and a short set of instructions. Remember to read these very carefully so you know what to prepare, which could be on anything included in this unit. It is highly likely you will need to analyse and evaluate some data.

As the guidelines for assessment can change, you should refer to the official assessment guidance on the Pearson Qualifications website for the latest definitive guidance.

## Sitting the test

The test will be supervised and your work will be kept securely during any breaks taken. Listen very carefully to any verbal instructions you are given and thoroughly read the instructions for the test.

You will be instructed to produce one or more of the products defined by the command terms. You will need to demonstrate ability to:

- analyse data
- analyse management information
- identify and apply management principles.

Check you have everything you need for the test and arrive in plenty of time.

Plan out your time to ensure you get chance to proof read and correct any mistakes before handing in.

| Command or term | Definition |
|---|---|
| Executive summary | A brief but comprehensive synopsis of a business plan or proposal. |
| Formal report | This is a report written for an audience in appropriate business language, layout and style. |
| Presentation | Using software to prepare the materials for a visual presentation. |

▶ Remember, a pass mark requires you to rationalise the styles and skills required in different management and leadership situations.

▶ You will also need to show you understand the factors influencing management and performance of the workforce and how to apply them in the workplace.

▶ Make sure you justify the recommendations proposed for business improvements, which must be related to management and leadership principles.

## Worked example

## Part A: Set task brief

You are working for the quality department in a manufacturing company which produces high energy drinks. Your boss, the quality manager, has asked you to carry out quality checks of each department starting with sales to contribute to a report on the continuing viability of the business. You will need to:

- identify the issues in this case study and carry out preparations for completing the tasks relating to this unit
- spend approximately six hours on this research (check exact times available with your tutor, as this may change).

> Read this carefully! Make sure you understand exactly what you need to do ahead of starting your preparatory work on Part A.

> Think about how you will make the best use of both the space and time you have available.

## Part A: Set task information

### Activate Drinks Case Study

High energy drinks are often associated with healthy lifestyles and leisure-type activities. The sports industry is also associated with consuming high energy drinks as a means to sustain intensive activities. Activate introduced their range of energy drinks in early 2000 and business went well, increasing sales year-on-year until 2012 when they started to decline.

> It's important to highlight any numbers in the text as you may need to refer to quantitative data.

> Make sure you have fully understood what you need to do from the set task brief. You need to look at the viability of the business and so this piece of information about how well the business is doing is crucial.

Although competition between brands is fierce, with Red Bull being a market leader, sales overall are up by 6.7% in the USA alone in the year from 2013.

The sales team has doubled since the year 2000 to 20 personnel, overseen by a Sales Director who was promoted from being Production Manager in the factory. The sales team have either been recruited externally or internally from other non-sales-related roles.

> Note that the information about the Sales Director might be important as it gives you background about a previous role which might just be relevant later.

As the Activate brand was a new concept, which was introduced as a totally new line for the business long established in manufacturing the bottles for other high energy drink manufacturers, the leaders made the strategic decision to make and package in-house rather than only make and distribute to drinks manufacturers.

As sales have fallen and the Sales Director has been unable to confirm the reasons for this, the quality department have stepped in to investigate the possible reasons for this decline.

> It might be important to refer to the history of the product later and also the history of the business as a manufacturer.

Make sure you research all terms you do not understand or know little about.

You will need to spend time thinking about the likely reasons behind them.

One of the theories the quality team are keen to explore is the structure of the sales department which has been operating in a laissez-faire manner. Although the current leader has a managerial background, the context of manufacturing is not the same as managing a sales team and dealing with customers directly. As business grew rapidly there was little time for any training and only two of the team, who were recruited externally, have any sales experience and both from the retail sector.

The Sales Director reports that the department is extremely frantic and that everyone has kept busy dealing with enquiries, talking to production, chasing suppliers for raw materials and never enough time for meetings, appraisals and other 'stuff' which, the Director quotes, 'gets in the way of the day-to-day business'. When asked about the benefits of employing two team members with sales experience, the Sales Director is quick to respond that they are young and both worked in a different sector although have some useful qualities.

Think about what the Sales Director might be implying here. It could indicate how the sales department operates as a culture.

You might want to practise interpreting graphs; perhaps you have some you can refer to from maths lessons?

In response to the Sales Director reporting that the department is always extremely busy, the quality team have asked for records of staff attendance to check whether the pressure and amount of work is too great for the number of staff employed. The only records available are for the six months starting 2015, due to, as stated by the Sales Director, the pressure of work and lack of apparent support from the administration team or HR.

| SALES DEPARTMENT ABSENTEEISM | | | | | | |
|---|---|---|---|---|---|---|
| | Jan-15 | Feb-15 | Mar-15 | Apr-15 | May-15 | Jun-15 |
| # on payroll | 19 | 18 | 17 | 17 | 17 | 18 |
| # sick | 0 | 6 | 8 | 3 | 0 | 1 |
| # maternity | 1 | 1 | 1 | 1 | 1 | 1 |
| # holidays | 2 | 1 | 1 | 2 | 0 | 1 |
| # compassionate leave | 0 | 2 | 1 | 0 | 1 | 1 |

## Part B

## Activity 1

Following the research you have undertaken, you will need to produce a report for your quality manager. In your report you should identify the key issues and include recommendations for the sales department. The boss of the organisation has made it clear that removing Activate as a product line is unlikely as too much has been invested in its production although is open to suggestions which lead to an increase in sales.

(Total for activity 1 = 44 marks)

> Plan out the structure for your report, making sure you have all the necessary headings ending with a conclusion and recommendations. Include a contents page and don't forget your references.

## Activity 1 Answer:

There are a number of issues that this report will investigate in relation to the falling sales of the Activate brand and the reduction in sales. Quality checks were undertaken to ...

I will discuss the following key issues:

- inappropriate leadership style
- sales team has limited sales experience
- lack of delegation
- possible conflict between Sales Director and team members with sales experience
- lack of formal procedures
- weak management skills
- poor planning and organisation.

From the evidence gathered... the sales department operates under a laissez-faire leadership style (fact) and this appears to impact on the effectiveness and efficiency of the department...

...Due to the lack of procedures in the sales department, the monitoring of staff attendance was overlooked until .... Therefore, although it could be initially assumed that the workload was too great for the number of employees, the sales department was operating on ... percentage of staff...

My recommendations moving forward include upskilling the Sales Director to build on production knowledge in a sales context. This will ensure that they are able to both understand the concerns of staff they are responsible for but also allow them to understand the data coming from the team. ....restructuring the sales team to operate in a transformational style, this change will....

....retaining or reskilling the sales team members with little sales experience. This will not only upskill the workforce but may help with motivation. This may help with sickness absenteeism, which is quite high from the data provided....formalising appraisal procedures....

> You may find it useful to tick off each aspect as you refer to it in the report and then strike through again when you have made a recommendation associated with the finding.

> Ensure you only include the facts where making a judgement otherwise make it clear when it is your opinion. A useful term to use when relating to opinions or where there is insufficient evidence to be absolutely sure is to refer to what the findings 'suggest'.

> When using terminology always make sure you're using it in the correct context!

## Activity 2

Prepare a maximum of five slides with speaker notes for a presentation which contributes to a meeting between the quality manager, organisation boss and Sales Director. Your contribution will:

- provide an evaluation based on the data from staff absenteeism
- propose a systematic approach to managing the human resources
- explain the impact of managing change on the potential sales opportunities.

(Total for activity 2 = 44 marks)

## Activity 2 Answer:

*Rather than lots of words, you may want to include a diagram here to show how the new structure could look.*

| Slide 1 | |
|---|---|
| Slide content | Sales department staffing and structure<br><br>The proposal is to move to a transformational structure. This will allow... |
| Speaker notes | The following proposals to be discussed: building on the skills of existing staff with support for team members and managers from experienced mentors in similar positions. |

*This may be another place where you could consider including a diagram. Using a diagram makes it easier for the audience to interpret the data.*

| Slide 2 | |
|---|---|
| Slide content | Staff absenteeism<br><br>The analyses of the staff absenteeism table indicate that the sales team does not operate on full capacity though further exploration is required to identify staff turnover. |
| Speaker notes | Discuss limitations of the data: only one-sixth of the period between the three years from the end of 2012 to the end of 2015. |

*Any recommendations you make should be backed up by the evidence you have already discussed. Be prepared to justify any recommendations you make!*

| Slide 3 | |
|---|---|
| Slide content | Recommendations<br><br>Review the current procedures and policies<br><br>Identify periods where current staff allocation is not meeting needs. ... |
| Speaker notes | Expand on the periods where we're busy – make sure they realise how crucial that is... |

| | Slide 4 |
|---|---|
| Slide content | HR strategy<br><br>1 carry out TNA of sales department<br><br>2 undertake appraisals<br><br>3 evaluate job roles and skill levels<br><br>4 review job descriptions<br><br>5 implement sales and management training programme<br><br>6 set sales targets<br><br>7 implement quality monitoring system |
| Speaker notes | 1 the TNA will identify existing abilities and how these align to the needs of the organisation. Gaps in skills and understanding will be used to inform training plans and team structure<br><br>2 appraisals will provide the opportunity for staff to assess where they think they belong in the organisation, what training they need and their aspirations for their careers<br><br>3 job roles. |

When you discuss staff training, the type of training may be different for each individual, especially for the Sales Director. Consider how the manager will feel if attending the same training as subordinates and what the training is meant to achieve.

Ensure you refer to the key terms you have learnt about in your studies, such as upskilling, reskilling etc.

In slide 4, you might add to your speaker notes where you will make links between the quality monitoring system and some examples of what the system could comprise. For example, proposing the company works towards IiP, with a brief explanation of why and how the business and department will benefit.

| | Slide 5 |
|---|---|
| Slide content | Culture and managing change<br><br>*From discussion with line managers we have established the following concerns....* |
| Speaker notes | Discuss relationships between proposed changes to department operations and managing change.<br><br>Make links to Herzberg's theory and how recognizing staff contributions will impact on future sales and setting sales targets. |

When you talk about culture or any other terms, remember to elaborate on what you mean in this context. It's helpful to assume that your audience won't necessarily know what you mean or how you are relating it to the current situation.

You could produce an executive summary. First you need to identify the main points, highlighting the business case, the main issues and providing an overview of actions to be taken. Begin with an introductory sentence. Make sure that the points you make are relevant to the activity. Use examples of positives, negatives and any outstanding issues. Use transition words such as 'next', 'before', 'for example', 'to sum up' to connect sentences. Proof read your work for presentation, spelling and grammar.

## Further reading and resources

Adair, J. (1979) *Action-centred leadership*, Gower Publishing Ltd

Blanchard, K. (2011) *The one minute manager meets the monkey*, Harper

Blanchard, K. and Spencer, J. (2015) *The new one minute manager*, HarperCollins Publishers

Cooper, R. (2015) *Decision making: the ultimate guide to decision-making!*, CreateSpace Independent Publishing

Cumbay, T. (2014) *Managing all-in-one for Dummies*, John Wiley and Sons

Department for Education and Skills (2003) *21st century skills: realising our potential*

Fuller, C. (2008) *A toolkit of motivational skills: encouraging and supporting change in individuals*, Wiley-Blackwell

Goleman, D. (1995) *Emotional intelligence: why it can matter more than IQ*, New York: Bantam Books

Goleman, D. (2001) 'An EI-based theory of performance' in *The Emotionally Intelligent Workplace*, Jossey-Bass

Scouller, J. (2011) *The three levels of leadership: how to develop your leadership presence, know how and skill*, Management Books 2000 Ltd

## Websites

**www.businessdictionary.com**

Dictionary of useful business terminology.

**www.ons.gov.uk/ons/index.html**

Official national statistics from the Office for National Statistics.

**www.b2binternational.com/publications/competitor-intelligence/**

Article on how to find competitor and market information.

**www.ifs.org.uk**

Institute of Fiscal Studies – providing information from independent research on economic performance.

**www.ilo.org**

International Labour Organization – provides data on projects and employment policies at a global level.

**www.oecd.org**

Organisation for Economic Co-operation and Development – provides extensive data on skills and statistics on human development, life expectancy and inequality from 34 countries.

**businesslinks.co.uk**

Company directory from Business Links, allowing businesses to advertise to each other.

**www.citb.co.uk**

Construction Industry Training Board.

# Business Decision Making 7

# Getting to know your unit

**Assessment**
You will be assessed by a task set and marked by Pearson.

Everyone has to make decisions for themselves every day of their lives and the same is true in business. During this unit you will learn about business decision making. You will acquire the knowledge and learn how to apply the skills you will need to make informed decisions based on interpreting data and reaching solutions. This unit will also help you to understand how to predict possible consequences and identify flaws in arguments or misrepresentations of information or data. It will enable you to make links with all the other business units you are studying and appreciate the importance of decision making and planning in a business and social environment. You will gain a foundation of transferable skills for any future employment and study.

## How you will be assessed

This unit is assessed under supervised conditions. You will complete a set task based on a case study/business scenario.

The information you will be given will include some numerical data which you will need to analyse and use for calculations. The information could be about any business-related scenario in any business context. You may be asked to make a decision about any business aspect.

The second activity will require you to summarise your business plan to convince potential investors. You may be asked to produce some slides and speaker notes which clearly demonstrate your ability to justify your reasoning, identify and assess the risks and articulate your plan to the likely audience. You will need to demonstrate your ability to financially forecast and identify factors which impact on the decisions you make. You will be expected to use reliable sources of information and reference all your sources fully. Overall your outputs will need to be fit for purpose and business-like.

Both activities will need to be completed within the time allocated. You are likely to need to devote more time to some areas than others. Remember to allow time to check any calculations for accuracy and self critique your

decisions and proposals as if from another point of view. It is vital that you ensure you format your work accurately especially where numerical values are being portrayed.

As the guidelines for assessment can change, you should refer to the official assessment guidance on the Pearson Qualifications website for the latest definitive guidance.

This table gives the areas of essential content that you must be familiar with prior to assessment.

| Essential content | |
|---|---|
| A | Business plans |
| B | Decision making in business |
| C | Use of research to justify the marketing of a business |
| D | Efficient operational management of the business |
| E | Understand the importance of managing resources |
| F | Creation and interpretation of financial forecasts |
| G | Viability of a business |
| H | Demonstrate business skills/IT skills |

## Getting started

Making decisions involves a series of complex actions and processes. During this unit, list different types of business decisions required and expand the list to include the reasons for those decisions and the methods and sources of information involved in making them. It would be useful to also make a note of those decisions which were bad decisions and why, together with those which resulted in having a significant positive impact.

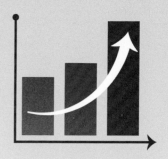

 # Business plans

A **business plan** is a formal document or statement about the intentions and purpose of the business. The plan should include the reasons for the business and how the goals will be achieved. It is likely to include some information and background about how the business idea came about and, as business plans are not just for new businesses, the plan might include the history of the business and how it has evolved over time. A business plan is required by funders and stakeholders as it will describe the intentions for the future of the business.

## Business ideas

Business ideas can emerge at any time during the life of a business. An idea sparks the inception of a business, although many ideas never become fruitful just as many business ideas do not become a success. Business ideas can be justified in different ways.

### 'Start-up' business

A 'start-up' business is where a new business idea is associated with one or more of the following.

▶ Gap in the market – A gap in the market might lead to a business when, through research and development, or an **entrepreneur** spotting it, there is an opportunity to infill between products or services. One example is an emergency light for scuba divers to see when their tanks are low on air. Many new businesses, or extensions to existing businesses, emerge in this way, for example a safety helmet for surfers. In some cases, a business offers a service or product which does not appear to be a new idea as it seems so obvious.

▶ Competitors – Keeping a close eye on what your competitors are doing can create a new business idea. New business owners Sue Youn and Ben of Yogiyo Korean sauces followed a similar pathway as entrepreneur Levi Roots, who is the founder of Reggae Reggae Sauce, when they started a new business selling Sue Youn's family-made Korean sauce in 2015. Competition for specialist coffees and health drinks has led to new business start-ups and **franchise** opportunities, such as those promoted by Costa Coffee and Starbucks.

▶ Current trends – Business ideas emerge when a gap in the market arises due to current trends driving up demand. One such example is technological labour-saving devices; this has led to several businesses starting up manufacturing or distributing household robots. Examples include cleaning and mowing the lawn, or it might be simply for fun or as a conversation piece, such as the Christmas 2015 hype to own a BB-8 (a Star Wars decoration).

**Key terms**

**Business plan** – a written document that comprises all areas of a business proposal.

**Entrepreneur** – a person who sets up a business, taking a financial risk in the hope of making a profit.

**Franchise** – an authorised business arranged to operate as an agent for another company's products or services.

▶ Likely demand – Business ideas can also arise by anticipating a likely demand for a product or service. This might occur when a gap in the market is possible because of another business operation. For example, an increased demand for somewhere to play tennis, as a result of the UK's potential success at major events, could be forecast as an opportunity to turn waste ground into a commercial tennis court. Another example might be that, when celebrity chef Jamie Oliver campaigned for a tax on sugary drinks, a business idea emerged to find alternative ways of sweetening drinks or manufacturing drinks to fulfil the current demand. When the UK government announced a sugar tax in its 2016 spring budget, it is possible that some businesses were already anticipating a likely demand for an alternative source in readiness for the tax introduction in 2018.

> **Research**
>
> Try out the NHS sugar app (which you can download from the NHS Change4Life website). Identify an opportunity in the market for a low-sugar or sugar-free product.

## 'Developing' business

Business ideas are required for developing a business. A business needs to evolve over time to maintain a market share and demand for its services or products. For example, a garage servicing and repairing cars will rely on technology to diagnose problems and assist in remediation. As consumers all have higher expectations about the service they receive and the products they believe they need, businesses need to respond to those expectations. Other factors also influence how businesses develop.

### ▶ Changes in the economic climate

Changes in the economic climate drive and influence how businesses develop and how they succeed or fail. When the government announced the need for more homes, offices and retail outlets which could sustain the long-term future of Britain's growing population, the construction industry had to find ways to build sustainable infrastructure, ie buildings and services which will last for many years.

One such change in the economic climate is the introduction of the sugar tax previously mentioned. Business ideas may well emerge to develop a business, such as ways to respond to the changes in the demand for different raw materials or processed products which can be used to manufacture these alternative drinks.

M&S identified an opportunity when they introduced their 'Dine in for Two' promotion as an alternative to eating out during a recession when consumers had less disposable income yet still wanted the occasional treat.

### ▶ Trends

Businesses are influenced by trends and changes in lifestyle. One such example is the clothing industry. Fashion dictates the majority of clothing that is manufactured, the materials used and the styles that appear in the shops. Trends also develop business ideas by the way products are manufactured, from the machinery and technology used and the way businesses are run. Profits drive a business and organisations are constantly striving to become more efficient and productive while reducing costs. Job roles change and one such example is the way that managers are now often required to perform their own administrative tasks whereas until the early to mid-1990s it was still fairly routine for businesses to employ secretaries.

When Ocado introduced its unique home service grocery delivery, in response to changes in the way people run their lives and fill their leisure time, other businesses, such as Iceland, Tesco and Asda followed suit.

▶ How did this business idea respond to current trends?

▶ **Competition may force diversification for survival**

**Diversification** may be forced upon a business and require the organisation to develop whether it wants to or not, purely to survive. If the competition is taking your market share, perhaps because they have diversified their services or products and your business has not moved with the times, then it is possible that it will fail. When Woolworths closed stores in late 2008 and ceased trading in early 2009, it was claimed the reason for its failure was because it had not diversified and continued to operate as it had for generations. Of course, diversification may not always be a good thing. Traditional outfitters, corner shops and specialist services do exist as they have a **niche** market and diversifying could be criticised by their loyal customers.

**⏸ PAUSE POINT**　　What business ideas can you identify which were short lived as they met a current trend but failed to diversify or develop?

　　　　**Hint**　　Read about how Dutch electrical giant Philips got ideas for their products. What happened to their business and why?

　　　　**Extend**　　What new business ideas have emerged due to changes in the economic climate?

## Purpose and structure of the business

Every business, no matter how small, needs to have a clear purpose and structure. The structure is like a framework which joins all the parts together. Even the smallest of businesses such as a street shoe cleaner has a structure. A business may have limited or unlimited liability. If the business is limited liability, the owners/shareholders are only responsible for the debts of the business up to the value of their stake in the business. So if a shareholder has invested £1000 to start up a business, and the business has limited liability, that shareholder is only responsible for debts of the business up to £1000. If the business has unlimited liability, the shareholder who invested £1000 could be liable for any amount of the business's debts. The purpose is to perform a service cleaning people's shoes. The structure would be described in the parts shown in Figure 7.1.

> **Key terms**
>
> **Diversification** – alternative products or services which differ from the traditional or routine operations, products and services.
>
> **Niche market** – a small group of customers for a specialised item.
>
> **Micro business** – a business employing up to nine members of staff.

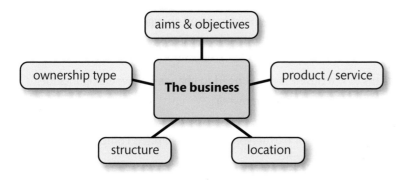

▶ **Figure 7.1:** Even the smallest businesses need a structure

## Aims and objectives

The aims and objectives of a business describe how the organisation plans to achieve its goals. Every business needs aims and objectives – just as every lesson you attend has aims defining the purpose and outcome of the lesson and objectives are planned to identify how to achieve the aim. Although these aims and objectives might be less formal in a **micro business**, every business must have a purpose and outcome.

## Product/service

The next part of the framework identifies the product or service the business provides. Without a clear framework, some businesses can lose focus – this was much of the criticism aimed at Woolworth's.

> **Discussion**
>
> Which businesses can you recall where you were not clear about their main focus? Perhaps you have wandered into a retailer and out again, feeling confused about their purpose. Discuss with a peer.

## Types of ownership

Businesses are owned in one of three ways: private, public and not-for-profit, and how they are owned can help define the purpose of the business. For example, a not-for-profit business is usually related to a charitable organisation such as BBOWT (Berks, Bucks and Oxon Wildlife Trust), a regional organisation with the purpose of protecting local wildlife. Larger charitable organisations include OXFAM.

Privately-owned businesses can vary from micro to **macro businesses**. Examples at micro level include local garages, trades such as hairdressers, plumbers, decorators and electricians. Macro businesses include Virgin Atlantic and construction and agricultural machinery giant JCB. Health food chain Holland and Barrett is also privately-owned and forms part of the largest private organisation (the Carlyle Group) in the world.

 **PAUSE POINT**  What publicly-owned businesses can you identify?

> Hint
>
> You will have learnt about some publicly-owned businesses and what the term means earlier in your course. Look back through your notes to remind yourself.

> Extend
>
> Can you name any businesses that changed their ownership? Why did they do so? For example, search online and look at Jessops in 2013.

## Reasons why a business may need to change its ownership

During the life of a business its ownership might change due to various reasons. For example, the business might be sold to another investor, perhaps because a **capital investment** is needed and the current owner cannot or chooses not to invest further.

Other reasons why a business might need to change its ownership include:

- age, death or divorce of current owner
- change of business operation
- change of sole trader or partnership to private limited company possibly for financial and legal reasons
- a corporate buyout where another organisation or group of people invest in the ownership of the business
- **merger** with another business
- business failure.

## The structure of the business

### Flat

A flat structure is a simple example of how a micro business might structure the personnel which make up the organisation. Larger businesses are not excluded from any type of structure but each has advantages and disadvantages.

> **Key terms**
>
> **Macro business** – a large employer, possibly employing over 250 members of staff.
>
> **Capital investment** – funds (money) paid into a business to further its development to meet its goals.
>
> **Merger** – when one or more organisations combine operations and financial arrangements and change ownership.

> **Link**
>
> See also *Unit 1: Exploring Business* on business structure.

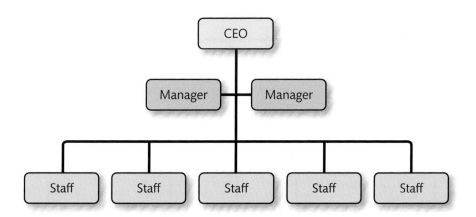

▶ **Figure 7.2:** An example of a flat structure: there is only one level of management between the CEO and the staff

## Matrix

The matrix type of structure is complex. It brings together teams of people depending on their abilities to work on specific projects. BT puts together teams of employees to work on projects, as does Google. Other examples include sporting teams such as football clubs Manchester United, Real Madrid and Bayern Munich, and CASCAR, Canada's stock car touring division.

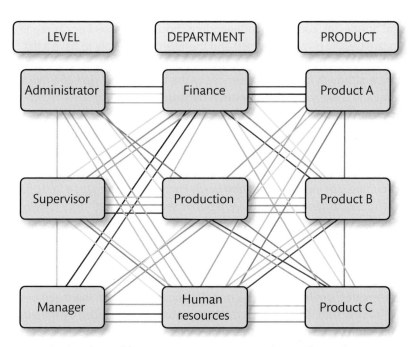

Each coloured line represents a team made up of members from one or more of the levels, departments and products

▶ **Figure 7.3:** An example of a matrix structure

## Hierarchical

As the name suggests, this structure shows a hierarchy of responsibility and authority showing who is responsible for what and who has authority to make decisions regarding business operations. This type of structure is fairly easy to understand and, as Figure 7.4 shows, there is one person with overall responsibility and authority for the business and everyone else has a clear position in the organisation.

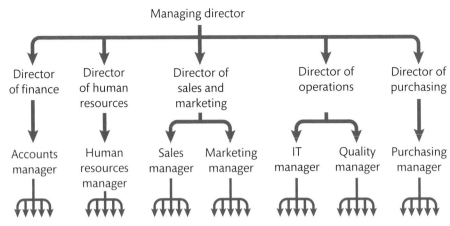

▶ **Figure 7.4:** An example of a hierarchical structure

### The location of the business

Where a business is located will help determine its purpose and structure. For example, a business structure might be influenced by the geographical culture of its location and the purpose of a business can also be determined by its location. One example is the number of fresh fish restaurants in seaside towns, another is the curiosity shops you can still find in the backstreets of tourist areas, but a small business renting out sun loungers would not be found in the middle of a city.

#### Local

Small, local businesses, such as an independent shop, hairdressers or car repair workshop, are usually privately-owned and therefore most likely to have a flat structure. Some local businesses might also be franchises. However, your local council office, although it provides a service to the local area, is part of a much bigger organisation and is likely to have a hierarchical structure.

#### National

Many businesses are part of national and international organisations and fewer smaller, local businesses remain, possibly due to the competitive market situation. National businesses will have a variety of structures which may depend on the corporate culture. For example, the John Lewis Partnership operates a fairly flat structure whereas, as mentioned above, a public sector local authority is likely to structure its operations hierarchically.

#### International

**Link**

See also *Unit 5: International Business*.

International businesses offer their products or services globally. Amazon is one example of an extremely well known, international business and it runs its operations as separate entities, similar to that of a matrix structure although managed overall by a fairly flat structure. This type of structure is possibly influenced by the business distributing through the internet rather than direct through a number of outlets. Another international business example is British Airways. This also operates a fairly flat structure, which was introduced after a significant change in management in 2008.

---

**⏸ PAUSE POINT**   What are the purposes and structures of your favourite businesses?

**Hint**   List those you visit most and search for their structures and aims using their websites and other corporate material.

**Extend**   Search online for more information about hierarchy and the different ways that well-known companies organise their operations. Why do they organise themselves in this way?

---

# Evaluation, justification and synthesis of business ideas

At the start of a business, an investment is made in its future that is not purely financial but also emotional and physical. None of the stages a business goes through can be undertaken lightly and without well-informed or justified decisions being made. Even when a snap decision is made, a complex, **cognitive** process has taken place.

Each of the units you have been studying involve levels of evaluation, just as when you make a purchase or consider upgrading your mobile phone, even if no additional fee is required. When you evaluate, you are cognitively processing information and drawing on new knowledge. The information you have processed, the amount and the quality of that information is then used to justify the decision you make. This complex process is **iterative**, as represented simply by Figure 7.5.

**Key terms**

**Cognitive** – acquiring and processing information which is undertaken mentally.

**Iterative** – an iterative process is one where you come to the desired result by means of a repeated cycle of operations.

**Synthesise** – to combine two or more components, such as information.

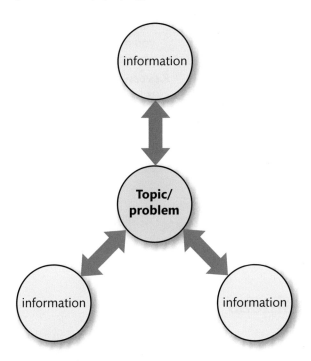

▸ **Figure 7.5:** Iterative cognitive cycle

**Research**

You can learn more about problem solving techniques and cognition by searching online.

Information can inform or generate a problem or issue to resolve; any decision to be made is a problem-solving activity. When you acquire knowledge you will need to process it, and the more knowledge you gather the more you will need to **synthesise** it. You may have heard this term before, in particular when studying subjects like English literature. It means combining information, such as from two chapters of different books, to develop a conclusion around both pieces of text.

A business needs to evolve, which could be in response to any one or combination of reasons: new ideas, developing the business or as with British Airways, restructuring or changes to ownership. Each or all of these factors will be used to form a decision, for example the type of restructure which will best respond to market forces or the personnel within the business. If a business changes premises, perhaps due to expansion, then another set of decisions will be required through an evaluative process.

Arborist (tree specialist) Anthea, has taken over the family nursery from her elderly uncle. As it is the only nursery in their medium-sized town, Anthea would like to expand the business into a landscaping company. She has identified likely demand from corporate operations landscaping their grounds to families looking to re-landscape their personal spaces. She's also noticed an increase in TV programmes about garden landscaping and lots of news reports about a tree disease that will mean another species is likely to become popular. Many new homes have been built in the town recently as well.

Anthea thinks she will have to increase the number of employees, initially from three to ten, and expand the nursery's premises. She knows she will need to produce a business plan to help her secure additional funding and might need assistance in determining how best to manage a larger workforce. Anthea knows a lot about her market but she has little training or knowledge about formal business operations. You have been hired to help her ensure she makes the correct decisions in planning the next steps of her business and assist in writing the business plan. You will need to help Anthea identify the aims and objectives of her business and also identify what pieces of information she should examine closely to make sure she's making the right decisions. You will need to write a conclusion for Anthea, using the information you have gathered, to justify her business decision to expand.

### Plan
- Where are you going to begin?
- What information have you been given?
- What else are you likely to need?

### Do
- Have you organised everything so you do not feel overwhelmed by what you are being asked to do?
- Do you have all the information provided?
- Have you kept a checklist of what you need to do and the time you are allocating to complete everything?

### Review
- What did you gain from undertaking this activity?
- What worked well and what not so well?
- How will you ensure you can repeat the processes or actions that worked well?

# B   Decision making in business

Decision making plays a significant part in business and the decisions made can make or break a business. There are many examples of situations where decisions have resulted in business growth, increases in market share and market leadership. But there are also instances where bad decision making has resulted in loss of potential growth and even led to closure, for example the oversight by Kodak in 1975 when one of its engineers invented a digital camera and decided it would have limited demand.

## Sources for data collection

There are two types of research: primary and secondary. The difference between them relates to whether the research is original to the organisation conducting the research (it gathered the data) or whether it came from another source (the data had already been gathered). Within these categories, information can either be internal (from inside the organisation) or external (from another organisation or source outside the organisation).

> **Link**
>
> See also *Unit 1: Exploring Business*, *Unit 2: Developing a Marketing Campaign*, *Unit 19: Pitching for a New Business* and *Unit 22: Market Research* for more on types of data and data collection.

## Primary sources

Primary research is information that the business has gathered first-hand and that has not been gathered before. Therefore the data is original in that although the questions in a survey might be repeated, the responses are new information. Even if the information gained from the methods used is similar, or the results are the same, it will still be considered as original and current. Primary sources can be derived internally and externally using a variety of methods.

Internal primary research data sources include:

▶ production costs

▶ sales figures

▶ employee records such as CVs and appraisals

▶ repeat customer details.

External primary research methods include:

▶ customer responses from trials of new products or services

▶ questionnaires and surveys such as online feedback forms

▶ interviews and focus groups

▶ mystery shoppers.

## Secondary sources

Secondary research uses data and information that has been collected before, either from within the organisation (internal) or by another organisation (external). Secondary research is sometimes referred to as 'desk research' and sources include those shown in Table 7.1.

▶ **Table 7.1:** Types of secondary research

| Types | Internal | External |
|---|:---:|:---:|
| Reports from sales and regional representatives | ✓ | |
| Previous marketing research | ✓ | |
| Trade journals and websites | | ✓ |
| Books and newspapers | | ✓ |
| Industry reports from industry associations and government departments | | ✓ |
| Census data and public records | | ✓ |

▶ Internal examples include business data on customers and financial records which can be obtained from loyalty cards, such as those used by Boots, Nectar and Avios. Loyalty cards offer rewards, often in the form of vouchers or points to be exchanged for other goods, services or leisure activities. Data collected can include sales records which identify customer preferences and information about how people like to live their lives. These enable a business to market similar products or sell the data to other organisations, such as those selling insurance or financial packages.

▶ External examples include commercially published reports such as those produced by the government which inform market and economic trends. Data collections and publications are also provided by the Chamber of Commerce on a smaller scale, which are of particular interest to small and medium-sized enterprises (SMEs) and micro business owners. International data collection and statistical analysis is provided by organisations such as the Organisation for Economic Co-operation and Development (OECD) and the Office for National Statistics.

> **Link**
>
> Information on mystery shoppers can be found in *Unit 14: Investigating Customer Service.*

Businesses need to be aware of the limitations of secondary research as the basis for making decisions as it may no longer be relevant.

## Storage

There are rules about storing as well as how we use data. This doesn't just mean whose data we can and can't share as set out in the Data Protection Act but also the length of time we must keep data.

### ▶ Security of information

Information should be kept secure in accordance with the nature and sensitivity of that information. In business, there is a legal requirement to store information securely and there are rules dictating how information is stored and for what period of time, according to different industries.

> **Reflect**
>
> How would you feel if you knew someone had access to your personal information? Especially if that information was something particularly personal that you thought no one else knew.

Requirements for storing data electronically are also changing. In addition to passwords, data encryption and permissions rights, there are also rules depending on the frequency and methods used for keeping information secure.

### ▶ Legislative

It is crucial that businesses are up to date with the legal requirements around data storage; the consequences of disregarding these are severe. The main legislation in relation to storing information is the Data Protection Act 1998 and the Computer Misuse Act 1990.

### ▶ Regulatory and ethical issues

Government regulations vary according to the country where the business is registered or located. However, businesses will need to ensure they frequently monitor impending changes to any legislation or regulation, which they can do via electronic alerts. There is an ethical imperative for all businesses to keep information secure; oversights can happen although they are not excusable.

> **Reflect**
>
> Have you ever considered that simply sharing a friend's phone number or address with a third party, without your friend's knowledge or permission, however innocent this might be, is unethical and illegal? Have you ever put someone on the spot and asked them for their password perhaps to use their phone or email address, without realising you are breaking the law?

There have been several instances where businesses have unlawfully sold customer data to other businesses without permission and the law was changed in an endeavour to prevent such unethical practice. The process of trawling through data and using it for other means which is passed to a third party is known as data mining.

## Analysis, comparison and evaluation of data

As data collection is now so widespread, much of the data that is collected might not ever be analysed. Data collection in business, however, should have a defined purpose to ensure it is not a worthless exercise.

To inform a business plan, the data will be analysed and comparisons made with other sources to check its reliability and validity. Once analyses and comparisons are made, it is possible to evaluate what can be learned from the data. Probably the most important stages are to plan, identify and prepare – as shown in Figure 7.6.

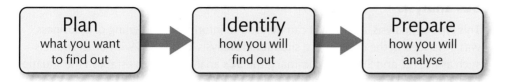

▶ **Figure 7.6:** The 'PIP' model

Collecting data is probably the easiest part of the process and requires a structure to be able to manage the data without becoming thoroughly overwhelmed. Once the analyses have been undertaken, the comparisons and evaluation are used to predict consequences, provide reasonable alternatives and justify the solutions.

**Link**

See also *Unit 2: Developing a Marketing Campaign* and *Unit 22: Market Research*.

⏸ **PAUSE POINT**  When have you carried out your own research? What stages did you follow? What would you do differently next time?

**Hint**  Perhaps you researched booking a holiday or choosing this course? Jot down the data you gathered and where you got it from. How did you synthesise the information, make comparisons and form your evaluations? What criteria helped you make a decision?

**Extend**  Prepare and carry out a small-scale research activity to find suitable kennels for your young puppy, who must stay indoors, while you are away.

# The use of business models to aid decision making

Theoretical models are often used in business decision making. This is to ensure that decision making follows a consistent structure which has been tried and tested many times before rather than a random set of actions which may cost the business in lost time and effort. Business models can also help managers to recognise where there are gaps in their knowledge or processes which need to be filled before implementing a decision which could fail. You will have already learnt about two of the following four business models in this section so now you will consider them specifically in a decision-making context.

**Links**

For more on business models see:
- *Unit 1: Exploring Business*
- *Unit 5: International Business*
- *Unit 6: Principles of Management*
- *Unit 19: Pitching for a New Business.*

## Porter's five forces model

In *Unit 1: Exploring Business*, *Unit 5: International Business* and *Unit 19: Pitching for a New Business* you looked at Porter's five forces model and how it is used to evaluate the position of a business in terms of its competition. Five categories are considered:

▶ existing competitive rivalry between suppliers

▶ threat of new market entrants

▶ bargaining power of buyers

▶ power of suppliers

▶ threat of substitute products (including technology change).

In terms of decision making, analysis and evaluation, using this model as a framework provides prompts which will help to interrogate your data. For example, the analyses have been undertaken and you have begun to form your evaluations which you will consider in relation to each of the five categories.

## 5Cs analysis

This type of analysis, and how it can be used to inform the marketing of a business, was described in the context of a situational analysis, combined with other models such as PESTLE and SWOT. In summary, the **5Cs** analysis aims to establish the situation of a business as part of the overall decision-making process.

Each category is analysed by responding to questions which seek to identify, for example, the components that make up each of the 5Cs (see Table 5.6 in *Unit 5: International Business*). This type of analysis is used to inform business operations as it focuses on current internal operations using data and statistics.

> **Key term**
>
> **5Cs** – company, collaborators, customers, competitors, climate

## Ansoff Matrix

This model is used to enable a business to make decisions about the opportunities for growth in the market place. A business would consider using this model when wanting to evaluate and justify opportunities for introducing new products or for product growth.

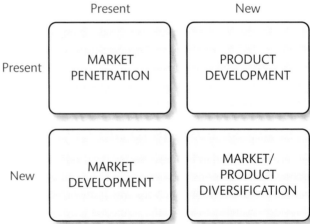

▶ **Figure 7.7:** The Ansoff Matrix (from Strategies for diversification, *Harvard Business Review*, 35(5), pp. 113–24 (Ansoff, I. 1957), with permission from Harvard Business School Publishing)

The purpose of this model is to assist with decision making by considering whether the product is new or existing or whether the market is new or an existing market. Its founder, H. Igor Ansoff, developed the model to help focus on four main areas in decision making: market penetration, product development, market development and diversification.

## Boston Matrix

The fourth model you will learn about in relation to decision making at this stage is the Boston Matrix. The Boston Matrix (also known as the BCG Matrix due to its 1970s founders – the Boston Consulting Group) is concerned with both the market share and market growth.

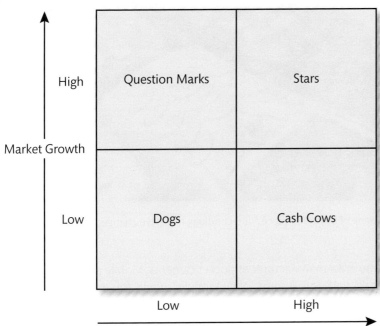

**BCG Matrix**

▶ **Figure 7.8:** The Boston Matrix
Source: The Boston Consulting Group, adapted from The BCG Portfolio Matrix from the Product Portfolio Matrix, © 1970, The Boston Consulting Group (BCG)

This model is used to aid decision making by helping predict where a business should invest in the future. The matrix helps with analyses concerned with market trends and considering opportunities for increasing market share. The terms used roughly translate to:

▶ question marks – no or little profit but could become stars or cash cows as they are in a growth market

▶ stars – could become stars of the business with some investment

▶ dogs – low market share and low market growth but do not require much investment

▶ cash cows – the most profitable and low market growth.

For example, what should a business do when an existing product, which has proved to be profitable and popular, is likely to lose its popularity according to current trends; while a new product is costly to produce and market, produces very little if any profit, but is situated in a growth area? Where would the business place its investment? This model helps those decision-making processes.

▶ Can you think of any other pieces of technology that have changed from 'cows' to 'dogs'?

**PAUSE POINT**

Imagine you are a manufacturer of pocket cameras. Mobile phones have increased ability to take and store photos. What model(s) would you use to help you to decide the pocket camera's future?

Hint

Try each of the four models using this scenario. Which one works best or is a combination more effective? Is there an order to which models you apply?

Extend

Select a model or models for a similar scenario: you are now responsible for the future of Fujifilm Instax camera range.

## Techniques to analyse data effectively for business purposes

You have been learning about types of data sources and different business models to aid decision making. In this section, you will learn more about some of the techniques used to analyse data. You will probably have used some of these terms during maths activities and in exams or assignments undertaken previously. You will start with the meaning of some of the values.

### Representative values

The term refers to a series of steps or calculations to establish the overall value of a dataset which may have been collected through primary or secondary sources. These representative values are used to present findings and justify recommendations to help decision making. For example, we are told in advertisements about the number of people who prefer brand X to brand Y; the evidence presented is usually as a percentage of the total number surveyed. In sales reports, we are often presented with the proportion of sales or the average sales over the last six months etc. These values are then used to identify trends over time.

## Mean, median, mode

There are three common procedures – **mean**, **median** and **mode** – used to establish representative values.

### Worked example

Calculating the mean.

**Step 1**: Add up the **raw data**: 5, 2, 6, 8, 6, 7, 2, 4, 9, 3.
Total = 52

**Step 2**: Count up how many values are in the list.
Total = 10

**Step 3**: Divide the total sum (Step 1) by the total number of values (Step 2).
52 ÷ 10 = 5.2
The mean is 5.2

Depending on whether a decimal place is required, this figure would normally be rounded up or rounded down, depending on the value after the decimal place. The standard rule is that any number up to 0.5 will be rounded down, therefore this answer would be 5. Decimal values of 5 and above will be rounded up to the next whole number. In mathematical terms, whole numbers are referred to as integer numbers.

| Key terms |
| --- |

**Mean** – the average of all the figures (mathematically referred to as values), arrived at by adding all the values together and dividing them by the number of values in the list.

**Median** – the middle amount, not the average but the middle in a set of values when placed in numerical order.

**Mode** – the value (figure) that appears most commonly in a set of figures. The mode is also referred to as the modal value.

**Raw data** – original data collected before analysis is undertaken.

### Worked example

Calculating the median.

In a simple case where there is an odd number of values in a list, then take the middle number. However, where there is an even number of values in the list, as in our example, then the process is slightly different:

**Step 1**: Re-write the original numbers provided: 5, 2, 6, 8, 6, 7, 2, 4, 9, 3 into numerical order.
2, 2, 3, 4, 5, 6, 6, 7, 8, 9

**Step 2**: Find the middle two (pair) numbers.
The pair here is 5 and 6.

**Step 3**: Add them together = 11

**Step 4**: Divide the number in half
11 ÷ 2 = 5.5

The median in this example is 5.5

This means that half of the list is comprised of numbers greater than 5.5 and the other half comprises numbers valued at less than 5.5.

## Worked example

Calculating the mode.

**Step 1**: Re-write the original numbers provided: 5, 2, 6, 8, 6, 7, 2, 4, 9, 3.
2, 2, 3, 4, 5, 6, 6, 7, 8, 9

**Step 2**: Find the values that appear most often. In this example, 2 and 6. Therefore the mode (or in this case bimodal) are both 2 and 6.

The mode will only be determined where any number is repeated more than once, otherwise there is no mode. A mode is only useful if there are some values repeated more than others and not where all numbers are repeated the same number of times. If there are more than two modes then this is referred to as multimodal.

> **Tip**
>
> You can learn more about how to apply these terms from online sources or by joining a forum such as Dr Math.

Of course, when working with larger datasets, you may be comparing two or more sets of data to identify the mode, mean or median.

### Calculation from raw data and frequency distributions using appropriate software

There are many tools for performing calculations using software available on a variety of digital devices as well as the traditional calculator or even mental arithmetic.

Using software does not replace the need to understand how calculations are performed and the formulae used. It is important that you are able to estimate the answer as a form of validation, rather than just relying on software to give you the answer.

> **Key term**
>
> **Frequency distribution** – the number of times a set of values occur and the spread of occurrences over a range of situations (or values).

Nevertheless, when working with large amounts of raw data, technology and appropriate software are invaluable and enable enormous amounts of data crunching to take place in seconds, which would have been impossible not so long ago. Some of the software used to perform **frequency distributions**, the most commonly used method of displaying analysed data, depending on the type and purpose of data, include those shown in Table 7.2.

▸ **Table 7.2:** Example software used for helping analyse data

| | | Microsoft Excel | Sage | Microsoft Access | SPSS | NVivo |
|---|---|---|---|---|---|---|
| Examples of context | Numerical and graphical | ✓ | | | | |
| | Accounts | | ✓ | | ✓ | |
| | Customer details, sales records | | | ✓ | ✓ | |
| | **Statistical** | | | | ✓ | |
| | Qualitative | | | | | ✓ |

> **Key term**
>
> **Statistics** – the result of complex analyses of raw data, often confused with being the term used to define the actual raw data.

When using software to analyse data, it is important to remember that the analysis and evaluation of the results still rely on people's insights. For example, NVivo (Table 7.2) is a specialist software package used to identify frequency distribution of words, terms, phrases etc. It is extremely useful when analysing very large amounts of qualitative data, such as customer feedback, and is used mostly in research studies, especially in higher education.

SPSS (Table 7.2) is a sophisticated software package produced by IBM and used by many major organisations for aggregating all business administrative activities and data in one central system. It requires considerable training and, as with any software package, the data coming out is only as reliable as what went in.

> **Reflect**
>
> How often do you check for errors when inputting data? Have you ever assumed an answer must be right because you used a calculator, but did not consider whether you may have put in the wrong numbers?

### Using the results to draw valid conclusions

After using various techniques to analyse the data, the next stage is to use the results to determine the conclusions and support the decisions to be made. For example, Fujifilm Instax may seek customers' feedback to determine whether or not the company should continue to manufacture that camera. The organisation could analyse sales figures but this will tell them little without customer feedback, especially feedback from those customers who decide to buy a different product. These results will help the business make a decision about their future plans and will be used when applying the business models to help with those decisions.

Using different techniques to help with the analysis of data is also likely to require you to make comparisons of the analyses. For example, you may need to compare trends from sales figures with the comments that customers make. This will involve analysing both quantitative and qualitative data.

## Measures of dispersion

This is the term given to the spread of the dataset and there are statistical methods for finding this out.

### Standard deviation for small and large samples

The standard deviation means the amount that the values vary beyond the norm. The standard deviation for a small sample might be significant whereas the larger the sample, the smaller the deviation might appear. To calculate the standard deviation requires a calculation based on finding the square root of the variance. To calculate the variance there is a mathematical formula:

$$\text{Variance} = \sigma^2 = \frac{\Sigma(x_r - \mu)^2}{n}$$

The standard deviation is the square root of the variance.

## Worked example

Take the values used earlier to calculate the mean: 5, 2, 6, 8, 6, 7, 2, 4, 9, 3. The mean was 5.

**Step 1:** Take each value in turn and subtract the mean from the value (eg 5 – 5; 2 – 5 etc).
0, –3, 1, 3, 1, 2, –3, –1, 4, 2

**Step 2:** Square each of the results from Step 1 (multiple by themselves) to get rid of any minus signs.
0, 9, 1, 9, 1, 4, 9, 1, 16, 4

**Step 3:** Add up all the results from Step 2.
Total = 54

**Step 4:** Divide the total in Step 3 by n, which represents the total number of numbers (10)
$54 \div 10 = 5.4$

**Step 5:** To arrive at the standard deviation take the square root of the answer you arrived at in Step 4.
$\sqrt{5.4} = 2.3$

> **Tip**
>
> You can learn more about standard deviation and practise some tasks by going online and trying some revision maths.

### Typical uses (statistical process: control, buffer stock levels)

As you can see, there are complex processes for making decisions and using calculations. Some of the typical uses for this statistical process include:

▶ **Control** – such as controlling stock levels by not placing orders for the same product in the same quantities without deviating. Looking at trends over time might suggest that the month of August is generally cooler and wetter than July and September. Therefore an organisation selling outdoor BBQs may make a decision to reduce stock levels in August, although may increase them slightly and temporarily for September, especially if weather forecasts are good. The statistical process would be used to manage stock attrition especially with the onset of autumn and fewer BBQs being sold as winter approaches.

▶ **Buffer stock levels** – by analysing the data and studying the trends over time, the standard deviation might suggest that additional stock needs to be ordered and available as a buffer. For example, a leisurewear company selling swimwear, sun lotion and sun hats would analyse weather forecasts, for changes in summer temperatures and other patterns in previous sales, such as school and Bank holidays or special sporting occasions like the Olympics, so that they can cope if there is suddenly a greater demand for their products.

Business leaders may be able to guess at the weather, using personal experience, and make a decision but should never do so. The data will confirm a theory or break a theory and the statistical analysis is required to substantiate any business decision made.

> **Link**
>
> See also *Unit 2: Developing a Marketing Campaign* for more on the uses of research data.

# Calculation

There are multiple calculations to be performed when undertaking statistical processes. These will involve the use of quartiles, percentiles and correlation coefficient.

▶ **Quartiles**: this means to put the data in order or size, then divide the values into four equal parts. Using the data used earlier, we have 10 values, so the first quartile comes between the second and third value (since 10 ÷ 4 = 2.5). This means it comes between 2 and 3. The second quartile is the fifth value (since 2.5 × 2 = 5) so it is 5 in this case. The third quartile comes between the seventh and eighth values (since 2.5 × 3 = 7.5) so it is between 6 and 7 in this case.

| 2, 2, | 3, 4, | 5, 6, 6, | 7, 8, 9 |
|---|---|---|---|
| 1st quartile | 2nd quartile | 3rd quartile | 4th quartile |

These represent:

| 1st quartile = 2.5 | 2nd quartile = 5 | 3rd quartile = 6.5 | 4th quartile = 9 |
|---|---|---|---|

Presenting information as quartiles is done to demonstrate the spread and uses a concept which represents the median (which is the second quartile).

▶ **Percentiles**: a percentile is a value below which a given percentage of observations fall. For example, if we take the data above, the 50th percentile is 5 and is the value up to and including which 50% (half) of the values fall. Similarly, 75% of the values fall up to and including 6.5.

| 1st quarter = 2.5 | 2nd quarter = 5 | 3rd quarter = 6.5 |
|---|---|---|
| 25th percentile | 50th percentile | 75th percentile |

The important point to remember with calculating percentiles is that the data must be in order if representing, for example, height or weight. In the example used, the values may be related to sales figures for each of ten months, possibly a seasonal business which closes over the two coldest (or hottest) months of the year.

▶ **Correlation coefficient**: a number that gives an idea of the degree of relationship between two variables. Values of the correlation coefficient vary between –1 and 1. A value of 1 means that the two variables are directly related (if you plot a graph showing the two variables there will be a straight line with gradient 1). You might get such a relationship between sales of ice cream and temperature (as temperature increases so do sales of ice cream). A value of –1 means that there is a negative correlation between the two variables – such as relationship might also be found between sales of ice cream and temperature, but this time sales of ice cream decrease as temperature decreases.

**Research**

Learn more about using statistical data from using the website Explorable. There is an app you can download for easy access.

---

**PAUSE POINT**    Which parts of data analysis have you found easy? Which parts have you found harder?

Hint    You can get more practice by trying out the examples from the website Maths is Fun.

Extend    Try practising statistical analysis using data from the ONS and OECD to find out, for example, the trends for births or the deviation in gender split of the UK population or perhaps business trends using BIS reports.

# Appropriate formats for decision making in a business context

After analysing the data, it is important to present it in different and appropriate formats for the decision making process.

## Creation and interpretation of graphs using spreadsheets

Graphical representation is a fairly common way of presenting information for making decisions as it is easier to understand and process the information. When you use graphs, you are more able to visualise patterns in data, extract trends and interpret the data to use in making decisions. However, initially it is important to understand the difference between the different types of graphs and their purposes and to consider the potential audience. The suitability of different colours, shapes, fonts and sizes must be considered carefully as these may not be accessible to everyone.

Creating graphs and charts is made relatively easy with spreadsheet software and the range of templates that come as standard. A simple way of creating a chart in most spreadsheet software is highlighting the data area and pressing F11. However, you should be aware that this will randomly produce a chart without ensuring that it is appropriate and fit for purpose.

> **Tip**
>
> Select the graph type according to the type of data, its purpose and the intended audience.

Here you will explore four types of graphs.

▶ **Line graph**: these types of graphs are used to identify trends over time. In Figure 7.9 the monthly sales figures are used to portray the trends over the last ten months. Assume for the purposes of this exercise that the figures represent the amount of revenue taken (in £000s) for sales of afternoon tea at a stately home between the months of February and November. The other two months, January and December, they were closed for urgent refurbishment.

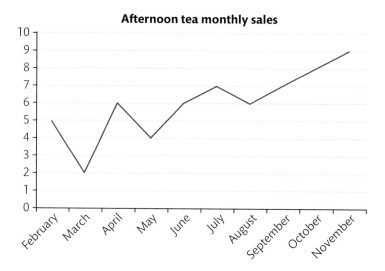

▶ **Figure 7.9:** An example of a line graph

If you study the graph in Figure 7.9 you will see almost instantly that sales grew from August to November and the least successful months during this period were March and May. By presenting the figures in this way, decision makers are prompted to ask questions, such as:

1   Why are there peaks and troughs in those months?

2   What made sales grow from August?

3   Why did May show significant decline following a particularly successful month?

Although this line graph does not display any references along the **axis** other than the title and each of the **series labels**, these can be added during construction or afterwards. It is common to include a **legend** and any labels which help to identify the information being presented.

### Tip

Avoid cluttering your graphs with too many labels. If you have included too many then double click into the graph to highlight the image and press delete. If you make a mistake, select undo (Ctrl Z).

If you find it hard to distinguish between the labels for the axis, the simple way to remember is that the X axis runs 'a cross' and therefore the Y axis must run up and down.

▶ **Pie chart**: this type of graph is probably the one most commonly used incorrectly. A pie chart is for presenting percentages as opposed to raw data and can only be used for representing single sets of figures. They are easy to interpret and can instantly be recognisable and familiar. Figure 7.10 shows the figures used above represented in a pie chart.

### Key terms

**Axis** – the sides of the graph which run horizontally and vertically and are represented by X (horizontal) and Y (vertical).

**Series labels** – the series are the data types and the labels are the names attached to the series, in this case the value of monthly sales figures and the months of the year, along each axis.

**Legend** – the term attributed to a key or list of terms and meanings (such as used in Figure 7.11 for the colours which represent each month in the chart) where an explanation is required.

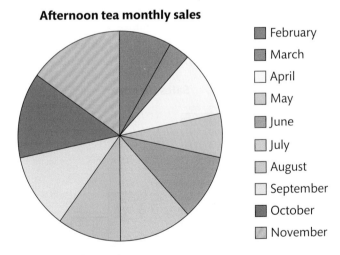

**Afternoon tea monthly sales**

- February
- March
- April
- May
- June
- July
- August
- September
- October
- November

▶ **Figure 7.10:** An example of a pie chart

When looking at the pie chart you can instantly interpret the data and recognise patterns in the monthly sales figures. Even the smallest months for revenue are distinguishable. The percentages in pie charts always add up to 100. Any decimal places will be rounded up or down depending on the number placed after the decimal.

In Figure 7.10, for the purposes of being able to visualise quickly, the labels have been added against each slice of the pie chart. These can be added during the construction of the graph or simply by reformatting the graph afterwards.

▶ **Bar charts**: these types of charts are commonly used to represent blocks of data, such as monthly sales figures, and are easily understood, especially for anyone with a visual impairment. When using a spreadsheet chart template, the bar chart runs horizontally whereas you may have more commonly referred to a vertical series (labelled in templates as a column chart) as a bar chart.

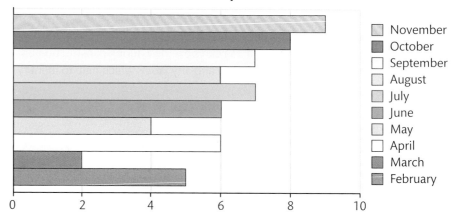

▶ **Figure 7.11:** An example of a bar chart

In Figure 7.11, the monthly sales figures, running horizontally, are displayed as even numbers and an adjustment to show every figure can be made by extending the size of the chart or by reformatting by double clicking into the various places on the image and selecting the options from the shortcut menu if using the mouse.

▶ **Histograms**: these types of graphs are similar to bar charts but group numbers into ranges. So, for example, a business might draw a histogram to show daily sales takings as shown in Figure 7.12. This type of graph can be found in the templates labelled as a column chart. A business may decide which range to present, depending on the decisions to be made. A histogram is used to display number ranges or frequencies but when the data is in categories then a bar chart should be used.

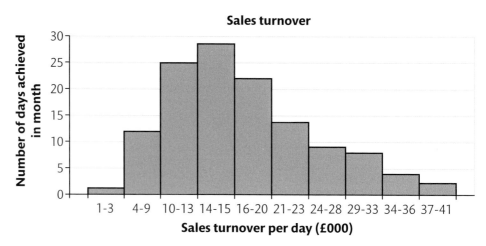

▶ **Figure 7.12:** An example of a histogram

## Scatter (XY) graphs and linear trend lines

These are used for **extrapolating** for forecasting (to check reliability). Scatter graphs are often used to establish whether or not there is a relationship between the X and Y axes. So far you have just been representing very simple information in your graphs using just the monthly sales figures. This time you will be using three lots of information by repeating the monthly sales figures, and months of the year but also including the number of days where special events fall throughout the year such as Mother's Day, Father's Day, Valentine's Day and Bank Holidays.

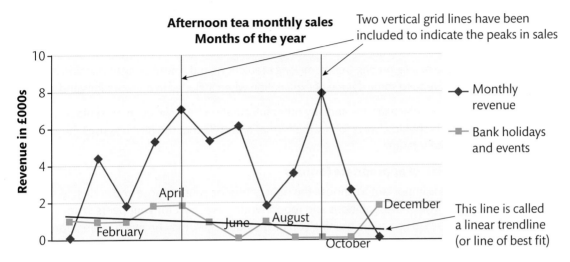

▶ **Figure 7.13:** An example of a scatter (XY) graph

The scatter graph in Figure 7.13 shows two sets of data, referenced by the legend and the label on the Y axis for the sales figures (in £000s). This graph also displays the two months when the hotel was closed for refurbishment represented by the starting point at zero and the end point also at zero sales. Only the labels for alternate months are also displayed to avoid cluttering the graph with too much information whilst providing a helpful reference point.

The trends representing the Bank Holidays and events are identified by what are referred to as linear trendlines (also called 'line of best fit'). The addition of a trendline (by selecting a series and choosing 'add trendline' from the shortcut menu), enables a quick visualisation of the pattern of events. Using linear trendlines provides data extrapolation for forecasting as it provides an element of reliability when making those decisions. Therefore a steady incline or decline over the year will help the business analyse the success of their afternoon teas and help them decide whether to keep offering them.

> **Tip**
>
> To learn how to create scatter graphs in Microsoft Excel®, try using the help function (F1) or by learning from online tutorials.

**Ⅱ**    **PAUSE POINT**    Which of these graphs did you find the easiest to interpret and which the more difficult? Why?

     **Hint**    Study each graph without reading the explanations and note what you can interpret from the data. Compare your findings and identify what you can as a collective group of charts.

     **Extend**    What function do the other graphs offered as Microsoft Excel® templates perform? Try representing data as a pivot table – what benefits do they provide and how do they enhance or replicate the function of graphs?

Tip

You can learn more about how to produce and use charts from the Maths is Fun website.

## Presentations and report writing

Link

See also *Unit 19: Pitching for a New Business* for more on preparing for and delivering presentations.

Graphs and charts are very useful for presenting information, prompting debate and analysing or interpreting trends, making predictions and contributing to decision making, but they require some degree of explanation when included in presentations and reports.

The way in which graphs and any other information is displayed in presentations and in reports should always follow the format and style that the business uses throughout its documentation.

### Utilisation of appropriate formats

Just as it is important to choose the right graph for your purpose and audience, the same is true of presentations and report writing. A report for your peers in your team, perhaps on some training you have undertaken, may be much more informal than a report you have been asked to produce for your manager. The same is true of presentations.

Tip

You can learn more about using outline in Microsoft Word® by searching online.

Another way to ensure you follow the appropriate format for a report or presentation is to use a template or, in the case of a presentation, to create a master slide containing all the relevant formatting and house style. There are multiple ways of ensuring you utilise the format required by the business when using presentation and word processing software, such as creating styles for all the headings and using 'outline view' to create a framework for your report.

It is absolutely vital that every report you produce is thoroughly proofread to ensure there are no errors and especially no omissions.

### Presentation software and techniques

The most commonly used software for creating presentations is Microsoft PowerPoint, though a number of other software packages are beginning to be more widely used. Not every business will use Microsoft and therefore it is useful to know what else is available. There are different software packages available for producing presentations, some of which are free. These include Prezi, Emaze, Presentia, Haiku Deck and PowToon. These presentation packages are becoming more popular. Some of the pitfalls when using presentation packages include:

▶ too much information

▶ information text too small or slides too cluttered for the audience to read

▶ too many features which cause confusion

▶ too much time and attention paid to animation and transition over quality of the content.

The golden rule with any presentation is to include only five or six bullet points of headline information. Therefore, although graphs are commonly used in presentations, any detailed explanation should be kept for the speaker's notes.

### Theory into practice

Explore alternative software for creating presentations and select one to produce three or four slides to convince a peer of the reasons for not using a mobile phone.

# Software-generated information for decision making in an organisation

Since the introduction of computers and technology, enormous amounts of data can be collated and crunched, saving significant time and enabling access to more information than ever before.

Apart from the bespoke software systems which exist in some organisations, there are several off-the-shelf systems which businesses rely on to process large amounts of information and generate reports. The information generated is used to aid decision making at strategic levels of the business.

## Management information systems

Computers and information-processing tools are used for operational, tactical and strategic levels of the business. Management information systems (MIS) are used to inform strategic decision making. Strategy is determined at higher levels of organisations, informing tactical plans and for operational teams to implement. MIS are used to organise and manage data by departments. Therefore Human Resources may use the system to contain all the staff records and generate reports such as:

▸ performance records
▸ appraisals schedules and outcomes
▸ promotion matching.

The registration and enrolment department in a college is likely to use the system for a different range of reports based on student information, such as:

▸ payment details
▸ course enrolments
▸ achievements and certification
▸ attendance
▸ leavers.

Organisations such as your place of study will use this information to strategically plan for ways of increasing attendance, punctuality and achievements, as well as many other aspects of their business planning.

## Project management

Project management is about structuring a clear and concise method for planning, implementing and concluding a project. The project management triangle (see Figure 7.14) shows how the elements time, cost and scope of a project are related. Projects can be large or small and there are numerous specialist software packages available, at differing levels of sophistication. Software available includes Microsoft Project, Intuit, Smartsheet, eTaskMaker and Wrike.

These are used to remind project planners of key dates, milestones and provide a ready built system which helps manage every aspect of the project management process.

Project management can be managed using paper-based systems, depending on the project's complexity, therefore not always requiring automated software. Readily available software includes spreadsheets and databases.

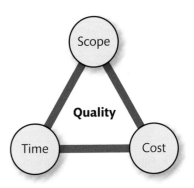

▸ **Figure 7.14:** The project triangle shows the three elements that must be considered when planning a project

## Networking and critical path analysis

Networking is the process of linking information or systems and people together to ensure all necessary information can be gathered into one place to use and share as appropriate. For example, a business selling components to a car manufacturer will need to know when to purchase or make more components in readiness for future orders. Therefore if the sales database does not link to purchase and production information any decisions made will be fragmented and could cost the business dearly.

A **critical path** analysis (CPA) relies on having the information in one central place so networking analysis can be undertaken to manage complex operations within their time constraints. Business operations involve projects as an ongoing function and a CPA is used to assess risk of projects failing or not meeting completion schedules. Each of these aspects is required to carry out a CPA:

▶ a full list of everything to be undertaken in the project

▶ the length of time each activity will need to be completed

▶ the relationships between each activity which indicate their dependency on each other.

The CPA performs a calculation based on the length of the overall project and the earliest and latest that an activity can start and finish without extending the length of the project.

### Gantt charts

Gantt charts are widely used as planning tools in business and even in leisure. It is not entirely unusual to see a rough plan setting out a timetable of activities, almost like a home-made calendar, especially for leisure activities like gardening.

The useful thing about a Gantt chart is that it is immediately visual and by using patterns, shading or colours it can help with project planning. Gantt charts, or something similar, are often used in academic organisations for displaying timetabling and room arrangements as a very simple and meaningful tool which requires little if any training to understand it.

| ID | Task Name | Duration (weeks) | Nov 2016 1W | Dec 2016 1W | 2W | 3W | 4W | Jan 2017 1W | 2W | 3W | 4W | Feb 2017 1W | 2W | 3W | 4W | Mar 2017 1W | 2W | 3W | 4W | Apr 2017 1W | 2W | 3W | 4W | May 2017 1W | 2W | 3W | 4W |
|---|---|---|---|---|---|---|---|---|---|---|---|---|---|---|---|---|---|---|---|---|---|---|---|---|---|---|---|
| 1 | Situation Analysis | | | | | | | | | | | | | | | | | | | | | | | | | | |
| 1.1 | Company Analysis | 2 | | ▓ | ▓ | | | | | | | | | | | | | | | | | | | | | | |
| 1.2 | Customer Analysis | 3 | | ▓ | ▓ | ▓ | | | | | | | | | | | | | | | | | | | | | |
| 1.3 | Competition Analysis | 5 | | ▓ | ▓ | ▓ | ▓ | ▓ | | | | | | | | | | | | | | | | | | | |
| 2 | Ventures | 3 | | | | | | ▓ | ▓ | ▓ | | | | | | | | | | | | | | | | | |
| 3 | SWOT and PESTLE | 4 | | | | | | | | | ▓ | ▓ | ▓ | ▓ | | | | | | | | | | | | | |
| 4 | Market Segmentation | 6 | | | | | | | | | | | | ▓ | ▓ | ▓ | ▓ | ▓ | ▓ | | | | | | | | |
| 5.1 | Product | 2 | | | | | | | | | | | | | | | | | | ▓ | ▓ | | | | | | |
| 5.2 | Price | 2 | | | | | | | | | | | | | | | | | | | | ▓ | ▓ | | | | |
| 5.3 | Promotion | 4 | | | | | | | | | | | | | | | | | | | | | ▓ | ▓ | ▓ | ▓ | |
| 6 | Execute | 4 | | | | | | | | | | | | | | | | | | | | | | | ▓ | ▓ | ▓ |

▶ **Figure 7.15:** An example of a Gantt chart

**⏸ PAUSE POINT**   What tools do you rely on to make decisions? Do you use manual or electronically-based tools and techniques? Why? How could you make the process more efficient and reliable?

**Hint**   Try using a different approach or technique to plan ahead for your future.

**Extend**   Create a Gantt chart to provide a structure to use for making decisions.

## Financial tools

In Table 7.2, Sage was referred to in the context of data analysis. Sage became synonymous with accounting functions, especially in smaller businesses. Accountants and administrators use Sage to contain their supplier and customer details and all the transactions associated with them. Reports can be generated routinely to provide the financial state of the business as it links into the organisation's bank statements and provides information on cash flow (which can be used for **cash flow forecasting**), frequency of repeat orders, outstanding payments and invoices and when they become due for payment etc. Other financial tools which generate reports to aid decision making include:

▶ net present value – how much the money in the business is worth today, not how much it might be worth in the future if invested

▶ discount cash flow – the value of the money in the business once invested and the interest has been added into the total

▶ internal rates of return (IRR) – the amount of return after investment based on cash flows of a project or at an internally chosen interest rate.

Other financial tools include:

▶ financial statements such as those generated by the bank

▶ financial ratios (which provide more in-depth analysis and can indicate the strengths and weaknesses of a company)

▶ management accounts – which are routinely and frequently (often monthly) generated by accountants and presented to management for reviewing business performance and making decisions about the future.

> **Key term**
>
> **Cash flow forecast** – a document that shows the predicted flow of cash into and out of a business over a given period of time, normally 12 months.

## Assessment practice 7.2    `A01`  `A02`  `A03`

Your family owns a small fish and chip shop in the centre of a market town surrounded by villages, farms and small industrial estates in South Wales. The nearest major town is Swansea, which is around 12 miles away. Although the fish and chip shop generates a fairly consistent income, you believe there is room for growth. You need to present a well-justified plan to your father as your idea will involve some investment into the business.

You have an idea to provide home deliveries like other takeaway businesses provide. You have found out about the costs of buying or leasing a vehicle for deliveries but know other costs will also exist. Your figures exclude VAT as you are a VAT-registered business and you know you will have to estimate the mileage to calculate the potential fuel costs.

▶ **Table 7.3:** Vehicle cost planning

| Citroen Berlingo 1.6 litre | Initial payment | Monthly payments for 24 months | Final payment | Road tax | Service costs |
|---|---|---|---|---|---|
| Finance lease | £109 | £109 | Zero – hand back the vehicle | £130 per year | Zero |
| Contract hire | £109+ | £109 | £5000 and keep the vehicle or penalty for early withdrawal | Zero | £30 per month |

You have located some data online and intend to research further, along with information about the age of the local population which may be of use in determining the future for the business.

You will need to provide:
- a presentation justifying your proposal based on the use of at least one business model to justify your decisions
- an analysis of the data provided and any relevant additional sources of information to support your proposal.

*Plan*

- How will you approach the task?
- What resources do you need to complete the task?
- How confident do you feel in your own abilities to complete this task?

*Do*

- Are you recording any problems you're experiencing and looking for ways/solutions to clarify queries?
- Can you make connections between what you're reading/researching and the task, and identifying the important information?
- Can you understand your thought process and why you have decided to approach the task in a particular way? Can you explain this reasoning when asked?

*Review*

- Can you explain how you would approach the hard elements differently next time (ie what you would do differently)?
- Can you explain what skills you employed and which new ones you've developed?
- Can you use this experience in future tasks/learning experiences to improve your planning/approach and to monitor your own progress?

# Use of research to justify the marketing of a business

**Links**

See also *Unit 1: Exploring Business, Unit 2: Developing a Marketing Campaign, Unit 14: Investigating Customer Service* and *Unit 22: Market Research* for more about the uses of research.

*Unit 2: Developing a Marketing Campaign* covers marketing and how research is fundamental to informing marketing decisions and practices. Marketing is a dynamic field and is integral to the success of a business and therefore it cannot be undertaken lightly or without evidence to substantiate and inform the decisions made about how to promote the business.

## Types of research

As you have seen already, there are two types of research: primary and secondary. Within these categories, information can also be internal – from inside the organisation, or external – from another organisation or source outside the organisation.

**Key terms**

**Quantitative data** – data consisting of numbers, responding to what, where and why questions.

**Qualitative data** – data providing context and information about how or details about why (customer comments).

The tools used to gather and analyse the data will need to be appropriate for the type of research. For example, undertaking research using data from financial reports will rely on methods for analysing **quantitative data**; you are unlikely to create a questionnaire or run a focus group. If you are seeking customer feedback, however, this will require a different set of tools, techniques and skills to analyse the **qualitative data** gathered and interpret the meaning. Each of these factors will require careful consideration and planning (and decision making) before embarking on the research.

### Primary research

Primary research consists of information and data that the business has collected first-hand (it is first or primary). Internal primary research data sources include:

▸ sales figures for the business' own products

▸ customer data held on a central database.

External primary research methods include:

▶ surveys and questionnaires such as online feedback forms and interviews

▶ observation techniques and mystery shoppers

▶ focus groups or trials of new products for gathering feedback.

## Secondary research

There are multiple sources for secondary research and they should always be referenced in acknowledgement to the creator of the material.

▶ Published reports – these could be financial reports from other organisations so marketeers can analyse the information and make decisions about ways to maintain or increase their own market share.

▶ Back data – also known as historical data is used by organisations and researchers to identify business and economic trends which influence the decisions they make about ways to market products and services.

▶ Industry reports – may include those relating to health and safety, which will enable a business to promote a safety device in a targeted area in response to risks or accidents. Other reports might include, for example, the intended demolition of an old office block, which would allow a construction business to target their services for rebuilding or purchasing the land.

▶ Government data – a vital source of information for how to market your business. The government data reports provide information regionally, nationally and globally and combine data from other sources which is also routinely and widely gathered and analysed. Data on economic growth or changes in legislation can be used by marketeers for pricing strategies and product development or diversification.

▶ Consumer reviews – these can build or break business reputations. Businesses which exploit positive customer reviews can benefit significantly without necessarily spending money on expensive adverts but rather by using their own website and comparison websites to promote their services or products.

---

**Tip**

Primary research should never be undertaken without the permission of those contributing. Rules for seeking written consent of an adult if children are involved in research are available online from the Ethics Guidebook website.

There are special guidelines for some professions, such as the medical profession, from the General Medical Council.

**Link**

Read about how to ensure data validation and reliability in *Unit 2: Developing a Marketing Campaign*.

---

**❚❚ PAUSE POINT**   What research activities have you undertaken? What methods and tools did you use? How did you analyse the data?

**Hint**   Remember that any research involves a series of activities, even choosing somewhere to live or how to get to your place of study.

**Extend**   Prepare and carry out a focus group with some peers on another course. What preparation will you need and how will get the most from the data you gather?

## Competitor analysis

Keeping a close eye on your competitors is an important aspect of market research. Businesses are interested in knowing what sells, what does not and what the risks are – based on the competition. Watching your competitors closely can also inform product development; an obvious example is that of the technology sector.

Businesses research and analyse the effect of competitors on their business to establish the following:

▶ The effect on the product/service to be offered – the price that competitors charge and any offers they apply will have an effect on product sales. Noticeably, during and since the recession, prices have been reduced and sales are more frequent while retailers compete for the market share.

▶ Pricing strategies – businesses will use competitor information to determine how they price their products or services. Some prices are fixed and businesses have little control other than possibly introducing enticements to encourage customers to spend more when visiting their premises.

▶ Location – when using competitor analysis for how competitors impact on a business, the data being analysed must be recognised in accordance to where competitors are located. For example, a jeweller in Hatton Garden in central London will have access to a different clientele from a jeweller located in a rural market town. Therefore the location alone will not be an exact comparison.

▶ Comparison websites aid businesses by gathering data on their behalf through customer feedback, which also enables businesses to see what customers think of their competitors. For example, there are insurance, travel and utility websites such as comparethemarket.com, TripAdvisor and uSwitch.

## Trends

Analysts search for trends in the data over varying periods of time. These can depend on the product or service, the type of business and length of time the business has been operational.

For example, a new start-up business will be monitoring its own data and making comparisons with competitors almost constantly whereas a large organisation may gather data but analyse and seek trends routinely, on a monthly basis. Businesses and government continue to look for trends over a longer period of time, usually referring to the last three to five years as a measure.

### Economic trends

There are different types of trends to be measured in data and one is the national economic trend. This information will subsequently impact on the business so it will help predict future business opportunities. Electronic data on economic trends are available from numerous sites and particularly government sites such as the Office for National Statistics (ONS) and their collation of data forecasts.

### Market trends

Market trends identify the movements of the investment market over time. These trends use financial data to forecast the direction for future investment by basing their predictions on past performance and where to place investments. For example, if a business invests in a commodity such as gold which has fallen in price over time and appears to be continuing its decline, then investors have to make decisions about whether to buy more stock while prices are low and before they start to rise, to leave it longer and buy at an even cheaper price or to sell the stock they already have before they lose more money.

Market trends are analysed and used for forecasting the price of oil which has a major impact on the economic capability of businesses around the globe as it impacts significantly on their operational costs.

**Link**

See *Unit 2: Developing a Marketing Campaign* for more about market intelligence, the process of gathering, analysing and using competitor data to inform business decisions.

**Research**

You can read more about market trends by searching online.

### Social trends

These are possibly harder to predict as there are so many variables in society. Nevertheless, there are considerable amounts of data collected continually to assist with monitoring and analysing social trends. The data, collated and analysed by the ONS, provides information about the demographic of the UK population which is then compared with that of European countries and globally, such as shown below.

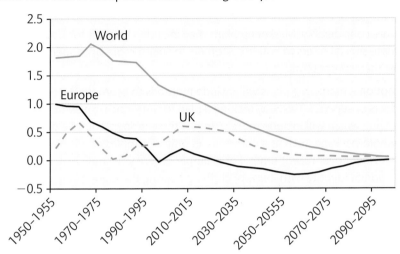

▶ **Figure 7.16:** Predicted percentage population growth – UK, Europe and worldwide (from *World Population Prospects*, Department of Economic and Social Affairs, United Nations Secretariat, United Nations)

This graph indicates that the global population is predicted to continue on its decline to the end of this century. Such information can be used by organisations to make decisions about their operations, however, the thing to remember is that by the time information is gathered, analysed and published it could be considered out of date. However, these analyses also provide predictions about the future growth in the population and the likely demographic associated with that growth based on trend data. Therefore organisations such as the construction industry will make decisions about their market based on data analyses like these.

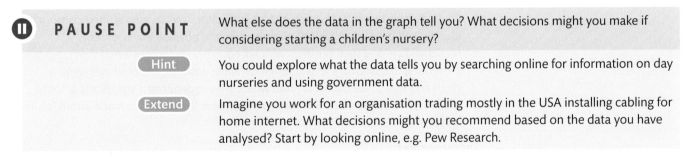

**❙❙ PAUSE POINT**

What else does the data in the graph tell you? What decisions might you make if considering starting a children's nursery?

**Hint**

You could explore what the data tells you by searching online for information on day nurseries and using government data.

**Extend**

Imagine you work for an organisation trading mostly in the USA installing cabling for home internet. What decisions might you recommend based on the data you have analysed? Start by looking online, e.g. Pew Research.

# Marketing plan

A marketing plan can be devised in many different formats, for example as a Gantt chart, so long as it has the key components. The titles used for each column might vary, along with the order of each one, and some might include much more detail. Where the plan involves more than one aim, then a separate plan may be used, each one linking to the other. Plans might also be broken down into more detail against each resource perhaps in order to monitor and measure progress.

Marketing plans are based on the marketing mix. The extended marketing mix comprises seven elements known as the 7Ps.

**Links**

See also *Unit 2: Developing a Marketing Campaign* for an example of a marketing campaign plan; *Unit 19: Pitching for a New Business* for the marketing mix and the 7Ps and *Unit 22: Market Research*.

**Elements of the 7Ps**

▶ Product – successful businesses recognise they need to constantly improve or develop the products they offer. The marketing plan will include methods for informing product development, diversification of the range and those products which should not be changed.

▶ Price – is the one element of the marketing mix that produces revenue; the others generate costs. The amount of money consumers are charged to acquire a product can vary considerably. Marketing plans may include strategies for how and when to promote special offers to entice customers to spend more or to spend with them rather than competitors.

▶ Promotion – marketing plans will include methods to promote the organisation's products or services. This may include a plan for introducing new or updated packaging which will include more than just the wrapper around a product but the whole 'package' such as a corporate identity. Examples of this have become more evident over recent times. For example, where you study may have a form of corporate identity with items of clothing bearing the logos of the organisation, codes of conduct being practised etc.

▶ Place – the location where a product or service is offered or promoted will form part of the marketing plan. This could mean where premises are located or advertising is placed or the position on a shelf in a supermarket.

▶ People – are the face of an organisation and successful businesses recognise they need to constantly improve the service they offer alongside their products in order to benefit from repeat business. It is now standard for companies to offer a level of customer care to assist with any product queries or issues. For example, banks often have a member of staff dedicated to greeting customers, resolving minor issues and assisting with automated transactions.

▶ Process – the purchasing process for a particular product or service can be a key part of the promotional mix. Many companies use technology to improve the service they offer customers: they might help customers to create accounts quickly (to avoid providing the same information each time they buy something) and to track orders so customers can see when their purchase will be delivered.

▶ Physical environment – businesses plan for better ways to market their corporate identity and product or service offer through the physical environment. McDonald's is one such business which frequently undergoes a makeover, promoting to customers its modern look while ensuring the premises remain clean and well presented in an area where they experience a significant amount of traffic. Marketing plans are used to implement the decisions made about future investment.

**Target market**

A successful marketing plan requires knowledge about the target market. For example, John Lewis and Primark know who their shoppers are and where to target their marketing.

**USP**

This is a unique selling point and more recently evolved to unique selling proposition. Identifying a USP enables a business to market their services or products more effectively. Examples of businesses which promote their products or services by using a USP include Samsung and its mobile phone range with its ability to increase memory for additional storage of photos and Dyson offering a guarantee for life on its vacuum cleaners.

## Segmentation

This involves having a focus for the business and the marketing plan should target the business market according to its segment. So the clothes retailer New Look targets its teenage female market, which is likely to generate the greatest revenue.

---

**⏸ PAUSE POINT**

How do businesses promote their USP? How did they determine they had a USP among other, similar products/services?

**Hint**

Explore the websites and adverts of KwikFit; Oil of Olay; Body Shop; Waterstone's. Make notes about their USPs, any key terms they use and how each business presents their USP.

**Extend**

Use the 7Ps to initiate a marketing plan for B&Q's black and white campaign. Start by reading more about them online.

---

### Assessment practice 7.3     `A01` `A02` `A03`

PoundProducts, a shop which sells products for a pound or less, entered the market place at the start of the recession in a medium-sized town in the south-west of England. Business owner Marta and her husband Rhom anticipated a niche in the market with families struggling to make ends meet while also providing a quick option for workers to buy their lunches by automated cash receivers to avoid long queues.

However, Rhom and Marta are considering their future business plans as the country emerges from recession and there is competition from two other pound retailers who have opened over the last two years. Each has their own idea about where to direct the business. Rhom is keen to become a 'PoundandaHalf' shop so the range they offer can be wider. However, Marta has ideas about a change in operation completely and thinks they should diversify into environmentally friendly products, an area she is especially passionate about. Marta is confident that this is a growth market which will continue to attract consumers.

As they cannot agree, they are seeking help in making their decision. The one thing that remains static is their business premises as they have a lease secured for 22 years and have factored in their rent and estimated their rates for the next five years. General operating costs stay the same but the issues they are struggling with are:

- what to do with the £65,000 of stock they currently own on which an average profit of 250 per cent would be generated
- what products they could sell for Marta's business idea
- how to plan the timeframe for effectively closing down one business and opening up another without losing the relied upon income in the interim period.

Both agree, however, that they also need to consider the longer-term future of the business as they have seen the market change considerably in the last eight years together with changes in the local demographic and industry in the surrounding area. There are even talks of a 'new town' being planned just 15 miles away plus major road and rail networks in the county to support a potential population growth of 250,000.

Marta and Rhom have asked you to produce a presentation that:

- analyses each business idea, using the research above and any other research you gather online to show the advantages and disadvantages of each
- considers the issues listed above in relation to each business idea
- provides a rationale for moving forward with one of their business ideas.

### Plan

- What are the success criteria for this task?
- What resources do you need to complete the task?
- How can you get access to them?
- Do you need clarification about anything?

### Do

- Have you spent some time planning out your approach to the task at hand?
- Do you understand when to consider and when to be decisive (reflection vs action)?
- Can you make connections between what you're reading/researching and the task, and identify the important information?

### Review

- Can you draw links between this learning and prior learning?
- Can you explain what skills you employed and which new ones you've developed?
- Can you identify how this learning experience relates to future experiences (ie in the workplace)?

# D Efficient operational management of the business

There are frameworks which have been devised to assist businesses in the way they operate by providing a structure for efficient and to some extent, standardised operations. These frameworks include regulations and legislation which are mandatory as well as other frameworks designed to assist businesses in managing their quality processes. You will explore some of the more well known ones in this section.

**Links**

For more on the laws that affect business see *Unit 1: Exploring Business* and *Unit 23: The English Legal System*.

## Legislation

Legislation has a huge influence on the manner in which a business can operate. There is legislation which applies to the way every business operates, laying down rules and regulations ranging from how we price our products to how long we keep our documentation and electronic records. There are different types of legislation specific to the nature of a business and we shall explore some of those next.

### Relevant industry legislation

As mentioned a little earlier, there is legislation which relates to all businesses and there is also legislation which is specific to specialist industries. For example, a catering business would need to consider applicable food legislation, whilst the medical sector is bound to comply with legislation such as the Medical Act of 1983. Other examples are shown in Table 7.4.

▶ **Table 7.4:** Examples of industry legislation and who it affects and protects

| Legislation/regulation | Examples of business sector | Employees | Customers |
|---|---|---|---|
| Fair Trading Act 1973 | Generic | X | X |
| The Workplace (Health, Safety and Welfare) Regulations 1992 | Generic | X | X |
| Equality Act 2010 | Generic | X | X |
| Street Vendors Act 2014 | Generic | X | X |
| Food Standards Act 1999 | Hospitality | X | X |
| Care Act 2014 | Health, education, child minding | X | X |
| Data Protection Act 1998 | Generic | X | X |
| Consumer Rights Act 2015 | Generic | X | X |
| Health and Social Care Act 2015 | Health sector | X | X |
| Industry specific health and safety legislation | Construction | X | X |
| Supply of Goods and Services Act 1982 | Generic | X | X |
| Equal Pay Act 1970 | Generic and also represented by the Equality Act | X | |
| Food Labelling Regulations 1996 | Any providing food or drink | X | X |
| Import and Export Controls 2012 | Generic | X | X |

## Health and Safety at Work

One of the mandatory laws affecting every business type is the Health and Safety at Work Act of 1974. This law is also known by various labels which include HSWA, HSW Act, the 1974 Act and HASAWA. Therefore whether you own or are an employee (paid or volunteering) you must comply with the rules of this act, such as:

▸ how to safely dispose of chemicals and other products, even printer cartridges and batteries

▸ safety rules for exiting and entering premises

▸ wearing protective gear when in close contact with chemicals, fumes or in buildings under construction

▸ using ear defenders when using noisy tools, including at home

▸ making sure fire hazards are kept to a minimum

▸ noise levels, even in bars and at music events

▸ boat handling and diving procedures.

### Reflect

When did you last check your surrounding work area to ensure you and others were safe? For example, consider where you put your bag and other belongings at college; whether your chair allows sufficient room for others to pass, especially in an emergency; turning off any monitors not being used and adjusting window blinds to prevent glare etc.

▸ How might health and safety rules affect a concert such as this one?'

## Data protection

The Data Protection Act of 1998 is frequently monitored and reviewed for its relevance and to accommodate changes which impact on its promises. This Act requires that personal data is not shared without the permission of the individual it relates to and also provides individuals with permission to ask for information held about them by organisations. There are eight principles with which all records must comply, they must be:

▸ fairly and lawfully used

▸ used for limited purposes

▸ adequate, relevant and not excessive

▸ accurate and up to date

▸ not kept for longer than is necessary

▸ used in line with your rights

▸ secure

▸ not transferred to other countries without adequate protection.

Changes to the act now mean everyone is entitled to read their own medical records and the records held about them by their place of study. The people responsible for inputting the data must be aware of any consequences arising from sharing that data.

Legal developments affect businesses in a range of ways. For example, any changes to the Data Protection Act would affect any business that holds customer data, whether this is a supermarket or a dental practice. Similarly, businesses have to accommodate ongoing changes to equality laws in the way they market their products and services. For example, businesses might produce promotional literature in the different languages used by their target audience. They also need to ensure that images do not portray stereotypes and that their business goals do not discriminate against minority groups.

Have you ever inadvertently shared someone's data without permission?

List the occasions over the last week when you have talked to others, over the phone, face-to-face, text messages; or engaged in social media and introduced new 'friends' to each other.

How would you manage the situation if you realised that someone had shared your or a friend's data without permission?

## Employment legislation

As with all legislation, it is our responsibility to keep up to date with reforms and changes. The Employment Rights Act of 1996 has undergone further changes as from 2016, the first major reforms in over 20 years. Changes are instigated to keep in line with other legislation, for example the Equality Act of 2010 and Trade Union Bill of 2015. Employment legislation changes, which can vary according to the size of employer, include:

▶ requirement to publish gender pay gaps

▶ national living wage

▶ statutory paternal and sickness pay rates

▶ protection for apprentices

▶ illegal working.

### Research

Do some online research about:
- the Equality Act 2010
- the Trade Union Bill
- any changes to employment legislation in the last year.

Imagine you are working for a small business. Produce a brief presentation outlining how the above affect the operation of the business.

## Consumer legislation

The Consumer Rights Act of 2015 aims to simplify the rules by combining previously separate legislation: Sale of Goods Act, Unfair Terms in Consumer Contracts Regulations, and Supply of Goods and Services Act.

This Act came into force from 1 October 2015 and protects customers by imposing set rules for:

▶ refunds and timeframes

▶ remediation options

▶ replacements and repairs

▶ additional items sold or provided with the item of interest

▶ pre-contract information.

### Discussion

In a small group discuss the legislation and regulations of your place of study. Compare these with business legislation, perhaps from places where you or your peers work. Search for legislation associated with businesses where you would like to work when you have finished your studies.

## Case study

### For all the tea in China...

Henrietta Lovell started the Rare Tea Company in 2004. She had been working in logistics for a corporate finance company in the late 1990s, spending time in China and drinking a lot of tea. Ms Lovell, who now employs 12 staff, spent several years researching her market. She spent a year visiting farms all around the world and negotiating contracts. She now sells her teas globally and is famous for her English teas in China.

In China, particularly, classic British tea brands from the Rare Tea Company are in demand from mostly high-net-worth individuals, some of whom buy a year's supply of tea in advance. Now the company is even selling Chinese tea to China.

The Rare Tea Company tea is not always labelled as organic, though it often is, because Ms Lovell feels it would disadvantage the smaller farms. The company tries to ensure it works only with farmers using sustainable practices that benefit the land and the people who live and work on it. Moreover, because the cost of organic certification is so high for smaller farmers, Ms Lovell takes on the cost herself and gets her teas tested in Switzerland. 'So people know our teas are clean and pure and unadulterated. It can be hard to know in China if you're getting pure tea.' The company is also about to launch with five or six restaurants in Japan later this year.

Import duties can be crippling, she agrees, 'and for us to do retail it has to be at the higher end of the spectrum, but that's OK. The middle classes are burgeoning and they believe British brands stand for ethical business practice. And we're selling really, really good tea...'. (Source: 'Yes, this woman really does sell tea to China'. Routes to Growth, routestogrowthasia.com/2016/rare-tea-company/, © Cathay Pacific Airways Limited)

### Check your knowledge

1  How did Ms Lovell justify her business idea?

2  Where did Ms Lovell gather her research from and what methods were used?

3  What legislation would impact on Ms Lovell's global business?

4  What trends would have been likely to influence Ms Lovell's future business plans?

5  Which of the business models do you think would have assisted Ms Lovell in planning her future expansion?

---

**⏸ PAUSE POINT**    How do you rate your success in responding to the knowledge questions in this case study?

> Hint    Note the techniques and knowledge you relied on to carry out this task from what you have learnt so far. Identify what you need to go over again to secure your understanding.

> Extend    To what extent do you think the forecast for the future of the Asian economy, especially China, will affect Ms Lovell's plans?

## Quality issues

In order to keep customers, and attract new ones, a business must ensure the quality of the product or service and customer care. Quality management is the process where businesses put systems in place to ensure the quality of their product or service is consistent and to combat potential quality issues. You are probably aware of some of the quality systems where you study, such as the moderation or verification procedures to confirm the standard of assessment of your work is reliable and accurate.

> **Link**
>
> See also *Unit 6: Principles of Management* on quality management and standards, BSI and ISO.

Quality can be regulated by quality standards which are devised by bodies, such as professional organisations, to be used as a framework to control quality levels. These frameworks are not necessarily mandatory but are deemed important for several reasons.

▶ **Quality control** (QC) – the term associated with how the quality of products and services are controlled through a series of consistent monitoring processes. These control mechanisms might have been devised by the organisation themselves as an in-house set of procedures to check the quality is as they expect. For example, checking apples are free from blemishes and rejecting those which do not meet the internal standard for quality produce.

▶ **Quality assurance** (QA) – the process of planned checks which can also be designed as an in-house set of procedures. For example, checking apples are free from blemishes and rejecting those which do not meet the internal standard for quality produce and checking the process for checking the apples to establish any flaws in the process not just the apples.

Although very similar, QA is a component of QC procedures. The difference between QC and QA is that QC aims to locate incidences where quality is sub-standard and requires improvement or looks for ways in which further developments can be made. QA is about maintaining confidence in the processes and associated outputs by systematically planning for and sampling each aspect of business practices.

> ### Research
>
> Choose a business that has lots of information online. Research their quality processes and produce a one-page report outlining these. Compare your work with a partner to see similarities and differences with different business.

▶ **Benchmarking** – the process of measuring a standard against what is expected. Businesses rely on benchmarks to help inform them of, for example, how their products or services compare with other similar businesses. Of course the benchmark needs to be from a reliable source; this might be from government data, such as the Office for National Statistics (ONS), used to compare with national trends. Benchmarks are also taken from internal performance data. For example, a business would set sales targets based on percentage point improvements when compared with the previous quarter, half-year or three-year trends.

▶ **Quality circles** – a process for involving employees, usually those undertaking similar jobs or working in the same department, with problem-solving and resolutions. This can be a highly effective and efficient quality assurance method for unpicking an issue and getting to the heart of it, by listening to those most closely related. For example, listening to those employees who are directly customer facing, such as waiters in a restaurant or receptionists of a leisure centre.

▶ **Self-checking** or **inspection** – additional forms of quality control and assurance. These methods rely on individuals to check they are meeting the **service standards** set by the business. The business needs to ensure its employees know and understand what comprises the service standards and how to measure they are meeting expectations. One business which evidently instils its expectations in its employees is fast-food outlet McDonald's.

▶ **ISO 9000** – probably one of the most well-known of quality standards used by industry. These standards are internationally recognised for both quality management and quality assurance. They provide a framework for quality processes and checks for consistency of standards across the business. As they are internationally recognisable, businesses awarded the standard are able to present an assurance to potential and existing customers of the quality of their products and services.

> ### Key terms
>
> **Quality control** – series of consistent checks to ensure products or services meet a predetermined set of criteria or standards.
>
> **Quality assurance** – planned and systematic checks of procedures and outputs.
>
> **Quality circles** – groups of employees who meet regularly to consider ways of resolving problems and improving production.
>
> **Service standards** – a predetermined set of measures which identify the levels of quality expected for business operations.

However, some businesses, especially smaller ones, may find the process of acquiring an ISO endorsement, and the regular re-assessment to show that standards have been maintained, not only time-consuming and burdensome but also a costly process. One of the disadvantages of not being a recognised, endorsed business is that some suppliers or manufacturers refuse to deal with businesses which are not ISO 9000 registered.

▶ **TQM** - designed to involve the whole company in evaluating what works well and what it needs to improve. The British Standards Institution (BSI) provides a series of quality products tailored to different aspects of industry. This includes, for example, a guide for management principles on how to organise the business structure which makes best use of the resources, including the workforce, to meet business objectives.

> **Key term**
>
> **TQM** – Total Quality Management.

**PAUSE POINT**   What quality measures can you identify at your place of study or in your place of work?

Hint   What quality issues have you identified or reported in the past? How did the organisation manage your complaint or respond to your issue? Perhaps they referred you to a copy of their quality standards.

Extend   Choose an organisation and research how they manage their quality processes and issues, for each of the mechanisms discussed.

# E   Understand the importance of managing resources

The term resources refers to physical, financial and human resources. Physical resources are tools, equipment, machinery etc; financial resources relate to budgets, cash flow and money matters; and human resources (HR) are the employees and any others who are involved in the business. In this section you will explore each of these starting with human resourcing.

## Human resources

> **Link**
>
> See also *Unit 21: Training and Development* for more on human resources.

Every business requires some HR even if it is a sole trader. As a business grows, many decisions have to be made about the management of HR. There is legislation to consider, which affects the way in which businesses operate, but also the process of managing people is complex and challenging. Each decision made is likely to impact in some way on HR.

### Staff requirements for efficiency

Decisions about appropriate levels of HR must ensure the business operates efficiently and effectively with minimum costs where possible. The types of decisions managers would make about the people they employ involves identifying the skills required for each job and comparing them with existing or potential staff. This might include introducing new manufacturing processes or services or when replacing or expanding the workforce.

## Wages/salaries

For many businesses, the wage bill is their highest cost, for example in a college the cost of employing tutors is likely to be greater than other costs. Wages are most likely to be paid on a daily or weekly basis. Part-time employment is more likely to be defined by an hourly or weekly wage. Salaries refer to a fixed regular payment, which is normally paid on a monthly basis. Normally, a salary is expressed as a full year amount. Businesses have to consider a number of different factors when deciding what pay to offer for a job role.

These will include, for example, the level of education and/or experience the role requires, how many hours they are asking the person to work and whether additions such as bonuses or overtime should be offered. These tend to vary between industries and most businesses in a certain industry offer similar conditions. For example, it is very common in banking to receive bonuses, unlike in the catering sector. Businesses will also need to consider what wages or salaries their competitors are offering. Many job adverts contain the phrase a 'competitive salary'. Businesses need to ensure that they are attracting the best candidates for a role, without offering them more money than the business can afford.

## Full time/part time

Managers need to make decisions about the arrangements for employing their staff, whether it is on a full-time or part-time basis. Although the number of hours which defines full-time employment varies according to the business, there are government guidelines restricting standard employment terms and conditions which exceed 48 hours per week averaged out over a 17-week period.

However, many organisations might offer overtime to cope with additional HR needs in order to make use of the knowledge of the skills and performance of their existing employees rather than taking on additional staff temporarily to cover for busier periods.

There are exceptions to these rules according to the nature of the job, such as the armed forces and specialist or emergency services.

Part-time work is harder to define as there is no set minimum which determines a part-time contract although it is usually defined as a maximum of 32 hours per week. However, there are rules about what can be achieved by part-time work and also the rights associated with part-time work since changes to the legislation in 2000 with the introduction of the Part-time Workers (Prevention of Less Favourable Treatment) Regulations.

## Recruitment process

Resourcing HR is a complex and time consuming task which needs a variety of skills. It requires many decisions before even meeting with potential staff. These include decisions about:

▶ duties that must be fulfilled

▶ impact on existing staff

▶ essential skills to undertake the work

▶ desirable skills

▶ affordability for the right person for the job

▶ availability of the right person for the job

▶ contingency for managing until new staff member takes up the post and is fully operational.

The recruitment process can be extremely lengthy and impact significantly on the smooth operation of a business. Larger businesses may offer incentives to attract suitably skilled individuals to move into the area as part of their **remuneration** package.

Making decisions about employing the right member of staff can detract from the day-to-day business operations, especially for a smaller business where most duties are undertaken by the business owner who is also responsible for carrying out most of the duties.

**Link**

See also *Unit 8: Recruitment and Selection Process* for more on the recruitment process.

**Key term**

**Remuneration** – money and benefits paid as part of work or employment.

▶ What preparations would you need to carry out to make the right selection?

## Training requirements

**Links**

See also *Unit 21: Training and Development* on training requirements and *Unit 6: Principles of Management* on upskilling.

Once staff have been recruited they are likely to need some training before they meet the efficiency and effectiveness expectations of the business. This training may vary according to whether it is required for inducting a new member of staff into the organisation's processes and systems, or showing someone the basics of their day-to-day job, and will have different costs as well.

▶ What different forms of training are there?

For example, a highly skilled and qualified member of staff might need a minimum straightforward induction training session whereas a lesser or unskilled staff member may need to have full training on equipment and machinery or with members of the public before they can begin functioning effectively.

**Reflect**

If you have a part-time job, what training did you require when you first began? What training have you had since and what was its purpose?

Every member of staff is entitled to some form of training or **upskilling** and the government has also produced rules about the organisation's responsibility to assist employees in seeking additional training while working. However, the first question to be asked is whether the training should be undertaken **in-house** or **externally**. It may seem obvious that if the training can be met internally then it must be more cost effective to do so. But it is necessary to consider the cost of external training in relation to the lost production time when using in-house staff, such as the line manager or a competent colleague.

Other factors include the skills of the member of staff in being able to train or teach another person and whether the training, such as that for health and safety, requires **accredited** trainers.

**Key terms**

**Upskilling** – to teach additional skills or enhance the skills one has already.

**In-house training** – usually training which is provided by another member of staff in the organisation or an external trainer contracted to deliver training in the organisation.

**External training** – purchasing training from an outside organisation, where employees are sent to receive training from another individual.

**Accredited** – a formal recognition such as a qualification, which validates the knowledge, skills or competence of the trainer or training.

Other factors to consider apart from cost when arranging training include:

▶ the skills and understanding relating to the business of external trainers

▶ time and logistics of sending staff on external training

▶ how the benefits and impact to the business will be measured

▶ whether the training should lead to a recognised qualification.

 **PAUSE POINT**

Do you know what your preferred employment might pay when you first start out? What is the potential for future earnings depending on your skills and qualifications and what training you expect to receive?

**Hint**

Explore your local job agencies and newspaper advertisements. You could also search online. TheNational Careers Service website is a good starting point.

**Extend**

Create a business plan for your future. Decide on your preferred employment route and create a contingency which offers alternative routes.

# Physical resources

Physical resources will vary, depending on the size and type of the business. For example, a cash and carry or online warehouse requires premises to store large amounts of products across a vast range of supplies. The warehouse is likely to require a large administration area, either onsite or elsewhere and staff facilities for the employees who receive, pack and distribute the goods.

On the other hand, a high turnaround service, such as a garage providing MOT and tyre services, may not require much in the way of storage as they can arrange to have their supplies delivered as they need them. A small office for administration and a workshop with toilet and possibly kitchenette might be the extent of their needs.

## Premises

When faced with the decision of whether to rent or buy premises, a poor decision could be an expensive mistake and tie a business into a long-term lease or a building it cannot sell on. Equally, leasing a building may not provide the security or flexibility required and any investment to be made, perhaps to accommodate business services or refurbishment of staff facilities, may be lost. However, the flexibility leasing can offer in terms of expansion or reducing the business accommodation or moving sites may also be an attractive consideration.

A business loan may secure premises at a cost that can be forecast, whereas leasing business premises may not offer the same security. If you choose to buy premises, they may also provide living accommodation.

A business decision such as this would also factor in the length of operation and future growth plans. If the business has responded to a trend or gap in the market, the business plan would need to demonstrate that the cost of premises is sustainable and not likely to cause disruption financially.

---

**Theory into practice**

Assume you are about to start trading as an online distributor of garden tools. You have an investor who is prepared to help you out for the deposit on leasing a building but you have also secured a two-year contract from a small chain of garden centres for your tools. Which would you do?

You could start by searching local commercial estate agents and property pages in newspapers. You could also search for information online.

---

## Equipment required

Whatever the business idea, there is always equipment required, even if it is just a printer, laptop, phone, vehicle, suitable clothing or business cards.

The type of equipment required will vary depending upon the type of business. Even a small business selling products from home will need to purchase equipment, for example, packaging and pens, and will need to pay for access to the internet. A larger business setting up an office in a town centre will need to bulk order stationery items as well as desk furniture and other general office equipment. The majority of equipment costs are likely to be ongoing and should be accounted for in the business plan. Purchases such as website set-up costs might appear to be a one-off but will incur ongoing costs for maintaining and upgrading. It may also be that specialist software or training on existing software, such as databases and accounting packages, is required.

▶ How do you think a business decides on the type of vehicle to choose?

## Vehicles

Vehicles might be required to run a new business and generate initial and ongoing costs as they require maintenance, repair, tax and insurance and fuel to operate. If vehicles are leased, this is also an ongoing cost. As a business grows, the original vehicle may have to be replaced or added to. These costs should not be unforeseen but should be planned into the everyday management and forecasting of the business.

A sensible strategy is to make arrangements with a local garage to maintain the business vehicles. This could benefit a business in several ways, for example by providing:

▶ preferential rates and treatment

▶ **payments on account** (which can help a business better manage their cash flow so they can settle the outstanding bills when they receive payment from their **creditors**)

## IT hardware and software

All businesses require some form of dedicated hardware and software to manage their operations and this will require frequent maintenance and occasional updating. One of the many benefits of **cloud** computing and cloud storage is that some of the technical expertise formerly required in-house and ownership of software can now be replaced by using cloud services. There is still an ongoing cost incurred for these services although a business may calculate that these services are more cost efficient than purchasing stand-alone software.

Over time the IT hardware will require maintenance and replacing on a fairly frequent basis. **HMRC** make tax allowances for equipment classified as capital investment, but the cost of replacing, upgrading and expanding the range of IT hardware must be allowed for in the operational management of the business.

## Suppliers and cost of equipment

You may be surprised to learn that suppliers are also classified as physical resources. This is because without your suppliers your business would not be able to function. Take, for example, a mobile coffee shop – it must have supplies of coffee and milk to operate.

Until a business is operational and has built up a reputation, it is likely that a payment on account system will be offered by the supplier. Sufficient funds need to be readily available to purchase the supplies in order for the business to generate revenue. There are many other bills to pay, including those known as on-costs, such as utilities, wages and all those costs that will not wait or attract extended payment periods.

**Link**

See *Unit 3: Personal and Business Finance* for more on capital investment.

# Financial resources

Financial resources are essentially the money that a business has to buy the things it needs and can include cash, credit and any other assets and **liquid securities**. Businesses have to make many decisions about the way they manage their financial resources. One of the common oversights of small business owners is failing to accurately and routinely allocate a portion of their income for payment of taxes and, where applicable, VAT payments.

**Key term**

**Liquid securities** – assets which can be turned into cash quickly and hold relatively stable values.

## Sources of finance

There are many different sources of finance available for businesses. Some will depend on the age and size of the business. Venture or start-up capital is required to start a business. Investment capital is used by both start-up and existing businesses to finance the purchase of equipment or to finance business growth. Existing businesses with a proven track record can seek further investment from banks and other businesses by forming partnerships and cooperatives. Businesses which are built on sustainable resources, such as energy supply, have also benefited from government assistance over recent years, such as for solar panels and wind farms. All businesses need working capital to cover the day-to-day running costs for the business.

**Link**

See *Unit 3: Personal and Business Finance* for more on raising finance, including hire purchase and leasing options.

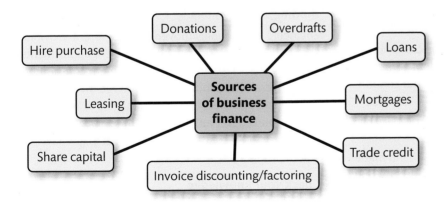

▶ **Figure 7.17** – Sources of business finance

Different sources of finance are used for short-, medium- or long-term needs. For short-term needs, sources which are paid back in less than a year, such as trade credit, overdrafts, and invoice discounting/factoring can be used. Medium-term needs, that can be paid back in one to five years, can be met by using leasing, hire purchase or a bank loan. Long-term needs, which need to be paid back in more than five years, can be covered by commercial mortgages or raising share capital.

## Start up and running costs

Start-up businesses require sufficient funds not only to prepare for and start trading but also to maintain a sustainable business operation. The costs involved in starting a business include buying equipment, deposit for renting premises, taking out necessary insurance, and setting up any publicity. Ongoing costs include rent and other premises costs, staff wages, and monthly bills for utilities. Banks are in the business of loaning money and require a well-thought through and justifiable business plan which demonstrates confidence in the ability to repay any loan in full and make the ongoing payments throughout the duration of the loan. The government also offers incentives to start-up businesses.

Venture capitalists also seek to invest in business opportunities. Possibly some of the most well known include those represented by the BBC TV programme *Dragons' Den*. These investors are looking for viable and innovative business opportunities where they believe they can guarantee a significant return on their investment by providing their expertise and access to business contacts.

### Research

Search online and learn about some of the successful outcomes from businesses which successfully and unsuccessfully pitched their ideas to the Dragons.

## Case study

### On yer bike!

The folding Brompton Bike is bought by customers all over the world and is especially evident at railway stations and in major cities including central London. The Brompton Bike strapline line is 'one bike, made for you' offering a custom-built machine to suit your individual frame and need.

Every bike that Brompton manufacture is hand made. Brompton's history can be traced back to 1975, when the inventor and founder, Andrew Ritchie, created prototypes of Brompton bikes from his bedroom in London. Each bike is hand brazed by a skilled craftsman and has a 'signature' which they stamp on the parts of the bike that they work on.

In order for every bike to be roadworthy and meet customer expectations, Brompton Bikes have routine quality control and assurance systems in place which involves every member of staff taking responsibility and ownership in their contribution. As each component is

manufactured, the individual stamps their identification on the component so it can be traced back to them. This enables any faults identified in the future to be traced back to their origin so that investigations can be undertaken and corrections made. Employees strive for perfection and modifications to any imperfections provide opportunities for further research development.

Every member of the business gets involved in the life journey of the Brompton Bike. Even the MD might be on the shop floor, checking on progress, talking to staff, trying out bikes and getting involved in meetings about new designs, customer orders, resolving issues and showing around visitors.

Engineers are routinely moved on to different activities and work with new teams and in different departments. That way staff learn how their involvement contributes to the overall end product. At each stage they are trained and upskilled, enabling managers to manage their resources so every department can be covered when demand increases or absenteeism might have halted productivity.

### Check your knowledge

1  What is the USP of Brompton Bikes?

2  What types of quality checking do Brompton Bikes utilise?

3  What business model does Brompton Bikes operate to manage its resources effectively?

4  Why do you think Brompton Bikes made the decisions they have to operate their business using the model described?

**Creation and interpretation of financial forecasts**

In the previous section, you started to consider how financial resources are managed, the types of costs involved in running a business and examples of where to source finance. In this section, you will learn about using financial data for making decisions about how to operate business on a daily basis and how to predict financial viability and opportunities by forecasting.

## Creation and analysis of a sales forecast

Businesses collect sales data which helps them to assess what has happened and to forecast what will happen next.

### Use data to predict sales over a 12-month period

When a business collects and analyses the data it generates, such as income from sales, it can use the data to predict potential sales over the coming months. The data used often represents the previous 12 months, but depending on the type of business it may use data over the last three years or even longer, especially if the business is seasonal or influenced by, for example, a change in government.

Study the figures for a small florist in the Cotswolds in Figure 7.18 and think how they might be used to predict sales over the next year:

**Link**

See also *Unit 3: Personal and Business Finance* for more on financial forecasting.

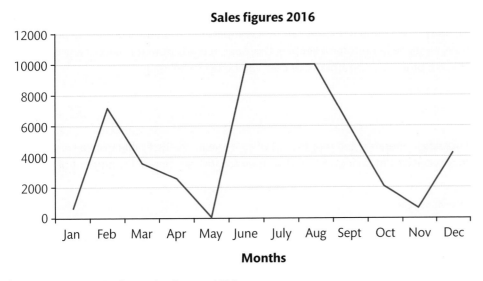

▶ **Figure 7.18** – Sales figures for the year 2016

Poppy, the owner of Blooming Marvellous, collated the figures into a spreadsheet which has been graphically reproduced to study the trends and analyse the sales performance. Poppy can make several predictions based on the data for the forthcoming year. These include the following observations:

▶ peak sales periods are associated with religious and celebratory occasions, such as Valentine's Day, Easter, Mother's Day, summer weddings and Christmas

▶ quiet periods provide opportunities for Poppy to take her holiday, redecorate the premises or consider other ways to promote her business such as 'the wedding anniversary florist of choice' or partnering with the local undertakers when funerals often peak around the winter months

> opportunities for Poppy to increase her sales beyond the forecast may exist if she is able to increase her stock and expand her workforce in preparation for the peak times.

Ⅱ PAUSE POINT    What other decisions might Poppy make based on her past sales performance?

Hint    Go online to explore other sources of information, such as the Florists' Review.

Extend    If you have a part-time job, or a mentor, ask if you can see their sales forecast or ask how they use their sales data.

## Create and interpret a cash flow forecast

> **Link**
>
> See also *Unit 3: Personal and Business Finance* on cash flow forecasts.

Cash flow forecasting enables businesses to plan effectively for the incoming and outgoing of funds, such as revenue from sales and payments that need to go out on time, including employees' wages, taxes, national insurance etc. No matter how small the business, a cash flow forecast is essential to ensure bills can always be paid and the business stays solvent.

### Creation of a cash flow forecast from data given

Businesses create a cash flow forecast based on the data they gather based on their income (cash in) and expenditure (cash out). If you consider every single purchase and sale must be accounted for, this can be a complicated and time-consuming process. This is a very valid reason for keeping thorough records from the start of any new business, otherwise the amount of data can be overwhelming.

## Worked example

'Rest Awhile' is a successful bed and breakfast operating ten months out of every year. The first table from a very simple example shows the income they receive from their guests and, as they are VAT registered, the amount of VAT they have received on those sales.

▶ **Table 7.5** Rest Awhile income for the previous year

|  | Jan | Feb | Mar | Apr | May | June | July | Aug | Sept | Oct | Nov | Dec |
|---|---|---|---|---|---|---|---|---|---|---|---|---|
| Sales | 0000 | 5000 | 6000 | 6000 | 6000 | 7000 | 10,000 | 12,000 | 10,000 | 8000 | 0000 | 10,000 |
| VAT on sales | 0000 | 1000 | 1200 | 1200 | 1200 | 1400 | 2000 | 2400 | 2000 | 1600 | 0000 | 2000 |
| Total cash in | 0000 | 6000 | 7200 | 7200 | 7200 | 8400 | 12,000 | 14,400 | 12,000 | 9600 | 0000 | 12,000 |

This second table shows the cost of purchases Rest Awhile needs to make to operate their business and the amount of VAT they have paid on these purchases which can be reclaimed from HMRC.

▶ **Table 7.6** Rest Awhile costs for the previous year

|  | Jan | Feb | Mar | Apr | May | June | July | Aug | Sept | Oct | Nov | Dec |
|---|---|---|---|---|---|---|---|---|---|---|---|---|
| Purchases | 2000 | 2000 | 3000 | 3000 | 3000 | 3000 | 5000 | 6000 | 5000 | 3000 | 4000 | 4000 |
| VAT paid | 400 | 400 | 600 | 600 | 600 | 600 | 1000 | 1200 | 1000 | 600 | 800 | 800 |
| Total cash out | 2400 | 2400 | 3600 | 3600 | 3600 | 3600 | 6000 | 7200 | 6000 | 3600 | 4800 | 4800 |

## Analysis of a cash flow forecast

A cash flow forecast can be used to predict consequences of business actions and suggest and justify solutions. It is especially useful in planning to manage risks associated with the flow of cash in and out of a business.

Predictions rely on assumptions being made based on trends and other data sources. For example, the florist business owner can make assumptions that the summer will be the most popular time for weddings and that Mother's Day and Valentine's Day will also be a peak sales period. Therefore Poppy could predict sales based on these assumptions although she would need to consider other factors which will affect her profits, such as changes to the cost of supplies and utilities and any change to government taxes and business rates.

Poppy would use these figures to calculate her profits and potential to invest further in the business. A cash flow forecast may be used to predict consequences for the business in the short term, medium and longer term. These terms may represent six months for a small, start-up business although more likely one year. Medium and longer term, usually portray a three- to five-year plan and sales targets are based on these predictions.

Figure 7.19 is an example of the cash flow forecast Poppy might produce.

Planned investment over 3-year period of staged payments each of £20,000

Cash in the bank brought forward from current year

|  | Jan | Feb | Mar | Apr | May | June | July | Aug | Sept | Oct | Nov | Dec |
|---|---|---|---|---|---|---|---|---|---|---|---|---|
| Cash brought forward | 20,000 | | | | | | | | | | | |
| Cash in | 1,000 | 5,000 | 6,000 | 6,000 | 6,000 | 10,000 | 10,000 | 12,000 | 10,000 | 8,000 | - | 11,000 |
| Cash out | 25,000 | 2,500 | 2,000 | 2,000 | 3,000 | 4,000 | 2,500 | 3,000 | 2,500 | 2,000 | 1,000 | 2,000 |
| **Cash balance** | **-4,000** | **2,500** | **4,000** | **4,000** | **3,000** | **6,000** | **7,500** | **9,000** | **7,500** | **6,000** | **-1,000** | **9,000** |

Figures shown as a minus figure (often represented enclosed in brackets) are negative (deficit) values.

▶ **Figure 7.19** – Blooming Marvellous 12-month cash flow forecast

Poppy can make certain predictions and resolutions from her 12-month forecast, having taken into account her existing ideas to purchase earlier, market her business to a wider audience and allow for potential rate increases:

▶ planned investment for an extension to existing premises will leave her with a deficit if she goes ahead in January, unless she can delay payment

▶ continued investment on this scale will result in little funds by year 3 but if delayed will restrict business growth and cost more when additional funds are available

▶ successful marketing and earlier purchasing of supplies may increase sales in currently dry months by years 2 and 3

▶ additional staff will lead to increased outgoings but enable more customers to be served, resulting in more sales.

**Reflect**

What else do you think Poppy has overlooked? What alternative solutions does she have to ensure she remains profitable in the longer term?

Other considerations for Poppy include:

▶ contingencies for non-payment of invoices although the majority of her business is paid at point of ordering

▶ further increases in business rates and taxes

▶ maintenance costs and fuel increases

▶ alternative suppliers needing to be sourced at prices higher than currently paid.

# Creation and interpretation of a break-even chart

A break-even chart is a visual representation which demonstrates at what point the business is not making a loss or a profit. For example, the situation Poppy could find herself in at the end of year 3 if sales do not increase and costs continue to rise. As you will learn or may have already learnt about in *Unit 3: Personal and Business Finance*, a break-even analysis studies the figures to assess at what point a business may cease to be profitable or even viable before it gets to that stage.

## Creation of a break-even chart from data given

**Link**

You learnt about drawing a break even chart in *Unit 3: Personal and Business Finance*.

To produce a break-even chart let's imagine the owners of the Rest Awhile bed and breakfast have calculated the cost per unit which represents the amount each guest on average must be charged in order to cover all outgoings but without making any profit; this is known as the break-even point.

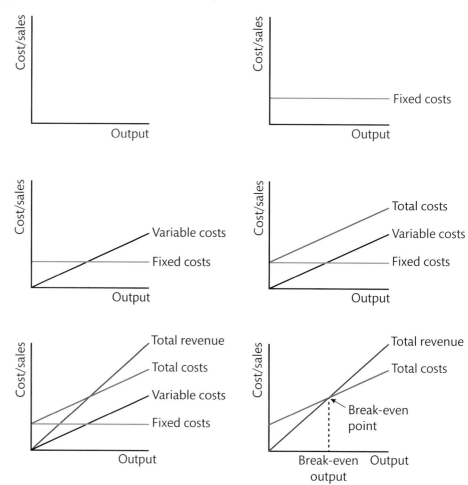

**Tip**

You could learn how to make a break-even chart from online tutorials.

**Figure 7.20:** Completing a break-even chart

## Analysis of a break-even chart

The data portrayed in a break-even chart can help businesses to predict consequences and the future financial success of the business by suggesting and justifying solutions. For example, if the chart displays a point at which costs exceed the income, then the business will no longer be sustainable. Before getting to this point, business decisions would have to be made about how to prevent that from happening.

One way is to increase prices but that solution may not be sustainable either. Your customers may not buy as many products or seek your services if prices are no longer competitive. Products which have fixed prices will prevent you making decisions about increasing prices so alternative solutions will need to be found.

### Worked Example

Amrit runs a Pilates class at his local village hall. It's a fairly new venture which he hopes to provide on more occasions and eventually extend to other villages so he can give up his full-time job and do what he loves. Amrit's fixed costs are £2000 per annum and his variable costs are based on the number of people joining his class on a weekly basis which he has averaged out over the six-month period he has been operating, amounting to £4 per person (or unit) with a variable cost per unit of £2.50.

Contribution per unit = selling price – variable cost

Contribution per unit = £4 - £2.50 = £1.50

Break-even point = Fixed costs divided by Contribution per unit

Break-even point = $\dfrac{£1,000}{4}$ = 250 clients

£1000 represents the six-month period.

Based on these calculations, Amrit must have 250 clients to break even over a six-month period and 500 over the course of a year. This leaves him with no income at all and therefore would not be sustainable. If his client numbers drop rather than increase then he will make a loss; if the client numbers increase he will make a profit.

Amrit knows that January can be a particularly good time for the leisure industry but as he started his business at that time he realises he did far too little promotion to ensure a healthy client group to allow for some drop outs as the time went on. He also has to allow for holidays and sickness periods when client numbers will be unstable. Amrit has not allowed for any increases in his variable costs, such as rent of the village hall as he has been offered a fixed rent for the next two years.

Amrit has several decisions to make:

▸ increase his price by just 50p per session per client
▸ charge clients an upfront fee of £30 for each six-week period
▸ increase the number of clients at every session
▸ offer an annual membership for an attractive fee which makes him a profit
▸ source another area for his classes which may attract more clients
▸ run additional sessions at the current location.

### Theory into practice

Using the cash flow forecast you created a little earlier, produce a break-even chart and analyse at what point you could run out of funds if you failed to monitor your income and outgoings closely. What changes can you make to ensure that does not happen?

Draw a break-even chart for Poppy based on the data tables you have been given. At what point does Poppy's business only break even if she continues to invest at the same rate annually according to her plan?

**Hint** You can find out more about forecasting and cash flows online (for example at Business Plan Hut).

**Extend** Produce a cash flow forecast and break-even chart for the Blooming Marvellous florist assuming the planned extension building costs increase by 25% over years 2 and 3.

**Tip**

Did you know you can produce a break-even analysis using Microsoft Excel by applying formulas known as goal seeking? You can learn how to do this online.

## Creation and interpretation of an income statement

Figure 7.21 shows a statement of comprehensive income for the year ended 30 April 2015. What expenses do you think a business might include under the heading 'miscellaneous'?

| Statement of comprehensive income for the year ended 30 April 2015 | £000s | £000s |
|---|---|---|
| Sales | | 411,529 |
| Less cost of goods sold | | |
| Opening inventory | 34,993 | |
| Purchases | 128,129 | |
| Closing inventory | 21,445 | |
| | | 141,672 |
| **Gross profit** | | 269,852 |
| Less expenses | | |
| Rent and rates | | 37,554 |
| Wages and salaries | | 96,221 |
| Telephone and postage | | 1,359 |
| Distribution | | 31,593 |
| Advertising | | 15,579 |
| Miscellaneous expenses | | 28,452 |
| Depreciation | | 17,848 |
| Total expenses | | 228,696 |
| Revenue income | | 0 |
| **Net profit before tax** | | 41,246 |
| Less tax | | 8,250 |
| Operating profit after tax | | 32,996 |
| Retained profits | | 30,996 |
| Distributed profits | | 2,000 |

▶ **Figure 7.21:** Statement of comprehensive income for year ended 30 April 2015

## Creation of an income statement from data given

Every single transaction a business makes must be accounted for – no matter how small or seemingly insignificant. The income statement will be used by businesses for many procedures, such as checking viability, calculating when to pay invoices, ensuring employees' wages can be paid on time and for planning the future of the business.

Creating an income statement for your own records can be fairly simple using technology. A small or start-up business may not require specialist software in the first instance as it can use spreadsheet software such as Microsoft Excel.

Consider the type of income statement Amrit might create for his Pilates business by studying the example shown in Figure 7.22.

> **Tip**
>
> You can learn more about creating income statements from online tutorials.

Income statement 1 January 2016 - 31 January 2016

| Date | Transaction details | Cash in | Cash out | Total |
|---|---|---|---|---|
| 02/01/2016 | Opening balance | | | 2,300.48 |
| 02/01/2016 | Rent | | -166.67 | 2,133.81 |
| 04/01/2016 | Equipment | | -532.78 | 1,601.03 |
| 08/01/2016 | Clients' payments | 16.00 | | 1,617.03 |
| 08/01/2016 | Petrol | | -48.82 | 1,568.21 |
| 10/01/2016 | Stationery | | -32.54 | 1,535.67 |
| 15/01/2016 | Clients' payments | 24.00 | | 1,559.67 |
| 17/01/2016 | Petrol | | -24.65 | 1,535.02 |
| 18/01/2016 | Printing flyers | | -72.40 | 1,462.62 |
| 18/01/2016 | Floor mats | | -76.00 | 1,386.62 |
| 18/01/2016 | Extension lead | | -11.99 | 1,374.63 |
| 22/01/2016 | Clients' payments | 20.00 | | 1,394.63 |
| 29/01/2016 | Clients' payments | 20.00 | | 1,414.63 |
| **Balance** | | | | **£1,414.63** |

▶ **Figure 7.22:** Income statement for Amrit's Pilates business

## Analysis of an income statement

Income statements can be analysed to predict consequences and suggest and justify solutions. As you can see from Figure 7.22, Amrit's bank balance may look fairly healthy but if he continues to bring in very little income his balance will soon be depleted. Amrit's income statement shows the costs his business has had in January for purchasing equipment and which are unlikely to be a monthly expense. This kind of information is crucial for businesses to predict how their income statement may look in future months. This allows businesses to consider the consequences of certain actions, for example the purchase of more equipment or the renting of another site. A clear and accurate income statement allows businesses to justify these decisions as they can predict the possible outcomes from what has happened in the past.

# Creation and interpretation of a statement of financial position

A **statement of financial position** provides a snapshot at a given moment in time of a business' assets (what it owns or is owed) and its liabilities (debts) which can be used to assess its financial viability.

| | Cost | Accumulated depreciation | Net book value |
|---|---|---|---|
| | £ | £ | £ |
| Non-current assets | | | |
| Premises | 218,000 | 28,880 | 189,120 |
| Fixtures and fittings | 38,500 | 15,800 | 22,700 |
| Vehicles | 19,500 | 19,500 | 0 |
| Current assets | | | |
| Stock | | | 34,294 |
| Debtors | | | 21,455 |
| Cash at bank | | | 0 |
| Cash in hand | | | 381 |
| **Total current assets** | | | **56,130** |
| Less current liabilities | | | |
| Creditors | | | 17,881 |
| Overdraft | | | 12,389 |
| **Total current liabilities** | | | **30,270** |
| Working capital (current assets – current liabilities) | | | 25,860 |
| Non-current liabilities | | | |
| Bank loans | | | 50,998 |
| Net assets (Non current assets + working capital – non-current liabilities) | | | 186,682 |
| Financed by | | | |
| Capital | | | 60,000 |
| Retained profit | | | 126,682 |
| Capital employed | | | **186,682** |

▶ **Figure 7.23:** Example of a statement of financial position

A statement of financial position provides financial information which is used to assess the strengths and weaknesses of the business and is used to inform important decisions made about its future and the future of its employees.

A statement of financial position is usually produced by an accountant and contains the business' value and information about **assets**, **liabilities** and **equity**. If a business seeks extra funding, perhaps from a bank or investor, it is highly likely they will need to provide their latest statement of financial position and probably those over previous periods of time to demonstrate the stability and growth of the business.

Potential investors will use the information contained within the balance sheet and possibly use other financial reports to determine whether or not the business is worth investing in, especially as they would want to check the accuracy of the statement of financial position. If you have watched the BBC2 TV programme *Dragons' Den*, the type of financial information the Dragons ask of potential business investments relates to the statement of financial position. This method of presenting the value of a business would be created at any time out of the normal routine if called upon by managers, accountants, HMRC or for potential investment.

---

**Key terms**

**Assets** – a thing, property or person of value to the business which when calculated provides the value of the business overall.

**Liabilities** – sums of money owed by the business such as loans, mortgages, outstanding expenses and taxes.

**Equity** – the value remaining after deducting the business' liabilities from its assets.

---

## Creation of a statement of financial position from data given

To create a statement of the business position financially, all the financial data would be gathered and presented in a predetermined order.

Each of the categories would provide the value at that specific moment in time, therefore any assets such as property or shares would require a valuation or reliable calculation performed by an accountant who would take into account any increase or decrease in value since the previous valuation. The order in which the assets, liabilities and equity appear on the statement of financial position is consistent:

- non-current assets
- current assets
- current liabilities
- non-current liabilities
- net assets.

Matt owns a mobile mechanical service, called 'Solutions', which diagnoses engine problems on-site. His first year's statement of financial position is shown in Figure 7.24.

| Assets | |
|---|---|
| Cash | 25,408 |
| Supplies | 1,819 |
| Debtors | 5,153 |
| Total | 32,380 |
| **Liabilities** | |
| Taxation | -2,614 |
| Creditors | -4,803 |
| **Equity** | |
| Total | **24,963** |

The value of the supplies Matt has as stock

Those who owe money to Matt's business (in red because Matt does not have this money yet)

Matt's tax liabilities to be paid in July

Value of outstanding invoices

▶ **Figure 7.24:** An example of a simple statement of financial position for mobile mechanic 'Solutions'

## Analysis of a statement of financial position to predict consequences and justify solutions

The statement of financial position for 'Solutions' provides the total equity once Matt has paid all outstanding debts and assuming all outstanding income will be received into the business. The statement of financial position will be used by managers at all levels to determine the decisions made about the business in the short, medium and long term.

For example, Matt may need to purchase further equipment for his business. If Matt was to spend the cash in the business account (currently £25,408) he would not have sufficient funds to pay his debts and the business would go into deficit. However, by analysing the sales and cash flow forecast, Matt would be better informed about his financial position and more able to justify the decisions he makes about his business. For example:

▶ the amount of financial investment the business will sustain

▶ when sufficient funds should be available to purchase additional equipment

▶ how long the business could survive if some or all of its debtors fail to pay their debts to the business

▶ how much of a contingency fund Matt should maintain in the business account to avoid paying **overdraft** costs.

**Key term**

**Overdraft** – the financial term given to the deficit in a bank account which occurs when more funds are taken out of the account than exist in it. Also known as 'in the red' as negative figures are often shown in red ink.

**Research**

Go online and find out more about the role of financial analysis from sites such as Flex Study.

**ⅠⅠ PAUSE POINT**

What predictions and decisions would you make based on the financial records for 'Rest Awhile' and Amrit's Pilates business? What further information do you need to justify your decisions?

**Hint**

Create a statement of financial position template for both businesses. Enter the data from the statements to identify gaps.

**Extend**

Use the search term 'Statement of financial position' to explore further examples of these.

## Assessment practice 7.4

### What's the big issue?

The Big Issue is a social enterprise which offers homeless people the opportunity to sell copies of the organisation's magazine in return for a small financial return for their time.

In 2015 an entrepreneurial company combined forces with the Big Issue in London to train a small group of homeless people as baristas on mobile carts, giving a free coffee with every magazine sold to generate income for the homeless. The business has since expanded to several major cities.

This joint venture has since recognised a gap in the market by offering an online coffee ordering service for freshly roasted coffee beans delivered to your doorstep in batches of timely subscriptions from a week up to a year. Each venture provides a homeless person with the chance to earn some money to assist them with something they have identified is important to them on their journey back into work and stable living. From the revenue they generate, from sales of the magazine, coffee and deliveries, vendors receive a contribution of up to 80 per cent towards their goal from The Big Issue Foundation. The pie chart in Figure 7.25 is a typical example of the percentage of people that continue their journey in a variety of ways by receiving grants.

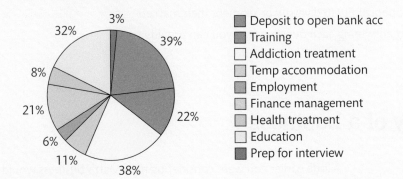

▶ **Figure 7.25:** Grants from the Big Issue Foundation

There are plans to expand these operations to provide more opportunities for work in return for grants but the charity needs to remain viable. The logistics of this operation are considerably more complex than before and you have been asked to analyse the figures from the previous four months' trading to help with the decision making whether to expand and, if so, by how many vans over what period of time. The charity's aim is for every person to receive a grant of some sort and it has included the numbers of those registered in the local area for the next potential mobile coffee van or vans.

▶ **Table 7.7:** Trading figures for the *Big Issue* for four months

|  | September | October | November | December |
|---|---|---|---|---|
| Number of potential vendors | 840 | 790 | 784 | 920 |
| Average grant received by each beneficiary (vendor) | £25 | £25 | £25 | £25 |
| Price per magazine | £2.50 | £2.50 | £2.50 | £2.50 |
| Cost to produce each coffee | £0.30 | £0.30 | £0.30 | £0.30 |
| Mobile van and equipment overheads | £200 | £200 | £200 | £200 |
| Average number of magazines sold per van | 10,000 | 10,000 | 10,000 | 12,500 |
| Price of cups per 1000 | £5 | £5 | £5 | £5 |
| Cost to produce magazines per 5000 | £300 | £300 | £300 | £310 |

The charity suggests calculations are based on an average of four months costs, revenue and potential profits. They are currently running two vans with five vendors on each van. The initial cost of each mobile van is £7500.

The charity wants to know:

1  How much does each beneficiary need to raise in order for the charity to remain in profit and cover its costs?

2  What is the potential for expansion based on an average over those four months?

3  How many vans would they require to reach their ideal target of every homeless person working on the vans in order to receive a grant, also based on the average?

They are also interested to know:

4  Is the coffee idea sustainable?

5  Is there some other opportunity to diversify or segment their market?

Produce a written report answering each question that you can provide to the charity.

# G  Viability of a business

A little earlier you were considering how Matt's business would soon be in danger of becoming unviable if he assumed he could spend the money in the bank account without considering the financial position of the business in more detail. In this section you will be learning about making decisions which support the viability of a business rather than rash decisions which can risk the future of the business.

**Research**

Search online to learn more about the 27,000 or so businesses which have collapsed during and since the recent recession.

When interpreting and analysing a statement of financial position it is also useful to consider working capital because this is a measure of the firm's ability to meet day-to-day expenses. The statement of financial position is a useful indicator of how effectively management are running the business.

# Ratio analysis

Ratio analysis allows for a more meaningful interpretation of published accounts by comparing one figure to another. Ratio analysis also allows for both inter-firm and intra-firm comparisons. Ratios will be used by internal stakeholders such as managers and employees, as well as external stakeholders such as investors and creditors.

## Liquidity ratio

This is calculated using the following formula:

$$\frac{\text{current assets} - \text{inventory}}{\text{current liabilities}}$$

The liquid capital ratio is thought to be a tougher measure of a firm's liquidity. Like the current ratio, it shows the amount of current assets in relation to current liabilities, but it does not include inventory. This is because inventory is considered to be the hardest current asset to turn into cash quickly. The result is expressed as $x$:1.

---

### Worked Example – Freedom Designs Ltd

Current assets = £55,130

Stock = £34,294

Current liabilities = £30,270

$$\text{Acid test} = \frac{£55,130 - £34,294}{£30,270} = \frac{£20,836}{£30,270} = 0.68$$

This means that, for every £1 the business owes in short-term debts, it only has 68p in liquid assets (current assets excluding stock). This figure shows the firm to be **illiquid**, as it could not meet its short-term debts if immediate repayment was demanded. A fashion retailer is likely to have a large amount of its current assets in the form of stock, due to the nature of the firm.

---

**Link**

You learnt about measuring liquidity, profitability ratios and measuring efficiency in *Unit 3: Personal and Business Finance*.

**Key term**

**Illiquid** – not easily converted into cash.

**Fixed assets** – items that have a predetermined fixed price for a period of time, such as a loan or perhaps parcel of land or building.

## Profitability ratio

A profitability ratio measures the profitability of the business.

## Performance ratios

Performance ratios measure how well a business turns its assets into revenue. They include these ratios.

$$\textbf{fixed asset } \text{turnover} = \frac{\text{revenue}}{\text{value of property, plant and equipment}}$$

$$\text{sales revenue per employee} = \frac{\text{total sales revenue}}{\text{total number of employees}}$$

## Interpretation of ratios calculated

The higher the value of the ratios described in the section above, the better the business is performing.

**⏸ PAUSE POINT**

Practise the calculations for liquidity, profitability and performance using the formulas you have been learning about.

**Hint**

Use the formulas to calculate your financial position based on your own data. This will help you remember how to use the formulae and manage your own finances.

**Extend**

Explain the reasons for producing financial statements and list the possible assets the Rest Awhile business is likely to own.

# Threats and 'what if' scenarios

When you make decisions, you often rely on scenarios to help play out what the conclusion might look like depending on the route you take, rather like playing a computer game.

By considering the threats associated with not taking action, as well as those which arise when you do take action, you can make decisions which lead to what you believe will be the most desirable outcome.

## SWOT analysis to identify possible threats

One of the more familiar tools you can use to help identify the possible threats associated with your decision making, such as whether the business will remain viable, is a SWOT analysis. You will have learnt about and used this technique in other units.

**Links**

For SWOT analysis see also *Unit 1: Exploring Business* and *Unit 19: Pitching for a New Business.*

> **Theory into practice**
>
> Produce a SWOT analysis for Amrit's desire to expand his Pilates business to other locations and compare with a second SWOT analysis for Amrit to remain at one centre but extend the number of sessions offered.

## 'What if' scenarios

Sometimes it can be helpful to use 'What if' scenarios to analyse how a proposed business/business development could be affected in a variety of alternative situations. To make decisions based on thorough analyses, our cognitive processes consider the options available to the given scenario. For example, when you were first preparing to attend your place of study, or perhaps for a part-time job, you would have considered how you would make your journey to arrive on time and which route you would take.

Although it sounds very simple, this process would have involved a number of what if scenarios to provide a suitable solution. For example, you may have considered different means of transport or walking routes. You may have considered what to do in alternative situations, such as public transport not arriving on time or at all or difficult weather conditions etc.

Imagine a farmer whose livestock is about to give birth. The farmer has considered the 'what if' scenarios such as the impact of extreme weather conditions and availability of skilled employees if any births occur at night or veterinary assistance is required with problematic births. These situations may seem fairly routine but the variables associated with them may result in unforeseen consequences, impacting on the future viability of the farm. For example, the farmer may be relying on income from selling on the newborn livestock. If there is a high mortality rate, the farmer may not be able to sustain the farming costs for the rest of the year.

> **Research**
>
> Carry out some research to find out about the impact on farms as a result of unforeseen outbreaks from foot and mouth disease in 2001.

## PESTLE analysis

Another tool used by businesses to aid decision making is the **PESTLE** analysis. It can be used to identify possible risks/opportunities for the proposed business/business development.

The PESTLE analysis tool is used to examine the external environment which can be used by businesses to identify the possible risks (or threats) and the opportunities for developing or maintaining a business. For example, Amrit's PESTLE analysis for expanding to other village centres might look something like the example shown in Table 7.8.

> **Key term**
>
> **PESTLE** – political, economic, social, technological, legal and environmental.

▶ **Table 7.8:** PESTLE analysis for Amrit

|  | **Risk** | **Opportunity** |
|---|---|---|
| **Political** | The media could decide fitness activities such as Pilates do not benefit society as much as previously thought. | Fitness is high on government agenda to combat obesity. |
| **Economic** | Rates for hire of the halls could spiral beyond expectations and become unaffordable. | While interest rates remain low, the business can grow by keeping client fees at attractive prices. |
| **Social** | Some locations may have a population demographic which is averse to public displays of fitness activities. | Many clients attend such leisure classes to meet new friends. |
| **Technological** | High profile celebrities promoting Pilates classes which can be held at home without the need for a trainer. | Create own fitness DVD fairly cheaply using own technology which can generate more revenue or used to add value to client's fee. |
| **Legal** | Health and safety laws may restrict Pilates activities to regulated centres. | Use regulations, such as Equality Act, to offer discrete sessions to groups who may otherwise be marginalised. |
| **Environmental** | Some centres may be demolished due to dangerous substances found in the structure of the building eg asbestos. | Work with the local authority to expand range of centres used such as schools, colleges, church halls etc. |

**❚❚   PAUSE POINT**     What conclusions can you draw from Amrit's PESTLE analysis?

> Hint    If you were Amrit, what would you do based on the financial and other information you have gathered?

> Extend    Produce a PESTLE analysis for a bicycle shop. What are the risks and opportunities? What recommendations would you make to ensure the continuing viability of the business?

**Links**

For more on PESTLE analysis see also *Unit 1: Exploring Business, Unit 2: Developing a Marketing Campaign, Unit 5: International Business* and *Unit 19: Pitching for a New Business.*

## Contingency plan

A contingency plan is one which provides alternative solutions or routes to take based on the outcomes from analyses such as the PESTLE, SWOT and other tools. Take for example your decision about how you travel to your place of study or work. One day your bus or subsequent buses might not arrive due to a major incident, or perhaps the train derails. If you usually walk, what would you do if you broke a limb and could not walk? You need a contingency plan.

**Reflect**

Have you ever been late for your place of study or work? Did you forget to set an alarm or did the battery go flat overnight? What contingency plan will you put in place to ensure it does not happen again?

### Creation of a contingency plan

A contingency plan needs to accommodate all eventualities, meaning that it involves numerous complex decisions and solutions. The plan is likely to involve several stages and a process that is repeated for different scenarios. For example, every business relies on some form or forms of utilities to function which are taken for granted as always being available.

Imagine a children's nursery and the problems which immediately arise if there was a problem with the supply of water or electricity. The contingency plan would not only need to provide alternative solutions to keep children fed and watered but also clean and hygienic. The plan would need to involve details such as antiseptic wipes and appropriate toilet facilities. If it was decided that the nursery must close, then the nursery would need some means of contacting parents, many of whom are unlikely to be able to collect their children at a moment's notice.

From an administrative point of view, all the children's records and the financial accounts would require a routine system of back-up. Some records would need to be readily available (and up to date) in other forms, such as parent details, in order to make contact for alternative arrangements.

 **PAUSE POINT**

All businesses need a contingency plan for staffing – often called a succession plan. What type of contingency plan do you think is in place should your tutor need to take unexpected leave for sickness or an emergency?

**Hint**

Ask HR (at your place of study or work) for a copy of the organisation's contingency plan or procedure for covering unexpected events.

**Extend**

Create a contingency plan for Rest Awhile if they had a week-long period of power failure due to extreme weather conditions. Compare this with one created by someone else in your group.

## Assessment practice 7.5

AO1   AO2   AO3   AO4

Jewels of Persia has been operational for three years and during that time has grown from a £2000 investment into a business with current assets of £112,260. The business is based in the east of England and prides itself in providing a design and make service of Islamic clothing for women.

The financial statement for Jewels of Persia shows current liabilities of £60,540. Owners Anya and her sister, Jamalia, have been debating whether to expand the business into their nearest out-of-town shopping mall as a trial for further expansion. Although they have been offered an attractive start-up rate of £12,000 in the first year, this will increase by 50 per cent in year 2 and be doubled by year 3. Jamalia has provided a sales forecast in their first year of £150,000 which is 20 per cent more than they currently sell.

However, Anya has an idea that their business should offer the same service to men and wants to develop this side of the business before committing to premises outside where they are currently located. She is worried that they would not be able to cope with a disparate business although their brother is keen to join the business and prepared to invest £10,000.

The sisters have asked you to help them decide on the best way forward by providing them with a report on the viability of the options they are considering. To do this you will need to:

- create a statement of financial position
- undertake a ratio analysis which identifies their existing liquidity status
- investigate the potential for their business idea based on the local demographic
- carry out a PESTLE and SWOT analysis for three 'what if' scenarios
- present proposed solutions for the outcomes from the PESTLE analyses
- create a contingency plan based on at least two outcomes
- initiate a list of resources the business is likely to need for the two options proposed.

The sisters have asked that the report you provide be sufficiently professional and comprehensive to present to their bank if they need to secure additional funding.

### Plan

- How confident do you feel in your abilities to complete this task?
- Do you understand what each task is asking of you?
- What resources do you need to complete the task? How can you get access to them?

### Do

- Are you spending enough time on each task?
- Have you checked that the figures in the statement of financial position are correct?
- What strategies are you employing to produce your PESTLE and SWOT analyses? Are these right for the task? Are they working? If not, what do you need to do to change this?

### Review

- Can you say whether you had everything you needed to succeed?
- Can you explain which elements you found the most challenging?
- Does your report look professional? Is there anything you would present differently in the future?

# Demonstrate business skills/IT skills

The business skills you will be expected to demonstrate to your employer are numerous but probably some of the most important skills you will need to make decisions on include:

- problem-solving
- innovation
- creativity
- communication
- thinking
- teamwork.

Your ability to be computer literate is easily overlooked, especially when computers are evident in just about everything people do. However, using IT effectively and as efficiently as required in business might be different from your own experience; it also requires the right decisions to be made. In this section you will learn about some of the decisions associated with business and IT skills.

# Business skills

As just stated, business skills are numerous and crucial to your ability to be viewed as a valuable asset to the organisation. You should remember that every business activity provides you with the opportunity to further develop your skills.

## Consideration of all key factors and alternative approaches

Imagine that the skills you need for business are your tools. Whatever role you take on, you may have to stop and decide which tool or skill you will need and this will require a set of decisions to be made.

This is only part of the decision making process. Possibly the most important part is reviewing whether those tools were used skilfully or whether something else might have been more suitable. This process of reflection is invaluable when striving for continual improvement.

> **Discussion**
>
> With a peer, discuss how often you devote time to reflecting on practice. Do you make a conscious effort to learn from your efforts and improve upon them in different ways?

Table 7.9 displays a range of skills and behaviours you may apply to different situations.

▸ **Table 7.9:** Skills and behaviours for different business situations

| Situation | Behaviours | Skills |
|---|---|---|
| Customer complaint | Sensitivity | Listening<br>Empathy<br>Note-taking<br>Problem-solving<br>Teamwork |
| Emergency | Calmness<br>Orderly<br>Systematic | First aid<br>Communication<br>Telephone<br>Teamwork |
| Locating stock | Conscientious<br>Systematic<br>Procedural<br>Diligence | Problem-solving<br>Thinking<br>Record-keeping<br>Teamwork |
| Dietary request | Non-judgemental<br>Sensitivity | Listening<br>Note-taking<br>Creativity<br>Innovation<br>Problem-solving<br>Teamwork |

In terms of the approaches used in business to make decisions, social science theorists refer to three main approaches:

▶ vision-led: clear image or procedures of how to deal with the situation

▶ plan-led: criteria or objectives are defined based on analyses of methods

▶ consensus-led: outcomes from discussions with other stakeholders.

Although this might appear to simplify these approaches, it is likely that you will need to determine the skills you will need and the factors which influence your decision on which approach to take. For example, your employer may have provided you with a procedure for managing a customer complaint, but it depends on the nature of the complaint and the behaviour of the customer as to how you actually manage the complaint to ensure a satisfactory outcome for all parties.

> **Research**
>
> You could search online to read more about these approaches.

> **Theory into practice**
>
> Over the next week or so, observe and listen to how customers' requests are managed in different environments and situations. Make notes about each situation and how they were dealt with and, in particular, identify all the skills both parties used to reach a conclusion.

> **Reflect**
>
> Which occasions resulted in a satisfactory outcome as a result of the skill of the employee? What business skills did they employ particularly effectively and how?

## Consideration of risk (legal, reputation, financial) when making final recommendations/judgements

In the previous section you looked at threats and risks and how they can identify opportunities as well as help with the decision making process for business development and sustainability. Now consider the factors associated with risk and how they can impact on final recommendations or the judgements made about the future.

▶ **Legal**: you have no control over the legal factors which are imposed on you and your business operations but they will impact on your decisions. For example, businesses which have relied on sponsorship from the tobacco or alcohol industry would have been irresponsible to have overlooked the government bans on advertising from the early 2000s and future planned changes in legislation.

▶ **Reputation**: the importance of building and maintaining the reputation of a business should not be underestimated. Examples of businesses that did not sufficiently consider the risk to their business which impacted on their reputation include some of the telecommunications and transport businesses in the UK. Businesses such as Virgin took decisions to reduce their expanse of airline travel to a much more limited service to retain viability without cutting back extensively on the customer in-flight service.

▶ **Financial**: in the section above on financial forecasting and statements of financial position, you were asked to consider several scenarios to assess business viability. Some of the examples provided involved making decisions about expanding or diversifying business operations. A business must be aware of government intentions from the annual budget and reviews. The outcomes of these might include changes to the tax laws and, in previous years, these have included almost immediate changes to national insurance contributions, corporation tax and VAT. An example of this, and a concern for many businesses, especially the smaller organisations, was the introduction in April 2016 of the National Living Wage. Any business which did not include a calculation in their forecasting based on earlier announcements found it impacting on their business practices.

How aware are you about potential risks to business relating to legal intentions?

Learn more about government intentions by looking at the government website, particularly the section on legislation.

Explore how changes to the US government pose both threats and opportunities for UK businesses.

# Use IT skills to create appropriate documentation

Most people need to be able to use some form of technology in their daily working practices. Possibly one of the key skills many people are not taught routinely is how to touch type to use a computer keyboard correctly and accurately. However, it is not just the process of using a keyboard but selecting the right software and documentation to meet business expectations. In this section, you will learn a little more about selecting the right IT tools for the job.

## Appropriate software for the production of a formal business report/executive summary

Each business may have its own preferred rules and agreed style for producing business reports and you should make sure you are fully aware of these before beginning. One of the first points to consider is the purpose of the report as it could be, for example:

▶ narrative

▶ financial

▶ visual

▶ summary

▶ evaluative

or it might be for one of many other purposes, generated perhaps in a set format using standard office software such as Microsoft Word or Excel.

A financial report, for example, might be routinely generated through accounting software such as Sage or Intuit, particularly if the organisation is fairly small. Some micro businesses might use Microsoft Excel to produce forecasts while accountancy firms often use bespoke software but produce a summary of accounts for their clients in a word-processed report.

Larger organisations often use management information systems (**MIS**) which combine all the organisation's operations through one single IT system. **SAP** is another example which combines financial operations with general information about customers and suppliers and provides the business with reporting tools and processes.

## Appropriate software for the production of a presentation

There are many different types of presentation software available, as discussed at the beginning of this unit (see the section Presentation software and techniques). Standard Office packages often come complete with presentation software and the features are fairly simple to apply with tutorials explaining how to use them effectively.

However, the term 'presentation' does not automatically mean using presentation software. For example, a financial presentation from an accountant to the Board of Directors, who will make decisions about the viability of the business, may be more appropriate using financial reports generated from the accounting software.

---

**Reflect**

Would you like to be able to learn to touch type? Why do you think it is important to use a keyboard correctly?

**Discussion**

With a peer or in a small group, discuss the risks associated with not using a keyboard correctly.

**Key terms**

**MIS** – management information system.

**SAP** – systems, applications and products; a data processing system.

---

What specialist presentation software does provide is an integrated system to other software, such as audio and video software, spreadsheets and databases. The benefits of sophistication made easy are, as in this case, that portions of reports, graphs, videos and websites etc can be linked into the presentation. When a link is embedded into the presentation, such as a graph, any changes made to the spreadsheet are automatically updated in the presentation providing the link has not been broken.

> **Tip**
>
> Always check whether you want the link to remain embedded and automatically updated. If you are intending to retain all previous versions of an image such as a graph, you will need to either remove the hyperlink or re-create the spreadsheet to generate a new version of the chart. Deleting the data in the spreadsheet may also remove it from the graph.

## Programmes/software packages for production and manipulation of financial information, generation of graphs and 'what if' scenarios

As software has become more sophisticated over recent years sections from one software package to another can be integrated, resulting in several benefits.

▶ Technology provides a simulated reality of paper-based processes. For example, if you wanted squared paper or a spreadsheet for accounting but were writing a report, you would select a spreadsheet package such as Excel to produce the financial section and integrate it into Word where you produced the narrative. Using a spreadsheet for text is limited and does not form the same function as a word processing application.

▶ Integrating text and images from one software package to another is recognised by the software and may behave in a similar manner by copying the formatting and functions across from its source. For example, a section of spreadsheet containing formulas will transport into a word processed document without losing the values.

▶ Spreadsheet packages might be credited with enabling non-accountants to better manage their financial affairs than ever before. When spreadsheet packages such as Excel first appeared with a graph and chart wizard, the use of this visual representation became commonplace and a fairly simple process to produce. However, the interpretation of the graph and using the right chart for the job is a skill that is also required in business.

▶ Presenting graphs and 'what if' scenarios using software packages provides decision makers with alternative ways to study the data and better visualise situations which impact on the business.

 **PAUSE POINT**   How adept are you at creating graphs and the right formulas?

>    Hint   Learn more about creating graphs from online tutorials.
>
>    Extend   Produce a graph for Amrit's business income statement (Figure 7.18) if his rent increased to £195 per month from next January.

# THINK ▶FUTURE

**Brendan Murphy**

Trainee conveyancer

Brendan has just started working for a solicitor as a trainee conveyancer. He never dreamt he would become a professional but they were impressed with his ambition and said he had the skills and qualifications that matched what they wanted.

Before completing his National Diploma in Business, Brendan asked the careers advisor what options were available, thinking he would probably work in retail or estate agency. But the advisor said he could do an Advanced Apprenticeship in legal services or a foundation degree and he chose the apprenticeship as it offered hands-on experience which has obviously paid off! His new employer said they were looking for someone who is diligent and well organised and particularly someone who can make the right decisions about when to involve the client and when to deal direct with other solicitors.

What Brendan found especially useful about the National Diploma was the breadth of knowledge he gained about business. He thought he wouldn't really need the finance information but found that finance and especially maths is crucial. He is now developing a wider range of skills in the workplace and is grateful to the apprenticeship for that. He feels able to talk confidently with other professionals, including bankers and solicitors, and is gaining in knowledge about how to use the technical language involved in this line of work. He is really looking forward to the next stage of his career and the training he will get to become a qualified solicitor.

## Focusing your skills

When Brendan's employer said they needed someone who was diligent, he hadn't really thought about the job being more than an administrator. However, as he is now dealing with legal documentation every day, he realises how important it is to check everything because:

- a property purchase is a client's largest expense and errors could be very costly
- everything related to a purchase or sale is legally binding and there are hefty penalties for getting it wrong
- any mistakes could also cost the client money in interest, loss of earnings from rent or extra payments on mortgages or fees
- he has to make sure everything that comes into the office is valid, reliable and there are no gaps in information. His studies really helped him understand how to evidence and verify everything.

**Looking ahead**

There is a lot to learn and he mustn't be impatient. Brendan needs to settle into the firm first and make sure to listen and learn from everyone. At the moment he is doing all the basic jobs in order to learn as much as possible. Two of the secretaries have been there for a long time and their experience is priceless. His plan is to:

- take every opportunity to learn from those around
- learn from his mistakes
- search for the best method and location to study for the degree he plans to do after his apprenticeship
- start researching distance learning and part-time degree study.

What skills do you think Brendan will rely on to get the most from his degree course and apply himself fully in his job?

# Getting ready for assessment

This section has been written to help you to do your best when you take the external examination. Read through it carefully and ask your tutor if there is anything you are not sure about.

## About the test

This unit is assessed under supervised conditions. Pearson sets and marks the task.

As the guidelines for assessment can change, you should refer to the official assessment guidance on the Pearson Qualifications website for the latest definitive guidance.

You will need to prepare:

- a word-processed formal report
- a document outlining four presentation slides with speaker notes.

## Sitting the test

Make sure that you arrive in good time for your test and that you leave yourself enough time at the end to check through your work. Listen to, and read carefully, any instructions you are given. Marks are often lost through not reading instructions properly and misunderstanding what you are being asked to do. There are some key terms that may appear in your assessment. Understanding what these words mean will help you understand what you are being asked to do.

| Command or term | Definition – what it is asking you to do |
|---|---|
| Business Plan | A written document that comprises all areas. |
| Executive Summary | Brief but comprehensive synopsis of a business plan or an investment proposal. |
| Formal report | This is a report written to an audience in appropriate business language, layout and style. |
| Presentation | Using software to prepare the materials for a visual presentation. |

- Always make a plan for your answer before you start writing. Sketch this out so you can refer to it throughout – remember to include an introduction and a conclusion and think about the key points you want to mention in your answer. On this plan, think about setting yourself some timeframes so that you make sure you have time to cover everything you want to – and, importantly, have time to write the conclusion!
- Make sure that you understand everything being asked of you in the activity instructions. It might help you to underline or highlight the key terms in the instructions so that you can be sure your answer is clear and focused on exactly what you've been asked to do.

Try and keep your answer as focused on your key points as possible. If you find your answer drifting away from that main point, refer back to your plan!

# Preparing for your assessment

- You will be given a short set task brief. Read this carefully before attempting any questions.
- You can use a calculator and will have access to a computer but you must work on your own.
- You might be given the tasks to do over more than one session.

Don't forget to revise the formulas you have been learning about as you will not be able to take them into your exam.

During your external assessment you will be provided with a set task brief and some background information.

✓ Read all parts of the brief and the background information carefully.

✓ Highlight or underline key words.

# Sample answers

Look at the sample activities which follow and the tips on how to answer them well.

## Set task example

### Set task brief

You have been selected for an interview for a Management Trainee position. As part of your assessment day you have been asked to complete this task to show your understanding of how business decisions are made.

You are required to read the scenario and documents provided and then you will be asked to reach a decision and prepare a business plan in a formal report format and some presentation slides.

On the following pages you will find information relating to a business start-up for a small business offering a vacation rental in France. You need to consider the background information carefully to create a business plan.

## Background information

Mark and Alex bought a rural cottage (known as a Gite) in France to run as a holiday business because they wanted a change in career and something to do as they approached retirement. They longed to live in the Loire Valley and decided upon running the Gite as a means of generating an income whilst realising their lifelong dream. They continued to charge the same rate as the previous owners of €100 per night for double occupancy.

Read the brief carefully and make notes about the important information you are likely to need. You may find it helpful to jot down any key information you think you will need and ideas about how to present your work as you read the brief whilst it's fresh in your mind.

You may need to refer to this later to justify an increase in prices, especially if there is any refurbishment or investment undertaken by the current owners.

This piece of information on price is probably going to be crucial to any calculations you need to make. You will also need to note the current exchange rate which is likely to be listed somewhere in the brief.

Their cash in and out figures are shown in Euros, as represented here:

| | Jan | Feb | Mar | Apr | May | June | July | Aug | Sept | Oct | Nov | Dec |
|---|---|---|---|---|---|---|---|---|---|---|---|---|
| **Total cash in** | 600 | 1300 | 3900 | 6400 | 7000 | 7000 | 12,100 | 14,800 | 11,500 | 8000 | 700 | 6000 |

This second table shows the net cost of purchases to operate their business. The current rate of VAT in France is currently the same as in the UK.

> You will be expected to know what the current rate of VAT is in the UK. If the amount in France was different, you would be provided with this information if needed.

| | Jan | Feb | Mar | Apr | May | June | July | Aug | Sept | Oct | Nov | Dec |
|---|---|---|---|---|---|---|---|---|---|---|---|---|
| **Purchases** | 2000 | 2500 | 3500 | 3500 | 3500 | 4600 | 5200 | 5800 | 5200 | 2500 | 2500 | 3500 |

Alex and Mark have differing views about how to develop the business. Mark is keen on putting in a swimming pool and has received several quotations already, averaging €15,000. Mark is convinced that the inclusion of a swimming pool will justify an increase of €20 per person per night.

Meanwhile Alex has been exploring other ways they can develop their property and receive an income at the same time as the potential for a grant.

He has downloaded some information from the internet which he wants you to summarise in your report and show in the forecast how it will benefit them all round:

---

**Incentives for the installation of solar panels on your French home**

…giving an entitlement to a 50 per cent tax credit, an interest free loan, potential eligibility to a grant, and the possibility of a modest tax free annual income. As a rule of thumb, 3kW is equivalent to around 25m² of photovoltaic solar panels, which would cost around €25k to install… As the resale price of the electricity you sell back…is around five times greater than the price you pay through your meter……the amount of income that could be generated each year is in the order of €1500/€2000. The French government has offered an interest free loan of up to €30k.

---

> This could be a red herring as you have not been given any financial data for a grant. However, in your 'what if' scenarios you could refer to this as a potential opportunity to reduce the investment costs. However, the tax free loan is important to note as Alex and Mark can avoid paying interest and possibly invest their own money wisely to gain interest elsewhere.

Alex and Mark have asked you to look at the data they have provided and make some recommendations about what developments they could undertake.

Other options they have discussed include:

- a refurbishment of three bathrooms, estimated cost €7500
- hire of a mini bus to collect guests from the airport at a cost of €12,500 per annum (but recouping an overall 5 per cent on the cost per double room)
- addition of another Gite by converting an existing barn for which they have received quotations of €28,000 but know a contingency budget of 25 per cent is likely to be needed.

The addition of another Gite would accommodate up to a family of eight which equates to four adults and four children at a maximum of €600 per night based on current prices.

They are both in agreement that they want the greatest return for their investment and, having just received some good news that an elderly relative has bequeathed them £32,000 on the proviso it is spent wisely, they are keen to get started.

## Activity 1

Using the information provided, prepare your business plan for Mark and Alex's Gite business. Mark and Alex have asked for help with progressing their business ideas and have realised they do not understand very much about their financial situation.

In order to help them make some well considered business decisions, they have asked you to produce a report for them, demonstrating:

- their annual VAT liability in Euros
- their annual profit last year in pounds sterling
- their average sales and purchase figures
- an evaluation of the current financial status identifying opportunities for further investment.

You should present your plan in the style of a formal report that could be read by potential investors. Your report should be word processed and clearly structured.

(Total for Activity 1 = 52 marks)

> The first thing you will need to do is perform the calculations. You might find it useful to produce a list of the ones you need to do and either do the easiest ones first or in the order you need to present the answer.

Important to note this as the figures are very basic and vague. Check and double check exactly what the figures are before making any calculations.

You will need to identify which software will be the most suitable or whether you will need to integrate sections from other software into a word-processed report.

Make sure you work back any calculations you make to check you have used the right formula.

Make sure you highlight or circle what you need to do and allocate time for each part.

Tick off each outcome as you have completed them so you do not miss anything.

## Activity 1 Answer:

Introduction

Financial status of the business

To establish the financial status of the Gite business, I have gathered together the first year's trading figures. These are presented here as Table 1. All figures in Euros.

Table 1

|  | Jan | Feb | Mar | Apr | May | June | July | Aug | Sept | Oct | Nov | Dec |
|---|---|---|---|---|---|---|---|---|---|---|---|---|
| Total cash in | 600.00 | 1300.00 | 3900.00 | 6400.00 | 7000.00 | 7000.00 | 12,100.00 | 14,800.00 | 11,500.00 | 8000.00 | 700.00 | 6000.00 |
| VAT on sales | 100.00 | 216.67 | 650.00 | 1066.67 | 1166.67 | 1166.67 | 2016.67 | 2466.67 | 1916.67 | 1333.33 | 116.67 | 1000.00 |
| Sales (cash in VAT) | 500.00 | 1083.33 | 3250.00 | 5333.33 | 5833.33 | 5833.33 | 10,083.33 | 12,333.33 | 9583.33 | 6666.67 | 583.33 | 5000.00 |
| Purchases | 2000 | 2500 | 3500 | 3500 | 3500 | 4600 | 5200 | 5800 | 5200 | 2500 | 2500 | 3500 |
| Net profit (sales – purchases) | -1500 | -1416.67 | -250 | 1833.33 | 1833.33 | 1233.33 | 4883.33 | 6533.33 | 4383.33 | 4166.67 | -1916.67 | 1500 |

To calculate the sales income you will need to use a formula to work out how much of the total cash in will remain after VAT has been paid. To do this, divide the cash in figure by 1.2 and take the answer away from the cash in figure.

Cash in ÷ 1.2 – cash in = sales

From this analysis, the annual net profit in Euros is €21,233.31 = 21,233.31
The VAT they can reclaim on purchases is 0.2 × €44,300.04 = 8860
This means the annual profit is €21,233.31 + 8860 = 30,093.31
In pounds sterling, this is 30,093.31 × 0.8 = 24,074.65.

Do not forget that when you calculate the profit you need to add in the VAT that they have paid on their purchases which they can claim back from the government. The formula you need to convert from euros to pounds sterling is euros × 0.8 = pounds sterling.

The average monthly sales figure is €5506.94.
The average monthly purchase figure is €3691.67.

Graph 1 shows how new profit varied throughout the year.

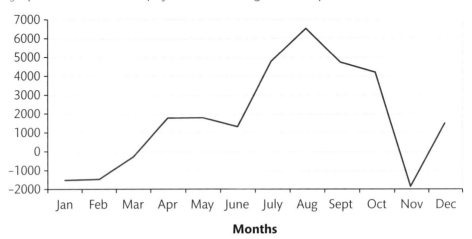

**Months**

This shows that maximum profits were made during the months of July, August and September. However, investment in new facilities needs to be made when sales are lower so that as few guests as possible are inconvenienced by the work.

Options to consider

1. Addition of a swimming pool (assuming an increase of €20 per night on last year's cash in and same occupancy rates).

   Cash in and sales figures are shown in Table 2.

Table 2

|  | Jan | Feb | Mar | Apr | May | June | July | Aug | Sept | Oct | Nov | Dec |
|---|---|---|---|---|---|---|---|---|---|---|---|---|
| Total cash in | 720.00 | 1560 | 4680 | 7680 | 8400 | 8400 | 14520 | 17760 | 13800 | 9600 | 840.00 | 7200 |

You would then complete this table with the figures as in Table 1 for VAT on sales and sales.

This option entails an initial cost of €15,000.
The projected figures are as follows. (Assuming pool installed in January when occupancy rate is lowest, and that other purchase figures remain the same as last year.)

You would now add the cost of the swimming pool as a purchase in the January column of the table.

2. Refurbishment of three bathrooms

3. Hire of a minibus

4. Addition of another Gite

You would consider each of these options in turn and decide which was likely to bring most return on the investment, before making your final recommendations.

## Activity 2

Summarise the viability of your business plan in a way that will convince potential investors. Present your summary in the form of a four-slide presentation with speaker notes. (Total for activity 2 = 18 marks)

## Activity 2 Answer:

| Slide 1 | |
|---|---|
| Slide content | Scenario<br>Swimming pool v no swimming pool:<br>Cost XXXX; Potential additional income generated XXX;<br>Contingency budget...XXX; Advantages....disadvantages... |
| Speaker notes | Flag that data has been analysed to ensure accuracy with currency changes. The calculations used included... |

You might include a small table here to show the risks and uncertainties to the business for each idea Alex and Mark have given. The table could provide a template for each scenario so there is a consistent approach to how you present your scenarios and findings.

If you are asked for a certain number of slides think about the best way to present information. If you have more than one scenario, but only four slides, you might want to put all your scenarios in one table on one slide.

| Slide 2 | |
|---|---|
| Slide content | Strengths/Weaknesses<br>Existing business....<br>Potential for expansion....<br>Feasibility of the conversion in time.... |
| Speaker notes | Some of these ideas, such as xxxx are desires rather than justifiable business decisions which will either generate more income or sustain income growth over time. |

Your speaker notes should be prompts for providing the detail which you would not include in your slides. You might prepare another slide with the financial forecast. Alternatively, you could prepare a graph showing the existing financial situation with the current guest rates and what the future could look like if there is investment in your proposal.

| Slide 3 | |
|---|---|
| Slide content | Opportunities/Threats<br>Increase client numbers<br>Increase existing client rates by...<br>Possible loss of guests due to building work... |
| Speaker notes | The opportunities outweigh the risks but we should be aware that the risks are substantial. The timing of the building to coincide with the peak period means that... |

Using a tool such as a SWOT analysis will help you focus on the key points of your business plan and help you to make appropriate recommendations.

Your speaker notes should include your justifications for your recommendations. This will demonstrate your ability to think critically and objectively.

| | Slide 4 |
|---|---|
| Slide content | Recommendations<br>1. Move forward with Scenario....<br>2. Include a budget of...<br>3. Propose starting building work on... |
| Speaker notes | The justification for scenario 1 is that we can.... The bulk of the budget will be funded through.... |

## Further reading and resources

Heath, C., Heath, D. (2014) Decisive: How to make better decisions, Random House Business

Jones, D. (2014) Decision making for dummies, John Wiley & Sons

Jones, N. R. (2000) The Decision-Making Pocket Book, Management Pocket Books

## Websites

- www.mindtools.com/pages/main/newMN_STR.htm
  A variety of business strategy tools.
- www.openmynewbusiness.com/business-plan-guide
  Advice on writing a business plan.
- http://smallbusiness.chron.com/important-factor-influencing-decision-making-35584.html
  Information on making decisions as a small business.
- www.mathsisfun.com
  Online tutorials and guidance on maths calculations.
- http://word.mvps.org/FAQs/Formatting/UsingOLView.htm
  Find out about using outline in Microsoft Word
- www.excel-easy.com/examples/scatter-chart.html
  How to create scatter charts in Excel.
- www.wisegeek.org/what-are-market-trends.htm
  Information on market trends.

People who set up their own businesses are often called entrepreneurs. They are expert at exploring potential business opportunities. They are able to select viable business ideas and prepare an appropriate business plan that they can pitch to potential investors. These steps are crucial for creating new businesses, and this unit will give you the opportunity to develop your skills to enable you to put together a business plan and pitch for funding.

## How you will be assessed

This unit will be assessed through two assignments. The first will be research and preparation which will lead on to the second, practical assignment. Throughout the unit, there will be assessment practices for you to undertake that will help towards your final assessment tasks.

To obtain a Merit or Distinction, it is important that you take notice of what is being asked of you at each grade. For example, the Merit criteria ask you to analyse the work that you undertake and the Distinction grade will require you to evaluate your work.

Your tutor will set your assignments, made up of a number of tasks that will cover all of the learning aims at each of the Pass, Merit and Distinction grades for the unit.

You will be required to produce a portfolio of evidence that supports specific recommendations for a micro-business start-up that you will go on to develop in order to pitch for funding. This portfolio of evidence will contain details and actual records of your research methods and a number of different types of analysis as well as the risk evaluation that you will be asked to complete. This will culminate into a business plan that you will be required to produce.

Presentation will also form a part of the assessment as you will need to present a final pitch for funding of your chosen micro-business.

The assignments set by your tutor will consist of a number of tasks designed to meet the criteria in the table. They are likely to include a written assignment but may also include activities such as:

▸ creating a portfolio of evidence to include all of your research, analysis, risk assessments and any other documents you have created to plan for and deliver your business pitch

▸ creating a business plan

▸ delivering a professional presentation of your pitch for the funding of your micro-business.

## Assessment criteria

This table shows what you must do in order to achieve a **Pass**, **Merit** or **Distinction** grade, and where you can find activities to help you.

| Pass | Merit | Distinction |
|------|-------|-------------|

**Learning aim** **A** Explore potential ideas for a micro-business start-up

| Pass | Merit | Distinction |
|------|-------|-------------|
| **A.P1**<br>Describe the potential business opportunities for a micro-business start-up.<br>**Assessment practice 19.1** | **A.M1**<br>Analyse the internal and external factors associated with a selected micro-business start-up.<br>**Assessment practice 19.1** | **A.D1**<br>Evaluate the internal and external factors associated with a selected micro-business start-up.<br>**Assessment practice 19.1** |
| **A.P2**<br>Review the factors that need to be considered to start up a micro-business.<br>**Assessment practice 19.1** | | |

**Learning aim** **B** Develop a business plan for a viable micro-business start-up

| Pass | Merit | Distinction |
|------|-------|-------------|
| **B.P3**<br>Explain your marketing plan for a selected micro-business.<br>**Assessment practice 19.2** | **B.M2**<br>Analyse the financial and marketing plans for your micro-business.<br>**Assessment practice 19.2** | **B.D2**<br>Evaluate your plan for a micro-business and justify your conclusions.<br>**Assessment practice 19.2** |
| **B.P4**<br>Explain how legal and financial aspects will affect the start-up of the business.<br>**Assessment practice 19.2** | | |

**Learning aim** **C** Carry out a pitch for funding for the chosen micro-business

| Pass | Merit | Distinction |
|------|-------|-------------|
| **C.P5**<br>Pitch for funding to start up a micro-business.<br>**Assessment practice 19.2** | **C.M3**<br>Effectively present an individual pitch to negotiate funding for a micro-business start-up, analysing audience feedback and viability issues.<br>**Assessment practice 19.2** | **C.D3**<br>Demonstrate individual responsibility and effective self-management in the preparation, delivery and review of the presentation of a high-quality pitch.<br>**Assessment practice 19.2** |
| **C.P6**<br>Review the viability and risks of the start-up using audience feedback.<br>**Assessment practice 19.2** | | |

## Getting started

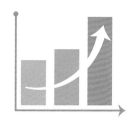

There are an estimated 4.9 million small businesses in the UK and entrepreneurs, whether famous or not, will all go through the same processes of identifying potential business ideas and creating business plans to take their ideas into reality. The skill in finding the most suitable investors who will be willing to invest in any business is an important factor as is the way in which the pitch for this funding is made.

## A  Explore potential ideas for a micro-business start-up

### Micro-business start-up idea exploration

It is crucial, before you can go forward with a business idea, that you believe in your idea 100 per cent and can transfer the passion you have to other people who you will need along the way, such as investors and those who you may need to employ.

Some inexperienced and new entrepreneurs may have a clear idea of what they want their business to be, but others may have no idea at all. Some ideas come from a long held desire, some are 'found accidentally' and some are generated by following steps to grow and develop ideas.

### Idea generation for new products, services and/or market for business opportunities

There are five areas from where ideas can be generated.

▶ Technical breakthrough: this is where ideas are generated from pioneering technical areas that are generally outside the public domain, such as the military, space exploration or Formula 1 motor racing. The very best industry experts with technical expertise are employed by such organisations to provide innovative and specific solutions for pioneering or ground-breaking innovations. Businesses are then generated from this. For example, the memory foam mattress was developed from the need to offer astronauts a comfortable sleeping platform and ABS brakes were originally designed for aircraft. Formula 1 then took on the ABS braking system for their racing cars and developed it further, which enabled car manufacturers to develop the braking systems that we have in our cars today.

▶ Non-technical idea development: this is where ideas are taken from something that already exists, but with a new way of using it or taking it to market. For example, the jewellery industry has taken on a new concept in the way that customers can build their own items, such as bracelets and necklaces, with the option to spend according to their budget. Pandora and Links of London are two examples of companies that have embraced this. Another example is companies that have been created to use people's wish to recycle rather than throw items away. They offer to pay for used items, such as ink cartridges and mobile phones, and then refurbish them before selling them again through their own websites.

▶ Ideas from another environment: this is where entrepreneurs have seen items and services in other countries, cultures or areas of interest that they know would open up a whole new market. For example, sushi started as a street food in Tokyo back in 1824, moved into restaurants in Japan and then the first conveyor belt sushi restaurant opened in Waterloo station in 1994. Another example can be seen in the way that clothing shops, created in particular areas, selling clothing and accessories

▶ How has sushi developed from being a street food in Japan?

for local hobbies and needs, have developed their businesses into great success stories. For example, the founders of Saltrock discovered that the demand from surfers for their clothing went beyond their expectations within North Devon, and now have 42 stores across the South West/South Wales, and FatFace, which started with two young men selling shirts and sweat shirts in the Alps, and now has over 200 stores in the UK and Ireland.

▶ New concepts for jewellery have created new customers and markets.

▶ Serendipity: this is where business ideas come through unintentional routes, or even by accident. Did you know that Marmite came about because it is a by-product of beer? In the 19th century Justus Von Liebig found that yeast extract, a by-product of brewing beer, could be concentrated, bottled and eaten and, over the years, the product has grown into the success you see today. Another example is how the Post-It note came about. In 1970, Spencer Silver was trying to develop a strong glue, when he ended up with a weaker product. He found that this weaker glue would stick, but then become unstuck very easily. About four years later he noticed a friend of his using paper markers in a music book that kept slipping, so his glue was used and he realised that after the markers were removed from the book they had not damaged the pages. This was the beginning of the Post-It note, which was first launched in 1979.

▶ Purposeful development: this is where there is a heavy investment in developing new ideas, products and/or services. Established businesses will have departments dedicated to producing new or improved products. For example, leading supermarkets employ scientists and chefs to develop some of their own brand products, such as ready meals. They invest in laboratories and commercial kitchens and employ industry experts and scientists for the development of new products. Another example is technology. Apple are constantly working on new ideas and innovations to add to the products they offer: for example, think about the iPad. The iPad was launched in 2010 and very quickly was improved with newer models; then came the iPad Mini and now the iPad Pro. Each, Apple would argue, is an improvement on the model before it and still the company continues to design and develop new products.

### Research

There are many more examples of products and/or services that have been generated from each of the five areas above. Carry out research online to see if you can find another example from each of these five areas.

**❚❚ PAUSE POINT**

Looking at the five areas from where ideas can be generated, which areas are your ideas most likely to originate from?

**Hint** Create a table with a heading for each of the five areas and write each of your ideas underneath the relevant heading.

**Extend** See if any businesses using your ideas already exist. Investigate how they are operating and if you would be duplicating what is already established, or if you could improve it and offer something better.

### Decision matrix: generation of selection criteria and scoring for business opportunities

As you try to come up with an idea for a new business, many ideas will pop into your head, some of which will be relevant and some which will be less important. There may be things that you have not even thought about in these early stages that you will need to consider. These ideas need to be organised and a decision matrix is a good way to do this.

A decision matrix is a tool that helps you to weigh up the different factors that need to be considered before taking a micro-business from the initial ideas stage into something that you can use to work on and then develop into a serious proposition and, ultimately, into a business plan.

The decision matrix requires you to list all of the options you have within your new business idea and also factors that you need to take into consideration. Each of these factors should be weighted in order of importance.

See Table 19.1 for an example of a decision matrix used to establish which options would be best for an individual who has the idea of starting up a business making and selling bunting and other soft furnishings and who wants to establish which would be the best products to move forward with.

The weighted ranking for each of the factors must be made according to the needs of the business and the importance they will have to the overall success. In the example shown, the most important factor that has been taken into consideration is space in the stockroom and, therefore, it has been given a low weighting. This would be because space is limited and many large items would be difficult to store, so the weighting reflects this. The next area of value is the cost and availability of materials. These factors have been weighted with equal importance. The time taken is next, followed by the skill to make the items, which is weighted as the least important. This might be because all of the options or items listed are considered to be well within the skills base of the business owner or staff that will be employed.

The next stage within the decision matrix is to score each of the options according to the different factors, based on the knowledge of the individual who is creating the new business, or on their research if they do not already know. These scores are based on a scale of 1 to 5 in Table 19.1, below, and have then been multiplied by the weighted ranking to give an overall score. The higher the score, the more viable the product, and the lower the score, the less viable the product. For example, bunting has scored 4 for the cost of the materials, as fabric scraps can be used, which are relatively inexpensive, and 5 for the amount of space, as there is plenty of space available. However it has been scored 1 for the amount of time it will take to make, as making bunting is a time-consuming job.

▶ **Table 19.1:** A decision matrix for a business start-up making bunting and soft furnishings

| Factors | Cost of materials | Availability of materials | Time required to make item | Skill required to make item | Amount of space needed in stock room | Total scores |
|---|---|---|---|---|---|---|
| **Options** | weighted ranking 3 | weighted ranking 3 | weighted ranking 4 | weighted ranking 5 | weighted ranking 2 | |
| Bunting | 4 × 3 = 12 | 4 × 3 = 12 | 1 × 4 = 4 | 3 × 5 = 15 | 5 × 2 = 10 | 53 |
| Cushions | 4 × 3 = 12 | 4 × 3 = 12 | 3 × 4 = 12 | 4 × 5 = 20 | 1 × 2 = 2 | 58 |
| Table cloths | 1 × 3 = 3 | 1 × 3 = 3 | 5 × 4 = 20 | 5 × 5 = 25 | 3 × 2 = 6 | 57 |
| Tea towels | 2 × 3 = 6 | 2 × 3 = 6 | 5 × 4 = 20 | 5 × 5 = 25 | 4 × 2 = 8 | 65 |
| Peg bags | 3 × 3 = 9 | 3 × 3 = 9 | 3 × 4 = 12 | 4 × 5 = 20 | 4 × 2 = 8 | 58 |
| Door stops | 4 × 3 = 12 | 4 × 3 = 12 | 3 × 4 = 12 | 4 × 5 = 20 | 2 × 2 = 4 | 60 |
| Weighting: low number = negative high number = positive | | | Scores: low number = negative high number = positive | | | |

**❚❚ PAUSE POINT**

From the table above, which option is the most viable to make in the new soft furnishings business? Give your reasons.

Hint — Put the total scores in order and list the options from most viable to least viable.

Extend — Are there more factors that could be considered and added to the decision matrix? What additional value would your additional suggestions give to the overall results?

# Models for business opportunities

Business activity can be considered as primary, secondary or tertiary, depending on the nature and structure of the business. Sometimes it can be a combination, or all three. It is important for an entrepreneur to understand and know how each of the three different types of activity can contribute to a business, so that they can focus on what is most important to them and identify what opportunities might be available should they need to develop and/or diversify their business.

## Business activity

### Primary activity

This is where businesses use natural resources as their main product, for example an arable farming business where the farmer will grow the crops using his land, which forms the basis of the business. Another example is the salt mining industry; Winsford Rock Salt Mine in Cheshire has been operating as one of the longest operating mines in the UK and provides salt for the roads in icy conditions and for other purposes.

### Secondary activity

This is where manufacturing and/or construction is the main activity of a business. In these businesses, products will be made using raw materials or parts that they order in. There will be many stages of production that may happen within a whole business, or may be distributed across several businesses. These businesses cover many different areas, including furniture, books, clothing and cars. A furniture manufacturer is likely to make and produce their products in totality as they buy in the raw materials, such as timber, padding and fabrics and then employ skilled craftspeople to make the furniture. An example of this can be seen in a company called

▶ Winsford Salt Mine is an example of a primary activity. Can you think of other examples?

Distinctive Chesterfields, based in West Yorkshire. In contrast to this, the automotive industry has businesses that manufacture components for vehicles, and then other businesses buy these component parts and bring them to their production lines in order to produce whole vehicles. Honda, in Swindon, is an example of a car manufacturer that has a car production plant and a separate engine manufacturing plant.

### Tertiary activity

Businesses that offer services such as estate agents, insurance companies and travel agents are all undertaking tertiary activity. These businesses rely on interaction directly with their customers who are usually the end users. They may also have a business-to-business model where their customers are other businesses that require their services.

Some businesses will be focused and have one main activity, which could be primary, secondary or tertiary. However, there are also examples of businesses diversifying or needing to expand in order to remain successful. For example, a farmer may decide to make his own cheese and other dairy products that can be sold in a farm shop created in one of the farm buildings. The farm in this example is demonstrating all three types of activity. There are several farms that have been successful in diversifying their businesses beyond just traditional farming, such as Wykes Farm in Somerset and St Helen's Farm in Yorkshire.

> **Link**
>
> You will have learnt about the different types of business activity in *Unit 1: Exploring Business*.

> **Research**
>
> Look at the websites of the different farm businesses, such as Wykes and St Helen's, to find out more about the products and services they offer.
>
> Identify the primary, secondary and tertiary activity that is taking place in each of the businesses.

**PAUSE POINT**

Write a brief explanation of primary, secondary and tertiary business activities. Think of an example of one type of industry for each and then a business that might use more than one of the three main activities.

Hint

Research online to find examples of different businesses that engage in primary, secondary and tertiary activity and of at least one more business that uses more than one, or all three, of these activities.

Extend

With the examples you have found online, identify ways in which the business could diversify into other activity areas to grow and develop the business.

> **Key term**
>
> **Robotics** – the use of robots within a production line. Quite often the manufacturer will be involved in the development of the robots, as they are required to conduct specific and specialist tasks within the process of the production line, which is likely to be unique to the organisations.

### Processes

It is important to be aware of the processes that are involved in specific businesses. These are manufacturing, outsourcing, sourcing and channels to market.

### Manufacturing

Manufacturing takes place when raw materials, ready-made components and/or parts are made into a finished product or products on a large scale, using a production line that involves machinery. People are employed to operate the machinery, although, more and more manufacturers are now using **robotics** in their production line. What may appear to be the simplest of processes could well use a production line with robots. This includes consumer goods ranging from food and drink to technology gadgets, such as mobile phones and tablets. The milk industry has used production lines and robotics for many years, so that the milk and the container are not touched by human hand from the time when the cow is milked through to when the carton or plastic bottle is delivered to the supermarket.

> ### Research
>
> Look at different manufacturing production lines online. See how many different industries you can find that use production lines and robotics. Are they all large companies? Can you find any family-run businesses that are in manufacturing?

### Outsourcing

Outsourcing is when an organisation uses other businesses and individuals to supply them with products and/or services rather than manufacturing their own, or they may use a combination of their own products and services as well as outsourcing in order to meet demand and to accommodate fluctuations in their business. For example, car rescue organisations, such as the AA and RAC, have their own employed mechanics with a fleet of rescue vehicles and also use a network of local garages and rescue services across the country. In other examples, businesses may offer their own clothing range, but outsource the making of this clothing to another company. Think of Marks and Spencer, which have their own brand name for clothing, household goods and food; however, they do not actually make or manufacture anything. All M&S products are outsourced to a variety of specialist companies, chosen for their ability and expertise in each of the product areas.

Outsourcing is also used by businesses for services that are necessary for the smooth running of their own business, for example, the payroll, or an employee support line. These types of service are outsourced for a variety of reasons. A large organisation is likely to use outsourcing for economies of scale where it may be more cost effective to use a payroll specialist, such as Ceridian. This company will guarantee that the payroll is accurate and that employees are paid on time, as well as ensuring that everything completed is in compliance with employment law.

Smaller organisations are likely to outsource to a payroll company for their expertise and convenience. It may be that the company does not have a payroll expert and wants to concentrate on the core elements of the business rather than what may be a complex area of the business for them to understand.

### Sourcing

All businesses have a level of sourcing that they have to undertake, where they research and find the products they need in order to operate. Even if a business is going to manufacture its own products, it will still need to source the raw materials needed to make those goods. In a large organisation, sourcing is likely to be undertaken by a dedicated department, such as buying, whereas, in a smaller organisation, the owner or a senior manager might source what is required. Sourcing can be undertaken in many different ways, from researching online to travelling overseas to go and see, touch or experience the products before deciding whether to purchase.

When sourcing products and/or services, there are many factors to consider, such as suitability of the product, price, value for money, colour, feel, touch, functionality, quality, ethics, how popular it would be with the target market and continuity of supply. Five of these factors, with the impact they can have on a business, have been listed in Table 19.2.

▶ **Table 19.2:** Factors to consider when sourcing and possible impact on a business

| Factors to consider in sourcing | Impact it can have on a business |
|---|---|
| Suitability of product | When sourcing a product, suitability is very important. Is the product fit for purpose? Will it do what it says it will do? If the product is to sell on to customers, will it suit the target market of the organisation? If the product is to use within the manufacturing of a product, will it meet the needs of the production line? |
| Cost | Cost is a very important part of the decision-making process when sourcing. Can the business make a profit once the item has been paid for? Can there be an appropriate markup to allow for a profit, and that will not make the item prohibitively expensive for the customer? |
| | If sourcing for a production line, is the cost of the item in line with the overall manufacturing budget? |
| Quality | Is the product built to last? Will it meet the expectations of the customer if sourcing for a retail environment? |
| | Is the item of sufficient quality to meet the needs and demands of a production line? |
| Ethics | Businesses are increasingly becoming concerned with how a product has been made, for example in clothing manufacturing the general public is becoming increasingly aware of young children working in squalid conditions to make budget high street fashion clothing. Businesses are now questioning the origins of such items, whether for the retail market or for the production line. |
| Continuity of supply | Businesses need to know the probability of a supply being available in the future. For some businesses, their strategy is to source unique items, and so the fact that they would not be able to buy the product again is a positive factor. This is likely to be in a retail outlet where one-off pieces of art or clothing are the unique products sold. |
| | Other businesses have a strategy where they promote the fact they can offer the same products for a guaranteed period of time and this can be very important for their customers, – think of chinaware and dinner services. Customers would not be happy if they could not replace a broken plate or cup from an expensive six piece set, even after a few years. In manufacturing, the business is likely to want reassurance that the part or item being sourced will be available for a considerable period of time. |

### Channels to market

Businesses must consider how they are going to get their goods and/or services from the point of production to the end user, and who the customer, or consumer is. It may be that they can sell directly to the customer, but, even if this is the case, the business still needs to consider how that might be done, for example online using a website, face to face in a shop or by phone using a contact or call centre. For other businesses, it may be necessary to use a wholesaler and/or a distributor, and some businesses might also need to use a combination of some of these **supply chains** (see Figure 19.1).

> **Key term**
>
> **Supply chains** – the sequence of processes to get a product or service from production to the consumer. This is likely to involve a network of businesses and services to produce and move a product through the channels to market, in order to be made available to the customer.

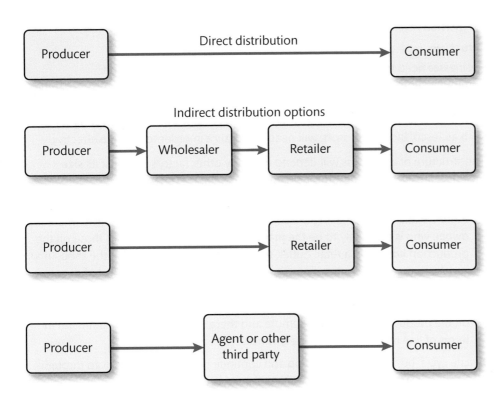

▶ **Figure 19.1:** Different products need different channels to market.

▶ Producer to consumer: this is the most straightforward channel and is likely to work for certain sectors, for example farms that run their own farm shops or a small craft businesses.

▶ Producer to retailer to consumer: there are some companies that choose to avoid using a wholesaler, such as Oak Furnitureland. This is an established business selling oak furniture to the public via their website and through a chain of their own branded stores across the UK. They have a large distribution centre and employ their own teams who deliver their products directly to their customers' homes.

▶ Producer to wholesaler to retailer to consumer: the food and clothing sectors are likely to use wholesalers. The wholesaler will source the products and buy them from the producers, who may be from around the world. They then store the products or goods in large warehouses before selling them on to the retailer. Using a wholesaler means that the retailer can offer a wide range of products to their customers in a cost-effective way, because they are purchasing their items to sell from a small number of wholesalers, who are offering a wide range of worldwide products. The wholesaler will buy in the products at a certain price and sell them on to the retailer at an increased price, all of which is clearly detailed in the financial transactions.

▶ Producer to distributor to retailer to consumer: in many ways, the distributor behaves in a similar way to a wholesaler, in that they will source products to sell on to retailers. The main difference is that the distributor has more of an interest in the goods being sold and will be proactive in the promotion and development of the sales of the products they are handling. A distributor is more likely to take a percentage amount of the products sold from the retailer in return for their services. This means that the amount paid will be determined by the efforts and success of the distributor.

**Link**

*Unit 1: Exploring Business* covered the different types of organisational structure that businesses operate. Look there to remind yourself of flat, matrix and holocratic structures.

**Key terms**

**Public Limited Company (PLC)** – PLCs offer shares to the general public and have a limited liability. Their stocks can be acquired by anybody. A company must follow strict government rules and regulations to become a PLC.

**Size** – number of employees in an organisation. Classifications for business size include micro, small, medium and large.

## Organisational form

### Structure

Businesses need to have a structure outlining the lines of authority and communication channels. The size of the business is likely to be a large contributing factor to its structure. A small, family-run business is less likely to have a formal and complicated structure, but, a large multi-national **Public Limited Company (PLC)**, such as Tesco, BP or Microsoft, will need a structure in order to operate effectively.

The structure of a business will depend on many other factors than just its **size** – including life cycle, strategy, business environment and even values.

▶ Size: the fewer employees in an organisation, the fewer levels of management there are likely to be, making the company structure 'flat'. An example is where the owner, who is also likely to be the managing director, will work with those on the production line, or, in a retail outlet, they could both be working in the shop. In a very large organisation, the managing director will work with a board of directors who look after different areas of the business and they will have senior managers reporting to them. The chances of the managing director knowing those who work on the production line is quite remote and there will be a chain of command in terms of line managers across the business.

▶ Life cycle: businesses that develop and continue to grow are likely to go through a series of structural changes, creating life cycles that they are continuously going through and emerging from. Large and small organisations are affected by life cycle structures that are influenced by factors such as business growth, a need to save costs, to become more effective or to reflect industry changes, such as becoming more mechanised and therefore requiring fewer managers.

▶ Strategy: a business may decide to have a smaller structure so that it can react quickly to market changes and keep ahead of its competitors. Another organisation, however, may decide to have a larger structure so that each area or department can become specialists in different areas of the business.

▶ Business environment: in fast-paced sectors, it will be important to have a smaller, slicker structure to ensure that the business can react to any market changes, whether expected or unexpected. The demands of the customer may also influence the structure of a business, based on the business environment.

### Roles and responsibilities

Whether the business is large or small, there is likely to be some kind of a structure. Within this structure, the roles and responsibilities of each level of management and job role must be clearly defined so that everyone is clear on what is expected of them in terms of performance, skills and behaviour. These roles and responsibilities are likely to be written down in larger organisations, and to be part of the job description for each role within the organisation. This ensures transparency and fairness when dealing with promotions, staff development and any concerns that a manager may have about the performance of one of their team.

In smaller organisations, roles and responsibilities are less likely to be so defined, as employees may be asked to undertake a variety of tasks as the need arises. In these situations, the employee is likely to be much closer to the senior manager or owner of the business and so communication channels remain open and accessible to raise any concerns around roles and responsibilities.

## Case study

### Scott's dog grooming business

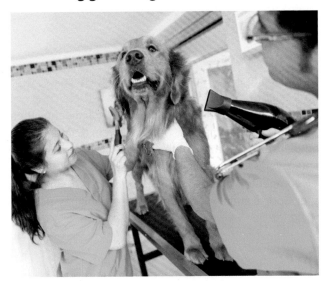

Scott has decided to start up his own dog grooming business. He has undertaken some market research and established that there is a local need, as pet owners have expressed an interest in the services he plans to offer.

As well as dog grooming, Scott plans to sell pet accessories and offer dog-sitting and walking services.

Scott was unsure on where and how to start his business in terms of what he should do first. A friend introduced him to a decision matrix, and so he used this as a basis to help him make the correct decisions in starting up his business.

Scott is able to use a large room for the dog grooming and there will be sufficient space to set up a small shop in the corner of the room, so accommodation, although important, is not a significant consideration in making decisions. He is on a budget, so setting-up costs are a big consideration that need to be controlled and the level of skill required for different areas of his business are quite varied. Scott is aware that he needs a qualified dog groomer, so he must consider the level of skill that is required for each of the four areas of his business should he need to employ anybody. Scott has completed the decision matrix to be able to get a good idea of costs that will be involved. He has weighted the factors between 1 and 5 and each of his options between 1 and 5.

Below is his completed decision matrix.

|  | Tools required weighting 4 | Accommodation weighting 2 | Outlay (cost) weighting 5 | Level of skill weighting 5 | Total |
|---|---|---|---|---|---|
| Dog grooming | 5 × 4 = 20 | 5 × 2 = 10 | 1 × 5 = 5 | 5 × 5 = 25 | 60 |
| Pet accessories | 1 × 4 = 4 | 4 × 2 = 8 | 5 × 5 = 25 | 3 × 5 = 15 | 52 |
| Dog sitting | 1 × 4 = 4 | 0 × 2 = 0 | 3 × 5 = 15 | 1 × 5 = 5 | 24 |
| Dog walking | 1 × 4 = 4 | 0 × 2 = 0 | 3 × 5 = 15 | 1 × 5 = 5 | 24 |

From completing the decision matrix, Scott could clearly see that the high risk, high cost areas of the business would be the dog grooming and pet accessories area of the business, whereas the dog sitting and dog walking were low cost and low risk.

Although the highest risk to the business is the dog grooming side, Scott feels that it is important to get this part of the business off the ground. He thinks that he may be able to outsource a qualified dog groomer to come in and work on the days that there are appointments, rather than employ anyone full time. Scott plans to do some of the dog-sitting and dog-walking services himself and then employ one person who can help him with the dog walking and the running of the shop.

For the pet accessories shop, Scott will need to establish where he can buy the items that he would need to stock his shop.

### Check your knowledge

1   Are there any other factors that Scott should consider within his decision matrix?

2   Looking at the decision matrix, what are Scott's high risk areas?

3   Does Scott have any other 'outsourcing' options?

4   What channels to market would Scott be using for each of his four areas of his business?

5   If Scott was to put a personnel structure in place, what would be its biggest contributing factor?

# Factors to be considered when setting up a micro-business

There are several different factors that you need to consider when setting up your own micro-business.

### Capabilities and core competences

Successful businesses will have a unique set of capabilities that set them apart from their competitors: these are known as their core competences. These core competences are what make an organisation a leader in their field, what define them and make them so successful. This is the organisation's internal strength. Managers of such organisations will complete an assessment of the company's internal and external environments. The manager is looking for strengths that meet the needs of their customers and that their competitors will find difficult to replicate. Think of Apple and their design capabilities, or Google and their search engine capabilities. Both are leaders and experts in their field.

### Time constraints

There are many tasks to complete, with deadlines to meet, when setting up a business. An entrepreneur must think about the order in which tasks need to be completed and the time each of these tasks will take, as they will work long hours when setting up their business and will not be able to do everything at once. Tasks need to be prioritised to ensure that those that will take a long time to complete are started far enough in advance so that they can be completed on time. For example, marketing materials may need to be ordered many months in advance of the business opening date to ensure that they are delivered on time, and accurately. Allowing an appropriate amount of time will ensure that the materials can be designed professionally, be carefully checked and given a final sign-off before going to print. It will ensure that expensive mistakes are avoided. Entrepreneurs will start with a project plan listing everything that they need to do, how they are going to do it and by when it needs to be done.

### Financial constraints

Obtaining sufficient funding is a real challenge for entrepreneurs. To be able to start up any business, money is needed for items such as logos, websites, recruitment and staffing, merchandise and premises – to name just a few. Budgets need to be set to establish how much money is required for the start-up and how much money is actually available. From this, the entrepreneur can prioritise where the money should be spent and where it can be saved. It might be that budgets are reduced for certain areas: for example, for someone opening a shop, a cutting edge website would be a nice thing to have, but, in reality, the shop and merchandise is more important, so the website can be scaled down until after the business has opened. Alternatively a web-based retailer requires the website to be the main 'shop window' to the business, and so, in this case, budgets in other areas would be reconsidered, such as the quality of the paper-based marketing materials. Costs should be put onto a project plan along with the time scales and tasks that have to be completed.

### Potential stakeholder influences

Stakeholders are any people who have a direct or indirect interest in the business, or who are likely to be affected directly or indirectly by the business. There are primary, secondary and key stakeholders and the type of business may decide which category the stakeholder falls into.

▶ How do you find the money you need to start up a business?

▸ Primary stakeholders: these are people who are likely to be affected either positively or negatively, such as landlords or neighbours of the business, the local authorities or the police. For example, a nightclub business is likely to work closely with the local police to ensure that their facilities and customers are not negatively affecting the local neighbourhood. The police, in this example, could have an effect on the business in terms of opening hours if the law is not complied with.

▸ Secondary stakeholders: these are people who are likely to be indirectly affected by the business, either because of the nature of the business or the activity that it undertakes. For example, a jewellery business is likely to ensure that their premises are secure by having metal shutters fitted to reduce the risk of burglary (and the workload to the police). This would require another business to put in the shutters. Another example would be a business working with the local authorities to ensure that recycling and/or refuse collection is effective and efficient.

▸ Key stakeholders: these people may or may not belong to either of the two groups above. In either case, they will have a negative or positive effect on the business and are the group most likely to have a direct influence on the business. Key stakeholders are likely to be funders, such as a bank, loan company or trust that has given a grant. They could also include investors into the business who may hold shares, or who have given their time in lieu of payment in return for a say in the business. For example, when setting up a new business, the entrepreneur is likely to work with their funder and gain their approval for large items of expenditure or long-term investment, such as website costs or advertising contracts.

---

**Ⅱ  PAUSE POINT**  What four factors must be considered when setting up a micro-business? List these factors and make notes for the key points.

Hint  If you are not sure, read through this part of the unit again and take notes for each of the four key points.

Extend  Which points are most important to a new micro-business? Put them in order of importance, giving reasons why you have put them in this order. If you think they are of equal importance, explain why.

## Access to physical resources

Some businesses are very dependent on physical resources, while others are not; it will depend on the strategy, nature and activity of the business. Access to these resources can be challenging when starting up a business, as an entrepreneur may need to prove to the supplier that they are genuine and have credibility in terms of funding, expertise or status. The supplier is likely to have a personal interest in ensuring that their equipment is used correctly and safely, or that their products are being sold in an appropriate setting and within the law. For example, a fitness gym has a responsibility to ensure that anyone using their equipment has received an induction from a qualified member of staff before being allowed to use the equipment. The supplier of this equipment is likely to ensure that the gym is following these procedures. Another example would be that suppliers of vitamins, or health food supplements, are likely to insist that retailers selling their products have fully trained staff who are compliant with any age-restricted products and who can advise customers accurately before selling the product.

Table 19.3 below demonstrates how, within the same sector, different types of businesses will have different needs for physical resources.

| Type of business | Level of dependency on physical resources | What needs to be considered when setting up a micro-business in terms of access to physical resources? |
|---|---|---|
| Membership gym offering fitness solutions to a local area where customers can call in at their convenience. | High – most modern gyms are fitted out with a range of exercise equipment. In order to meet customer demands, there is usually more than one example of each machine. A variety of exercise equipment is needed to ensure that a full body workout can be obtained.<br><br>The room in which the exercise takes place must be of a certain size to hold all of the equipment and the temperature has to be maintained at a comfortable level. | Which fitness equipment to buy?<br>Quality of the equipment.<br>Best price that can be obtained.<br>Availability of the equipment and how long will it take to be delivered?<br>Training offered by the supplier?<br>Can the equipment be seen and experienced in advance of purchase?<br>Which manufacturer to buy from? |
| Retail shop selling fitness products and clothing on a high street. | Medium – the retail premises would need to be of a sufficient size to hold stock and display items effectively. There will be an amount of racking, shelving and display equipment to purchase. | Which products to buy that can be stored and displayed in the shop and that will be popular with customers?<br>Which wholesalers to use that will give the best price?<br>Where can the necessary racking, shelving and other display equipment be purchased?<br>Can items be purchased online, or is it necessary to visit the wholesaler to see and touch the products? |
| Internet-based retail website selling clothing and fitness related items. | Low – an internet-based company requires an area to store their stock, although, in some cases, they can order what their customer requires directly from the supplier. For example, if the website sold gym exercise bikes, it is likely that the item would be dispatched directly from the supplier and not be held as stock by the internet-based company. | Which products will be kept in stock?<br>Which products can be dispatched directly from the wholesaler?<br>Which suppliers are going to offer the best deals?<br>Can all transactions be conducted over the internet, or is there a need to go and see the products before purchase?<br>Which suppliers will give the best discounts? |

## Availability of IT

Most businesses are likely to need and use information technology (IT), and some businesses will be totally dependent on IT. The internet and telephone are a minimum requirement for most businesses, regardless of how remote they are, as they will need to communicate with at least their customers and suppliers. Other businesses will use IT in every aspect of their business and would not be able to survive without it. Think of a business that you may not associate with IT, say Costa Coffee or Lush: both have walk-in retail outlets where their customers call in to purchase their products.

Costa Coffee has a loyalty scheme that it runs through its website, and Costa encourages its customers to sign up to their electronic loyalty scheme. The website also gives details of different coffee products and promotions. IT is used to deliver marketing messages directly to their customers via emails and texts.

Lush has a website selling its products and giving information on a variety of areas besides their actual products. Customers can leave feedback on products they have tried, find out about the returns policy, and even what career opportunities are available.

There are other businesses that you do associate with IT, such as the travel industry. As well as using technology to advertise their businesses, IT is used to book and to manage accommodation, transport and other associated ancillaries, such as business trips. In these types of industries, IT is used heavily by everyone in the supply chain, from the customers to the employees and the suppliers. Think of booking a holiday. The travel agent will book the holiday on behalf of the customer using a computer, the tour operator will manage the booking using a computer, the aircraft flying the customer to their destination will use a computer and the airports at each end will use computers.

Small businesses usually rely heavily on IT as it is a cost-effective way to launch a business with the use of the internet and social media. Continuity can then be maintained using these same channels of communication for updates on the business, promotions and other marketing activity.

The main factors to consider in the availability of IT are likely to be:

▶ internet speed – is fibre optic available, or just cable internet?

▶ cost – can the business afford the equipment? Will it have to be purchased in stages?

▶ compatibility – are the devices and equipment used by the business and its customers compatible? For example, using an iPad and/or a PC-based computer.

▶ capability of the technology – is the technology being used by the business 'fit for purpose' or does new software need to be developed? For example, a training company may need a bespoke program to record and deliver its training.

▶ timescales – has sufficient time been allowed by the business to ensure that all of its IT is in place before launching?

## Environmental influences

Government legislation and policies are just one example of the type of environmental influences that can affect the start-up of a micro-business. For example, in 2015, the government changed Insurance Premium Tax (IPT) from 6 per cent to 9.5 per cent. This affected all businesses selling insurance policies, as they were required to charge the additional tax to their customers and ensure that any paperwork explaining how much tax was charged on insurance premiums had been updated. It affected not just insurance brokers but any business selling insurance, such as travel agents, or electrical retailers selling insurance policies to cover breakdowns on products like washing machines or fridges.

The economic influences in a local area, the national situation or events on a global scale can also influence businesses. Think about exchange rates or interest rates. Most businesses will borrow money, particularly at the start-up stage when costs are high and income can be limited. If interest rates suddenly rise at any stage of the start-up it will mean that costs will rise; this will have a direct influence on the business, which may then need to reconsider its business plan or budgets. An example of a positive influence on a business would be when there might be grants available through local council initiatives to support new micro-business start-ups and these could have set criteria that must be met. New businesses may need to alter their business plans to ensure that the criteria are met for such grants and these changes are likely to enhance and improve the business plan.

Other environmental influences include social and technological factors. For example, the local social make-up of an area will have an influence on what type of businesses are likely to succeed. Souvenir shops, for instance, are going to be successful in areas where there are many tourists. Think of the souvenir shops that can be seen in Oxford Street, London. These business owners know that Oxford Street is a tourist destination and there will be a demand for the souvenirs that they sell. Technology is an area that is constantly developing and this can influence the ways in which businesses operate. For example, Apple have created technology where customers can pay using their mobile phone – this would not have been possible in the past. Most new micro-business start-ups will plan to have an internet presence even if they do not intend their customers to purchase from it.

▶ Small businesses are very reliant on IT.

**Link**

Find out more in the section: Market analysis and planning.

## Internal risks

A business should be aware of any internal risks in order to plan for them and to be able to reduce the impact to the business as much as possible. The types of internal risks include the following.

▸ Human, performance issues: ineffective management or leadership can pose a large risk to an organisation, which may lead to costly mistakes or customer complaints. Training and development programmes can be offered and put into place to motivate those members of staff and, therefore, reduce the risk.

▸ Human, dishonesty issues: these can be managed to a degree. Some employers use 'chance' mechanisms to be fair yet firm with employees or any visitors to their site. These are likely to be used when the employer has small but expensive items in its stock list. An example used by one employer involves the employee rolling a dice and if it lands on a certain number that is chosen for the day, then the employee is searched. Otherwise, they are free to go home as usual. Other businesses may reduce the risk by using CCTV or security personnel.

▸ Technological issues: these could include sudden, but necessary, changes in systems and processes for the distribution of services or goods. It may be that a piece of equipment or a device has broken, or that it has become obsolete. The risk can be reduced in these circumstances by keeping technology up to date and by replacing it before it becomes obsolete.

▸ Physical factors: equipment that is used within a business may break or wear out over a period of time. Businesses can plan against these risks by servicing equipment regularly and making repairs as soon as possible. There should also be an amount of money in the budget to allow for the replacement of equipment and other physical resources.

## External risks

External risks may be harder to manage as they will be outside the control of a business. However, being aware of the main factors can help a business to prepare and plan for how they might reduce any risk. External risks link very well to a PESTLE analysis, as explained later in this unit. They include the following.

▸ Economic events: examples would be energy cost rises, or the price of a worldwide commodity on which a business depends rising steeply. If the suppliers of coffee beans were to raise their prices drastically because of a coffee bean shortage, think about the effect this would have on coffee shops. Another example would be an interest rate rise. If a business relies on an overdraft facility to operate, rises in interest rates could add a significant cost to the business that would affect profits – unless this cost was passed on to the customer by increasing prices, and that could affect sales.

▸ Political factors: when there is a change of government, or a change in government policy, it can affect a business. For example, a change of government policy in funding for the care of the elderly could lead to a care home organisation having to restructure the way in which it operates to continue to meet the funding requirements.

▸ Natural factors: natural disasters around the world can have an effect on large and small businesses. For example, an earthquake in the Far East is likely to disrupt travel to that area and, in turn, this would have an effect on a tour operator offering holidays to that destination. Another example is a global honey bee disease, affecting the bee population, which would have an effect of the supply of honey. This could also drive the price up and/or making it difficult to source.

**PAUSE POINT**   What are the main factors to consider when setting up a micro-business? Put them in order of priority, starting with the most important. Give your reasons why.

Hint    What factors are likely to affect the business that you are thinking about developing? What are positive and negative factors?

Extend    What can you do to maximise your opportunity on the positive factors that you have identified? What will you need to consider to reduce the risk from the negative factors?

## Assessment practice 19.1    A.P1  A.P2  A.M1  A.D1

You have been given a window of opportunity to explore potential ideas for setting up a micro-business, either from home or in the local area where you live, with a maximum of up to four employees. In order to establish your idea, you should complete a decision matrix, stating at the top of each matrix where your ideas have been generated from.

You will then describe the model for each business potential that you explore in terms of the business activity, the processes you will use, and the organisational format. You should also identify and review at least four factors that you will need to consider within your potential micro-business.

As part of your research, you will analyse four internal and external risk factors, evaluating the benefits and extent to which they could be a risk to your selected micro-business start-up. You should research a number of different start-ups and use these as examples when exploring your business idea.

There is a strong possibility that you will need to present your research work in the future to potential funders, or at least refer back to your original notes as you gather more evidence to equip you with information to pitch for your recommended business. Therefore you should construct and develop a well-indexed portfolio that consists of all your research notes, analysis and evaluations of risk factors, decision matrices and any other notes that you have created and developed whilst exploring your business opportunities and making your final recommendations.

### Plan
- Where are my ideas going to be generated from?
- Which decision matrix will I use and what are the factors and options that I need to consider for the business?
- Is there anything that I need to go over to ensure that I fully understand what I have to do, such as the different factors to be considered when setting up a micro-business?

### Do
- Where can I go for advice on micro-business start-ups? Who can I speak to?
- Can I see progress in the plan I have put together?
- Do I fully understand the different factors to enable me to analyse and evaluate?

### Review
- Was my plan realistic? Did I allow sufficient time?
- Is there anything that I still do not fully understand in exploring potential ideas for a micro-business?
- What have I learnt from this assignment that will be useful to me when I need to move forward with my business idea?

## B  Develop a business plan for a viable micro-business start-up

In this learning aim, you are going to move forward from exploring potential ideas into actually developing a business plan for a viable micro-business start-up. There are several aspects that you need to learn about before you can draw up a viable and meaningful business plan, and it is important that you have a full understanding around each of these areas. There are four distinct areas that you will explore, including market analysis and planning, and the legal and financial aspects. Finally you will look at the evaluation of a micro-business start-up and the importance of this for the success of the business plan.

As you work through this section, you will be asked to relate your learning to the micro-business that you have already recommended as a result of the assignment you completed for learning aim A.

## Market analysis and planning

**Link**

See *Unit 22: Market Research.*

The beginning of a business plan should set out an analysis of the marketplace in which the potential new start-up business is to be situated. It should explain who the target market is, the current business environment, where possibly a PESTLE analysis can be undertaken as well as the marketing mix and unique selling points that the business will offer. Primary and secondary research are also an important factor in the planning process.

### Target market definition

Part of your market analysis is likely to include defining who your intended customers will be. This is known as your target market. You need to know who your target market is, in order to know who your customers are and what their needs and expectations will be.

▶ Expectations: what standard of service will they expect? What will be the anticipated level of quality for the product they are likely to purchase? Will they expect to order online, or walk into a shop? Will discounts be expected?

▶ Shopping habits: where does the customer currently shop? What time of day? What types of products do they buy and how often? Do they like discounts or loyalty cards? Is quality more important than cost? Is cost more important than quality?

▶ Demographics: where is the customer likely to live? For example, in the countryside, towns, villages, cities or a mixture? What type of house are they likely to live in? For example, a flat, two-bedroomed house, five-bedroomed house? What is their educational background? What earnings bracket are they in?

▶ Segments within the target market: can customers be categorised into groups, for example by age or gender?

▶ Who is your target market?

All of this information is important to ensure that any new business is located in an appropriate location and setting, and that it will offer products or a range of products to meet the needs and expectations of its customers – the target market.

## Secondary and primary research

Part of your planning will be to undertake research. Both secondary and primary research are useful tools that should be used for finding out as much information as you can about every aspect of any business start-up. There are benefits and drawbacks of using both types of research and it is likely that your budget, constraints, the nature of the research or even what is easily available to you will determine whether secondary or primary research is the best option.

▸ **Table 19.4:** Using primary and secondary research

|  | **Secondary research** | **Primary research** |
|---|---|---|
| What is it? | A collection or summary of existing research. It is important that you check the source of the research and that it is credible. A good way of doing this is by obtaining a second piece of secondary research that backs up the first, or to compare it with some primary research. | New research that is carried out to answer a specific question. It usually involves surveys or questionnaires that may be delivered through the post or conducted face to face with the general public. |
| Benefits? | It means that someone else has already done the counting for you. It cuts down all of the 'foot work' and means that you can get accurate information without too much effort. | The information is going to be up to date and relevant to the issues or question being asked. It is likely to be accurate. |
| Limitations? | Sometimes you have to pay for the information, so the benefit of paying for secondary research versus undertaking your own primary research needs to be weighed up. The credibility of the research does need to be checked as you will be relying on the results. | Primary research can be very time consuming as it can involve teams of people who go out to areas such as towns or shopping centres to gather the information over a period of time, sometimes hours, or sometimes days. |
| An example? | If you want to know the population of a town or area, there are websites that will give you this information. The most reliable websites are likely to be government websites which will have details of censuses and other research that has already been undertaken. | If a business wants to know what the general public thinks about their products, they will have canvassers based in the street who stop the general public to ask them a set list of questions. |

**❚❚ PAUSE POINT**  Think about your target market. Who will your customers be? What will they want from your business? What will they expect from your business? Will they be prepared to travel to get to you? Where do they live? What types of houses are they likely to live in?

Hint  Build up a customer profile and write down the characteristics, listing what your customers' expectations are likely to be, their lifestyles and the types of products and services that they are likely to be already using.

Extend  Can you see the link between defining your target market and undertaking secondary and primary research? How will the research help you to answer some of these questions? What secondary research will be useful? What primary research will you need to undertake?

**Link**

See *Unit 2: Developing a Marketing Campaign* and *Unit 22: Market Research*.

**Link**

See the section: Factors to be considered when setting up a micro-business.

## Business environment

Strategic tools used in market analysis and planning can help you to see the bigger picture in which your new business is likely to operate. They can help you to identify any challenges and/or opportunities which will allow you to plan for the future. The two main tools used are Porter's Five Competitive Forces and PESTLE, which are both explained below.

### Porter's Five Competitive Forces

Michael E. Porter is an economist, researcher, writer and tutor based at Harvard Business School in Boston, USA. Throughout his long career and work at Harvard, he has developed a concept of strategy and written many articles and books, including *The Five Competitive Forces That Shape Strategy*. This strategy has been used by many governments and business leaders worldwide. In his book, Porter explains how there are five important forces to be considered when thinking about a competitive strategy. These forces determine competitive power in a business situation and are:

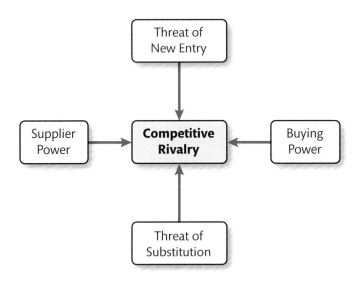

▶ **Figure 19.2:** Porter's competitive forces.

▶ Supplier power – this is about how powerful those who supply either goods or services to your business might be. Think about the goods and/or services that you are going to need to purchase for your business: are they only available from a handful of suppliers, or are they available from many suppliers? This will determine the strength of the supplier and how much power they may hold over you. Are they able to drive up the price you pay because their goods are in demand and very few suppliers offer them? Will they be able to dictate to you when the goods will be available because of long waiting lists? The more niche the product, the more power the supplier is likely to have over you and your business.

▶ Buyer power – this is about those buying from your business, i.e. your customers. How easy would it be for them to drive the price down? Think about the number of buyers/customers your business might have and how important each buyer/customer is to you and your business. Are your buyers/customers likely to switch their loyalty to another business, or share their business between yours and that of a competitor? If you only deal with a handful of powerful buyers, there is a possibility that they could dictate the price of your goods and/or services to you.

▶ Competitive rivalry – you need to think about the number of competitors you might have either locally or nationally, or even globally if you are doing business online. You must also think about the products and/or services that your competitors offer and their capabilities. Are they experts in their fields, or is there room for a large improvement, where your business could gain ground? Think about your likely competitors. If they offer the same products and/or services and are as good as your own business, then, unless you offer a very good deal, your customers are likely to use your competitors just as much as they do you, meaning that you have little power. However, if nobody else can offer the products or services as well as your organisation can, then you would have great strength and power.

▶ Threat of substitution – how easy would it be for your customers to substitute the product or service that your business will offer? If your customers could find another solution, and so not need your services, then you have very little power; however, if there is no alternative, then you have great power. For example, a business offering website design and creation may see their customers seeking alternative solutions where they can use an 'off-the-shelf' website design package based around a simple framework that can be purchased online, which the customer can populate with their own content. If your customers are able to find a substitution for the products and/or services of your business, then you have little power; if they cannot, then you have great power.

▶ Threat of new entry – how easy would it be for other, new businesses to enter your market? If there are very few start-up costs for your business, and very little time is required to set it up, then this is likely to indicate that others may also set up businesses similar to yours very quickly and effectively. If this is the case, it can lead to a weakening of your position within your market. However, if your business has start-up barriers such as cost, niche expertise or a requirement for specialist technologies, then you are more likely to be in a position of strength.

---

**Research**

Organisations such as Facebook, Nike and Ralph Lauren have used Porter's five competitive forces. Look at the case studies on **www.trefis.com**.

What can you learn from each of these case studies that would be useful when conducting your own analysis of the five competitive forces that will affect your micro-business start-up? What are each organisation's strong areas and positions of strength from the five competitive forces? Where are the vulnerable areas for each of the businesses?

---

**PESTLE**

A PESTLE analysis is another strategic tool that can be used as part of the planning stage when setting up a business. This will help to establish what environmental factors are likely to influence the success and running of the business and what needs to be taken into consideration.

Table 19.5 below explains the PESTLE factors and gives examples.

▶ **Table 19.5:** PESTLE

**Link**

You learnt about PESTLE in *Unit 1: Exploring Business*, *Unit 2: Developing a Marketing Strategy* and *Unit 5: International Business*.

| PESTLE | Explanation and examples |
|---|---|
| P | Political factors<br><br>The political situation of a country and the world in relation to the country may have a direct impact on a business. Government initiatives and policies may change, such as laws and taxes, and these may have a direct impact on a business. For example, when fuel duty is increased, this has a direct impact on businesses that use a lot of fuel, such as bus companies or leisure centres that operate swimming pools. |
| E | Economic factors<br><br>The economic situation of a country, such as inflation and interest rates, should be assessed in order to identify any areas that are likely to affect a business. For example, when interest rates are low, it is a good time for a business to borrow money. However, the business should assess the situation ahead to see if there are any indications that interest rates may rise as this would mean additional costs to the business. |
| S | Social factors<br><br>This involves looking at the mindsets of different countries and/or areas of the same country. A type of business may be very successful in one area or particular country, but not so in another. This could be directly related to a variety of social issues such as cultural factors, gender, demographics or social lifestyles. These need to be studied by businesses in order to get a full understanding of the market and their potential customers. |
| T | Technological factors<br><br>As well as being aware of technological changes, businesses need to be aware of their customers' expectations and ability to use technology. For example, many businesses have developed 'apps' that their customers can download and use to make purchases or book holidays, such as Premier Inn and Laura Ashley. |
| L | Legal factors<br><br>Changes in legislation happen from time to time, and it is most important that businesses are aware of any changes and remain compliant. For example, there may be a change to health and safety or discrimination laws that will affect all businesses. |
| E | Environmental factors<br><br>These include geographical location, climate, weather, pollution, recycling and use of green or eco-friendly products and practices. Businesses must be aware of their obligations, such as recycling, and the impact that this may have on their business. Another example would be climate: a sailing school will only be able to operate safely in good weather, so the calculation of the likelihood of poor weather needs to be factored into the planning and forecasting for the business. |

 **PAUSE POINT**

What are the Five Competitive Forces that Porter identifies? What does PESTLE stand for?

**Hint**

Read through the page and take notes to enable you to really understand these two strategic models.

**Extend**

Identify strong and weak areas related to Porter's Five Competitor Forces for your business ideas. Complete a PESTLE analysis.

## Alicja's party-planning business

After reading an article about Porter's Five Competitive Forces, Alicja has decided to apply this strategic business tool to her new start-up business. Her business idea is to offer party services to the local community and to sell party accessories online and in a locally based shop.

The party services will cover all types of parties for all ages. This will include children's parties, through to any type of celebration party, such as 18th birthdays, weddings and other special occasions.

Alicja plans to rent a building that will include an office for her to work from and a shop front for selling all types of party accessories and to act as a 'reception' for personal callers who may wish to talk though their party requirements. She is also hoping to find a large enough building so that an area can be used as a warehouse for the internet side of the business.

The third part of the business will be an online shop, where all types of party accessories will be offered.

This is Alicja's analysis of her business plans using Porter's Five Forces Analysis:

### Supplier power

* Alicja has undertaken extensive market research and has identified a number of websites offering party supplies that she will be able to use in the parties she organises and in her two shops. There is also a 'cash and carry' 30 miles away.
* She has researched all of the venues in the area that she is likely to use for all of the different types of parties she will offer.

### Buyer power

* Alicja has established that her nearest competitor is in the next town, 20 miles away, although there are a number of online businesses offering party accessories and party planning and organising. She thinks that this will mean that her potential customers are likely to shop around before making any purchasing decisions.

### Competitive rivalry

* To find out what her competitors offer, Alicja undertook a 'competitor visit', where she became a mystery shopper. From this, she was able to experience her competitors' products and services from the point of view of a customer. The party planning service was detailed. Alijca was welcomed into the premises, although all of the discussion took place over a high counter. Alicia plans to have comfortable chairs and offer coffee, both of which she did not experience with her competitors.
* She then went online to sample the websites. There were some excellent examples where the websites were easy to navigate with good search engines and excellent shopping online pages, but other websites were quite 'amateurish' looking and did not leave Alicja with the confidence to purchase anything from them.

### Threat of substitution

* Alicja felt that the unique selling points to her business were that she had been an events organiser for 10 years and so had a lot of experience in this area. She felt that she would be offering a far more personal service in the planning of the parties in the way that she would greet her customers and create an atmosphere for them to relax in during the initial consultation with her.
* Alicja couldn't see any real threat of substitution, as the type of customers that would use her party planning services would not want to organise their own parties, unless money got tight. For those customers who did want to plan their own parties, she had the walk-in and online shops that would cater for them.

### Threat of new entry

* The walk-in and online shops were going to be a new venture for Alicja, but one that she felt she would pick up quickly as there did not seem to be too much to the setting up of it, as long as she knew which products to market. Her only concern was that if she could start the business up so easily, did this mean that others could also set up a similar business?
* The party planning part of the business, Alicja felt, could only be run successfully by someone who had relevant experience. She would be able to train any new employees using her experience to impart her knowledge to them. Alicja thought that this area of the business was more specialist.

**Check your knowledge**

1 Reading through Alicja's comments, identify the strong and not so strong areas within each of the Five Competitive Forces. Give reasons for each of your answers.

2 If Alicja asked your advice on whether she should start all three areas of her business at the same time, what would you recommend? Explain why you would make these recommendations.

3 Which of the environment factors from the PESTLE analysis are going to affect Alijca's business the most? Identify the negative and the positive influences.

**Link**

See *Unit 2: Developing a Marketing Campaign* and *Unit 22: Market Research.*

## Marketing mix

There were initially four, but now there are seven, elements that make up the marketing mix. E. Jerome McCarthy, an expert in marketing, created the Marketing 4Ps model that has been used throughout the world and is recognised by many business schools. It is about putting the right product for the right price, in the right place, at the right time.

▶ **Figure 19.3:** The marketing mix.

▶ Product – goods and/or services created to meet the needs of a target market. It is important that research is undertaken to ensure that the product or services being offered are in demand and will continue to be in the future. Product development should be ongoing to ensure that it continues to be in demand. Think of the gaming industry: the manufacturers are continuously developing new software with better technology and graphics, while the retailers are stocking them to meet the growing demands of their customers.

▶ Price – is a very important component of the marketing mix. The product must be priced to meet the expectations of the target market, while, at the same time, ensuring that the business can make a profit and survive. A new business will need to research its competitors to establish the pricing that is already established within the sector, looking at both the low and high pricing ends of the market. For example, if a new business is going to be offering bed and breakfast, do they offer value rooms at a budget price, or deluxe rooms at a much higher price? In both examples, the rooms will be priced to meet the expectations of the guests.

▶ Place – includes distribution as well as placement of the goods. This requires a thorough understanding of the target market and the products that must be accessible to them. This means ensuring that the goods and/or services are positioned and distributed to locations and through channels that the customer is likely to use. This includes the following.

  ▶ Intensive distribution – this is when the product is stocked in the majority of outlets. Think of Cadbury's chocolate. You will find their bars in every supermarket and shop selling sweets across the country.

  ▶ Exclusive distribution – luxury goods fall into this category where they may be placed in just one or two select outlets, such as Harrods or Liberty.

  ▶ Selective distribution – this is somewhere between intensive and exclusive distribution, where the producer will sell their goods and/or services through a number of similar outlets, such as John Lewis, Debenhams and other similar department stores.

  ▶ Franchising – this is where a right is given to use a certain business model for a certain period of time. Think of Starbucks and McDonald's. Both of these internationally recognised organisations sell franchises to people who wish to run their own business.

▶ Promotion – businesses will advertise their products and services in many areas such as the television, newspapers, magazines, radio, online adverts and bill boards. It is important that the business chooses the most appropriate medium and timing of their advertising. Think about television adverts. When football matches are being broadcast, the adverts are likely to be directed at other interests that football fans are perceived to have, such as cars, whereas, for children's programmes, the adverts will be for toys and games.

▶ How many brands can you think of with intensive distribution?

The 7Ps model builds on the 4Ps model by adding People, Process and Physical Environment. These additional areas are aimed at the service industries, although may be appropriate for other types of business.

▶ People – this includes everyone who may be involved within a business and the target market, e.g. employees, management, customers and suppliers. If a business looks after all of the people who are working in the business, or are directly connected to the business, then they are more likely to be happy, enjoy their jobs and respect the business, which will lead to a 'people' culture within the business. A positive people culture will lead to excellent customer service.

▶ Process – having efficient and realistic processes in place will ensure that the services offered by a business are cost effective while continuing to meet the demands and needs of the customer. For example, a hotel must have processes for each of its departments, such as housekeeping, restaurant, kitchen and front of house, to ensure that the guests receive a seamless service.

▶ Physical environment – a business that encourages and invites guests on to its premises should think about the impression it gives to its customers. Is it comfortable? Is the environment suitable for the types of customers who are going to visit? Are the facilities suitable? Think about when you go into a bank. There are often play areas for children so that parents can continue their business knowing that their children are safe and occupied for the few minutes that they need to complete their transaction. At the same time, the bank has a professional feel, being clean, tidy and colour coordinated.

### Unique selling points (USPs)

When a successful business can offer something to its customers that cannot be offered by another competitor, this is known as a unique selling point (USP). For example, the Dyson USP was to be the first to offer high-tech domestic appliances, such as bagless vacuum cleaners. As other manufacturers developed this technology, Dyson continued to develop its products to stay ahead in the sector. Dyson went on to develop the first 10-second hand dryer and, more recently, developed a bladeless fan heater.

**PAUSE POINT**

What are going to be the most important elements of the 4 or 7Ps for your micro-business?

**Hint**

Write down all of the seven points and list under each point what you will need to consider for your business.

**Extend**

Establish your USPs and compare this to your target market's expectations and the list you have made of the 7Ps. How will you promote your USPs using the marketing mix? How will you be able to maximise the opportunities that your USPs will give your customers using the marketing mix?

**Link**

See also *Unit 23: The English Legal System* and *Unit 1: Exploring Business*.

## Legal aspects

### Business legal forms and liability insurance

Below are the most common legal forms that a business can consider.

▸ **Table 19.6:** Common types of business form

| Company form | Explanation |
|---|---|
| Sole trader | This is the simplest form of business set-up. The owner of the business owns the assets of the business and is responsible for all of its liabilities and debts. The individual is classed as self-employed by HMRC and must file a tax return, where any profits from the business are treated as personal income, which is subject to income tax and national insurance. |
| Partnership | This is when two or more people set up a business with the intention of making a profit. Partners usually draw up a legally binding partnership agreement detailing the amount of capital each has invested into the business and how profits and losses will be distributed between the partners. Partners share the risk, costs and responsibilities of being in business. |
| Limited company | This is the most common legal form in use for running a business. On incorporation under the Companies Act 2006, a company is required to have two constitutional documents.<br>• A Memorandum, which records the fact that the initial members wish to form a company and agree to become its members. The Memorandum cannot be amended.<br>• Articles of Association – often just referred to as the Articles – which are essentially a contract between the company and its members, setting the legally binding rules for the company, including the framework for decisions, ownership and control. The Companies Act 2006 provides significant flexibility to draw up articles to suit the specific needs of the company, provided it acts within the law.<br>A limited company is owned by its members (those who have invested in the business) and they have a limited liability meaning that the company's finances are separate from the personal finances of their owners and, as a general rule, creditors of the business may only pursue the company's assets to settle a debt. The personal assets of the owners are not at risk. |

**Source:** http://www.nationalarchives.gov.uk/doc/open-government-licence/version/3/

**Discussion**

There are other legal forms available which may be more suitable for the needs of your business. Obtain a copy of the Department for Business Innovation & Skills (BIS) *A Guide to Legal Forms for Business* – November 2011. Discuss the different forms available and which would be most suitable for your micro-business. Give reasons for your answers.

## Liability insurance

This is the most common insurance taken out by small businesses. Public liability insurance covers the business if someone is injured in some way by the business or if somebody within the business damages third party property when carrying out work. The insurer will want to know the type of business to establish what type of policy would be best suited to the business.

Once a business employs at least one member of staff, it must have Employers' Liability Insurance in accordance with the Employers' Liability Insurance Act 1969. The insurance covers the business if an employee is injured at work, or becomes ill as a result of working for the company. Certain government departments are exempt, as are non-limited family businesses.

**Link**

See also *Unit 1: Exploring Business* section on liability.

## Consumer protection legislation

The law protects your customers against being treated unfairly, or when things go wrong. The following are all included within this legislation:

▶ credit and store cards

▶ faulty goods

▶ counterfeit goods

▶ poor service

▶ problems with contracts

▶ problems with builders

▶ rogue traders.

It is important that your business has policies and procedures in place to avoid, where possible, things going wrong or treating your customers unfairly, both of which can lead to customer complaints and claims against your business. For example, by buying products from a reliable source, a business is likely to avoid selling faulty goods. If they do mistakenly sell faulty goods, then having a robust returns policy in place will keep the customer satisfied and mean they are less likely to make a claim against the company. Another example would be to ensure that only skilled and qualified tradesmen are employed to carry out work for a customer.

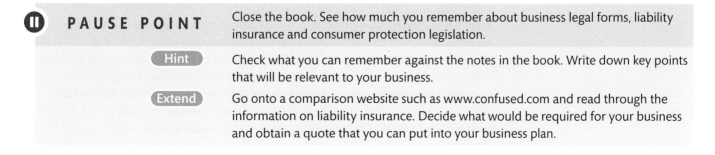

**PAUSE POINT**  Close the book. See how much you remember about business legal forms, liability insurance and consumer protection legislation.

**Hint**  Check what you can remember against the notes in the book. Write down key points that will be relevant to your business.

**Extend**  Go onto a comparison website such as www.confused.com and read through the information on liability insurance. Decide what would be required for your business and obtain a quote that you can put into your business plan.

**Link**

See also *Unit 23: The English Legal System.*

## Employment legislation

Table 19.7 below shows the main employment legislation that all businesses must implement. Larger organisations are likely to have written policies and procedures to ensure that their employees are working within the law. Smaller micro-businesses, that employ fewer than five people, will still have to adhere to the Acts, but will not be required to have written policies.

▶ **Table 19.7:** Employment legislation

| Legislation | Explanation |
| --- | --- |
| Employment Rights Act subsequently amended by the Employment Relations Acts of 1999 and 2004 | This Act states what the employee is entitled to:<br>• an itemised pay slip<br>• the national minimum wage<br>• terms and conditions of work must be set out in writing<br>• that there is protection against unfair dismissal at work. |
| Equality Act 2010 | This Act protects employees against discrimination on the grounds of gender. For example, job adverts, selection of employees, promotion of employees or training and development opportunities cannot be based on the gender of the individuals. There are exceptional circumstances: for example, a care company may advertise for a female care assistant to care for a female service user. It also makes discrimination on the grounds of race illegal. Organisations that employ more than 20 people must accomodate the needs of anyone who is disabled and ensure that they are able to access certain areas such as the working area and transport. A disabled person must not be treated less favourably than able-bodied individuals, as this is a form of discrimination. |
| Equal Pay Act 1970 | This states that men and women must be paid the same rate for doing exactly the same job. |
| The National Minimum Wage Act, 1998 | The minimum wage is increased each year in line with inflation, and employers must make sure that they check on the government website to know what the current minimum wage is and pay their employees at least the minimum wage. |
| The National Living Wage, 2016 | From 1 April 2016 anyone who is employed, aged 25 or over and not in the first year of an Apprenticeship, is entitled to the National Living Wage which is set by the government. For anyone under the age of 25, the National Minimum wage applies |
| The Working Time Directive, 1999 | Employees must be guaranteed that they will not work more than 48 hours in a week, and will receive four weeks holiday a year. Employees can elect to opt out of this working time requirement and work longer hours if they wish. |

## Health and safety legislation

Everybody in the workplace must take reasonable care of their own health and safety and that of others. However, employers also have a duty of care towards their employees and must ensure that they are aware of anything that might cause harm to them while they are doing their job. The employer must undertake risk assessments for every work area to identify potential hazards that may cause harm and then put actions in place to reduce these identified hazards. For example, protective clothing must be supplied by the employer, such as gloves, hard hat, steel toe-cap boots or overalls for employees who may be handling dangerous chemicals, or who are working in an area where objects could fall on them, such as in a warehouse. Another example would be that if there are chairs or tables blocking a fire exit, they must be removed immediately. There is also a requirement to undertake risk assessment for young people and pregnant women as they are likely to have specific risks. Health and safety training should be given to all employees in order for them to be able to do their job safely.

▶ Why do you need a hard hat in a warehouse?

The employer must also provide facilities such as toilets, washing facilities and drinking water to all of their employees. Where there are five or more employees, a Health and Safety at Work poster must be displayed for everyone to see.

## Data protection legislation

An employer must not disclose any personal information to a third party. Strict rules must be followed when handling personal data: computer systems must be password protected and paper records should be kept in a locked cabinet. In all cases, only authorised personnel should have access to personal records.

## Environmental protection legislation

This legislation covers three main areas.

▶ Pollution control – this sets out to control air, water and land pollution that can cause harm. For example, a manufacturing business must ensure that any harmful waste products do not enter local streams or pollute the surrounding land.

▶ Waste disposal – industrial and commercial waste must be disposed of safely. Any harmful controlled substances can only be stored once a licence has been obtained. For example, a road haulage business may wish to store its own fuel. This will only be allowed if the business holds a special licence.

▶ Statutory nuisances and clean air – this will apply to businesses that create dust, steam or smells that are deemed to be detrimental to health. The local authority must investigate if a complaint is made by a member of the public. If it is confirmed that the business is creating a statutory nuisance, then the business will be required to reduce the problem until it is no longer deemed a nuisance.

| | | |
|---|---|---|
| **Ⅱ PAUSE POINT** | | What employment, health and safety, data protection and environmental protection legislation is likely to be relevant to your business? |
| | Hint | Create headings, one for each of the different areas of legislation, and list your main points under each. See if the headings with most items listed beneath are the priority areas for your business. |
| | Extend | List your main priorities and create an action plan of what you will need to do to ensure that you meet the requirements of each of the legislative points. Explain how this will be relevant to your business plan, and any costs that may need to be built in. |

# Financial aspects

## Pricing policy

Any new business must consider their pricing strategy and policy. It is important to think in terms of the following.

▶ Market penetration – pricing to sell to an existing market to gain a higher market share. For example, supermarkets are very competitive and will reduce prices on certain items to create a price war. They do this to gain a greater market share over their competitors.

▶ Market skimming – pricing as high as possible where customers will be prepared to pay, and then reducing the price once these customers are proved to be satisfied, to attract a more price-conscious market. For example, with Apple products, the latest to the market is always expensive and usually higher than any competitors' similar products, yet customers are prepared to pay these high prices for the latest and most up-to-date phone or laptop. As new Apple products are developed, they take over these high prices and the original products are then reduced in price to become attractive to a more price-conscious market.

▶ Neutral pricing – pricing is set by the general market. This means that a company may not be maximising on the opportunity of a greater profit, as its pricing is similar to that of its competitors rather than what the customer might be prepared to pay. For example, consider small electrical goods such as kettles or irons. The majority are priced midrange and can be purchased in many different outlets. These are stable, consumer items that tend to be purchased out of necessity rather than desire.

## Sales forecasting

In order for a business to know how it will perform in the future, sales forecasting is very important. Sales forecasting will also inform the business of the resources and materials that are likely to be needed month by month, which will help in business planning. It also gives the business a chance to identify potential problems and opportunities, allowing it to take action. The main areas of a sales forecast are likely to include the following.

▶ A basis for sales forecasts – the starting point for a sales forecast is last year's business. From this, it is possible to see how many customers were gained and lost over the year, the average amount of sales per customer and any particular months that were busy or quiet. This is not possible for a new business, where the first year will be based on projection rather than last year's business. There is always a certain amount of guesswork involved for new businesses. However, the business plan must contain details of forecasting and can be used as the forecast tool for the first year in business.

▶ Sales assumptions – a business will make assumptions about the marketplace and their targeted customers through the research they have undertaken. Every year is different and so a business will need to think about any potential changes, such as possibly losing or gaining customers, as well as predicting the products and services that will generate sales, or those that have become unpopular and will not sell. For example, a clothing retailer will plan ahead on the fashion items it will stock. It needs to research fashion and trends likely to attract its target market and buy in suitable fashion items. The retailer will also predict its month-by-month sales, factoring in when customers are likely to buy certain items, such as summer holiday or Christmas party clothes and the time of year they are likely to be purchased.

▶ Avoiding forecasting pitfalls – it is important not to be over-optimistic. New businesses should avoid using the level of sales they need to survive as the sales figures in their forecast. It may take more than a year to build to the level of sales required, and this should be factored in. A new business also needs to consider if the business is actually viable: for example, a cafe will be limited to the number of people it can serve according to the space and amount of seating it has, and one person in the business can only serve a certain number of customers and work only so many hours in a day.

## Worked Example - Developing a Sales Forecast

There are three steps in creating and developing a sales forecast.

**Step 1**: Complete your sales assumptions.

**Step 2**: Break down your sales into specific areas such as market, product and geographical area.

**Step 3**: Predict likelihood of sales for each specific area.

## Worked Example

Here is an example of a hire company's 12 month sales forecast.

| | Jan | Feb | Mar | Apr | May | Jun | Jul | Aug | Sep | Oct | Nov | Dec |
|---|---|---|---|---|---|---|---|---|---|---|---|---|
| **Mechanical hire income** | 3500 | 4500 | 5500 | 5500 | 6500 | 7500 | 5500 | 5500 | 7500 | 8500 | 8500 | 6500 |
| **Non-mechanical hire income** | 1000 | 1000 | 1500 | 1750 | 2000 | 8000 | 2000 | 3000 | 3000 | 2000 | 2000 | 1000 |
| **Re-hire income** | 1400 | 2300 | 2400 | 2500 | 2600 | 2400 | 1750 | 2000 | 2200 | 2400 | 2500 | 1800 |
| **Transport - delivery and collection** | 670 | 960 | 1100 | 900 | 1200 | 1200 | 1300 | 1950 | 2000 | 2100 | 2200 | 1200 |
| **Consumables** | 1000 | 950 | 1010 | 1200 | 1300 | 1400 | 1200 | 950 | 1325 | 1200 | 1275 | 950 |
| **Repairs** | 200 | 400 | 450 | 475 | 1000 | 1500 | 2000 | 2100 | 1900 | 1875 | 500 | 300 |
| **Sales of new equipment** | 2000 | 1680 | 2300 | 2600 | 4500 | 1000 | 950 | 840 | 500 | 675 | 300 | 356 |
| **Fleet sales** | 0 | 0 | 0 | 2000 | 1500 | 950 | 0 | 0 | 0 | 1100 | 2000 | 0 |

Each area of sales and/or income stream has been identified above, with a forecast of the predicted income for each month.

The hire company will take into consideration local activity throughout the year and when hire of equipment will be in demand, such as WCs for the local country fair in June. It can be seen how non-mechanical hire income has been increased to 8000 to reflect this additional income.

This sales forecast is also predicting higher sales of mechanical hire towards the end of the year - this is due to research that tells the hire company that builders are very active leading up to Christmas to get jobs completed for customers in time for Christmas.

Fleet sales are predicted to be sporadic, as this is not the hire company's core business, but it does expect to sell some of the equipment from its fleet in some months of the year.

**PAUSE POINT**

Which of the three pricing policies are you likely to adopt in your business? Give your reasons why.

**Hint**    What will your customers be prepared to pay for your products and/or services? How does this affect your sales forecast?

**Extend**    Compare your target market's expectations of what they would pay to the figures in your sales forecast. Is your business viable? Can you, or should you, raise your prices? How can your pricing strategy and sales forecast be integrated into your business plan? Give reasons for your answers.

### Projected costs: set-up, fixed and variable costs

Your predicted sales need to be set against your predicted costs. A business will have a set-up cost, which will be a number of one-off expenses, and then there will be ongoing costs that will either be fixed or variable.

▶ Set-up costs – these include all the one-off purchases that a business needs to make to set up the business. It will also include other items that will become ongoing expenses, such as stock and replacement or repairs of equipment used within the business. For example, a retailer opening a new shop will need to invest in shelving and racking in order to be able to display the stock. It may also create a website and marketing materials, both of which will incur costs.

▶ Fixed costs – these are costs that will not change, but are necessary for the business to function. Examples include rent, council tax, insurance and telephone line rental. These costs will be incurred by the business regardless of the business activity taking place, so, when a shop is closed, it will continue to have to pay its fixed costs.

▶ Variable costs – these are costs that will vary according to the business activity, so, as business increases, costs are likely to increase in line. For example, the cost of massage oils or laundering of towels for a health spa will increase when they are busy and have many treatments booked.

**Link**

See *Unit 3: Personal and Business Finance.*

### Break-even forecast

A break-even point for a business is when total revenue equals its total costs. Once the break-even point has been reached, the business is then likely to start making a profit. Therefore, if a business can forecast its break-even point on a monthly basis it will give a good indication of when all costs have been covered and the business will start to make a profit. In some cases, the break-even forecast might be given yearly.

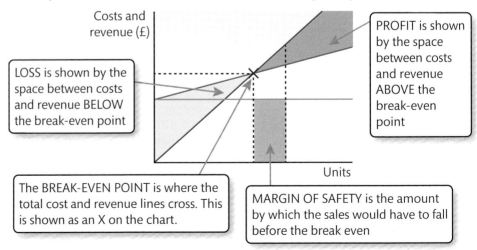

Costs and revenue (£)

LOSS is shown by the space between costs and revenue BELOW the break-even point

PROFIT is shown by the space between costs and revenue ABOVE the break-even point

The BREAK-EVEN POINT is where the total cost and revenue lines cross. This is shown as an X on the chart.

MARGIN OF SAFETY is the amount by which the sales would have to fall before the break even

Units

▶ **Figure 19.4:** Here is an example of a break-even chart showing costs and revenue against units sold for a business.

## Cash-flow forecast

A business needs to be aware of how much money is coming into the business and how much money is leaving the business, or being spent. It is important that money owed is paid to the business in order for its bills to be paid. When forecasting cash-flow, a business must be realistic about the number of sales it will make. It must take into account busy and quiet periods, where sales will increase or decrease, and any expected costs, such as equipment replacement, as well as having a contingency for unexpected costs, such as when equipment breaks down. Seasons and public holidays should be factored in, for example public holidays where the business may close down. Builders' merchants, for example, must consider when their customers, who are builders, will be on holiday and so cash flow will be reduced. Other businesses will be open to maximise the sales opportunities, such as retailers and cafes, therefore increasing their cash flow. This should be factored in against the costs, which may not be seasonal, such as fixed costs.

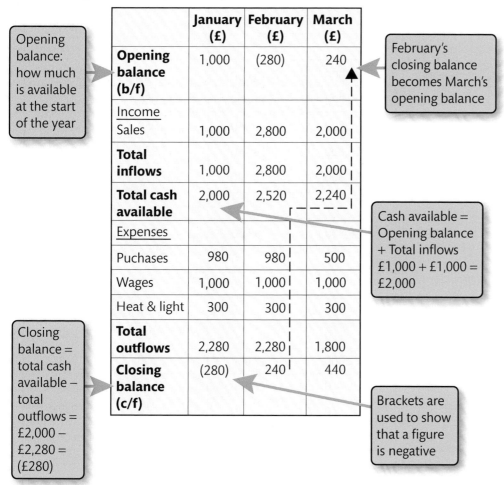

Opening balance: how much is available at the start of the year

February's closing balance becomes March's opening balance

Cash available = Opening balance + Total inflows £1,000 + £1,000 = £2,000

Closing balance = total cash available − total outflows = £2,000 − £2,280 = (£280)

Brackets are used to show that a figure is negative

|  | January (£) | February (£) | March (£) |
|---|---|---|---|
| **Opening balance (b/f)** | 1,000 | (280) | 240 |
| Income | | | |
| Sales | 1,000 | 2,800 | 2,000 |
| **Total inflows** | 1,000 | 2,800 | 2,000 |
| **Total cash available** | 2,000 | 2,520 | 2,240 |
| Expenses | | | |
| Puchases | 980 | 980 | 500 |
| Wages | 1,000 | 1,000 | 1,000 |
| Heat & light | 300 | 300 | 300 |
| **Total outflows** | 2,280 | 2,280 | 1,800 |
| **Closing balance (c/f)** | (280) | 240 | 440 |

▶ **Figure 19.5:** An example of a cash flow forecast

**ⅠⅠ PAUSE POINT**   What projected costs will you incur in your business? Can you explain what set-up costs, fixed costs and variable costs are?

**Hint**   Identify the set-up costs for your new business, as well as your ongoing fixed and variable costs. Check that all costs are necessary and you have not forgotten any. Speak to other similar businesses to check if your calculations are realistic.

**Extend**   Put together a break-even forecast and a cash-flow forecast for your business. Explain how you have reached the figures in your forecasts.

## Forecast opening and closing statement of financial position

A financial statement will be required by any potential investors, or anyone who already has a vested interest in the business, such as the bank or the local authority that may have given a grant. The financial statement will give an opening balance of the business for a specific period and will then list all the income and **expenditure** for that same period. Once the income has been added to the opening balance, and the expenditure taken away, what is left is the closing balance.

|  | January £ | February £ | March £ | April £ | Total £ |
|---|---|---|---|---|---|
| **Opening balance (b/f)** | 0 | (3,500) | (1,520) | 2,500 |  |
| Income owner's capital | 10,000 |  |  |  | 10,000 |
| Bank loan | 15,000 |  |  |  | 15,000 |
| Cash sales | 5,000 | 7,000 | 8,000 | 7,000 | 27,000 |
| Credit sales | 0 | 9,000 | 11,000 | 12,000 | 32,000 |
| Commission received | 0 | 800 | 950 | 950 | 2,700 |
| **Total inflows** | 30,000 | 16,800 | 19,950 | 19,950 | 86,700 |
| **Total cash available** | 30,000 | 13,300 | 18,430 | 22,450 |  |
| **Expenses** |  |  |  |  |  |
| Cash purchases | 8,000 | 9,500 | 9,500 | 3,500 | 30,500 |
| Credit purchases | 0 | 0 | 0 | 7,000 | 7,000 |
| Heat and light | 0 | 0 | 0 | 200 | 200 |
| Fixtures and fittings | 5,000 | 600 | 0 | 0 | 5,600 |
| Equipment | 5,000 | 0 | 0 | 0 | 5,000 |
| Drawings | 0 | 2,000 | 2,000 | 2,000 | 6,000 |
| Marketing | 3,000 | 0 | 1,200 | 0 | 4,200 |
| Premises costs | 10,000 | 0 | 0 | 0 | 10,000 |
| Insurance | 500 | 0 | 0 | 0 | 500 |
| Wages | 1,000 | 1,500 | 2,000 | 2,000 | 6,500 |
| Administrative costs | 1,000 | 750 | 800 | 1,250 | 3,800 |
| Overdraft interest | 0 | 70 | 30 | 0 | 100 |
| Loan repayments | 0 | 400 | 400 | 400 | 1,200 |
| **Total outflows** | 33,500 | 14,820 | 15,930 | 16,350 | 80,600 |
| **Closing balance (c/f)** | (3,500) | (1,520) | 2,500 | 6,100 |  |

▶ **Figure 19.6:** An example of a forecast opening and closing statement for a new business

## Capital structure to show investment necessary from potential investors

A business will have assets, or equity, that has a value; the business is also likely to have debts that will go against these assets. This is known as the capital structure. Potential investors will want to know the capital structure of the business to be able to establish the optimal value of the cost of capital. If the value of the assets is less than the debts of the company, it is not a viable business and investors will not want to invest their money into it. However, if the value of the assets is much greater than the debt of the business, the business is viable and investors are more likely to be interested.

## Forecast income statement for trading period

The financial performance of a business is measured using a financial, or profit and loss, statement that gives specific information on how a business has performed over a set period of time. This will include all money that has been received, known as **revenues**, and all money that has been spent. In order to attract investors, a forecast income statement will help to identify the revenue and expenditure streams of a business. This will then clearly show if the business is viable.

> **Key term**
>
> **Revenues** – all income that is received by a business whether sales, interest or any other source of income.

---

 **PAUSE POINT**    Write a paragraph to explain forecast opening and closing statements, what capital structure is and an income statement.

Hint       If you are unsure, reread the explanations, and do some further research online.

Extend       Practise forecasting by creating an opening and closing statement and an income statement. From this, calculate the capital structure. Relate these forecasts to your new business, where possible.

---

# Evaluation

Once you have created a business plan for your micro-business start-up, the next step is to evaluate the processes you have gone through. This will help you to identify any areas that you can improve and ensure that the figures you have calculated are correct and realistic.

> **Link**
>
> See also *Unit 1: Exploring Business* section on SWOT analysis and *Unit 5: International Business*.

## Marketing mix SWOT

A SWOT analysis is a useful tool to identify Strengths, Weaknesses, Opportunities and Threats to a business. It can be applied to most subject areas, and works really well when looking at the marketing mix model.

| Strengths | Weaknesses |
|---|---|
| Quality of product, experience of personnel | Need to expand knowledge base in some areas |
| **Opportunities** | **Threats** |
| Expanding customer base, impact of new technology | Competitors from overseas entering market |

▶ **Figure 19.7:** SWOT analysis can be applied to many business areas

By taking each element of the marketing mix, a business can identify the strengths, weaknesses, opportunities and threats that it has for each area. This will allow the business to set actions for areas that need improvement in the weaknesses and threats and maximise their strengths in areas where the business has strengths and opportunities.

## Financial forecasts

Evaluating the financial forecasts of a business plan will help to ensure that a business has accurately produced its figures for revenues and expenditure and that the business is a viable proposition. When pitching for funding, the financial forecasting will be scrutinised by the potential investors as they will want to know that their investment is safe and that the business will not only survive, but will become successful and profitable, giving them a good **return on investment**.

## Ratio analysis

### Liquidity analysis

Any potential investor will want to know that a business has sufficient income to pay its debts on a monthly basis. The more comfortably a business can pay its debts each month, the more successful the business is likely to be. Investors will want to know what the liquidity ratio is to be able to establish that a business is able to pay its monthly debts. This is calculated by taking the current **assets** of a business and dividing by the current **liabilities**, or the amount owed. Liquidity can be measured using the current ratio and the acid test ratio.

> **Key terms**
>
> **Return on investment** – the ratio between the amount of money invested and the profit received, usually given as a percentage.
>
> **Assets** – any items of value owned by an individual or business.
>
> **Liabilities** – obligations of a business, or amounts owed to its suppliers.

## Worked Example – Freedom Designs Ltd

Current assets = £57,130

Current liabilities = £30,270

$$\text{Current ratio} = \frac{£57,130}{£30,270} = £1.88$$

This means that, for every £1 the business owes in short-term debt (that is, its current liabilities), it owns £1.88 in current assets. The business therefore has sufficient liquidity to meet short-term debts.

Current assets = £57,130

Stock = £34,294

Current liabilities = £30,270

$$\text{Acid test} = \frac{£57,130 - £34,294}{£30,270}$$

$$= \frac{£22,836}{£30,270} = 0.75$$

This means that, for every £1 the business owes in short-term debts, it only has 75p in liquid assets (current assets excluding stock). This figure shows the firm to be illiquid, as it could not meet its short-term debts if immediate repayment was demanded. A fashion retailer is likely to have a large amount of its current assets in the form of stock, due to the nature of the firm.

### Profitability analysis

The profitability of a business is the difference between the money that it receives (revenues) and the money that it spends (costs). The difference is the profit the business is making. You must then consider gross profit and net profit.

Profitability can be measured using gross profit margin, mark-up and net profit margin.

## Worked Example – Freedom Designs Ltd

Sales turnover = £511,529

Gross profit = £369,792

Net profit = £51,246

Gross profit percentage of sales = £369,852 / £511,529 × 100 = 72.3 per cent

For every £1 Freedom Designs Ltd makes in sales, 72p is left as gross profit.
A fashion retailer is likely to have reasonably high costs of sales due to the nature of their product. If it was a service industry then you might expect this percentage to be higher.

$$\text{net profit percentage of sales} = \frac{£51,246}{£511,529} \times 100 = 10 \text{ per cent}$$

For every £1 Freedom Designs Ltd makes in sales, just 10p is left as net profit. A fashion retailer is likely to have reasonably high expenses due to the nature of their business. A retail business with a physical location (as opposed to e-commerce) may have high overhead costs such as premises and heat and light.

Another measure of profitability is return on capital employed (ROCE).

## Worked Example – Freedom Designs Ltd

Net profit before interest and tax = £51,246

Capital employed = £196,682

$$\text{ROCE} = \frac{£51,246}{196,682} \times 100 = 26 \text{ per cent}$$

This means that, for every £1 being used within the business, there is a return of 26p. This is certainly higher than you could expect from a bank.

▶ Gross profit – this is the turnover or revenue that a business receives less the costs of goods sold. Gross profit will not include any non-operating costs or items such as administration or accounts.

▶ Net profit – this is the turnover, or revenue of a business, less all of the costs, including any administration and other non-operating costs. Net profit is also known as 'the bottom line', as this is the actual profit that a company has made. Potential investors will be interested in the net profit of a business as they know that there are no other costs that have to be paid after the net profit for a set period.

### Sensitivity analysis

It is impossible to know if a business decision is going to be successful and profitable in advance. However, sensitivity and ratio analysis will help in reducing the uncertainty. Ask questions such as those shown in Figure 19.8.

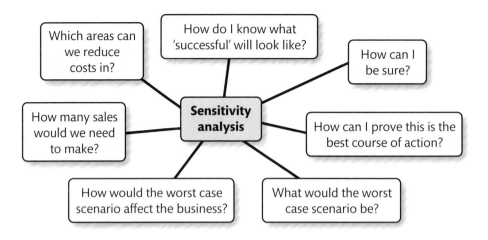

▶ **Figure 19.8:** Sensitivity analysis can help with decision making

Through addressing these questions, you are completing a sensitivity analysis. This will enable you to establish that the course of action you are planning is the most likely to succeed and, if there are any variations, the business is likely to be able to absorb them.

### Analysis of performance

This is where the strengths and weaknesses of a business are identified through understanding the key performance indicators that are established through the liquidity, profitability and sensitivity analyses. It is a form of financial statement analysis that will help in understanding the financial results and trends of the business over a period of time. By tracking operating and financial performance through these analyses, a business can see if it is growing or deteriorating.

 **PAUSE POINT**

What do you know about liquidity, profitability, sensitivity and ratio analysis? Write down the key points.

**Hint**

State what you have learnt and how you will apply each analysis to your business idea. Write down everything that you will need to consider for your actual business idea.

**Extend**

Undertake a liquidity, profitability, sensitivity and ratio analysis for your business idea. Give full explanations of your results.

## C Carry out a pitch for funding for the chosen micro-business

In this final learning aim, you are going to put everything that you have learnt into practise from the first learning aim. The business plan that you have developed while working through learning aim B will also be a key factor when you are completing this learning aim.

## Documents and materials for pitch

### Appropriate documents and materials that are detailed, appropriate, and relate to individual business proposal

When you put together a pitch for your new micro-business start-up, anything that you say during your pitch must be backed up with clear, written explanations that you can leave with your potential investors to digest at a later date. They may want to know more about a certain aspect of your pitch, and will look to your written documents to give a further explanation.

Any documents that you use must be appropriate and fit for purpose. You should adopt a professional style by typing up any explanations and using spreadsheets for figures. Use an appropriate font such as Arial, font size 11 or 12. What type of business are you promoting? Think about how your presentation can reflect your image. The presentation of your written pitch is as important as the verbal presentation you will give.

You should relate your pitch to your business proposal but also cross-reference data and analysis. You could also put a copy of your business proposal in with the written documents and materials that you intend to use as part of your pitch.

**Link**

See also *Unit 8: Recruitment and Selection Process* section on interview skills.

**Theory into practice**

Put a draft outline together of your business pitch. Talk to your peers to get more ideas of how you could improve your pitch.

## Documentation to support funding investment

Any figures that you quote during the presentation of your pitch must be backed up with written proof that the figures are robust, which, in turn, will prove that your business is viable.

All your figures and analysis must be accurately laid out in a way that is easy to understand, with sufficient detail to enable the potential investors to make decisions. You must make sure that you understand your figures and that they can stand up to questioning and scrutiny from any potential investor. Have you watched *Dragons' Den*? If those pitching for investment cannot answer the financial questions, the Dragons immediately become disinterested and say 'I'm out!'.

**❚❚ PAUSE POINT**     What documentation will you use for your business pitch? What type of image do you need to project to reflect you and your business? Do you have the IT equipment to produce a professional portfolio of documentation? Do you know how you will lay out each area of your analysis?

**Hint**     Research online for ideas on creating the documentation for your pitch. Search for financial forms that you could adapt.

**Extend**     Create a draft portfolio of your written business pitch. Check that it reflects the image you wish to give of yourself and your business.

## Evidence of exploration of potential questions and answers from potential investors

You should create a section in your portfolio of questions and answers (Q&As) that potential investors are likely to ask you. Put yourself in the investors' shoes. What would *you* want to know about your business? Are there any gaps in your business plan? Are there any weak areas that will not stand up to scrutiny?

Then consider your business again. What areas of the business do you want to showcase? Can you write a question around this area that can go into the Q&As?

Ensure that you cover the following areas by creating questions that you can answer fully.

- Risk – identify the risks to the business and create a question around these risks, giving full answers that will demonstrate how these risks will be removed, or reduced.

- Expectations for return – by creating a question, you will be able to explain the exact return on investment that the potential investor can expect.

- Share ownership and voting rights – potential investors will want to know if shares will be offered within your business and, if so, what the voting rights will be.

- Percentage of shareholding and control – you will need to be clear about what the percentages will be of the shareholding and who will have ultimate control of the business.

## Professional presentation skills

### Presentation, behaviour and conduct of presenter

You need to develop your presentation skills. The skills you need include speaking clearly and making eye contact with your audience.

▶ You are representing your business so your presentation must be professional and business-like.

When you give your presentation, you are representing yourself and your business. Your potential investor will want to believe in you as much as in the business, so, if you are not confident, or organised, the potential investor will think that your business is run in the same way. Here are some areas that you should concentrate on.

- Clothes – what you wear is so important. What image do you want to portray? You should dress smartly, making sure that your shoes are clean, while also reflecting the nature of the business. For example, if your business is in the sports sector, it might be appropriate to dress in smart sportswear whereas, if your business is in the health care sector, you may wear a white clinical coat. This will help you to set the scene.

- Attitude – be professional throughout your presentation. Treat all questions from your potential investors seriously: even if you think the answer is obvious, they will not. Smile and relax as much as you can, without becoming too casual or informal. Take a positive approach and be confident without making assumptions.

- Being business-like – what you wear, and your attitude, are part of showing appropriate business-like skills. Do not interrupt potential investors by cutting across their questions or ending their sentences for them. Be well prepared for the presentation by having all of your documentation in order and arriving in plenty of time to set up your presentation.

▶ Suitable for audience – research the potential investors that you will be presenting to. Try to find out their preferences, such as looking at figures, or having visual aids to demonstrate your products, and think about their specialist areas so that you can make this your focus. If you have an idea of their expectations, you will be able to build this into your presentation.

▶ Excellent preparation – be sure that you know all your figures and how you have arrived at them. Read through your presentation so that you become familiar with the content and will not need to read from your notes. Have any handouts clearly labelled and in the order that you will need them. Arrive early so that you can set up any equipment you might need during your presentation.

---

**⏸ PAUSE POINT**    What professional presentation skills come to you naturally and which ones are you going to need to work at?

> **Hint**    Ask friends, family and your peers, and perhaps a business mentor, for honest feedback on what skills they think you have.

> **Extend**    Put your first draft presentation together and practise using your business skills. Present to your family, friends or tutor and ask for their feedback. Take note of what they say and refine your presentation.

---

## Negotiation and communication skills

You may find that your potential investor does not offer the amount of money that you were pitching for. If this happens, then you will need your negotiation and communication skills to try to agree a deal. You will need to put a good argument together as to why you want the amount you are requesting. The potential investor is likely to argue back with the reason why they will only offer the amount they have suggested. This conversation will continue until an agreement can be made. Both parties will want to feel that they are getting a good deal out of any agreement and one that will take the business forward.

In order to be able to negotiate well, you need to be:

▶ well prepared and armed with information and figures that will back up your arguments

▶ prepared to enter into a discussion, listening to the arguments against your ideas and being prepared to negotiate

▶ clear on your goals and able to communicate these to your potential investor

▶ looking for a win–win outcome, which may mean that both parties need to 'give' a little

▶ open to agreeing a way forward with your potential investor

▶ able to implement the new course of action if, in agreeing, you have had to come away from your original plan to accommodate new ideas from your potential investor.

---

**Theory into practice**

Practise your negotiation skills with another learner, following the guidelines given above. What are the most difficult areas for you to negotiate? Which skills are you not so good at? Which skills are you good at? Practise these skills by carrying out a role play within your class, where you take it in turns to pitch for the funding and then be the investor. Arrange for a third person to observe the role play in order to give you feedback.

# Review and evaluation

In order to learn from the experience of presenting a new micro-business start-up pitch for funding, you need to review and evaluate it. This will help you to identify the areas that went well and the areas that did not go quite so well. You cannot do this on your own, as you will then only have your own perspective.

## Receive feedback on the business content of the pitch, analyse feedback and make amendments accordingly

You need to involve others in the review and evaluation process, including the potential investor. You should do this regardless of whether you were successful with your pitch. Even within a successful pitch, the potential investor may have identified areas that were weaker than others. You can also obtain feedback on the business content from others who have read through your business plan and documents.

Analysing feedback from as many sources as possible will give you a rounded evaluation of your start-up business activity, its business content and your presentation. You can review this feedback, and act upon it to develop and improve your business.

Any positive amendments that will improve your business and reflect the feedback particularly that from your potential investor, should be made to your business plan as soon as possible.

---

## Assessment practice 19.2

**B.P3** **B.P4** **C.P5** **C.P6** **B.M2** **C.M3** **B.D2** **C.D3**

Following on from your work in assessment practice 19.1, you are now going to expand on the business that you researched. You have been advised that a panel of local employers is interested in investing in a new business, and you are required to create and write a business plan that you will use as the basis for the preparation of your pitch for funding.

You must be able to explain, analyse and evaluate your business plan and demonstrate that it is viable. It should have a marketing plan that includes a market analysis and marketing mix analysis, as well as an explanation and analysis of all legal and financial aspects. A SWOT, sensitivity and ratio analysis should be used effectively to give an evaluation of how successful you predict the business will be. You should end with an evaluation of the contents of the business plan and provide justifications for your conclusions.

You will then go on to prepare and deliver your pitch for funding to a group of local business professionals. You should have with you all the documents and materials that you have created as part of your pitch and be prepared to negotiate for funding. Throughout your presentation, you must demonstrate professional business skills. At the end of the pitch, you should seek audience feedback from the panel so that you can complete a review and evaluation of the pitch, including an analysis of the viability and risks of the start-up. Any recommendations and modifications to your proposal and pitch should then be made.

You should demonstrate individual responsibility and effective self-management in the preparation, delivery and review of your presentation.

### Plan
- Do I know the order in which I am going to gather my information?
- What information for the pitch and business plan is going to be the most difficult to obtain? When should I start to I get this information?
- Who will I need to speak to, to gather more information for my business plan?

### Do
- Which documents and materials am I going to use for my business plan and pitch? Have I thought creatively about what I can use?
- Who can support me in ensuring that my figures are correct and that they show the business as viable?
- Have I booked time with those who can support me to listen to my presentation and read through my business plan?

### Review
- How successful was the pitch? Did I get the funding?
- Did I use my negotiation skills effectively?
- What would I do differently if I were to do this again?

# THINK ▶▶FUTURE

**Carly Roberts**
Owner of Bake Me Happy

Carly had always enjoyed baking and, using her financial services background, she could see an opportunity to start a baking business. Family and friends were her first customers and, from there, Carly's business began to grow. Carly needed to find out what legislation was relevant to her business, so that she would be operating lawfully. She started by talking to the local environmental health officer who sent her an information pack. Although cake making is 'low risk' Carly still needed the basics, which included hygiene training, allergy awareness training and public liability insurance.

Then Carly had to ensure that she had all the equipment required. She had to consider specific requirements related to her business. Carly ensured that her equipment was fit for purpose and suitable: for example, the size of the motor in her food mixer was more important than the look of it and it had to be able to mix the ingredients of the largest cake she would sell.

Marketing her business has included producing business cards and setting up a Facebook page. Individuals are now contacting Carly to order cakes and she is also supplying cakes to a local cafe. This gives two income streams: one that is constant (the cafe orders approximately ten cakes a week) and the other which can be extremely busy, or very quiet, where Carly receives orders from individuals. In quiet periods, Carly offers a 'treat box day' which she advertises on Facebook. In these boxes, customers can buy seven large slices of seven different cakes which she hand delivers. To keep interest and demand high, Carly only offers this monthly or bi-monthly and times the offer to come out on a Friday, ready for the weekend.

Carly recognises that it is easy to start up a business such as hers, and so she ensures that what she offers customers is of the very best quality with unique designs. Pricing is a very important aspect of the business, as Carly must ensure that there is an appropriate profit margin while still giving customers value for money.

## Focusing your skills

### Understand your business

Even micro-businesses have a level of complexity that needs to be understood in order to be successful.

- Take advice from experts and recognise what is essential to have in place, such as equipment, facilities and record keeping.
- Know what specific legislation will apply to your business and get this in place before you open for business.
- Undertake all training that is offered to you and take every opportunity to learn from others.
- Identify your strengths and limitations. Understand the roles within your business and recognise specialist services that you may need to 'buy in' or employ someone to do, such as book keeping, as well as roles that you can pass on to others without compromising the quality of products or services.

### Be prepared to work hard!

Having your own business is extremely rewarding and gives you the autonomy to make decisions and work the hours that you choose, although, in reality, you will probably end up working rather more hours than if you worked for someone else!

- Never stop thinking up new ideas. This will help you to stay ahead of the competition, increase sales in quiet periods and develop your business.
- Continue to update yourself on legislation and other initiatives that may affect your business – make this at least a monthly priority.
- Keep paperwork up to date. This includes the financial aspect and any legislative aspects, such as recording fridge temperatures twice a day for a catering business.
- Prioritise urgent tasks that must be completed even in busy periods and keep the less urgent tasks for quieter times. Focusing on the customers' needs will help you to know which tasks to prioritise.

# Getting ready for assessment

Maryam has always wanted to start her own business and was really keen to include this unit in her Business Studies course. She has had many ideas in the past, but was never sure how to go about developing them, and this unit has helped her to focus on the important aspects of starting a new business. Maryam was asked to explore up to four business ideas, one of which she took forward to write up a business plan and present a pitch for funding to a panel of local business professionals.

## How I got started

The hardest part for me was deciding on which idea to take forward. I asked my friends and family which idea they thought was the best, and got different responses from different people! I then realised that I needed to undertake my own research, both primary and secondary, so that I could make an informed decision. I found the decision matrix really useful in identifying the relevant and important parts of the business.

Once I had the basis of my business idea, I went back to my friends and family with some specific questions that would help me to refine my idea.

I then went back to the textbook to read up on the financial and marketing analysis. I had a rough idea of what it was all about, but wanted to be sure that I fully understood so that I could complete all of the financial documents and be able to answer questions on them at a later date.

As I was aiming for a distinction, I also completed a SWOT analysis, a sensitivity analysis and a ratio analysis. I went back over my notes to remember how to do this.

It was really important to keep an action plan going where I ticked off what I had done and highlighted what I still had to do. There were quite a lot of areas to cover for this assignment, so I had to be well organised right from the beginning.

## How I brought it all together

I started with my market analysis and then completed a PESTLE analysis and a SWOT analysis of the marketing mix. I found this really interesting but realised quite quickly that I needed to cover a lot of ground by speaking to people and then undertaking secondary research by doing online research.

Once I had completed all of the analyses, I compared them to see if there were any contradictions in my figures: for instance, the projected costs needed to be reflected in the cash-flow forecast and the income statement forecast.

For the legal aspects, I went back over my notes that I had taken in class and reread the textbook. When I was still unsure if any particular legislation applied to my business idea, I checked on the internet. I found that they all did apply, so spent time ensuring that my business was going to operate within the law.

I left the questions that I needed to create until I had completed everything else, so that I could see what questions would be useful to my potential investors. I also asked my family and business mentor to read through my business plan and ask me questions so that I could use this too.

Once I had gathered all of the information for the business plan and written it up, I concentrated on my pitch for funding and presentation. I enjoyed doing this as I like creating PowerPoint presentations and this allowed my creative side to come out. It was a bit scary thinking that I was going to have to present this to a panel of local business people; however, they were really supportive and, because I had prepared so well, I was able to answer most of the questions they asked at the end of the pitch.

## What I learned from the experience

▶ I should have started the assignment sooner than I did as I found that I could not speak to everyone I wanted to as they did not have the time to see me.

▶ The different analyses that need to be completed take time and need rechecking. I did all the checking myself and I would have benefited from having another pair of eyes on the break-even forecast as this did not tie in with the other forecasts. This was picked up by the panel, but luckily I was able to explain what the figures should have been.

▶ There were a couple of questions from the panel where I hesitated, and they said it would be better for me to say that I did not know the answer to their questions than to make up an answer on the spot that I could not prove. I will remember this for when I do another pitch.

## Think about it

▶ Are you sure that you fully understand each topic area for each of the learning aims?

▶ Do you have a clear plan of how you will complete the assignment and have you written this down with timescales and sufficient detail?

▶ Have you asked the right people to read through your work? Are they knowledgeable on the subject area? Will they give you honest feedback?

# Training and Development 21

# Getting to know your unit

Businesses need their staff to have the correct range of up-to-date skills and knowledge so they can perform effectively at work. There is a cost to the business, but it is a worthwhile investment to ensure newly appointed staff members understand their role and know what is expected of them and that established staff members are updated and developed to meet the demands of the business and enable them to progress in their careers.

## How you will be assessed

This unit will be assessed through two assignments. The first will be a presentation, based on the research that will be undertaken around training and development in a selected business. This will lead onto a second assignment, where an induction plan for a group of new starters into a business will be constructed. These assignments are designed to follow on from each other so that you can demonstrate an understanding of training and development and can apply this knowledge practically.

To obtain a Merit or Distinction it is important that you read carefully what is being asked of you for each grade and that you apply it to your completed work. For example, the Merit criteria ask you to assess and analyse various aspects of training and development, whereas the Distinction criteria ask you to evaluate. It is important that you understand the difference between assess, analyse and evaluate; if you are unsure, speak to your tutor.

Your tutor will set your assignments; together they will cover each of the learning aims within the unit at Pass, Merit and Distinction grades.

You will be required to provide evidence as you complete each of the assignments, and this is likely to be through written work, presentations, practical tasks and other notes that you may have, such as checklists and presentation notes.

The work set by your tutor is likely to include a written assignment, and may also include:

▶ creation and delivery of a PowerPoint presentation
▶ an induction plan for a group of new starters within a business
▶ collection of evidence that forms part of a new starters induction, such as checklists and information handouts.

## Assessment criteria

This table shows you what you must do in order to achieve a **Pass**, **Merit** or **Distinction** grade, and where you can find activities to help you.

| Pass | Merit | Distinction |
|------|-------|-------------|

**Learning aim  A ** Investigate training and development in a selected business

| Pass | Merit | Distinction |
|------|-------|-------------|
| **A.P1**<br>Explain why a selected business trains its **employees**<br>Assessment practice 21.1 | **A.M1**<br>Assess the reasons for training in a selected **business**<br>Assessment practice 21.1 | **A.D1**<br>Evaluate the contribution that training and development make to fulfilling the objectives of the selected **business**<br>Assessment practice 21.1 |
| **A.P2**<br>Describe how a selected business identifies training **needs**<br>Assessment practice 21.1 | | |

**Learning aim  B ** Examine the planning and delivery of training programmes in a selected business

| Pass | Merit | Distinction |
|------|-------|-------------|
| **B.P3**<br>Describe the types of training and development used by a selected business<br>Assessment practice 21.1 | **B.M2**<br>Analyse the likely costs and benefits of different types of training to a selected business and its **staff**<br>Assessment practice 21.1 | **B.D2**<br>Evaluate the likely costs and benefits of different training methods for individual needs in a selected **business**<br>Assessment practice 21.1 |
| **B.P4**<br>Explain the impact training has had on an individual in **a selected** business<br>Assessment practice 21.1 | | |

**Learning aim  C ** Develop an appropriate induction programme for a group of new starters in a selected business

| Pass | Merit | Distinction |
|------|-------|-------------|
| **C.P5**<br>Plan an appropriate induction programme for a group of new starters in a selected business using own research<br>Assessment practice 21.2 | **C.M3**<br>Assess the factors likely to make induction successful for new starters in the **selected business**<br>Assessment practice 21.2 | **C.D3**<br>Evaluate the likely impact of the induction programme on the business and the **individuals**<br>Assessment practice 21.2 |

## Getting started

What does training and development mean to you? Have you ever received training as part of your induction when you first started a job? Did you receive on-going training after that? Successful companies are likely to have detailed and comprehensive induction programmes, with further training and development available to staff members as they become experienced and ready to progress in their career.

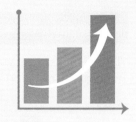

# A Investigate training and development in a selected business

**Key terms**

**Training** – acquisition of skills, knowledge and competencies as a result of teaching.

**Development** – process where an individual is able to grow, change and/or become more advanced in their skills and competencies.

## Training and development

Training and development is a term that is very often used in businesses. Some businesses are likely to have a training and development team, where in others this may be a responsibility of an individual and part of another role that they undertake. Before investigating this further, you need to understand the differences between **training** and **development**.

### Training

Training is crucial where an individual needs to learn essential skills in order to do their job. This might be in groups of formal training, such as classroom workshops or in less formal situations where an individual has a one-to-one session with a mentor or line manager. In all cases, the individual will be learning essential knowledge and skills in order to be able to carry out the basic functions of their job.

### Development

Development is likely to follow on after training and be part of an agreed plan over a period of time. Part of the development of the individual may include further training in order to learn new skills and gain further knowledge that will prepare them for additional responsibilities within their role or even a new role.

**PAUSE POINT**

Think about jobs you may have had. List training that you received, whether it was formal training or less formal one-to-one training.

**Hint**    Did this training help you carry out your job? Were there other areas of your job that would have benefited from further training? What difference would this have made to your performance?

**Extend**    Was this training followed up with a development programme? If yes, what development activities did you undertake? If no, were there development activities that you would have benefited from?

## Reasons for training

Focused and successful businesses are likely to have clear objectives detailing their goals and the vision that they wish to achieve over a set period of time. Any programme of training needs to be aligned to these objectives so that the workforce is equipped with the correct skills, competence and knowledge to be able to work effectively and efficiently towards these goals.

These overall objectives are likely be broken down for different aspects or departments of a business where the specific skills, competence and knowledge that may be required are different in each area.

## Strategic

The overall reasons for training will start at the **strategic** level. The business will have a main focus that is linked to its objectives, and a well-trained workforce that has excellent product knowledge and customer service skills is likely to help the business increase its profit and turnover and become a market leader.

▶ Increase profit: cost-awareness training will help an organisation to increase its profitability without necessarily increasing its turnover. For example, finance and budget training for store managers is likely to lead to their ability to control or reduce costs resulting in financial benefits to the company.

▶ Increase turnover: product knowledge, customer service and sales training are three key areas that businesses will invest in to ensure that staff are equipped to do their work effectively. A workforce trained in these areas is likely to increase the turnover of a business.

▶ Become market leader: businesses that are market leaders are likely to have a development programme that follows on from any induction training and incorporates further training. They train and develop the workforce to be specialists and offer consistent and exceptional customer service which helps the business maintain its position as a market leader.

## Operational

The strategic reasons for training need to be broken down into the different **operational** areas of a business as follows.

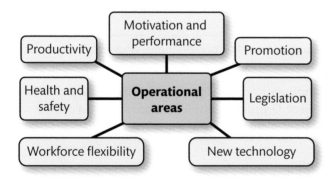

▶ **Figure 21.1:** There are many good reasons for training

▶ To increase productivity: successful businesses are likely to always be looking at new ways of working to increase output. They are likely to train and develop their workforce in order for them to adopt new ways of working. This could be following new systems and procedures for a manufacturing business or training the workforce to think differently in their approach for a sales-based company.

▶ To introduce new technology: most businesses are likely to use technology, which will need to be updated or completely renewed from time to time. The workforce will need to be trained in order to be able to use the technology effectively and efficiently to ensure the smooth running of the business.

▶ To improve health and safety: businesses have a duty of care to their workforce and customers and therefore it is essential that health and safety training is in place in order for the organisation to meet their legal requirements. Some individuals are likely to be trained beyond the basic levels depending on their health and safety role within the business, for example a dedicated and named first aider will receive further training so that they are equipped to deal with emergencies.

> **Key terms**
>
> **Strategic** – reasons that relate to the long-term or overall aims of the organisation.
>
> **Operational** – in use, or ready for use.

▶ Can you think of any industries where health and safety training is likely to be of crucial importance?

▶ To satisfy UK and EU legislation: different departments within a business will need to be aware of, and trained, in certain UK and EU laws and regulations so that they are operating within the law. For example, the staff in a human resources department will need training on employment law, whereas kitchen staff will need to be trained in food hygiene.

▶ To create a more flexible workforce by **back filling**: multi-skilling the workforce through training and development means that individuals are more valuable to a business as they will be able to work in more than one department. For example, a hotel may train its front of house staff to serve in the restaurant, behind the bar and in reception.

▶ To introduce **succession planning** for promotion: businesses with a medium to large workforce are likely to create training and development programmes to identify and equip those within the workforce who have the potential for, or are seeking, promotion. These programmes are likely to stretch and challenge the individual so that when a role at the next step up becomes available, they are in a good position to apply for it.

▶ To improve job performance and motivation: the appraisal system is used by many businesses where individual performance and motivation is discussed and recorded along with any training needs or desires. This may happen on a yearly or six-monthly basis and be followed up with monthly one-to-ones. This information is then collated across the workforce to create an organisational development plan, based on the collective training needs of the individuals within the business. This activity is likely to support the improvement of job performance and motivation. This system is often used as the basis for any bonus schemes or pay rises within the business, another important motivating factor for employees.

### Key terms

**Back filling** – a practice used by organisations, where staff are replaced from within the workforce who have been developed in order to step into a new role.

**Succession planning** – having a plan in place to fill a sequence of roles within a team or department. Organisations will develop more than one person for each role to allow for movement and changes within the business.

**⏸ PAUSE POINT**

List businesses that have a healthy profit and turnover and/or are market leaders. What are the indicators that make these businesses successful?

 Hint

What outward signs suggest to you that the workforce is well trained?

Extend

Can you identify any areas of the business where they could benefit from further training?

### Departmental

Whole departments are likely to have a training plan in place for their particular area in order to fulfil a collective need such as the following.

▶ To meet sales targets: a combination of knowledge of the products and/or services being sold and skills in selling is required in order for a department to meet its sales targets. Therefore successful businesses are likely to train their staff in more than one area. The workforce must have a thorough knowledge of any product and/ or service that they are going to be selling in order give them confidence to talk to their customers, which is likely to lead them on to being able to offer advice and additional sales. Sales training will also be given to ensure that the workforce is maximising the opportunities for increasing sales and that they are following the organisation's sales procedures. A good example can be seen with Apple shops. The staff are very knowledgeable about the computers and other products that they sell and once the sale is made, the staff member will offer additional products such as a protective cover or a yearly training package for the product just purchased. The staff member is well trained in the product, the sales technique of **up-selling** and the sales process to follow in using the hand-held device to take customer details and payment.

▶ To improve customer service: customer service training is often linked to meeting sales targets as detailed above, where it would be the third element along with product knowledge and sales training. A well-trained workforce that values its customers and knows how to ensure that the customer receives excellent service, exceeding their expectations, will lead to customer loyalty and repeat business. There are other organisations where sales may not be relevant, such as the NHS or a local government department but where customer service is just as important. These organisations are offering a service to the general public and part of their success measures will be based on customer feedback. By receiving specific training around customer service, these organisations are able to improve the service they offer and the experience received by those who use their services.

**Key term**

**Up-selling** – persuading a customer to buy something in addition to original purchase.

### Individual

Businesses experience continual changes and updating where individuals may need to equip themselves with new skills and/or knowledge to remain up to date. There will also be people within a business or organisation who require training based on their specific needs, such as to be up-skilled. In both cases, there are different reasons for individuals to need training.

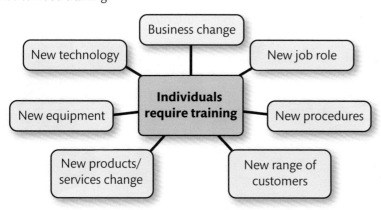

▶ **Figure 21.2:** People need training for a variety of reasons

▶ To prepare for change: there may be a re-structure within the business, meaning that roles and responsibilities may be changed, or increased to incorporate additional skills. There may be external changes that will have an impact on the business, which means individuals need training. For example, when insurance tax was introduced by the government, anyone working in the insurance industry had to be trained on how the tax was to be calculated, the rates and to which product the tax would apply. The government made announcements of the changes to be made which gave the insurance industry time to train their workforce.

▶ New job role: with promotion, comes additional responsibilities that are likely to mean new skills and knowledge required. The correct training will ensure that the individual is equipped with the skills needed to be effective in their new role. For example, a member of staff promoted from within their own sales team will have the skills and knowledge of how to operate within the team, but will need further training on management skills in order to be able to become an effective manager and gain respect from their new team.

- New equipment: when a business introduces new equipment, it is essential that the appropriate training is given to ensure the workforce operates it effectively and safely. For example, a waste transfer station may introduce a new machine to sort the recycling of different items of rubbish. There will be health and safety aspects to consider as well as the operating skills required by those using the machine. Training of the workforce in the use of the machine will ensure that the investment of the new equipment will be returned as efficiently and effectively as possible.

- New procedures: businesses are likely to introduce new procedures for a variety of reasons, such as to increase productivity, improve their service or due to external pressures such as legislation or market forces. A workforce will become ineffective if they are not using any new procedures that are put into place and so it is vital that an organisation identifies the skills and knowledge that are required in order for the new procedures to be implemented, and that there is a plan of training with a realistic timescale in place so the workforce is trained in advance of any new procedures coming into operation. For example, a bank introducing a new electronic banking system, to be used at the counter with customers, must ensure that all staff are fully trained before 'going live' to retain customer confidence and satisfaction.

- New products and/or services: when businesses diversify into new areas or introduce new products to an existing range it is likely to lead to their workforce requiring training in order for the new product and/or service to be successful and to give the workforce confidence in selling the new product and/or service. For example, when a coffee shop introduces a new type of coffee, staff will require skills training for using the coffee machine at the correct temperature and knowledge training for the taste the new coffee should have and what makes it special, so that they can then communicate this to the customer.

▶ New products or equipment mean staff have to learn new information and procedures

- New technology: when a business introduces new technology, it will only be effective if the workforce is trained to use it for how it is intended. The organisation selling the technology to the businesses is likely to offer initial training as they have experts who can cover all aspects of the equipment and programmes the workforce will use it for. This specialist team is likely to train identified IT experts within the organisation who will then train the rest of the workforce. For example, an organisation introducing a new Human Resources system into a business will train its key team members on how to use the system and they can then cascade what they learn from the training to other key individuals who will also be operating the system.

▶ New range of customers: a way for businesses to diversify and increase their sales is to make their product and/or service attractive to different types customers or to diversify into new products and/or services that may bring a new range of customers. For example, a holiday company wishing to attract new customers to their business may decide to offer a new activity for their sports holiday programme. The workforce selling these new holidays would need product knowledge training in order to be able to discuss customers' requirements and make recommendations. The new activity could also mean new locations, and therefore the workforce would need to be trained on what is on offer in the new locations in terms of facilities and entertainment.

---

**❚❚ PAUSE POINT**

What other reasons are there that a department or individual would need training? Give examples from jobs that you have had, or have now.

**Hint**

If you do not have experience of departmental or individual training, ask a relative or friend about the training they have received or that takes place where they work.

**Extend**

How did this training equip you, or those you asked, to improve the team's performance or individual performance to learn new skills and knowledge?

---

## Identification of training needs

### Training Needs Analysis (TNA) or Training and Learning Needs Analysis (TLNA)

Before undertaking a TNA, a business must be able to define the skills and knowledge that it requires its workforce to have. This is likely to be directly linked to the objectives of the business from which a clear definition of job roles and responsibilities can be identified and communicated to the workforce. A TNA should be an on-going activity, rather than a one-off, and form part of the training and development plan of a business. Training can only be effective and useful to an organisation, and the individuals within it, if there is an awareness of the skills that already exist within the workforce and where there are gaps within these skills. This activity is called TNA or TLNA. A TNA and TLNA is a health check on the skills, talent and capabilities of the business.

▶ It reviews current skill levels of staff: a review of skills across the whole business should be considered to identify current skills, knowledge and behaviours within the workforce. This will highlight any skills, knowledge or behaviours that may have gone unrecognised and identify any gaps. From a full review such as this, training can be designed and written to meet the needs of individuals to fulfil their current and desired job roles. For example, many businesses develop their next generation of managers from their existing workforce. Those individuals who wish to pursue a career into management can be identified while in their current role and undertake a first line manager course in order to learn the skills, knowledge and behaviours required before applying for the manager role.

▶ It identifies skills/knowledge gaps within the business/of an individual: once the review of current skills is complete, the results can be compared to the skills, knowledge and behaviours that are required for the business to operate successfully and what individual departments or areas of the business will require the workforce to do. This can also be used to identify and address any standards of work performance that are not being met.

▶ It looks at new skills that could take the business forward: businesses continuously need to keep themselves up to date with new innovations and to ensure they continue to meet the needs of their customers. With an effective training and development programme in place, a business can plan and prepare to ensure

**Link**

This section links to *Unit 6: Principles of Management*.

that its workforce is equipped to meet any new demands this may bring. A TNA will identify individuals who could increase their capacity by taking on further responsibility by delivering training to meet any new demands, and where there continues to be skills gaps, the business can recruit additional members of staff who already have these new required skills. For example, a car ferry company may decide to introduce a foreign exchange facility at the dockside. After completing a TNA of current staff, it was established that nobody had the skills required to manage the new facility, and so a foreign exchange manager was advertised, and the skills required were clearly outlined in the recruitment process.

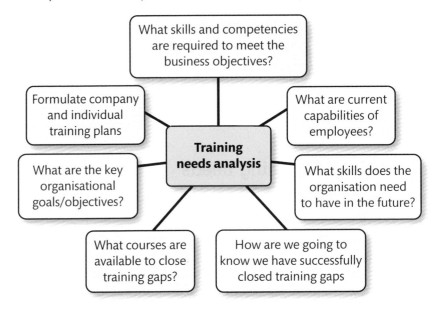

▶ **Figure 21.3** An example of how a TNA can be carried out

## Case study

### Planning and training

Daniel works in the training department of a large DIY store where he is part of a team that designs and writes training programmes for the workforce based in stores throughout the UK. He has been advised by his manager that the company is about to launch a new product range in the garden department which will include garden furniture and worktools.

Daniel has recently been through his own appraisal where he made known his wishes to develop his own skills further by being considered for any new projects or initiatives that might become available in the training department. So his manager has given Daniel this middle-size project where he will be responsible for writing the training for departmental staff in these new products.

His time-scales mean that the whole project has to be completed in three months, with the first proposal being written for his manager to read through by the end of the first month. This will give him a further two months in which to make any adjustments and complete his work to come up with a final proposal.

Daniel has put a plan together to help get him started and deliver his project on time.

- Complete a skills analysis of job roles to identify any common skills between the new products and the products that the company currently sells.
- Look at the current training offered by his department to establish if there is any overlap.
- Speak to a selection of area managers to find out what their expectations are on the performance of the department in terms of the workforce skills needs and budgets they will be expected to meet.
- Speak to the suppliers of the new products to establish if there are any specific training requirements that he should be aware of, such as health and safety, and if there are any training that the suppliers would be prepared to deliver.
- Recommend a delivery model to ensure the training roll-out is smooth and reaches the workforce across all locations as quickly as possible, but without compromising on the quality of the training and ensuring the workforce is fully trained and equipped with the appropriate skills.

Daniel completed his five-point action plan as detailed above and takes his first proposal to his line manager at the end of the first month. This is what he has established.

- Selling is already a part of the training programme, and the business already sells a budget range of garden furniture that complements the new range.
- The existing company sales and customer service training can be adapted and used in this new training programme.

- The area managers were really busy and this information is not yet available.
- The suppliers were very helpful and explained that they could offer product knowledge training on the features and benefits of the equipment. They could not offer specific health and safety training.
- His initial thoughts are to roll out the training to an identified geographical location to obtain feedback from them, before rolling out to the whole organisation.

**Check your knowledge**

Imagine you are Daniel's line manager. What advice would you give him regarding each of the five points above that he could work on in order to include in his final proposal?

1  What further TNA activity should Daniel undertake? What would the benefit be of this additional TNA?

2  What will he need to think about if he is going to use the existing company training? Consider the advantages and disadvantages.

3  How important is it that information is obtained from the area managers? State your reasons for your answers.

4  How much involvement should the suppliers have in the training programme? What is their influence likely to be?

5  Are there any pitfalls in the delivery model Daniel has suggested?  What other delivery models could he consider?

# B  Examine the planning and delivery of training programmes in a selected business

## Types of training

Training can take place in many different places and be conducted in many different forms in order to suit the needs of the business and individuals. Many businesses will have in-house training programmes and prefer to train their own workforce using their own training teams, or other experts within the business, whereas others will see the benefits in using external organisations to train areas of the workforce in specialist areas or to bring an 'outside' perspective or way of thinking to its workforce.

### Internal/in-house/on-the-job training

Internally-based training allows the organisation to use the skills and expertise that exist within the business. Individuals employed by the organisation to deliver their training, whether as dedicated trainers, or training colleagues as part of their everyday job, will have a sound understanding of the business and be able to communicate business messages related to the objectives and vision of the organisation.

▶ Who would you choose as a mentor?

▶ Induction: in order for an individual to understand their role, become familiar with their workplace surroundings and know what is required of them in their job, they need to go through an induction. In some businesses this may be over a prolonged period of time, whereas in others it may only be as short as half a day. It will depend on the nature of the business and the entry level of the individual as to the form and length of the induction. Larger organisations are likely to have a written and previously formulated induction that is standardised and used across the business, whereas in smaller companies inductions are likely to be put together for the individual as they are recruited.

▶ Coaching: this encourages the individual to think through certain situations in order to come to the appropriate conclusions. Many organisations use coaching as their preferred method of learning as it encourages autonomous thinking so that the individual becomes equipped to solve their own problems and understand the consequences of their actions with the limits of their responsibility.

▶ Mentor/buddy systems: these can be very useful for an individual when they are new to an organisation, or are looking for support in order to take on a new role and/or gain promotion. The mentor, or buddy, does not need to be the line manager and it usually works better if it is not. In some organisations the mentor or buddy is a trained individual who has this remit as part of their role, whereas in others the mentor or buddy may be chosen by the employee, based on their personal preference where they choose somebody who they can relate to and who they get on well with.

▶ Shadowing: when a new skill needs to be learnt, or an individual is new to their role, shadowing is an excellent way of learning about a job or role. Shadowing is quite often part of an induction and is planned in to allow the individual to observe different people within an organisation who are considered to be 'expert' or 'experienced' in their role and so able to demonstrate good practice with a positive approach.

▶ Peer training: in large organisations training is often cascaded from the training department in written form to be delivered locally by individuals who have the appropriate skills and knowledge. In other organisations, peer training may mean due to budget constraints, or the fact that there is no training department, the only person able to deliver the training works alongside the individual.

▶ Job rotation: graduate schemes are a good example of job rotation within training. The graduate joins an organisation and learns how each department operates in order to gain a full understanding of the business before moving into a more strategic role. For example, a graduate at a large coffee chain will learn how each department at head office operates by spending time and working in all of the departments. They will work in a coffee shop, learning the coffee making skills and eventually spending time as a manager to learn management skills. Job rotation may also be used by an organisation in order to develop the workforce, making it multi-skilled and meaning they can work effectively in different departments.

▶ Projects: internal projects are used by many organisations in order to complete activities that are part of the strategic vision and objectives of the business. Individuals may be seconded to undertake these projects, or the project may run alongside their everyday job.

▶ Business documentation: emails, leaflets and newsletters are likely to be used by organisations to communicate a consistent message, such as updates on health and safety or changes to systems and/or processes. It gives individuals a point of reference to be able to refer to as they learn about and implement the changes that are detailed in the documentation.

▶ Presentations: can be a useful tool when information needs to be communicated to the workforce that is consistent and instantaneous. This may be a communication from head office to the whole of the organisation around a specific and important topic, such as a company announcement.

▶ Wikis: forward-thinking organisations are likely to encourage the use of wikis via their intranet, where individuals can contribute to, and obtain information and knowledge concerning their organisation. There could be a frequently asked questions (FAQ) section, or it could be used to find group solutions or to develop standards across a company. For example, if an organisation is rolling out a new computer software program, a wiki could be set up for novice users to ask questions and describe any issues they may have, which can then be answered by the expert users within the organisation.

| ⏸ **PAUSE POINT** | Close the book, write down as many different types of internal, in-house and on-the-job training as you can. |
|---|---|
| Hint | Why would these different types of training be used? What are the benefits to the organisation and the individuals? How would a business use these different methods? |
| Extend | Why would a business need internally-based training? What are the benefits and the the limitations? |

## External/off-the-job training

Organisations may choose external training when they are introducing a new concept, system or new equipment to their business as they do not have the expertise internally. External, or off-the-job training, is likely to mean individuals attending training courses or similar activities away from their everyday place of work, either in another part of the building or at a completely different location.

▶ Secondments: larger organisations may offer individuals the opportunity to undertake a different role for a period of time to fill a temporary vacancy. This is usually a temporary promotion or an opportunity for an individual to work in a different area of the business at a similar or higher level in order to gain skills and knowledge in new areas. At the end of the secondment, the individual is guaranteed to be able to go back to their original position, although quite often because the individual has demonstrated new skills and gained a new level of expertise, a secondment can lead to a new role.

▶ E-learning/online learning: there are many online learning solutions available to organisations. Both larger and smaller organisations can take advantage of these flexible opportunities where individuals tend to work at their own speed and can plan when their training will take place.

▶ Vocational and professional courses: recognised courses are quite often linked to professional bodies, such as the Chartered Institute of Personnel and Development (CIPD) for human resources professionals or the Institute of Food Science & Technology (IFST) for those working in the food science and technology sector. These courses can cost several thousands of pounds and are seen as an investment by organisations who sponsor individuals to undertake such courses. The individual will be committing to a course that is likely to take a lot of their time, through attending formal workshops away from home and being required to complete comprehensive projects and assignments throughout the course.

▶ Conferences: this could be a whole organisation conference held annually to celebrate success and convey new messages for the year ahead, or for individuals to attend conferences connected to the sector in which they work, to learn about new initiatives and network with like-minded individuals from other, similar organisations. Attendees at a conference are quite often encouraged to contribute their ideas and experience through discussion and workshops.

- Seminars: these are used when there is information to be given or instruction for a certain sector. For example, an individual working in the insurance industry may attend a seminar to learn about new products and services being offered and how these are affected by new legislation. There are usually guest speakers chosen for their expertise to talk on specific subjects.

- Workshops can be used to introduce staff to new products

- Workshops: these are often run and delivered by an organisation for its workforce and might be a one-off or a series. Management training programmes are likely to consist of a series of workshops to cover topics such as coaching and developing a team, self-management, budgeting and report writing whereas one-day workshops may be more suitable for product knowledge training. Workshops are designed for inclusive learning where individuals are encouraged to take part in a variety of learning activities and the trainer becomes a facilitator for learning to take place. Larger organisations may hire in a specialist trainer to deliver workshops to its workforce because they can provide large groups of people and training rooms, making it cost effective, whereas smaller organisations may elect to send individuals to workshops being run by independent training providers and pay an attendance fee.

**ⅠⅠ   PAUSE POINT**

Have you or friends or family been offered external training by employers? What did you or they learn?

Hint

Research online for what external training organisations offer their workforce. Is there a common theme on topics offered?

Extend

What are the benefits of the workforce undertaking external training to the individual and to the organisation?

## Integration of strategies

Many organisations have formal plans in order to train and develop their workforce. These can take different forms and are likely to involve a combination of internal and external workshops and training. It is important that any training and development programmes reflect the needs of the business and the individuals, rather than becoming training for its own sake, or totally un-related to the environment or context of the business. This is more likely to be a concern when training is undertaken by a third party external to the business, but should not be taken for granted when internal training only is planned. Close working relationships between the business, training department and any third parties can ensure that all needs are met and that all training is 'fit for purpose' to help individuals learn the skills, knowledge and behaviours to do their jobs well and be productive. Having a robust review process in place can support the individual and should involve line managers and/or anyone who has an interest in the development and performance of the individual.

▶ Course of study with work-based learning: this type of training is offered by many organisations, both large and small, with the support of a private training provider or, in some cases, delivered by the organisation itself. These courses may be government-funded programmes, made up of different components, all designed to enable the individual to develop their skills and knowledge in their chosen occupational area. These programmes of study ensure that the individual is also developing their wider skills such as maths, English and ICT. For some sectors, such as policing or the NHS, there are programmes of study that form part of the initial training that must be completed before the individual is deemed qualified and competent in order to carry out their role independently.

▶ Day release systems: trades such as building, engineering, hairdressing and accountancy frequently use day release programmes where individuals attend a local college or training provider one day or evening a week in order to learn specific skills and knowledge. Individuals are given the opportunity to study towards and achieve nationally recognised qualifications; for example, AAT qualifications for accounting technicians.

## Training programmes

Organisations throughout the UK and in a variety of sectors offer employee training programmes. This is both to attract talented individuals to their business and to encourage those with potential and ambition within the organisation to develop and grow into more senior positions.

▶ Graduate training: there are many graduate schemes available and offered by many of the large employers, such as Marks & Spencer, Morrisons, Enterprise Rent-a-Car or even MI5! The graduate schemes are for those who have completed their university degrees and are often quite competitive and difficult to get onto. There are a variety of benefits such as a reasonable starting salary, on-the-job training, developing life-skills and confidence, the opportunity to meet senior managers and/ or directors of the business and being in a group of like-minded people.

▶ Management: trainee management programmes are offered to a wider population, such as those who have just left school and do not wish to go to university or who are already in the business and have shown potential. Management schemes can last up to 18 months and are likely to expose the individual to all areas of the business, such as operational roles, before moving on to managerial training and ultimately management roles.

**Link**

See the section: Internal/ in-house/on-the-job training on job rotation and internal training.

**Research**

Research organisations in at least three different sectors that offer graduate and management programmes.

What do different organisations offer the graduate or trainee manager? Are there any entry requirements? How long are the programmes? What opportunities are offered at the end of the programme?

**Link**

See the section: Training Needs Analysis (TNA) or Training and Learning Needs Analysis (TLNA) on TNA and identification of training needs.

# Costs and benefits of training and development

There will always be a cost attached to any training and this needs to be weighed against the benefits to the business and the individual. When training is compulsory by law, the business would have to absorb the costs and the benefit would be that the business can continue to operate lawfully. For example, a contractor must ensure that its workforce undertakes safety training and each individual passes a test before they can work on underground cables.

## Costs

### Planning

Effective training will be planned in advance, with sufficient time in order to design, write and produce materials. This means an investment in time and resources before seeing any benefits.

Training needs within a business have to be identified and assessed. This requires an investment of time and resources to identify what training is required and establish the training needs across the organisation as well as for the individuals in order to ensure the training is effective. An organisation may have a training department with the skills to undertake an internal TNA, or may have a budget that allows them to buy in the services of an external company to complete a TNA. A forward-thinking organisation will see the benefit of investing in this type of planning in order to ensure any training will meet the needs of the organisation and therefore be effective in its delivery and desired outcomes.

### Programme development and design

Once training needs have been identified, the next stage is to develop and design the training ensuring it is fit for purpose and will benefit the business and individuals. This will involve setting objectives, creating learning materials, handouts, activities and exercises that take into consideration a variety of learning styles and preferences of those attending the training. As well as the time involved, there will be a cost attached.

▶ Research: this could be undertaken internally, or the services of an external organisation could be bought in. Any investment in time of an internal training team member would need to be included in the budget for the development and design of a training course as well as the costs from any external organisations used.

▶ Purchase of training materials: training materials can be purchased 'off the shelf' that are written and professionally produced with workbooks, props and videos often part of the package. These types of training material packages can be quite expensive and so organisations may decide to develop their own training materials using training team members and then have the materials professionally produced. This is likely to reduce the cost of the training materials and ensure that company logos and the language used within the organisation is used within the training materials.

▶ Purchase of supplies: supplies that are associated with training programme development and design include a variety of items such as flip charts and marker pens, projectors, paper and refreshments. Some of these supplies will be essential whilst others will be a 'nice to have'. The trainer will need to consider what supplies will be essential for the training; this is likely to depend on the design and level of the course as well as the budget that is available.

### Delivery

There are many factors that are likely to have an impact on the delivery costs for training.

▶ Trainers: organisations that have their own training department or in-house trainers will have a budget in place to cover the employment of and other associated costs for their own staff. Although the cost of a trainer's time is already covered by using internal staff, training departments will often charge the budgets of other internal departments to design and develop training courses. Costs must still be controlled when training design and delivery is internal with accountability for the spend. The cost for external trainers can have a considerable range depending on the expertise, subject area and sector of the organisation. For example, experts considered to be leaders in their field can charge thousands of pounds for one day's training, whereas other lesser known trainers will cost much less than this.

▶ Training spaces: the type of venue and location will have an impact on the cost of training rooms and spaces. Central London hotels are at a premium and are likely to be very expensive whereas purpose-built training rooms in regional locations are likely to be less expensive. Where they have space, organisations may create their own training rooms, or areas that can be used for training. There will be an initial set up cost for such rooms and then ongoing costs for items such as maintenance, electricity and other running costs. For practical-based and/or specialist training, the training space may be an outside area such as an assault course for those undertaking physical fitness training as part of their job or a simulated environment such as a mock aircraft for air steward emergency evacuation training. The costs of creating these specialist training spaces, or hiring them from a third party, needs to be factored into the training budget.

▶ Refreshments: it will depend on the length of the training as to the amount of refreshments that may be made available. Whole day training is likely to include morning coffee, lunch and afternoon tea, whereas a half-day training is likely to include coffee and tea only. When outside venues are used, there is usually a choice of fixed lunch menus available that will have varying costs according to which is ordered. This allows for different budgets to be catered for. When organisations arrange to use their own venues, they may bring in outside caterers or advise the delegates that lunch will not be provided and that they are to make their own arrangements. Teas and coffees are usually supplied as standard, whatever lunch arrangements there may be. For residential courses where delegates are required to stay overnight, evening meals are usually provided. In some cases this will be charged as part of the course refreshments by the training organiser and, in other cases, the individuals may be required to purchase their own evening meal and claim back the costs through their expenses. Purpose-built training venues and conference centres often have a delegate rate which is an inclusive per person rate that usually includes the training room hire, all refreshments and any overnight accommodation. When there is a delegate rate offered, there is usually a minimum charge based on a minimum number of delegates.

▶ Technology such as wi-fi: purpose-built training centres are likely to offer up-to-date technological facilities such as wi-fi and wireless connections for the use of audio-visual equipment. Cameras linked to computers may be available to allow for a web-based link hook-up with another venue or group of people. Smart whiteboards and smart screens are often available where the trainer's notes can be either projected onto a wall or emailed to the participants after the training event. Lighting and air conditioning may be controlled via a computerised system and multi-screens be made available in larger venues. Training venues are likely to include wi-fi within the room hire, however, should any specialised technology be required, there is likely to be an additional cost.

▶ How important do you think it is that a delegate's technology needs are covered?

▶ Audio-visual (AV) equipment: training equipment is likely to include a laptop and projector as a minimum. Some venues will hire these items in addition to the room hire costs, whereas other venues will quote an inclusive room hire that includes the lap top and projector.

 **PAUSE POINT**

List the items that you are likely to require for delivering a day's training. How much planning time would be required to organise this? What other costs would you need to consider when planning this training?

**Hint**

What training facilities are available in your area? Find out the charges and what is included for a training room and refreshments at a local venue.

**Extend**

Put together a cost for a one-day training event in a venue local to you for a group of 12, based on the basic requirements you have identified above.

**Evaluation**

This is an essential part of the training cycle to help the trainer know what those who have attended the training feel about the training and what they say they have learnt. This gives the trainer an opportunity to follow up with any individuals, if there is a need, or to make changes in the training based on the feedback given. It is also good to know when the training has gone well and the individuals have benefited from the training.

Time spent evaluating the training: asking the delegates to give you feedback is just the beginning of the evaluation process. The information gathered should be acted upon in order to make any necessary changes to improve the quality of training delivery and any other aspects such as joining instructions, training room, venue etc. Time must be allowed for this information to be collated and any necessary adjustments and/or changes made by the trainer or training team. As this has an impact on their time, a cost has to be attached to this task, based on the cost to the business of the time spent in evaluating the training. It is possible that some organisations may use electronic evaluation software, such as Survey Monkey, for delegates to complete. Collation of feedback can then be generated electronically, however, this feedback does need to be read through and processed in the same way as paper-based evaluation. Some of these systems are free; however, in other instances, there can be a charge.

**Time**

Time can often be a hidden cost that must be considered and factored in when budgets are put together.

For example, the staff involved will be taken away from their day-to-day, productive work. This results in a cost to the business. This cost is factored into budgets when costings are put together for training. For example, a manager sending a member of staff on a week-long course must consider the cost to his budget. The manager may need to pay for cover by asking another member of staff to work extra hours.

## Benefits

For training to be effective, there must be benefits to the organisation and to the individuals. Effective training means that those who have attended are likely to be equipped with new knowledge, or knowledge that will make a difference when they return to work.

▶ Increased productivity: when individuals are trained on new or existing systems and procedures within their organisation, they are likely to find new ways of working to increase how much they or their team are able to produce, whether it is a production line or processing paperwork.

▶ Increased efficiency: a change in an individual's way of thinking or how they use the tools available to do their job through attending a training course can lead to increased efficiency.

▶ Better quality of service: forward-thinking businesses are likely to continuously monitor the delivery of the quality of service expected by their customers. They will invest in the training of their workforce to ensure they are customer service focused and confident in dealing with customers. In other situations, businesses may be reacting to customer feedback and recognise a need to invest in training to improve the quality of the service they are currently offering.

▶ Reduction in complaints: in order for a business to become successful, it needs to address customer complaints as quickly and efficiently as possible. If there are trends developing around the nature of the complaints, the organisation can react to rectify these issues. Training the workforce can help to reduce customer complaints, whether it is because of the quality of service or the quality of the products offered by the organisation.

▶ Higher morale: when the workforce is trained to a level that will ensure they can do their job well and effectively they are likely to be happy at work. They are likely to have a feeling that their organisation values them and wants to support them in their career path. A happy work force with a high morale is likely to be more productive and efficient. Whereas when there is very little or no training available to them, the workforce is likely to feel under-valued and that their company does not believe in them.

▶ Staff retention: recruitment can be very expensive once the cost of the advertising, interviewing and training of new team members is considered. It can cost an organisation as much as £2000 for every individual that is recruited. The amount that an individual earns is not the only reason why they may leave their employer. Lack of career progression and a comprehensive training programme is also an important factor to many employees. For example, large employers such as M&S or Rolls Royce will advertise to potential employees the full employment package and the benefits of being able to join a training programme that will be part of a wider career path.

Potential new employees who are starting out in their career, or looking for a career change, are likely to compare different organisations with what each has to offer them beyond the salary. Large organisations can see their rivals as competitors for staff as well as customers. By offering a full employment package, they hope to attract the most talented individuals. Employers who are serious about retaining their staff are likely to invest in a thorough and interesting induction to set the scene and create a good first impression which is then followed on with further training and development.

## Benefits of training

**Increased productivity:** Amaya (a team leader for a small business making confectionery) wanted to change the way her team was working with each other and with her. She attended a training workshop on managing a team and learnt new ways to coach her team and delegate tasks. This led to her team learning how to make their own decisions with new responsibilities and the result is that they are now producing 25 per cent more confectionery per week.

**Increased efficiency:** John has been working in an organisation for six months and was using the software for processing insurance claims as he was taught by his predecessor. His manager suggested that he attended a training course on the software program to ensure he was fully utilising it. The result of the training was that John learnt how to use the system in different ways and was made aware of other functions available within the software. On his return to work, John was able to use the software in different ways which saved him a great deal of time and his manager noticed that John was now able to process the insurance claims in half the time.

**Better quality of service:** Nathan (who works in the customer services department of a contact centre) was collecting customer feedback on the quality of calls. The data he had was showing that the contact centre was receiving 57 per cent positive comments in the feedback questionnaire, when the targets were set at 75 per cent. By reading through the comments made by the customers, he was able to establish the main themes that were leading to the low percentage ratings. These were: lack of friendliness by the phone operators, limited amount of knowledge around the products being sold, and the phone not being answered within an acceptable time.

Nathan called in the training manager and they decided to put a training workshop together for the contact centre telephone operators. They used the customer comments as a starting point for the training, spoke to the manager of the contact centre to get some ideas around working conditions and completed a TNA on the contact centre workforce which they compared against the job description.

The training was interactive, informative and gave those on the training an opportunity to discuss the impact of customer service. They came up with ideas to improve their attitude and behaviour while speaking to customers. It was agreed that they would follow up the session with product knowledge training.

After a month, Nathan looked at the customer feedback statistics and the positive comments had risen to 69 per cent. He continued to work with the contact centre staff with further training and setting up reviews for individuals to be able to discuss their development and ongoing needs.

It is now three months since the initial training and the customer comments scores are now over 78 per cent. The business is doing really well and the contact centre staff are taking a real pride in their work as they can see the direct improvement in the quality of service they are offering.

**Reduction in complaints:** Arek (training manager for a small hotel) was analysing customer complaints and noticed that customers were complaining that reception staff were not able to give very much information on local attractions. He arranged for the team of four receptionists to attend a two-hour training session being delivered by the local tourist information office to learn about tourist attractions in the area.

**Higher morale:** Louise left her last company because she had learnt her job through trial and error or by asking her colleagues to show her how to do things.

After nine months in the role, Louise decided to look for another job as she was becoming increasingly unhappy. She was successful very quickly and her new company had a full training and development programme. She was given a full induction in her first month followed by software and sales training. Within six months she was meeting her targets, she felt that her new company valued her as an individual and she noticed that everyone around her enjoyed their jobs and were happy at work.

II  **PAUSE POINT**   Discuss the costs and benefits of training at work with class members. Write down their ideas and compare with your own.

> Hint  Ask friends and/or family what training they have received at work and how this has benefited them and/or their employer. How does this compare to the discussions with your class?

> Extend  Research the case studies written at:
>
> www.training.dupont.com
>
> Compare the benefits these organisations have reported against what you have learnt in this section.

## Assessment practice 21.1    A.P1 | A.P2 | B.P3 | B.P4 | A.M1 | B.M2 | A.D1 | B.D2

You are part of a training team that designs, creates and delivers training to the workforce of a medium-sized business. You have decided to apply for the training manager's job that has just become available and think it would be a good idea to investigate the training provision, including induction, of a different business in order to gain fresh ideas and to use this as part of your interview for the promotion where you have been asked to deliver an innovative presentation on a topic of your choice. You identify two areas to investigate and research that you will eventually use as the basis for your presentation and you decide to clarify these two areas by dividing your work into part 1 and part 2.

Part 1 – you want to find out and explain why your chosen business is training its workforce and then identify and describe how they identify the training needs of the business and the individuals. You then decide to complete an assessment of the reasons found from your research as to why the business trains its workforce.

Part 2 – you want to be able to describe the types of training and development used by the business and decide to interview a member of staff where you ask them to talk you through the training that they have undertaken and explain to you the impact this training they have undertaken has had on them. Once you have established and written up this information, you plan to analyse the likely costs and benefits of the different types of training this business undertakes.

To complete your piece of work, you will collate all the information you have gathered from parts 1 and 2 of your research into a presentation that highlights the main points and has a summary with an evaluation of the contribution that training and development has made to fulfilling the company objectives and the likely costs and benefits of the different training methods the organisation has used for individual needs.

### Plan

- How will you decide which business to research and investigate?
- Do you have any contacts already working in a business who can introduce you?
- Have you put an action plan together listing what you will need to do and by when?

### Do

- Do you know how you should prioritise which actions on your action plan to complete first? Will this have an impact on the success of your assignment?
- Do you have a clear vision of the content of your presentation?
- Do you understand the likely costs and benefits of work-based training from what you have learnt in the classroom and that you can apply to your research?

### Review

- Have your covered each of the elements in parts 1 and 2?
- Does the presentation cover the main points that you want to cover and is there a full summary?
- Do you know the difference between analyse and evaluate and have you used them in the correct context in your work?

# Develop an appropriate induction programme for a group of new starters in a selected business

**Link**

See also the section: Internal/in-house/on-the-job training and induction on types of training.

## Induction

Induction is the process whereby employees adjust, or acclimatise to their jobs and working environment. Many businesses have an induction checklist to ensure that all areas of the job and the relevant parts of the business are covered whereas other businesses will take a less formal approach. Below is an example of part of an induction checklist.

| What? | Where? | When? | Person Responsible | Actions & follow up? |
|---|---|---|---|---|
| Company structure and who's who | | | | |
| Dress code, holidays and sickness reporting | | | | |
| Pension and health insurance | | | | |
| Health, safety and hazard reporting. | | | | |
| Data protection policy | | | | |
| Grievance and discipline procedures | | | | |
| Appraisals & 1-2-1s | | | | |

▶ **Figure 21.4:** Extract from an induction checklist

A checklist is a good idea as it allows the new employee to understand the different facets of their job and the business that they have joined. It is a point of reference and enables questions to be raised if all of the points are not covered within a reasonable amount of time. Depending on the complexity of the business and of the role of the new employee, an induction period can last for several weeks.

### Purpose

The purpose of induction is to ensure the effective integration of staff into, or across, the business for the benefit of both parties. A thorough and detailed induction is likely to retain new staff as they settle into the business and their new role. It will help to establish at an early stage the foundations and expectations of both parties in important areas such as values, integrity, corporate social responsibility and respect toward those working in the organisation. It is at the induction stage that the new employee will gain their first impression of the business they are now working for and this is likely to be a lasting impression. The training department has a responsibility to ensure inductions are fit for purpose by meeting the needs of the individual and the organisation. This will mean close communication with all departments in the business to understand what needs to be included in an induction and regular reviews and evaluation of the induction programme by obtaining feedback from everyone involved in the process, including the inductee and their line manager.

**Ⅱ  PAUSE POINT**  Close this book and write down your definition of what an induction is, what it might contain and its purpose.

> **Hint**  Open the book and check your understanding. If you were unsure of anything, read over the paragraphs in this section.

> **Extend**  Looking at the induction checklist, what other topics would you expect to see in a company induction? List these additional topics and keep in your notes for future reference.

# Benefits of a good induction programme and costs of a poor induction programme

An induction programme is **SMART** training that provides all the information needed by new employees, and develops the relevant skills, knowledge and behaviour that their posts require.

## Benefits of a good programme

A good induction programme will ensure that the new employee settles into the organisation as quickly as possible and becomes productive in a relatively short space of time. This benefits both the organisation and the new employee.

> **Key term**
>
> **SMART** – stands for Specific, Measurable, Achievable, Realistic and Time-bound.

> **Discussion**
>
> Before starting this section, hold a group discussion with your tutor and your class around what the benefits of a good induction programme might be. Prepare in advance for this discussion by writing down your thoughts in bullet points and bring this with you to the discussion. You may base your thoughts and notes on any personal experiences of induction.

The benefits of a good induction programme include the following.

▶ It helps the individual understand their role, the department they work in and the business as a whole – it can be quite difficult to describe to a new employee what their job will involve and how they should go about it. An induction plan can allow for different elements of the job to be covered in a logical sequence and over a period of time. Ways of explaining details of the department in which the new employee works can be built in; this may involve the new employee spending time with different people within the department and at some stage across the business. As well as getting to know the job, the new employee will also get to know their new colleagues and what their roles and responsibilities are. This is an important element of the induction that will help the new employee piece together who does what and how the current individuals within the department and across the business communicate and interact.

▶ Do you know the appropriate dress code for your workplace?

▶ It familiarises them with the physical environment, the culture and the business' procedures and policies. In the early days of new employment, the new employee will be unfamiliar with everyday activities that current members of staff take for granted. They will not know where to have lunch or coffee breaks or what is available in terms of vending machines, canteens or other facilities. The new employee needs to know if it is acceptable to take a cup of coffee to their work area, or if it is not permitted. The dress code is important; is business dress expected, or does the organisation have a relaxed approach in its dress code? Simple tasks can become difficult for the new employee to undertake, such as photocopying. They may not know how the photocopier works, or even where it is. The new employee needs to become familiar with policies and procedures set out by the organisation; these can usually be found in a company handbook, or intranet, along with other vital information to ensure the new employee settles into their new employment.

▶ It makes sure that employees understand their responsibilities, eg health and safety duties, contract of employment duties. Reading policies and procedures in the company handbook or intranet will not necessarily mean the new employee understands these policies. The new employee may be asked to complete a questionnaire around the policies and procedures they have learnt about since joining the company to demonstrate their understanding. Time should be built into the induction period for the new employee to be able to undertake their own research of the company policies and procedures and ask questions to relevant and knowledgeable personnel so they can check their understanding.

▶ It enables staff to quickly become more productive: a comprehensive and thorough induction will assist the new member of staff to become productive as quickly as possible. In the first few days or weeks, the new employee is likely to observe their colleagues and learn through watching what they do. This may be interspersed with training and/or spending time with certain colleagues who will give them background information on the company and/or department's policies and procedures. While the new employee is undergoing the induction, they are not able to work independently and this is costly to a business as the existing members of staff developing the new colleague are also probably being taken away from their job role, or at least being slowed down while they explain what they are doing to the new employee.

**Ⅱ PAUSE POINT**  How can a good induction programme benefit a company? How can it benefit an individual?

**Hint**  What are the most important parts of a good induction? How would you prioritise where to start in an induction to maximise benefits? Give reasons for your answers.

**Extend**  Put together an induction programme based on your priorities so that the order of the induction maximises the benefits to the organisation and the individual.

### Costs of a poor programme

When there are little or no induction processes in place, there are likely to be many costs to the organisation and the new employee. The new employee is likely to feel lost when starting in a new business, not knowing the processes or systems. It can also be quite stressful when all work colleagues are new and the new employee is constantly being introduced to new people where names are not yet familiar and have to be remembered. This can lead to unhappiness in the early days of new employment, which will ultimately have an impact on the organisation as the new employee will struggle to do their job well.

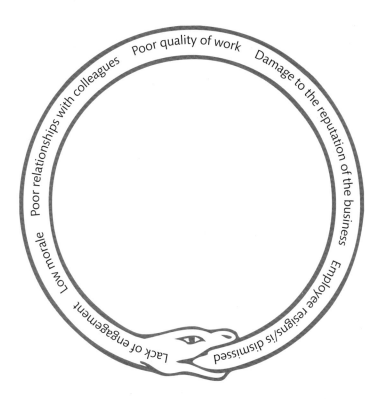

▶ **Figure 21.5:** There are serious implications of a poor induction process

## Case study

### New job for Chantelle

Chantelle was excited as she was due to start her new job with an estate agent in her local town. She arrived on her first day fifteen minutes before she was due to start as she was keen to make a good impression from the very beginning. She had been advised to come in at 10 am on her first day, although the office opened at 9 am and this would be her normal start time after her first day.

Everyone was busy as she walked into the office, although her new manager did make eye contact with her, making gestures for her to go through to the back office and make herself at home.

As soon as her manager was free, she greeted Chantelle and offered her a cup of coffee. She then produced a piece of paper that had lots of different headings and titles on, which was a list of everything that her induction was going to include. The manager explained that because Chantelle had been recruited as an extra member of the team, they didn't have a proper induction programme and so she had written down everything that she could think of that Chantelle would need to know about to create a checklist;

she planned to cover everything during the week.

Her manager explained that she was buddying Chantelle up with a member of the team, Mandy, who had been working at the estate agent for over ten years. Her manager explained to Chantelle that Mandy would go through all of the day-to-day routines in the office, as well as show her where the tea and coffee making facilities were and where to eat her lunch.

Chantelle spent the rest of the morning with Mandy, who talked her through the basic office procedures and ticked off the relevant parts of the induction checklist.

In the afternoon, Chantelle met up with her manager, who gave her the company handbook to read through and explained that she should sit in the office and observe everything going on for the rest of the day.

The manager planned to go through the company policies with Chantelle on her second day, which would include health & safety and the data protection act.

Below is a plan of the induction:

Monday – arrive at 10 am - go through office basics with Mandy

Tuesday – go through H&S and data protection with manager

Wednesday – spend time with different members of the team looking at their roles

Thursday – spend more time with Mandy to go through office duties

Friday – spend time with manager to discuss induction so far and review progress of the checklist.

**Check your knowledge**

1 What were the benefits to the company and to Chantelle in asking her to arrive at 10 am on her first day?

2 Do you think spending time with Mandy and then going through the company policies on the second day was the best order for these two activities? Give reasons for your answer.

3 What are the cost implications in conducting an induction in this way?

4 Would it be a worthwhile exercise in putting an induction programme in place for future employees? How could the manager include Chantelle in this? Explain your answers fully.

5 If you were asked to induct Chantelle, what changes would you make to her induction programme?

# Developing an appropriate induction programme

In this section, you are going to use all of the theory you have learnt about by going through the different stages of developing and creating an induction programme.

## Induction programme

The first stage is to think about who you will be inducting and what information they will require. Where will this information come from and how will it be useful to the new employee? How will it help them to understand their job and become productive as quickly as is possible?

▶ **Table 21.1** An example of an induction programme

| Items in an induction programme | |
|---|---|
| Pre-employment packs/letters/handbooks | Well-organised organisations are likely to provide these packs, letters and handbooks. It is important that any documentation is checked to ensure it is up to date and the most recent version being used. |
| Outline of job requirements | A job description or terms of reference is a good starting point for the inductor and inductee. This will ensure that the new employee is aware of all of the responsibilities within their role and that all aspects of the job are covered during the induction. |
| Explanation of terms and conditions | Sometimes, terms and conditions can be written in a formal language that may not be familiar to the inductee. It is useful if a knowledgeable person within the business can explain the terms and conditions to ensure the inductee fully understands the rights and responsibilities they have towards the organisation and that the organisation has to them. |
| Explanation of key policies and business objectives | Depending on the sector in which the organisation operates, there will be key policies and business objectives. These policies and objectives should be communicated to the new employee as soon as possible and at a time when it will be meaningful. |
| Organisational orientation | It is useful for new employees to be able to position themselves within the organisation in terms of senior managers, peers and those who may report to them. They need to be made aware of reporting lines. Company structures are quite often presented as a 'family tree'. It is a useful tool that can help to explain the different positions within the organisation and show who's who. |
| Physical orientation | Where things are in the building, things like canteen, lockers, rest areas etc, how to get in and out, staff bike and car parks etc. |
| Awareness of functions of the business | There will be different functions within a business; some that the new employee will communicate with on a regular basis and others where it may only be in rare circumstances, if ever, that they would need to communicate. By having an awareness of the different functions of the business, the new employee will have the confidence to know when it is appropriate to make contact and work with each function. |
| Meeting key employees | Induction is a good opportunity to meet key employees across the business as the new employee is likely to have time that can be set aside for this. These individuals can explain their role and how they may mutually work together in the future. |

▶ **Table 21.1** - *continued*

| Health and safety | Any business with more than five employees must have a written health and safety policy. It is the responsibility of the employer to ensure this policy is up to date and current. Training should be given where appropriate and the new employee has a responsibility to ensure they are aware of the health and safety procedures and that they follow them at all times. Employees are often required to read company health and safety policies on a regular basis and sign to say that they have read and understand them. In some circumstances it will be necessary to carry out a risk assessment for a new employee, such as a young person's risk assessment. |
|---|---|
| Practical information | Many aspects of a job can become taken for granted by those who already work within the organisation and it is this practical information that can help a new employee during their induction and the first few weeks. For example, it is useful for new employees to know where and when regular meetings are held, and the format that these meetings take. |
| Follow-up meetings | Regular reviews should be built into an induction programme to check on the progress of the new employee as well as their welfare. The induction can then be adjusted to meet the individual needs of the new employee and build in an opportunity to revisit any areas that are still unclear or that the new employee does not understand. |

⏸ **PAUSE POINT**     Close the book and list the items that should be included in an induction programme. Check and see if you were right.

> **Hint**     Write an explanation against each of the items of your induction programme. Check your explanation and note anything that you missed.

> **Extend**     Think about which order you would put these items into an induction programme. What will the new employee need to know early on? What information will the business wish to impart early on?

## Communication techniques

Communicating the different elements that make up an induction programme is important to ensure that the induction is interesting, informative and effective. There are different communication techniques that can be used within an induction programme that will keep it interesting for the new employee. An interactive induction programme will keep the new employee engaged and wanting to learn more about the organisation and their job.

▶ Presentations (PowerPoint/overheads/slides/videos): can be useful when there is a lot of information to impart and where a company message needs to be communicated across its workforce. The same presentation can be used for all inductions, whether they are one-to-one or group inductions. These presentations can then be posted onto the company intranet for future reference, or printed off and given to the new employee.

> **Discussion**
>
> You may have heard of the phrase 'death by Powerpoint'. In pairs, make a list of 'dos and don'ts' in regards to effective presentations. Think about what engages you when being shown presentations and what you think you should avoid.

▶ Talks: when groups of people are inducted at the same time, it can be useful to attend a talk. For example, a managing director may address a new group of employees to welcome them to the company, or an operations manager may give the new employees a talk on the objectives and vision of the organisation.

▶ Discussions: this would give the new employee the opportunity to discuss any issues that may arise as they go through their induction, or to discuss areas of interest such as policies and procedures to obtain a full understanding. For example, an organisation may build in discussion time within the induction programme. Subject areas may be decided in advance, or may be left open in order to accommodate any issues or areas of interest as they arise.

▶ Introductory one-to-ones: as the new employee goes through their induction, time should be planned in for them to meet key individuals within the business. By having one-to-ones, the new employee can get to know the key individuals and the key individuals can get to know the new employee. At this early stage, relationships are formed and communication channels are opened.

▶ Company documentation: it can be quite confusing for the new employee to understand and be aware of company documentation. If there is an intranet, company documentation is likely to be stored in a dedicated section; if not, company documentation is likely to be in a shared hard drive folder, or a paper-based file. Once introduced to the company documentation, the new employee should be encouraged to read through the documentation and become familiar with its layout, content and purpose.

▶ Visits: these could include visits to other departments or locations. These visits can be planned into the induction either at the beginning or at the end. A good induction programme will set out an agenda for the visit, with key information to be communicated by those being visited. There may even be a checklist for the new employee to ask questions and find out key information from their visit.

▶ Tours: this will help the new employee to become familiar with the business and give them an idea of how others are working within the business. For example, towards the end of an induction programme, it may be appropriate for the new employee to visit the company head office for a tour of the different departments. The new employee is unlikely to remember all of the people they meet during the tour, however it will give them a good oversight and help them to remember the different departments within the head office. They may also come away with contact names and numbers of key people they may need help from in the future.

▶ E-learning: this can complement the induction programme and allow the new employee to learn about certain topics such as health and safety training, or equal opportunities policy.

▶ Internet/interactive facilities: the internet is an excellent source of information and can be made available to the new employee throughout their induction. They could be set research projects to help towards their induction and understanding of the business. Electronic communications such as emails or other social media facilities that may be used by the business can be explained and used from quite an early stage. Logins for company software and email access should be sorted out as soon as possible after the new employee has started, or even in advance of their first day.

▶ Off-site training: it may be appropriate to send the new employee on a training course. This is a cost-effective way of an individual undertaking training if the expertise is not already within the organisation. If a group induction is being undertaken, the businesses may arrange to deliver off-site training for the group. This could act as an 'away day' or it may be that the business does not have the facilities to train on site.

**Theory into practice**

Talk through these different communication techniques within your group. Which of these have you and your class mates experienced with employers? Ask your tutor to join in by asking what their induction included and what communication techniques they experienced. See if you can find an example for each of the techniques listed.

## Stage of induction

The planning of any induction is crucial for it to be effective and ensure that the new employee settles into the business and their role. It is possible for the induction to start in advance of the new employee joining the company, for example, the company could send the new employee forms to complete asking for bank details and other personal information for the human resources department to ensure the new employee is on the payroll. From this initial point, the induction can be staged in order to plan what will happen in the first day, first week, first month and so on. The organisation should have a vision of when they would expect a new employee to be fully inducted and ready to work independently in order to be productive. Giving the new employee a checklist of what they will cover at each stage will help to reduce anxiety and manage their expectations of what will be covered and when.

▶ Pre-employment: the organisation is giving an impression of itself to the new employee from the very first communication when the offer of employment letter is sent. Ensure that letters are written professionally and give all the information that the new employee will need. The organisation can plan ahead, for example, by letting key employees know in advance that a new person is starting, and perhaps assign a mentor to guide and support the new employee in their first few days. The new employee's work area can be organised, comfortable and ready to use and name cards on top of all computers will help with remembering names.

▶ First day: this should cover all of the essential information that the new starter will need to know in order to operate at a basic level. For example, computer logins, ID cards (if required) and any special parking arrangements can be sorted during the course of the day. Supply a pen and notepad so that notes can be made.

▶ First week: meeting immediate colleagues and those in other departments can be planned during the first week. It is a good idea to plan how much information and how many people will be introduced to avoid overwhelming the new employee. There will be many new faces and names that they will need to remember. There will be many company policies and procedures that the new employee will need to become familiar with. Prioritise which are the most important and introduce those that are important during the course of the first week. Others can be planned in the first month.

▶ First month and beyond: once a new employee has the basics of the induction completed and they are beginning to know their way around the company and getting to know their colleagues, the induction process should still be ongoing. Reviews can be built in on progress and the learning that has taken place, as well as giving the new employee some responsibilities and to take control of their own learning. It is important that the new employee feels valued and welcome in the business as they continue with their learning and development.

 **PAUSE POINT**

Which communication techniques are likely to be the most used during an induction? How would these techniques help the induction to be successful?

Hint

Which communication techniques would you use at each stage of an induction? Give reasons for your answers.

Extend

Evaluate the likely impact that each of these techniques and stages are likely to have on the rest of the colleagues in the business, the business as a whole and the new employee.

The presentation that you completed in assessment practice 21.1 has been very successful. Your manager was impressed with the amount of research you had undertaken and the information you were able to gather.

In order for you to put your understanding into practice, he has asked you to prepare an induction programme that would be suitable for a formal induction of new employees to your business. He has asked that the plan includes a checklist of activities over a staged period up to one month that can be monitored and updated on an ongoing basis.

You will need to assess the factors that are likely to make induction successful and ensure these are fully covered in your plan. The plan should be fully documented and be accompanied by a written explanation of the benefits to each of the items you have included in the induction and the costs to the business if the plan is not implemented correctly or put into place. Your manager has also asked you to provide an evaluation of the likely impact of the induction programme on both the individual and the business.

## Plan

- Have you read through the assignment brief and fully understood what you are required to do?
- Can you remember the key points of how to develop an induction programme, in particular the factors that will make it successful?
- Have you put a plan in place with deadlines that will ensure you meet the assignment deadline?

## Do

- Do you have all of your research notes available from assessment practice 21.1?
- Do you have any key contacts that you can approach in order to discuss their experiences of inductions, both good and poor?
- Do you have a clear idea of what you would put into each stage of the induction process?

## Review

- Is your checklist achievable at each stage of the induction? Have you allowed sufficient time for new employees to digest information before moving on to the next stage?
- Have you ensured that the style of the induction will meet the needs of the individual and the business?
- Have you covered each part of the assignment brief, including induction checklist, documentation and written report?

# THINK ▶FUTURE

**Jenny Meredith**

Training and Development Adviser Screwfix

Jenny's first job was working in retail. She found that she really enjoyed the people element of her part-time job, helping her colleagues when they needed support at work and this led to her wanting to find out more about working in HR and training.

Her first role was an HR & Training Coordinator with the Co-op. Over several years, Jenny gained many skills in her training role and the Co-op sponsored her to complete a CIPD course which led to her being promoted to a Team Leader, looking after a team of trainers.

Eventually, Jenny wanted a new challenge and took on a national role with Screwfix. In this role, Jenny travels all over the country. Jenny is part of a team and has a joint responsibility for undertaking TNAs as well as designing, creating and delivering training to the Screwfix workforce. Jenny is involved in the Screwfix induction. She says 'the individual must be aligned to the business priorities and be supported in the early days of their employment with initial training and ongoing development'.

Jenny's work is not all glamorous and it can be hard work. The days can be very long as you may need to arrive up to two hours before the delegates on the day of the training to ensure the training room is set up and at the end of the day individuals may want to stay behind and talk to you one-to-one, (which you are happy to do) before clearing up!

# Focusing your skills

## Know what to expect

- Training and development roles are available across the whole of the UK. You need to decide which sector you would like to work in. Base this on what you are interested in.
- Working to deadlines is a regular feature in training and development, which can be pressurised. Be sure you are prepared to work in this environment.
- Staying in hotels during the week means staying away from home; this can turn into a regular routine for some training and development roles and will have an impact on your personal home life.
- Head office could be a long way from where you live, meaning that you have to travel for meetings and other events. Be prepared for early morning starts to meet these commitments.

## Prepare yourself by having the right skills and qualifications

This area of work is open to all levels of expertise and qualifications. Most organisations favour qualifications in subject areas relating to business areas, human resources or psychology. The skills required include the following.

- Being able to work with people of all levels is crucial as training is usually offered to all levels of the business.
- Good written and spoken communication skills that allow you to impart knowledge and skills as well as facilitate learning. Delegates must leave your training feeling that they have got something from it that they can take back to the workplace and make a difference.
- Using your initiative and being able to problem-solve. Sometimes equipment and handouts do not arrive at the venue, although it was arranged well in advance. You need the skills to overcome these problems so that the training is not affected.
- Organisation and planning skills. You will need to plan the training and deliver within the timescales you have allowed. You may have to book training rooms and ensure equipment is available. All training materials must be ready and printed off in advance of the training.

# Getting ready for assessment

Martin is interested in working in the human resources department for a large or medium-sized business. He would like to know more about training and development and so has decided to undertake this unit. It will help him to understand how training and development is put together and used by businesses as well as how induction programmes are planned and created for new starters to a business.

## How I got started

I was keen to investigate the training and development within a business. The hardest part was ensuring that I was asking the right questions to get the answers I needed to be able to complete my presentation. It would have been useful to sit down and write out some questions in advance of speaking to the different people.

I went back over my notes and read parts of the chapter again to be sure that I fully understood the different aspects of training and development as well as the induction process. I needed to recap on the benefits of a good induction programme and the costs of a poor induction programme.

My tutor gave us all a handout that explained the words assess, analyse and evaluate. I would really recommend finding this out as this helped me think about working towards a merit and possible distinction.

## How I brought it all together

The action plan that I put together, dealing with what I needed to do and by when was really useful in keeping me on target to complete on time. I was able to interview a selection of people and took notes as I went along. I kept these notes organised and made sure that my writing was neat enough so that I could re-read my notes later on when I came to write up the presentation. I wrote up my notes for 21.1 before putting the PowerPoint presentation together. I used a highlighter pen to identify the key points within my notes that I wanted to put into the presentation and this helped me to make sure that just key words were put on to each slide.

I practised the presentation at home to check the timings and help me become familiar with the content. It felt a bit strange doing this, but it was a really good way of finding out if the presentation flowed and if I understood the key points I had put in. I was able to 'fine tune' my presentation as I did make some changes after doing this practice on my own. I realised that some of the key points didn't mean anything to me when I went back over the presentation. I referred back to my notes and added a few more words to the key points to ensure I had enough information on the slide for it to make sense to me,

but not so much that it was difficult to read. I also put some images onto the slide to make it interesting.

Putting the induction programme together was also very interesting. I drew on my own experience as I have had three different part-time jobs and each induction was very different. This unit has helped me to understand and recognise the differences in my inductions and how each had a different impact on my time with the businesses. I took the best bits out of the inductions I had experienced and put these into my assignments. I added to my experiences from what I had learnt from this unit to ensure that I covered all of the points in the assignment.

## What I learned from the experience

▶ Having a deadline for each task means you can see if you are on target to complete by the hand-in date. This took away the stress and meant that I actually enjoyed the assignment.

▶ When undertaking research, know what you want to ask those you interview before you are with them.

▶ When I do another PowerPoint presentation, I will not use so many animations. It detracted from the points I was making in the presentation and at times I was confused and not sure what was coming on the next slide, or if all of the information had been shown on the slide I was on.

▶ Print out a copy of the presentation notes – I didn't know I could do this until after the presentation.

## Think about it

▶ Have you set realistic timescales and arranged to meet the right people for your research?

▶ Does the assignment make sense to you? Ask your tutor if you are unsure about anything.

▶ Have you done enough work to get the grade you are aiming for? Is there anything you could add that would push your work to the next grade?

# Glossary

**Accredited:** formally recognised by a regulated qualification.

**Active listening:** paying full attention to what someone is saying so that you can paraphrase and respond to the important points.

**Appraisee:** the individual being appraised.

**Appraiser:** the individual carrying out the appraisal.

**Aptitude:** the natural ability to do something.

**Assets:** a thing, property or person of value to the business which when calculated provides the value of the business overall.

**Attrition:** loss that is natural although it may be unexpected through death, sickness or retirement.

**Authoritarian:** enforcing strict obedience to authority.

**Autocratic:** controlling, not taking views of others into account.

**Autonomy:** the freedom to make decisions and take action, independent of others.

**Axis:** the sides of the graph which run horizontally and vertically and are represented by X (horizontal) and Y (vertical).

**Back filling:** a practice used by organisations where staff are replaced from within the work force who have been developed in order to step into a new role.

**Belongingness:** an emotional feeling of belonging to a community or group.

**Brand:** a distinctive name or trademark that is given to a particular product or service.

**Break-even:** the point at which costs and income are the same.

**Business plan:** a written document that comprises all areas of the business proposal.

**5C's:** company, collaborators, customers, competitors, climate.

**Capital investment:** the amount of money that needs to be spent on investment in asserts such as land, buildings, machinery or technology.

**Cash flow:** the amount of available money flowing in and out of the business. Having positive cash flow means that a business can always pay its costs. If a business has a negative cash flow for a long time it means that it is spending out more cash than it receives in income and this can lead to the business not being able to cover its shorter term costs.

**Cash flow forecast:** a document that shows the predicted flow of cash into and out of a business over a given period of time, normally 12 months.

**Cloud:** a virtual server for accessing and storing data via the internet.

**Cognitive:** acquiring and processing information which is undertaken mentally.

**Commodity:** a raw material or product that can be bought or sold.

**Compassionate leave:** time off work granted to someone as a result of particular distressing personal circumstances, especially the death of a close relative or partner.

**Competence:** to do something to the level required which meets the predetermined standard.

**Continuing professional development:** training that individuals engage in to enhance and develop their professional abilities.

**Continuum:** something that continues with gradual change over time.

**Creditors:** people or businesses which owe money to a business.

**Critical path:** the sequence of project activities which add up to the longest duration.

**Delegate:** (when used as a verb) to assign tasks or responsibilities to another person.

**Democratic:** a style of leadership that involves team members in decision making.

**Deployment:** using something or someone in a useful way.

**Depreciation:** the amount of value that an asset loses over time due to wear and tear/use.

**Development:** process where an individual is able to grow, change and/or become more advanced in their skills and competencies.

**Diversification:** alternative products or services which differ from the traditional or routine operations, products or services.

**Drilling down:** in statistical terms this refers to analysing the more detailed data which has been summarised to produce the headline data.

**Empathy:** the ability to understand and share the feelings of another.

**Entrepreneur:** a person who sets up a business, taking a financial risk in the hope of making a profit.

**Equity:** the value remaining after deducting the business' liabilities from its assets.

**Expenditure:** the amount of money a business spends.

**External training:** purchasing training from an outside organisation where employees are sent to receive training from another individual.

**Extrapolation:** to extract information based on relationships with different variables. Enables an estimation for future predictions.

**Fixed assets:** items that have a predetermined fixed price for a period of time such as a loan or perhaps a parcel of land or building.

**Franchise:** an authorised business arranged to operate as an agent for another company's products or services.

**Frequency distribution:** the number of times a set of values occur and the spread of occurrences over a range of situations (or values).

**Headcount:** the number of permanent employees.

**HMRC:** Her Majesty's Revenue and Customs.

**Hot desking:** allocating desks to workers as needed on a rota or flexible working system.

**Illiquid:** not easily converted into cash.

**In house training:** usually training which is provided by another member of staff in the organisation or an external trainer contracted to deliver training in the organisation.

**Intonation:** what can be inferred from, or is implied by an indication of intention of communication.

**Iterative:** an iterative process is one where you come to the desired result by means of a repeated cycle of operations.

**Legend:** the term attributed to the key or list of terms and meanings where an explanation is required.

**Liabilities:** sums of money owed by the business such as loans, mortgages, outstanding expenses and taxes.

**Licensee:** a business that has been given permission to manufacture or market services on behalf of the licensor.

**Limited liability:** having a restricted amount of money that a business is liable for that can be paid out if the partnership goes wrong. This means that the directors do not put their own personal wealth at risk if the partnership were to go wrong. Each individual business going into the partnership only has a set level of financial responsibility in the event that the partnership does not work well.

**Liquid securities:** assets which can be turned into cash quickly and hold relatively stable values.

**Logistics:** the movement of people, goods or facilities.

**Macro business:** a large employer possibly employing over 250 members of staff.

**Market intelligence:** factual information based on analyses and evaluations of multiple data, providing a big picture view of the economic climate which is used for planning, forecasting and to enable decision making.

**Mean:** the average of all the figures, arrived at by adding all the values together and dividing them by the number of values in the list.

**Median:** the middle amount, not the average but the middle in a set of values when placed in numerical order.

**Mentee:** the one being mentored.

**Merger:** when one or more organisations combine operations and financial arrangements and change ownership.

**Micro business:** a business employing up to nine members of staff.

**MIS:** management information system.

**Mode:** the value that appears most commonly in a set of figures. The mode is also referred to as the modal value.

**Model:** copy, behave in a similar way, and replicate the intentions of the vision.

**Mystery shopper:** a person employed undercover as a customer to assess the quality of goods or services.

**Niche market:** a small group of customers for a specialised item.

**Non-accredited:** does not lead to a qualification.

**Objective:** based on facts and not influenced by personal feelings, tastes or opinions.

**Operational:** in use, or ready for use.

**Optimising the work:** breaking down tasks into small chunks that can be timed so that workers know exactly what they are expected to achieve in a given timeframe.

**Overdraft:** the financial term given to the deficit in a bank account which occurs when more funds are taken out of the account than exist in it. Also known 'in the red' as negative figures are often shown in red ink.

**Paternalistic:** a management approach that involves a dominant figure who treats employees like members of an extended family and expects loyalty, trust and obedience in return.

**Payment on account:** a period of time before a business invoice needs settling in full according to the terms of the business such as 30 days or sometimes longer.

**Peripheral workers:** flexible working, contracted, not permanent.

**PESTLE:** political, economic, social, technological, legal and environmental.

**Piece work:** work that is paid for at a fixed rate (by the piece).

**Public limited Company (PLC):** PLCs offer shares to the general public and have a limited liability. Their stocks can be acquired by anybody. A company must follow strict government rules and regulations to become a PLC.

**Public sector:** the services provided on behalf of the government of a country that are mostly paid for through taxation, such as hospitals (in the UK, NHS), police, education and government itself.

**Quality assurance:** planned and systematic checks of procedures and outputs.

**Qualitative data:** descriptive data that cannot be measured numerically. For example, customer comments.

**Quality circles:** groups of employees who meet regularly to consider ways of resolving problems and improving production.

**Quality control:** series of consistent checks to ensure products and services meet a predetermined set of criteria or standards.

**Quantitative data:** data that can be expressed numerically. For example, the number of payments taken.

**Raw data:** original data collected before analysis is undertaken.

**Recession:** when the economic cycle of a country is declining, sales are falling, unemployment is increasing, output is reducing and interest rates are falling. At this time, inflation is also falling.

**Redundancy:** when an employee is dismissed because the company no longer needs someone to do their job.

**Remuneration:** money and benefits paid as part of work or employment.

**Return of investment:** the ratio between the amount of money invested and the profit received, usually given as a percentage.

**Revenue:** the amount of money that a company receives during a specific period of time.

**Robotics:** the use of robots within a production line. Quite often the manufacturer will be involved in the development of the robots as they are required to conduct specific and specialist tasks within the process of the production line which is likely to be unique to the organisations.

**SAP:** systems, applications and products; a data processing system.

**Self-employed:** a person who earns their living from charging fees or commissions rather than being employed or earning a salary.

**Series labels:** the series are the data types and the labels are the names attached to the series, in this case the value of monthly sales figures and the months of the year along each axis.

**Service standards:** a predetermined set of measures which identify the levels of quality expected for business operations.

**Size:** number of employees in an organisation. Classifications for business size include micro, small, medium and large.

**SMART:** stands for Specific, Measurable, Achievable, Realistic and Time-bound.

**Staff buy in:** employees not resisting change, willing and committed to business objectives.

**Statement of financial position:** a financial statement which states the value of the business.

**Statistics:** the result of complex analyses of raw data, often confused with being the term used to define the actual raw data.

**Strategic:** reasons that relate to the long term or overall aims of the organisation.

**Subcontractor:** a person or business that carries out work on behalf of another person or business.

**Subjective:** based on or influenced by personal feelings, tastes or opinions.

**Succession planning:** having a plan in place to fill a sequence of roles within a team or department. Organisations will develop more than one person for each role to allow for movement and changes within a business.

**Successional planning:** the process of identifying internal staff who have the potential to progress into higher and more responsible positions within the organisation.

**Supply chain:** the chain of organisations that link together to produce a product or service. The supply chain includes raw materials, information, processes and people. For example a yoghurt producer will have a farm for milk, and the chain will be between the farm and the manufacturer. The chain continues to the retailer to sell goods to the consumer and may also involve a distributor.

**Sustainability:** ability to function with sufficient resources and finance in order to maintain a certain level or rate.

**Synthesise:** to pull together and combine. For example, using information from different sources.

**Tender:** to invite bids from suppliers to offer a product or service.

**Time off in lieu:** a predetermined length of time as compensation for unpaid overtime.

**TQM:** Total Quality Management.

**Training:** acquisition of skills, knowledge and competencies as a result of teaching.

**Trait:** a distinguishing quality or characteristic.

**Up-selling:** persuading a customer to buy something in addition to their original purchase.

**Upskilling:** to teach additional skills or enhance the skills one has already.

# Index